ISBN 1-892051-17-6

MANAGING EDITOR
Claire Folkard

VP CONTENT MANAGEMENT
Chris Sheedy

SENIOR EDITOR
Jackie Freshfield

PRODUCTION DIRECTOR
Patricia Langton

KEEPER OF THE RECORDS
Stewart Newport

EDITORS
Rob Dimery
Peter Watts

PRODUCTION CO-ORDINATOR
David D'Arcy

RESEARCH TEAM
Stuart Claxton
Jerramy Fine
David Hawksett
Keely Hopkins
Della Howes
Hein Le Roux
Chris Marais
Sue Morrison
Jo Violette

DESIGN CONCEPT
Office Group NYC

FULFILMENT CO-ORDINATOR
Katie Stephens

COVER DESIGN
Ron Callow at Design 23

DESIGN
Karen Wilks

PRINTING AND BINDING
Printer Industria Grafica, SA,
Barcelona, Spain

PROOFREADING
Alyse Dar
Sasha Heseltine
Carla Masson

DTP
Juliet MacDonald

COLOR ORIGINATION
Colour Systems,
London, UK

HEAD OF PICTURE/MEDIA DESK
Betty Halvagi

AMERICANIZATION
Mary Sutherland

PHOTO ASSISTANT/DESIGNER
James Thackwell

INDEX
Indexing Specialists

LIBRARIAN/ARCHIVIST
Roger Wemyss Brooks

PICTURE RESEARCH
Maureen Kane
ilumi

ACCREDITATION Guinness World Records Ltd has a very thorough accreditation system for records verification. However, while every effort is made to ensure accuracy, Guinness World Records Ltd cannot be held responsible for any errors contained in this work. Feedback from our readers on any point of accuracy is always welcomed.

ABBREVIATIONS AND MEASUREMENTS GUINNESS WORLD RECORDS uses both imperial and metric measurements (metric in brackets). The only exception is for some scientific data, where metric measurements only are universally accepted, and for some sports data. All currency values are shown in dollars with the sterling equivalent in brackets except where transactions took place in the United Kingdom, when this is reversed. Where a specific date is given the exchange rate is calculated according to the currency values that were in operation at the time. Where only a year date is given the exchange rate is calculated from December of that year. The billion conversion is one thousand million. 'GDR' (the German Democratic Republic) refers to the East German state, which unified with West Germany in 1990. The abbreviation is used for sports records broken before 1990. The Union of Soviet Socialist Republics split into a number of parts in 1991, the largest of these being Russia. The Commonwealth of Independent States replaced it, and the abbreviation 'CIS' is used mainly for sports records broken at the 1992 Olympic Games.

GENERAL WARNING Attempting to break records or set new records can be dangerous. Appropriate advice should be taken first and all record attempts are undertaken entirely at the participant's risk. In no circumstances will Guinness World Records Ltd have any liability for death or injury suffered in any record attempts. Guinness World Records Ltd has complete discretion over whether or not to include any particular records in the book.

GULLANE
ENTERTAINMENT

A Gullane Entertainment company

GUINNESS
WORLD
RECORDS™

CONTENTS

06 INTRODUCTION
08 THE TOP TEN
   RECORDS OF 2002
10 HOW TO BE A
   RECORD BREAKER
14 GUINNESSWORLD
   RECORDS.COM
16 RECORD-BREAKING TV

HUMAN ACHIEVEMENT

20 HEROES AND
   LIFESAVERS
22 INSPIRATIONAL
   PEOPLE
24 SURVIVORS
26 COURAGE AND
   ENDURANCE
28 EPIC JOURNEYS

AMAZING FEATS

32 MARATHONS
34 TEAM EFFORTS
36 MASS PARTICIPATION
38 STRENGTH
40 SPEED
42 YOUNG AND OLD
44 BIZARRE SKILLS
46 WEIRD TALENTS

THE HUMAN BODY

50 REMARKABLE BODIES
52 MEDICAL MARVELS
54 MEDICAL TRIUMPHS
56 TRANSFORMED
   BODIES
58 SICKNESS AND
   DISEASE

POWERFUL WORLD

62 EARTH MATTERS
64 THE ENVIRONMENT
66 WEIRD WEATHER
68 NATURAL DISASTERS
70 THE UNIVERSE
72 SPACE EXPLORATION

AMAZING NATURE

76 PHYSICAL EARTH
78 WATER WORLD
80 EXTRAORDINARY
   PLANTS
82 WONDERFUL
   WILDLIFE
84 ASTONISHING
   ANIMALS
86 INSECTS AND
   REPTILES
88 AQUATIC LIFE
90 PREHISTORIC LIFE

SOCIETY AND POLITICS

94 PEOPLE AND NATIONS
96 GOVERNMENTS
98 MODERN SOCIETY
100 RITES OF PASSAGE
102 RELIGION
104 TRAVEL AND
    TOURISM
106 LAW AND ORDER
108 MONEY

AMAZING OBJECTS

112 MICROWORLD
114 BIG IS BEAUTIFUL

116 LARGER THAN LIFE
118 COLLECTIONS
120 GADGETS
122 EXTRAVAGANT PURCHASES
124 OBJECTS OF DESIRE

BUILDINGS AND STRUCTURES

128 SKY HIGH
130 COLOSSAL CONSTRUCTIONS
132 FEATS OF ENGINEERING
134 HOUSES, HOMES AND HOTELS

PLANES, TRAINS AND AUTOS

138 AIRCRAFT
140 CARS
142 BIKES AND MOTORBIKES
144 BOATS AND YACHTS
146 TRAINS AND TRAMS
148 TRUCKS AND DUMPERS

MILITARY SERVICE

152 ARMED FORCES
154 MILITARY AIRCRAFT
156 NAVAL WARFARE
158 WEAPONS OF WAR
160 MASS DESTRUCTION

TECHNOLOGY AND SCIENCE

164 DIGITAL SYSTEMS
166 DIGITAL TECHNOLOGY
168 BIO-TECH AND GENETICS
170 EXTREME SCIENCE
172 LAB SCIENCE

ENTERTAINMENT

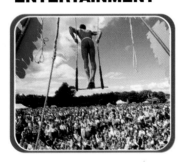

176 COMPUTER GAMES
178 THEME PARKS
180 FILM STARS
182 CINEMA
184 SPECIAL EFFECTS
186 POP MUSIC
188 POP STARS
190 CLASSICAL MUSIC
192 PERFORMANCE
194 TV AND RADIO
196 BOOKS AND NEWSPAPERS

SPORT

200 AMERICAN SPORTS
208 BALL SPORTS
220 ATHLETICS
228 WINTER SPORTS
236 MOTOR SPORTS
242 GOLF
246 RACKET SPORTS
250 WATER SPORTS
258 EQUESTRIAN SPORTS
260 AIR SPORTS
262 TARGET SPORTS
264 COMBAT AND STRENGTH
268 CYCLING
270 UNUSUAL SPORTS

272 INDEX
286 PICTURE CREDITS
288 ACKNOWLEDGMENTS

Welcome to Guinness World Records 2003! With over 1,000 new records and hundreds of exciting new pictures, this year's book is one of the brightest and best yet. We've added new chapters on Modern Society and Buildings and Structures, which offer a fascinating glimpse into our modern world, and the Sport section has been expanded to include a huge range of every activity imaginable, from international soccer to elephant polo!

But all the old favorites haven't been forgotten. There are mind-bending records on everything from the wonders of the human body to awe-inspiring facts on the natural world.

So delve into the wonderful world that is Guinness World Records and prepare to be astounded and inspired by the people who have deservedly claimed their place in history!

What could you break...?

Pictures from far left: a delighted Halle Berry with her Oscar at this year's Academy Awards; Rudolph Giuliani as Mayor of New York City; Edward Peter Hannaford with his record-winning French knitting; Olympic skier Janica Kostelic, holder of three gold medals.

FASTEST COMPUTER

The NEC Earth Simulator (below, right) at the Yokohama Institute for Earth Sciences in Japan is capable of carrying out 35.6 trillion calculations per second – around five times the speed of the previous record holder. Built by HNSX Supercomputers, a division of NEC, the computer is designed to simulate Earth's complex climate in order to predict climate change and global warming, both of which have serious implications for Japan. Its 5,104 processors are housed in cabinets that cover an area equivalent to four tennis courts.

FASTEST MEN'S 1,000-M SPEED SKATING

Gerard van Velde (Netherlands, below) skated 1,000 m in 1:07.16 at Salt Lake City, Utah, USA, on February 16 2002.

OLDEST VOMIT

On February 12 2002 a team of paleontologists led by Prof Peter Doyle (UK) announced the discovery of the fossilized vomit (right) of an ichthyosaur (ancient marine reptile). Found in a quarry in Peterborough, Cambs, UK, the 160-million-year-old vomit may provide an insight into ichthyosaurs' feeding habits.

LARGEST CURRENCY INTRODUCTION

On January 1 2002, 15 billion euro banknotes and 50 billion euro coins (with a value of more than €664 billion – $592 billion or £407 billion) were put into circulation in Austria, Belgium, Finland, France, Germany, Greece, Ireland, Italy, Luxembourg, The Netherlands, Portugal, and Spain, affecting 290 million people. Put end to end, the new euro banknotes would stretch to the Moon and back two and a half times.

MOST SPACEFLIGHTS BY AN ASTRONAUT

On April 8 2002, 54-year-old US astronaut Jerry Ross began his seventh space mission. He was flying as a crew member aboard the STS 110 mission of the space shuttle *Atlantis*, on a construction flight to the International Space Station. All of Ross's flights have been on the space shuttle. A retired Air Force Colonel, he was selected as an astronaut in 1980, and his first spaceflight was in 1985.

FASTEST TIME TO COMPLETE A MARATHON FOR WOMEN ONLY

Paula Radcliffe (UK, left) finished the women's race in the London Marathon on April 14 2002 in London, UK, in 2 hr 18 min 56 sec.

OLDEST PERSON TO CLIMB EVEREST

Tamae Watanabe (Japan, left b. November 21 1938) reached the summit of Mt Everest at age 63 at 9:55 am on May 16 2002. Watanabe reached the summit on its busiest day ever, when 54 other climbers reached the top of the 29,028 ft (8,848 m) peak.

OLDEST ROYAL

HM Queen Elizabeth the Queen Mother (UK, 1900–2002, below right) was the oldest member of the British royal family. She married Prince Albert (UK, later George VI) on April 26 1923 and on his coronation became the first British-born Queen Consort since Tudor times, as well as the Last Empress of India. She died on March 30 2002 at the age of 101. Her daughter, Queen Elizabeth II (below, left) celebrated her Golden Jubilee in 2002.

FASTEST $100-MILLION GROSS FOR AN ANIMATED FEATURE FILM

The computer-animated film *Monsters, Inc.* (USA, 2001, above) from Walt Disney Pictures and Pixar Animation Studios reached the $100-million (£68,636,036) mark at the US box office in just nine days after its release on November 2 2001.

LARGEST SIMULTANEOUS JUMP

To celebrate the launch of UK Science Year on September 7 2001 at precisely 11:00 am, 559,493 people began jumping up and down in 2,171 schools all over the UK for one minute (right). The total number of participants was 569,069. The extra numbers were made up by disabled pupils who contributed by dropping objects on the ground or hitting the ground with their fists.

BE A RECORD BREAKER

SO YOU WANT TO BE A RECORD BREAKER?

Guinness World Records 2003 is packed with extraordinary people achieving extraordinary feats. If reading this year's book has whetted your appetite to break a record or create a new one, then read on. Applying to become a record breaker has never been so easy. All you need to do is log on to www.guinnessworldrecords.com. But before you do, here are some things you may want to consider:

I COULD BREAK A RECORD – BUT WHICH ONE?

If you think you're made of record-breaking material but don't quite know which record to go for, it's time to get your thinking cap on.

The thousands of unusual records held in our database prove that being a record breaker is not just about being a top athlete or movie star! Maybe you could start a wonderful collection? This doesn't have to be expensive either – current record holders have collected sick bags or chewing gum wrappers! If you are interested in doing a group record, you could organize a huge poetry reading or do something that would help improve the environment, such as picking up litter.

You may even be a record breaker without knowing it. We have records for the most blood donated and the longest legs!

Another option is to create a record that is unique and requires an entirely new category. Our team is constantly on the lookout for new categories, particularly those that will be an inspiration to other people. What we look for is a challenge that is interesting, safe, and requires skill.

APPLY EARLY

Whatever your record, it is important that you apply to us early and contact us before your attempt. This is to give our researchers time to evaluate your suggestion and, if necessary, draw up new guidelines and consult experts who have special knowledge in that field.

You should also check with us shortly before you do your attempt to make sure that the record hasn't recently been set or broken. If you think you may already have set a world record, then contact us so we can decide whether your record is potentially valid before you send in any documentation.

GUIDELINES

For most of our current categories, Guinness World Records has specific guidelines to insure that all potential record holders make their attempts according to the same conditions that applied to previous challengers.

Your attempt has to be measurable, quantifiable, and breakable so that we can make fair comparisons with other record attempts. If the record you are interested in is not a current category and is of interest to us, we will draw up specific guidelines to make sure that we can consider it fairly.

DOCUMENTATION

Although some people break their record in front of millions of viewers on the Guinness World Records TV shows, the majority of potential record holders are obliged to follow our rules and regulations, and provide evidence of this with a clearly labeled VHS video tape (with the official timekeeper or continually running clock in view where appropriate). High quality color photographs or transparencies should also be submitted as documentation. If possible, get a local newspaper or radio station interested in your record so they can cover the event and, preferably, be present during the attempt.

All claims must be well documented. At least two independent witnesses are required, and these should be someone of standing in your local community such as a doctor, lawyer, or police officer. Any such witness must not be related to you. Choose someone who is relevant to your record. For example, if your record is to do with sports, invite someone from an appropriate sports body. Witnesses must be able to state they have seen the record take place successfully and that the guidelines have been followed. Guinness World Records cannot supply staff to monitor all record attempts but reserves the right to do so if it deems it necessary.

TAKING CARE

Safety precautions are another important factor. It is important to note that all record attempts are undertaken at the sole risk of the competitor. Guinness World Records cannot be held responsible for any (potential) liability whatsoever arising out of any such attempt, whether to the claimant or any third party.

CERTIFICATE

Everyone who breaks or sets a Guinness World Record receives a special certificate from us, acknowledging membership of an exclusive official body – Guinness World Record holders. Details of your record will also be added to our world-famous database for potential use in our book, on our website, or in other related material.

WILL I BE IN THE BOOK?

With tens of thousands of records in existence we are unable to publish all of them every year. We publish a different selection of records in each edition that we believe are most topical and will also be of most interest.

HOW TO APPLY

Our online service is the best way to submit your claim. Visit our website at http://www.guinnessworldrecords.com. All you need to do is fill in a simple form and follow the instructions that appear to send us your application. You will get an immediate response from us, and when you register your record attempt online we will give you a personal identification number so you can track your claim's progress via our website, where the most up-to-date information is held.

IF YOU DON'T HAVE ONLINE ACCESS

If you do not have access to a computer, then you can also easily contact Guinness World Records regarding your record attempt in one of the following ways:

Call us: 011-44-891-517-607

Fax us: 011-44-7891 4501

Or write to us: GUINNESS WORLD RECORDS
                    338 EUSTON ROAD
                    LONDON NW1 3BD
                    UNITED KINGDOM

THE FASTEST PENNY FARTHING IN THE WEST

Colorado's Steve Stevens is a major fan of Victorian penny farthings – he now owns 31 of them – but carried out his first US coast-to-coast ride on a conventional push-bike in 1985. "Afterwards I started reading about Thomas Stevens, who was the first man to ride across America on a penny farthing," says Steve. More than a century later, Steve set out to follow in his hero's penny farthing tracks.

He left San Francisco on May 26 2000 and arrived in Boston 29 days later, setting the record for the fastest trans-America ride on a penny farthing in the process.

It must have been punishing work to face strong headwinds on a penny farthing, while enduring the 100°F (38°C) heat. But Steve insists that he never even thought about giving up.

For his next ruse Steve is planning to participate in a Victorian Iron Man contest. He intends to wear a woollen Victorian swimsuit and ride a penny farthing in the cycling event!

The penny farthing was named after the smallest and largest UK coins in existence at the time of the bike's invention. Its name reflects the considerable difference in the size of the rear and front wheels.

THE FABULOUS BIKER BOYS

Political turmoil in Colombia and kidnapping threats threw Nick Alcock's and Hugh Sinclair's trans-America record attempt into jeopardy in 2001. The British biker boys had clocked up 6,000 miles in the month following their departure from Alaska on August 29 2001, but when they arrived in Panama they were warned about

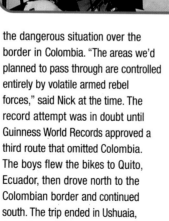

the dangerous situation over the border in Colombia. "The areas we'd planned to pass through are controlled entirely by volatile armed rebel forces," said Nick at the time. The record attempt was in doubt until Guinness World Records approved a third route that omitted Colombia. The boys flew the bikes to Quito, Ecuador, then drove north to the Colombian border and continued south. The trip ended in Ushuaia, Argentina, on October 15 2001, by which time the pair had covered around 15,000 miles (24,000 km).

FROM STRENGTH TO STRENGTH

English iron man Paddy Doyle began his prolific record-breaking career in 1987, when he completed 4,100 full press-ups with a 50-lb (22.7-kg) weight strapped to his back. He's broken numerous strength and endurance records since.

Paddy powered his way to yet another Guinness World Record this year. The martial arts expert and all-round strongman threw an incredible 4,104 full-contact punches and 1,560 martial arts kicks in just one hour. That works out at over three strikes every two seconds! Each strike was impacted on kick pads worn by one of Paddy's seven assistants – who had to alternate regularly because of the explosive force of the blows!

Paddy's planning to retire from record breaking in November 2002. And as a finale he has a string of speed endurance records planned.

ROLLIN', ROLLIN', ROLLIN'!

When most folks were washing the car, Texans Geoff Ackles and John Landers were pushing their full-weight Chevrolet Sprint around laps of the local neighborhood, in a bid to smash the record for 24-hour car pushing. In just over 17 hours of nonstop pushing the powerful pair managed to notch up a distance of 33.7 miles (54.2 km) – smashing the previous record held by two Italians, who pushed their car a distance of 32.6 miles (52.5 km) in 24 hours.

"My son was determined that we should break a record – and he suggested car pushing," Geoff says. "At first I thought it would be impossible but then slowly things started coming together. My neighbor, John Landers, agreed to help us, and I managed to get hold of a car that was really close to the minimum weight limit of 1,853 lb (840.5 kg) set by Guinness World Records."

Geoff was quietly confident after a test push – "but that was without a driver in as well." Five drivers took turns at front-seat duties during the record attempt. "Toward the end I was pushing with my eyes closed, I was just so tired," recalls the Texan record breaker. "When we crossed the finish line it was just about all I could do to raise my hands in the air."

LAWN MOWER MAN

Gary Hatter (USA) has been interested in lawn mowers since the age of 10. However, it wasn't until a back injury at 24 – which left him unable to continue working as a long-distance truck driver – that the idea of his record-breaking feat occurred to him. Gary needed surgery to prevent paralysis, an operation that would cost $100,000.

Having spent four years planning a trip to raise funds for his treatment, he set off on a $11,500 stock Kubota BX2200-60 mower, with a top speed of 9 mph (14.5 km/h), on May 31 2000 from Portland, Maine, USA. He drove through 48 contiguous states as well as Canada and Mexico and finally, after spending 260 days on the road, arrived at Daytona Beach, Florida on February 14 2001. Gary covered 14,594.5 miles (23,487.5 km) on his trek, breaking the previous record by more than 11,000 miles (17,702.8 km) and gaining himself a world record. Gary's machine clocked up 14 miles (22.5 km) to the gallon; the trip wore out three sets of rear tires and four sets of front tires.

Gary had his mower fitted with new equipment and lights to make it roadworthy. The only thing missing was the cruise-control, a problem he overcame by using a block of wood!

IS THE FORCE WITH YOU?

Jason Joiner, of Ealing, London, UK, a special effects expert who has worked on the recently made Star Wars films, has a collection of more than 20,000 Star Wars toys. And as if that wasn't enough, Jason also has one of the original C-3PO robots, an original R2-D2, and an original Darth Vader costume.

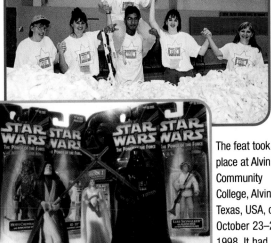

Just before his early teens, Jason developed an interest in the Star Wars movies and everything related to them. Like many of his peers, he began purchasing various types of memorabilia (including action figures, toys, books, and cards) with his hard-earned pocket money. But Jason's enthusiasm has not faded with time.

Jason has invested considerable time and money in organizing Star Wars collectors' fairs in England that help to fund his growing collection. He also heads a club of more than 2,000 Star Wars buffs. It just goes to show what a combination of passion, drive, and ingenuity can achieve!

THE CHAIN GANG

We've all made paper chains at least once during our lives – but it seems that some people just don't know when to stop! Sixty people made their way into the record books by constructing a paper chain measuring an incredible 51.8 miles (83.36 km) long and comprising 584,000 links – and all in 24 hours.

The feat took place at Alvin Community College, Alvin, Texas, USA, on October 23–24 1998. It had initially been proposed by ACC Child Laboratory School as part of the college's 50th anniversary celebrations.

The successful attempt beat the proposed target by 1.8 miles (2.9 km) and the previous record by 6 miles (9.7 km)! It also united the campus and the community as senior citizens, families, Girl Scouts, and church youth groups all joined forces to work four- and five-hour shifts apiece. Local businesses donated both the staples that were used to join the strips and food provisions for the participants, and the event was covered by local radio. The sponsorship and T-shirt sales from the event raised more than $5,000 for student scholarships.

RECORD-BREAKING FAITH

Ashrita (formerly Keith) Furman was born on September 16 1954 in Brooklyn, New York, USA. Ashrita confesses that he was a bit of a wimp as an adolescent and lacked direction until he embraced the teachings of the spiritual leader Sri Chinmoy. In 1974, by now a devout follower, he adopted the name Ashrita, which means "protected by God" in Sanskrit.

In 1978 Sri Chinmoy suggested that Ashrita attempt a 24-hour cycling marathon. The marathon enabled Ashrita to discover the resources that he could tap into through meditation.

Ashrita set his first world record in 1979 by carrying out 27,000 jumping jacks. Since then he has set around 60 world records, but now holds 14, as many have been broken. Ashrita has broken more world records than any other person. If he suffers extreme pain during a feat, he uses mantras to guide him and help him overcome it. By breaking records Ashrita believes he can free himself from his conscious mind and reach a spiritual plane.

SO WHAT'S NEW?

This year, your favorite records are just a
click away. Log on for details of thousands of
incredible record attempts, keep up to date
with all the latest record-breaking news, and
choose from hundreds of amazing video clips.

Plus, if you want to be a record breaker, apply
online for all the information and rules you
need. You can even track the progress of your
record using our new online claim system.
Who knows … this time next year you might
be a Guinness World Record holder!

FIND A RECORD
Looking for a specific record? Use our
keyword search to find one of the thousands
of Guinness World Records in the database.

BREAK A RECORD
Want to set a new world record? Click here
to tell us about your suggestion. If it's approved
by our researchers, we'll send you the relevant
rules and guidelines.

TRACK YOUR RECORD
Once you've applied to break a record,
follow the progress of your application
using our new tracking system.

VIDEO VAULT
Choose from hundreds of exciting video
clips and see some of the greatest
Guinness World Records come to life.

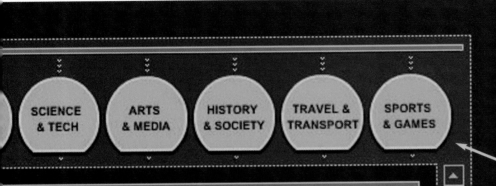

| SCIENCE & TECH | ARTS & MEDIA | HISTORY & SOCIETY | TRAVEL & TRANSPORT | SPORTS & GAMES |

ST HUMAN LAYERS ON A BED OF NAILS
Graber, Todd Graber, Chris Smith, and Doreen Graber
ned a four-person bed of nails at Tallmadge, Ohio, USA
8 October 2000. When the four had formed the four-layer
of nails, Lee was supporting an estimated ... <u>more</u>

ST POISONOUS FROG
nay be tiny but the multi-colored poison dart frog can be
al. The skin secretion of the golden poison dart frog
yllobates terribilis) of Western Colombia ... <u>more</u>

RTHEST DISTANCE WALKING ON WATER
ny Bricka walked on water and went without food for
ks - what was he thinking!? He walked across the Atlantic
an, starting out from Tenerife in the ... <u>more</u>

<<<<< **ON THE RECORD**

truly headstrong world record
On May 24, 1999 Evans set a
o have been head-balanced
a 159.6 kg (352 lb) Mini car for
ole or a gust of wind and I'd
n," explains John, who has
ilk crates, soccer balls, books

K A RECORD
ar Cube Skyscraper
t to be a Guinness World Record breaker? Why not try
ing the world's tallest sugar cube tower?

PRIVACY | CREDITS | CORPORATE

CHOOSE YOUR CATEGORY
Delve into the online archive and browse
through our collection of the world's most
amazing records – just choose the subject
area that interests you most.

DAILY RECORDS
Our researchers are always on the hunt for
the most astonishing, incredible, awesome
record attempts. Read our favorite stories
here each day.

ON THE RECORD
Dozens of new records are attempted
each week, so check back regularly
for all the latest news and updates.

PLUS ...
Discover top tips for breaking a record,
read interviews with record holders,
and meet the Keeper of the Records.

RECORD-BREAKING TV

There have been several TV series loosely based on GWR in the past – most notably, BBC TV's *Record Breakers*, and Sir David Frost's *The Spectacular World of Guinness Records*. However, in 1998 a major series was launched in the USA by Guinness World Records, *Guinness World Records: Primetime*. Since its launch, the American show has been screened in 28 different countries. It was closely followed by shows in Germany, the UK, Finland, Sweden, Denmark, Norway, France, Spain, and Japan. Every show is presided over by an official Guinness World Records judge who makes sure that rules are observed, and all attempts are accurately measured and timed. There are no tricks or illusions in the shows, just real people achieving incredible records.

1.
Vitaly Schnikers (Latvia) carried out 48 "Thomas Flanks" in one minute. His moment of gymnastic glory took place on the set of *Guinness – Die Show Der Rekorde* in Munich, Germany, on February 15 2002.

2.
Superbiker Joachim Hindren (Finland) is definitely going up in the world. At the studios of *Guinness World Records*, Helsinki, Finland, on October 20 2001, Hindren climbed a wall on to a platform 9.87 ft (3.01 m) high astride his trial motorbike.

3.
Tireless footwear tugger Teo, a Border collie, pulled 18 socks off the feet of a selection of people on the set of *Guinness – Die Show Der Rekorde*, on April 26 2002.

4.
Bundesliga team Energie Cottbus's Under-16 team scored 54 goals in two minutes with a header relay. Each team member headed the ball to the next teammate, and the last player headed the ball into a goal on the set of *Guinness – Die Show Der Rekorde*, on April 26 2002.

5.
Peter Wetzelsperger (Germany) smashed his way through a total of 64 coconuts in one minute with his bare hands on the set of *Guinness – Die Show Der Rekorde* on February 15 2002.

6.
Olympic diver Jan Hempel (Germany) executed a backward jump reaching a distance of 6 ft 7.1 in (2.01 m) on the set of *Guinness – Die Show Der Rekorde*, on February 15 2002.

7.
Slavisa Pajkic "Biba" (Yugoslavia) has developed the ability to pass an electric current through himself to power everyday household objects. On November 24 2001 "Biba" heated up a 0.5-fl oz (15-ml) cup of water from 77ºF to 20ºF (25ºC to 97ºC) in a record-breaking time of 1 min 37 sec on the set of *Guinness Rekord TV*, Stockholm, Sweden.

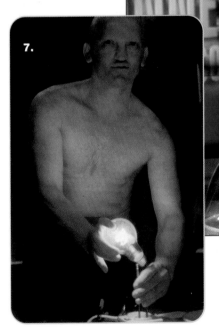

8.
Dean Sheldon (USA) held a total of 21 scorpions in his mouth for a time of 18 seconds on *Guinness Rekord TV*, on November 24 2001. His fearless feat broke his own record of 20 scorpions in the mouth.

9.
Soap bubble artist Fan Yang (Canada) created a world record 12 soap bubble domes inside one another at the *Guinness World Records* studios, Helsinki, Finland, on October 20 2001.

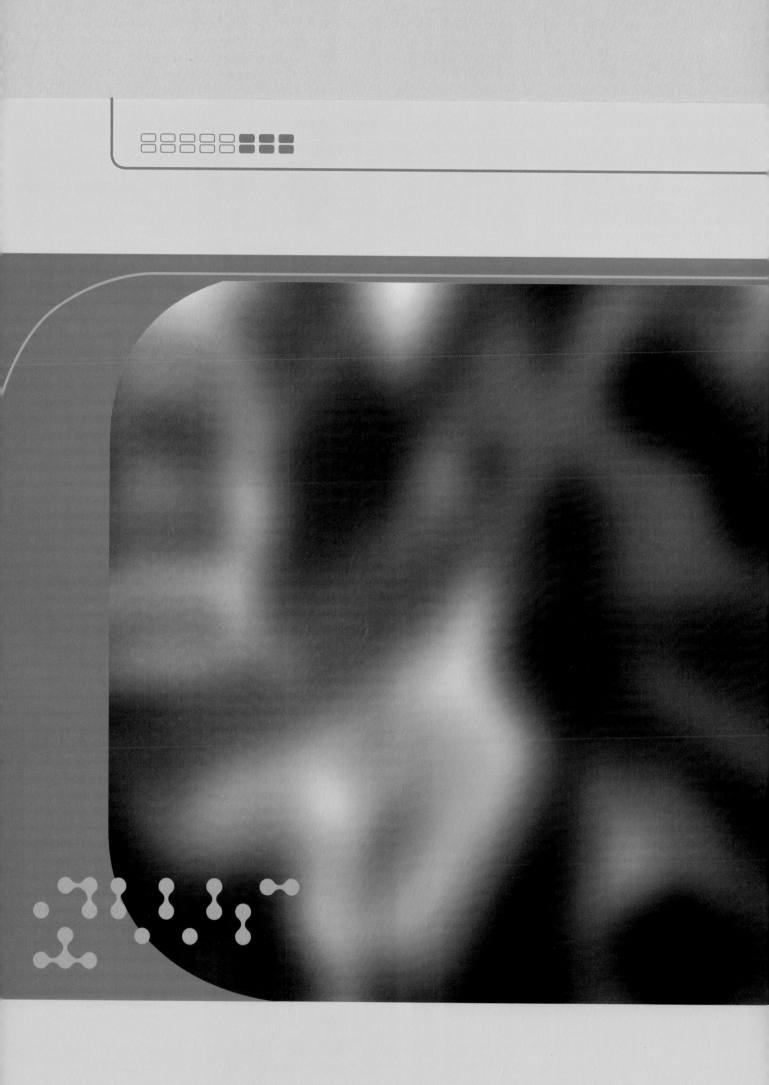

HUMAN ACHIEVEMENT

MOST MONEY RAISED FOR CHARITY IN A SPORTS EVENT

The Flora London Marathon (above), run annually since 1981 through the streets of London, UK, raises more money for charity than any other single sports event in the world. Around £156 million ($224 million) has been raised so far.

YOUNGEST GALLANTRY AWARD

At the age of 4 years 52 days, Ryan Woods (UK) became the youngest person to receive a bravery award when he was awarded The Royal Humane Society's "Testimonial on Parchment" in recognition of his brave actions during an accident in Portugal in July 1997. Ryan saved his grandmother's life by climbing for help when their car plunged down a steep cliff.

MOST DECORATED WAR HERO

Best known as a film actor, Audie Murphy (USA) was also the most decorated soldier in US history, winning 24 medals including the Congressional Medal of Honor. His exploits were the subject of the film *To Hell and Back* (USA, 1956), in which he starred as himself.

MOST CIVILIAN AWARDS

Reginald H Blanchford (UK) has received the following awards for lifesaving on land and at sea: MBE for gallantry in 1950; Queen's Commendation in 1957; Life Saving Medal of The Order of St. John in Gold in 1957, with gold bar in 1963; George Medal in 1958; Carnegie Hero Fund's Bronze Medallion in 1959; the OBE in 1961. He was made a Knight of Grace of The Order of St. John in 1970 and received the American Biographical Institute's Silver Shield of Valor in 1992.

YOUNGEST RECIPIENT OF THE VICTORIA CROSS

The earliest established age for the winner of a Victoria Cross is 15 years 100 days for hospital apprentice Andrew Fitzgibbon (USA). He was born on May 13 1845 and received his medal for acts of bravery carried out when he was a member of the Indian Medical Service serving in northern China on August 21 1860.

YOUNGEST RECIPIENT OF AN OFFICIAL GALLANTRY AWARD

Julius Rosenberg (Canada) was given the Medal of Bravery on March 30 1994 for foiling a black bear that attacked his three-year-old sister on September 20 1992. Age five at the time of the incident, he managed to save his sister by growling at the bear.

YOUNGEST NOBEL PEACE PRIZE WINNER

In 1992, Rigoberta Menchú Tum (Guatemala), an active political worker in labor and human rights groups, was awarded the Nobel Peace Prize, "in recognition of her work for social justice and ethnocultural reconciliation based on respect for the rights of indigenous people." At the age of 33, she was the youngest prize winner ever to receive this honor.

DEEPEST UNDERWATER RESCUE

Roger R Chapman and Roger Mallinson (both UK) were rescued from the submersible *Pisces III* after being trapped for 76 hours when it sank to 1,575 ft (480 m), 150 miles (241 km) off the Irish coast on August 29 1973. It was hauled up on September 1 by the *John Cabot* after work by *Pisces V*, *Pisces II* and the remote-control recovery vessel *Curv* (Controlled Underwater Recovery Vehicle).

MOST MONEY RAISED BY AN INDIVIDUAL IN A MARATHON

Retired executive John Spurling (UK) raised £1.13 million ($1.87 million) for the Animal Health Trust and the Lord's Taverners by running the London Marathon on April 18 1999.

LARGEST VOLUNTEER AMBULANCE ORGANIZATION

Abdul Sattar Edhi (Pakistan) began his ambulance service in 1948. Today, his radio-linked ambulance fleet is 500 vehicles strong and operates all over Pakistan, through $5 million (£3.05 million) funding raised annually.

GREATEST RESCUE WITHOUT LOSS OF LIFE

The greatest rescue without any loss of life was from the American vessel *Susan B Anthony*, which was carrying 2,689 people – all of whom survived – when it was sunk off Normandy, France, on June 7 1944, while being used as a troop ship.

EARLIEST MID-AIR RESCUE

Dolly Shepherd and Louie May (both UK) were part of a performing troupe who leaped out of balloons wearing parachutes. However, on June 9 1908, Louie's ripcord jammed following a jump from a hot-air balloon 11,000 ft (3,352 m) above Longton, Staffs, UK. Dolly saved her by bringing her down on her own single parachute.

LOWEST MID-AIR RESCUE

Eddie Turner saved an unconscious Frank Farnan (both USA), who had been injured in a collision after jumping from an aircraft at 13,000 ft (3,962 m). Turner pulled Farnan's ripcord at 1,800 ft (548 m), less than 10 seconds from impact with the ground, over Clewiston, Florida, USA, on October 16 1988.

LARGEST FUNDRAISING CHARITY

For eight consecutive years, the Salvation Army, USA (above), has raised more funds annually than any other charity. For the year ending September 1999, the total was $1,402 million (£855.22 million), the highest amount it has ever raised.

LARGEST SINGLE DONATION TO AIDS RESEARCH

The largest single donation to research into AIDS and HIV of $25 million (£15.08 million) was made by Bill Gates, founder of Microsoft, and his wife Melinda (both USA), in May 1999.

LARGEST MEDICAL CHARITY

The Wellcome Trust, established in 1936 as part of the will of Sir Henry Wellcome (UK), has an asset base of £12 billion ($19.46 billion). This large amount is due to the merger of Wellcome plc with Glaxo in 1995, which left the Wellcome Trust with a 4.7% stake in the new company, Glaxo Wellcome. The Trust has an annual expenditure of £400 million ($648 million).

OLDEST LIFE-SAVING ORGANIZATION

Britain's Royal National Lifeboat Institution (RNLI) was formed by royal edict in March 1824. Its lifeboatmen have to date saved over 135,000 lives.

MOST LIFEBOAT MEDALS

Sir William Hillary (UK), founder of the RNLI in 1824, was awarded a record four RNLI Gold Medals, in 1825, 1828, and twice in 1830.

MOST ARTISTS SAVED

Varian Fry (USA), known as "The Artists' Schindler," traveled from the USA to France in 1940 with a list of 200 prominent intellectuals and artists known to be in areas of Nazi-occupied Europe. He subsequently helped to save around 4,000 people from the Gestapo (the Nazi secret police), including some of the 20th century's most famous cultural figures: Marc Chagall, André Breton (both France), Max Ernst, and Nobel Prize-winning chemist Otto Meyerhof (both Germany).

OLDEST LIFEGUARD

James Janssen (USA, b. 1921) is the world's oldest lifeguard. A retired priest, James guards the Outing Club pool, Davenport, Iowa, USA, and teaches swimming and water aerobics.

LONGEST CAREER IN FIRE DEPARTMENT

Gustave Ebers (USA) served in the Rhinebeck Fire Department, New York, USA, as a volunteer fireman and treasurer from November 1932 until 1997. He died in 1998.

MOST FIRE PERSONNEL LOST IN ONE INCIDENT

According to the International Association of Fire Fighters, a total of 343 New York City fire personnel (surviving fire officers shown below) lost their lives in the unprecedented tragedy of September 11 2001, when two hijacked airplanes crashed into the twin towers of the World Trade Center in New York City, USA. The fire fighters' gallant rescue efforts saved thousands of lives. This was the largest single-event loss of life sustained by modern-day fire service personnel in war or peace time.

MOST VIEWERS FOR A SIMULTANEOUS CHARITY ROCK CONCERT

Live Aid, the largest simultaneous charity rock concert in terms of viewers, was organized by musician Bob Geldof (Ireland, above). Held in London, UK, and Philadelphia, USA, on July 13 1985, more than 60 of rock music's biggest acts played for free to approximately 1.5 billion TV viewers watching via satellite. The event was staged to raise money for famine relief in Africa.

OLDEST MALE ASTRONAUT

The oldest man to have traveled into space is John Glenn Jr (USA), who was 77 years 103 days old when he flew with the crew of STS 95 *Discovery* on October 29 1998. The mission lasted 11 days, returning to Earth on November 7 1998. In February 1962, Glenn became the first American to orbit Earth, in the spacecraft *Friendship 7*.

OLDEST FEMALE ASTRONAUT

The oldest woman in space to date is Shannon Lucid (USA), who was 53 years old when she took part in the space shuttle mission STS 76 *Atlantis* in March 1996.

She also has the distinction of being the only woman to have taken part in five space flights.

FIRST FEMALE PRIME MINISTER

The first woman prime minister was Sirimavo Bandaranaike (Sri Lanka), who became premier of Sri Lanka on July 21 1960 and also from 1970 to 1977 and from 1994 to 2000. Her daughter Chandrika Bandaranaike Kumaratunga (Sri Lanka) has been Sri Lanka's president since 1994.

OLDEST INTERNATIONAL HUMAN RIGHTS ORGANIZATION

Anti-Slavery International is the world's oldest human rights organization. Its roots stretch back to 1787, when the first abolitionist society was formed. The British and Foreign Anti-Slavery Society (BFASS) was officially created on April 17 1839 to crusade against slavery and the slave trade throughout the world. To this day, the organization continues the fight against human trafficking, traditional slavery, child prostitution, and all forms of forced and bonded labor.

LARGEST ENVIRONMENTAL FUNDRAISING EVENT

The Rainforest Foundation UK, established in 1989 by the musician Sting and his wife Trudie Styler (both UK), held a celebrity benefit concert in Carnegie Hall, New York City, USA, in April 1998. The concert included performances by Madonna, Elton John, and Billy Joel, and the street outside Carnegie Hall was renamed "Rainforest Way" to help promote Rainforest Awareness Week. The concert raised a record $2 million (£1.2 million) gross to provide aid for indigenous people worldwide and to contribute toward the preservation of the world's rainforests.

LARGEST SIMULTANEOUS BLOOD DONATION

The American Red Cross/University of Missouri Blood Drive, which was held at the Hernes Center Field House, Columbia, Missouri, USA, on April 7 1999, attracted a record 3,539 donors in one day. The drive yielded 3,155 productive units of blood in total.

LARGEST RALLY FOR RACIAL EQUALITY

On August 28 1963 civil rights leader Martin Luther King Jr (USA) led more than 250,000 demonstrators down the Mall in Washington, DC, USA. Following the march, King delivered his inspirational "I have a dream …" speech before the Lincoln Memorial. The rally was organized to promote equal civil rights for all Americans, irrespective of their race or color.

LARGEST LITTER COLLECTION

The greatest number of volunteers to collect litter in one location on one day is 50,405, along the coast of California, USA, on October 2 1993, in conjunction with the International Coastal Cleanup.

LARGEST AUDIENCE FOR A SPACE EVENT

The broadcast of the first moonwalk by the *Apollo 11* astronauts Neil Armstrong and Edwin "Buzz" Aldrin (both USA) on July 20 1969 was watched by an estimated 600 million people worldwide (about one fifth of the world's population at that time).

MOST FAN MAIL

After his solo nonstop transatlantic flight in May 1927, Charles Lindbergh (USA) received 3,500,000 letters. Although fan mail is usually associated with film idols and pop stars, no actor or musician has matched such a figure in his or her career.

BEST-SELLING DIARY

The Diary of Anne Frank has sold more than 25 million copies and has been translated into 55 languages. The diary is an autobiographical account of events that took place while young Anne and her family hid in an attic in Amsterdam, The Netherlands, to escape Nazi persecution during World War II. The book was first published by Anne's father, Otto (Germany), the only survivor of the family.

LONGEST INCARCERATION OF A FUTURE PRESIDENT

Nelson Rolihlahla Mandela (above) spent almost 27 years in prison in South Africa from 1964 until his release on February 11 1990. On May 10 1994, he became the first democratically elected president in South Africa's history.

ROYAL PATRON TO THE MOST CHARITIES

As of December 2000, Princess Anne, the Princess Royal (UK), was patron of 233 charity organizations. She is best known for her charity work with Save the Children UK, of which she has been president since 1970, and for her own Princess Royal Trust for Carers, which raises awareness of the UK's estimated 6 million carers.

EARLIEST ROCKET LAUNCH

On March 16 1926 at Auburn, MA, USA, Dr. Robert Hutchings Goddard (USA) launched a liquid-fueled rocket to an altitude of 41 ft (12.5 m) and over a distance of 184 ft (56 m). This feat effectively marked the first step toward spaceflight, transforming humanity's perception of the universe.

LARGEST RADIO AUDIENCE FOR RELIGIOUS PROGRAM

Decision Hour, a religious broadcast by the Baptist evangelist Billy Graham (USA), has been broadcast regularly since 1957, attracting an average radio audience of 20 million.

MOST CONDOLENCES POSTED ON THE INTERNET

A total of 580,000 people left messages on the memorial page of the official website of the British monarchy in September 1997, following the death of Diana, Princess of Wales.

MOST CAREER GOALS BY A FOOTBALLER

The most goals scored in a specific period is 1,279 by Edson Arantes do Nascimento (Brazil), known as Pelé, from September 7 1956 to October 1 1977 in 1,363 games. His best year was 1959, when he scored 126 times. The Milésimo (1,000th) came from a penalty for Pelé's club Santos at the Maracanã Stadium, Rio de Janeiro, Brazil, on November 19 1969, in his 909th first-class match. He added two more goals in special appearances.

Pelé has been actively involved in leprosy elimination campaigns in Brazil and has carried out extensive work for children's causes through the United Nations Children's Fund (UNICEF). Since his retirement in 1977, he has become an international ambassador for sports, working to promote peace and understanding through friendly athletic competition.

LARGEST FOOD DRIVE BY A NON-CHARITABLE ORGANIZATION

The 1,400 students of San Mateo High School, CA, USA, put together the largest food drive by a non-charitable organization from December 3–17 1999, collecting 214,713 lb (97,892.2 kg) of non-perishable food for the poor and homeless of San Mateo County.

LARGEST DONATION TO A SINGLE UNIVERSITY

The greatest donation to one university is $250 million (£176 million) to the University of Colorado, by the chairman and co-founder of software manufacturer BEA Systems, Bill Coleman, and his wife Claudia (both USA) in January 2001. The money will be used to set up the Coleman Institute for Cognitive Disabilities.

MOST OSCARS

Walter (Walt) Elias Disney (USA) has won 26 Oscars from 64 nominations. His studio's prolific output, including a host of classic cartoons as well as Oscar-winning documentaries, has had a major and lasting effect on the development of popular culture.

YOUNGEST ELECTED US PRESIDENT

At the age of 43, John F Kennedy (USA) became the youngest man ever to win the American presidency, as Democratic victor in the 1960 US presidential election. Winning by a narrow margin over Richard Nixon in the popular vote, Kennedy had the distinction of becoming the first Roman Catholic president. He was also the youngest president to die in office.

LARGEST DROP IN CRIME

In 1993, Rudolph Giuliani (USA, left) was elected the 107th mayor of New York City, USA. Under his indomitable leadership, New York City experienced an unprecedented reduction in overall crime. According to preliminary crime statistics from the New York City Police Department, between 1993 and 2001 murders in the city decreased by 66.63% and rapes dropped by 49.52%, while robberies fell by 67.56%. This is the largest drop in crime in more than 28 years of available data.

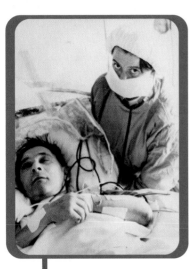

FIRST HEART TRANSPLANT PATIENT

The first heart transplant operation was performed on 55-year-old Louis Washkansky (South Africa, above left) at the Groote Schuur Hospital, Cape Town, South Africa, from 1 am to 6 am on December 3 1967 by a team of 30 led by Prof Christiaan Barnard (South Africa). Washkansky lived for 18 days.

LONGEST SURVIVAL WITHOUT FOOD AND WATER

Andreas Mihavecz (Austria) survived for 18 days without food and water. Mihavecz had been put into a holding cell on April 1 1979 in a local government building in Höchst, Austria, but the police subsequently forgot that he was there. On April 18 1979 he was finally discovered, close to death.

LONGEST ARTIFICIAL HEART TRANSPLANT SURVIVAL

William J Schroeder (USA) is the longest surviving artificial heart transplant patient to date. He survived for 620 days in Louisville, Kentucky, USA, from November 25 1984 to August 7 1986.

LONGEST TIME SURVIVED WITHOUT A PULSE

Julie Mills (UK) managed to last three days without a pulse in her vascular system, when she suffered severe heart failure and viral myocarditis on August 14 1998. Cardiac surgeons at the John Radcliffe Hospital, Oxford, UK, used a non pulsatile blood pump (AB180) to support her for one week, during which her heart recovered, and the pump was removed.

HIGHEST NON-VOLUNTARY G-FORCE ENDURED

Racing driver David Purley (UK) survived a deceleration from 108 mph (173 km/h) to zero in a distance of just 26 in (66 cm) in a crash at Silverstone, Northants, UK, on July 13 1977. He withstood a force of 179.8 g and suffered 29 fractures, three dislocations, and six heart stoppages.

HIGHEST PARACHUTE ESCAPE

Royal Air Force officers Flt Lt J de Salis and Fg Off P Lowe (both UK) made the highest ever escape in a parachute at 56,102 ft (17,100 m), over Monyash, Derby, UK, on April 9 1958.

LOWEST PARACHUTE ESCAPE

Sqn Ldr Terence Spencer (UK) made the lowest ever aircraft escape, at a height of 30–40 ft (9–12 m) at Wismar Bay, Germany, on April 19 1945. Spencer was blown out of his aircraft while attacking enemy planes in the Bay of Wismar. He landed in the sea and managed to swim ashore.

LONGEST FALL SURVIVED BY AN INFANT

In November 1997, 18-month-old baby Alejandro (Spain) survived a 65-ft 7-in (20-m) fall from the seventh-floor kitchen window of a flat in Murcia, Spain. He suffered only bruising, a broken tooth, and a split lip.

MOST HOSTAGES HELD

The largest group of hostages held by a terrorist organization numbered more than 500 people. They were detained by Tupac Amaru terrorists at the Japanese Embassy in Lima, Peru, on December 17 1996. Most of the hostages were released over time, and the final 72 were rescued when Peruvian commandos stormed the embassy on April 22 1997 killing all four rebels, including their leader, Nestor Cerpa (Peru).

MOST LIGHTNING STRIKES SURVIVED

A single lightning strike is made up of several 100 million volts (with peak current in the order of 20,000 amps). The only person to be struck seven times by lightning was ex-park ranger Roy C Sullivan (USA), the "human lightning conductor." His attraction for lightning began in 1942, when he lost a big toenail as the result of a strike. A second strike in 1969 resulted in the loss of his eyebrows, and in July 1970 his left shoulder was seared by a third strike. A fourth strike, on April 16 1972, set his hair on fire and a fifth, on August 7 1973, set his new hair on fire and seared his legs. His ankle was injured on June 5 1976 in strike number six, and on June 25 1977 he suffered chest and stomach burns with the seventh strike. In the USA, the average number of deaths from lightning is just over 100 a year.

LONGEST SOLO SURVIVAL ON A RAFT

Second Steward Poon Lim (Hong Kong) of the British Merchant Navy survived for 133 days after his ship, the SS *Ben Lomond*, was torpedoed in the Atlantic on November 23 1942. A Brazilian fishing boat rescued him off Salinópolis, Brazil, on April 5 1943, and he was strong enough to walk ashore.

LONGEST FALL SURVIVED IN AN ELEVATOR

Office workers Shameka Peterson and Joe Mascora (both USA) dropped 40 floors (about 400 ft, or 121 m) in four seconds down the Empire State Building, New York City, USA, when the cable of their elevator failed on January 25 2000. Stopping just four floors from the ground, both suffered only minor bruising during their ordeal.

HIGHEST FALL SURVIVED WITHOUT A PARACHUTE

Vesna Vulovic (former Yugoslavia, above) survived a fall from 33,333 ft (10,160 m) over Srbsk, Kamenice, Czechoslovakia (now Czech Republic), on January 26 1972, after the Boeing DC-9 she was working aboard exploded.

MOST LABOR CAMP ESCAPES

A former Soviet citizen, Tatyana Mikhailovna Russanova, now living in Haifa, Israel, escaped from various Stalinist labor camps in the former Soviet Union on 15 separate occasions between 1943 and 1954, being recaptured and sentenced 14 times.

LONGEST UNDERWATER SURVIVAL

In 1986 two-year-old Michelle Funk (USA) spent 66 minutes underwater, having fallen into a swollen creek. She went on to make a full recovery.

LONGEST MARCH

The longest march in military history was the Long March by the Chinese Communists, which lasted 368 days – of which 268 days were spent on the move – from October 1934 to October 1935. A force of around 100,000 people covered 6,000 miles (9,700 km) from Ruijin, in Jiangxi, to Yan'an, in Shaanxi. They crossed 18 mountain ranges and 24 rivers, reaching Yan'an with approximately 8,000 survivors as a result of continual rearguard actions against nationalist Guomindang (GMD) forces.

OLDEST EX-SERVICEMAN

The longest-lived soldier on record is John B Salling (USA) of the US Confederate Army; he is also the last accepted survivor of the US Civil War (1861–65). Salling died in Kingsport, Tennessee, USA, on March 16 1959, aged 112 years 305 days.

SURVIVOR OF LONGEST FALL DOWN A LIFT SHAFT

Stuart Jones (New Zealand) fell 23 stories, a distance of 229 ft 7 in (70 m), down an elevator shaft while carrying out structural work on the roof of a temporary elevator at the Midland Park Building, Wellington, New Zealand, in May 1998. Jones survived his dramatic fall, but sustained multiple injuries, including a broken hip, a compound fracture in his left leg, a broken left kneecap, and a broken rib.

LONGEST TIME TRAPPED IN A LIFT

On December 28 1997 Kiveli Papaioannou, who had recently moved from New York City, USA, to Limassol, Cyprus, found herself trapped in her apartment elevator for six days while she was on her way back from a shopping trip. The 76-year-old overcame dehydration and the cold by rationing the fruit, vegetables, and bread that she had in her shopping bag.

LONGEST HELD HOSTAGE

Terry Anderson (USA, below with his daughter Sulome) was held hostage in Beirut, Lebanon, for 2,454 days (6 years 264 days) by Hezbollah terrorists, until his release on December 4 1991.

FIRST WOMAN TO CLIMB MOUNT EVEREST

Junko Tabei (Japan, above) reached the summit of Mount Everest on May 16 1975. The first woman to climb the "Seven Summits" (the highest peak on each continent), she has also climbed 70 of the world's major peaks.

LONGEST SCUBA DIVE IN OPEN FRESH WATER

Between August 31 and September 3 2001 Daniel Misiaszek (USA) spent 60 hr 24 min submerged in Spring Lake, San Marcos, Texas, USA, using air only from underwater breathing tanks. The tanks were replaced throughout the record attempt by a team of 22 divers.

GREATEST DISTANCE WALKED IN 24 HOURS

At Albuquerque, New Mexico, USA, over 24 hours from September 18 to 19 1976, Jesse Castenda (USA) walked 142.25 miles (228.93 km).

The greatest distance walked over 24 hours by a woman is 131.27 miles (211.25 km) by Annie van der Meer-Timmermann (Netherlands) at Rouen, France, between May 10 and 11 1986.

LONGEST NON-STOP WALK

Georges Holtyzer (Belgium) walked 418.49 miles (673.48 km) in 6 days 10 hr 58 min, completing 452 laps of a 0.92-mile (1.49-km) circuit at Ninove, Belgium, from July 19 to 25 1986. He was not permitted any stops for rest and was moving 98.78% of the time.

LONGEST WALK BY A WOMAN

The longest walk by a woman was one of 18,840 miles (30,321 km) by Ffyona Campbell (UK) who walked around the world in five phases, covering four continents and 20 countries. She left John O'Groats, Highland, UK, on August 16 1983, returning there on October 14 1994.

FASTEST TRANS-AMERICA WALK

John Lees (UK) walked 2,876 miles (4,628 km) across the USA from City Hall, Los Angeles, California, to City Hall, New York City, in 53 days 12 hr 15 min between April 11 and June 3 1972. He averaged 53.75 miles (86.49 km) a day.

LONGEST DISTANCE WALKED ON STILTS

The greatest distance ever walked on stilts is 3,008 miles (4,841 km), from Los Angeles, California, USA, to Bowen, Kentucky, USA, by Joe Bowen (USA) from February 20 to July 26 1980.

GREATEST DISTANCE COVERED IN 24 HOURS IN A WHEELCHAIR

Iran-born Nik Nikzaban (Canada) wheeled himself over 77.58 miles (124.86 km) in 24 hours from April 6 to 7 2000. The endurance event took place on Handsworth Secondary School track, in North Vancouver, Canada. The track lane that Nik used was 1,362 ft 10.2 in (415.4 m) in length, and he completed 301 laps of the track.

FARTHEST ROUND-THE-WORLD WALK

The greatest distance claimed for a round-the-world walker is 34,501 miles (55,524 km) by Arthur Blessitt (USA), in more than 33 years since December 25 1969. He has been to all seven continents, including Antarctica, carrying a 12-ft (3.66-m) cross and preaching throughout his walk.

LONGEST TIGHTROPE WALK

The longest walk by any funambulist (tightrope walker) was by Henri Rochetain (France), on a wire 11,368 ft (3,465 m) long, across a gorge at Clermont Ferrand, France, on July 13 1969. The crossing took 3 hr 20 min.

FIRST PEOPLE TO REACH THE NORTH POLE

Arctic explorer Robert Peary (USA) is widely regarded as being the first person to reach the North Pole. Peary set off on his expedition from Cape Columbia, Ellesmere Island, Canada, on March 1 1909 with his associate Matt Henson (USA). On April 6 Peary made observations indicating that he had reached his destination. Although Frederick Cook (also USA) challenged his claim, asserting that he had reached the pole earlier that month, the US Congress acknowledged Peary's achievement in 1911.

FIRST SOLO EXPEDITION TO THE NORTH POLE

Japanese explorer and mountaineer Naomi Uemura became the first person to reach the North Pole in a solo trek across the Arctic sea ice at 4:45 am GMT on May 1 1978. He traveled 450 miles (725 km), setting out on March 7 from Cape Edward, Ellesmere Island in northern Canada. In February 1984, Uemura died attempting to become the first person to climb Mt McKinley, Alaska, USA, alone in winter.

FASTEST ASCENT OF MOUNT EVEREST

On May 21 2000 Babu Chhiri Sherpa (Nepal) made the fastest ascent of Mount Everest from base camp to its 29,028-ft (8,848-m) summit, via the south side of the mountain, in 16 hr 56 min.

During the same ascent, he also completed the longest ever stay (21 hours) at Everest's peak without the use of bottled oxygen.

MOST SOUTHERLY DIVE

On February 17 2000 nine members of HMS *Endurance* ship's company (above) undertook a dive at 77.11ºS, 32.59ºW in the Weddell Sea, Antarctica. The 32-ft 9.6-in (10-m) dive was in a water temperature of 29.3ºF (-1.5ºC).

FASTEST SOLO CIRCUMNAVIGATION BY A YACHTSWOMAN

Ellen MacArthur (UK) circumnavigated the globe in 94 days 4 hr 25 min 40 sec during the 2000 Vendée Globe yacht race, starting and finishing at Les Sables d'Olonne, France. She covered 24,000 miles (38,600 km) in her yacht *Kingfisher* from November 5 2000 to February 11 2001.

FASTEST SEVEN-SUMMIT ASCENT

Andrew Salter (UK) climbed the highest peak on each continent in 290 days. Between May 16 2000, when he reached the top of Mt Everest, Nepal, and February 28 2001, when he ascended Aconcagua, Argentina, he climbed Mt McKinley, Alaska, USA, on June 21 2000; Kilimanjaro, Tanzania, on July 12 2000; Elbrus, Russia, on September 1 2000; Puncak Jaya, Indonesia, on October 24 2000; and Vinson Massif, Antarctica, in November 2000.

MOST SOUTHERLY MARATHON

The Antarctica Marathon and Half-Marathon is the only sports event held on the most southerly continent. Operating since 1995, it takes place on King George Island, just off the Antarctic peninsula. Because the race takes place only in perfect weather, runners can use ordinary running shoes in the snowy conditions.

DEEPEST NO LIMITS FREE DIVE BY A WOMAN

The record depth for the dangerous sport of no limits free-diving by a woman is 411 ft (125 m) – deeper than Japanese submarines reached during World War II – by Audrey Mestre Ferrera (France) at La Palma, Canary Islands, Spain, on May 13 2000. Taking just a single breath she was underwater for 2 min 3 sec.

DEEPEST SEAWATER SCUBA DIVE

The deepest ever scuba dive was 1,010 ft (307.8 m) by John Bennett (UK) on November 6 2001. The dive took place off Escarcia Point, Puerto Galera, Philippines. The descent on a weighted sled took just over 12 minutes but the ascent took 9 hr 36 min.

FASTEST SOLO ROW ACROSS THE ATLANTIC FROM EAST TO WEST

From December 1969 to July 1970 Sidney Genders (UK) rowed from Las Palmas, Canary Islands, Spain, to Antigua, West Indies – a distance of 3,800 miles (6,115 km) – in 73 days 8 hours.

EARLIEST MANNED SPACE FLIGHT

The earliest manned space flight – ratified by the world governing body, the Fédération Aéronautique Internationale (FAI) – was by Cosmonaut Flight Major Yuri Alekseyevich Gagarin (USSR) in *Vostok 1* on April 12 1961. The take-off was from the Baikonur Cosmodrome, Kazakhstan, at 6:07 am GMT, and the landing occurred near Smelovka, near Engels, in the Saratov region of Russia, some 115 minutes later. Gagarin landed by parachute separately from his spacecraft 118 minutes after the launch, having ejected 108 minutes into the flight as planned.

MOST CONQUESTS OF MOUNT EVEREST

Apa Sherpa (Nepal) has successfully reached the summit of Mt Everest 12 times between 1990 and 2002.

YOUNGEST PERSON TO VISIT BOTH POLES

The youngest person to have visited both geographical poles is Jonathan Silverman (USA, b. June 13 1990, above), who reached the North Pole on July 25 1999 and the South Pole on January 10 2002, at 11 years 211 days of age. He traveled to the North Pole via a Russian ice-breaker and landed at the South Pole by aircraft from Chile.

FASTEST CIRCUMNAVIGATION OF THE WORLD IN A HELICOPTER

John Williams and Ron Bower (both USA) flew round the world in a Bell 430 helicopter in a record time of 17 days 6 hr 14 min 25 sec, at an average speed of 57.02 mph (91.76 km/h). They left Fair Oaks, London, UK, on August 17 1996 and flew west, against prevailing winds, finally arriving back at Fair Oaks on September 3 1996.

FASTEST MICROLIGHT CIRCUMNAVIGATION

Colin Bodill (UK, above right) flew around the world in a Mainair Blade 912 Flexwing microlight in 99 days from May 31 to September 6 2000. Bodill was accompanying Jennifer Murray (UK, above center) as she set the record for the fastest solo helicopter circumnavigation by a female. Along with co-pilot Quentin Smith (UK, above left), Murray had previously become the first female to pilot a helicopter around the globe – their 97-day journey lasted from May 10 1997 to August 15 1997.

LONGEST UNAIDED CROSSING OF ANTARCTICA

Alain Hubert and Dixie Dansercoer (both Belgium) are the only people to have crossed Antarctica – from the now defunct Belgian King Baudouin Base to the US McMurdo Base on the Ross Sea – with only a pair of skis and a parafoil. The 2,423-mile (3,900-km) journey began on November 4 1997 and ended on February 9 1998 after 99 days of struggling against ice storms and temperatures of below 14°F (-10°C).

FIRST POLE-TO-POLE CIRCUMNAVIGATION OF THE WORLD

Ranulph Fiennes and Charles Burton (both UK) of the British Trans-Globe Expedition were the first people to achieve a pole-to-pole surface circumnavigation of the world. Fiennes and Burton set out from Greenwich, London, UK, on September 2 1979, crossing the South Pole on December 15 1980 and the North Pole on April 10 1982. They returned to Greenwich on August 29 1982, having completed a 35,000-mile (56,000-km) trek.

GREATEST MANNED DISTANCE IN A BALLOON

The official Fédération Aéronautique Internationale (FAI) record for the farthest balloon journey is 25,361 miles (40,814 km) set by Bertrand Piccard (Switzerland) and Brian Jones (UK). The two piloted the *Breitling Orbiter 3* from March 1–21 1999.

When *Breitling Orbiter 3* crossed the "finishing line" of 9.27°W over Mauritania, northwest Africa, after a journey of 15 days 10 hr 24 min, it also became the first balloon to circle the world nonstop. As the first people to accomplish this feat, Jones and Piccard are also the holders of the record for the fastest circumnavigation of the globe in a balloon.

LONGEST LIFEBOAT JOURNEY

After his ship the *Endurance* became trapped by sea ice in Antarctica, Ernest Shackleton (UK) decided to abandon it, taking with him his 28-man crew. Three lifeboats headed for Elephant Island, 100 miles (161 km) north. Once there, and knowing that a rescue was unlikely, Shackleton chose five of his best men to sail the largest lifeboat, the 22.5-ft-long (6.85-m) *James Caird*, to a whaling station in South Georgia, 800 miles (1,287 km) away. They reached the island after 17 days, on May 19 1916.

GREATEST DISTANCE FLOWN BY A SOLO BALLOONIST

Steve Fossett (USA) flew 14,235 miles (22,909 km), launching in Mendoza, Argentina, and crash-landing in the Pacific Ocean, 500 miles (800 km) off the coast of Australia. The flight lasted from August 7–16 1998.

FASTEST ROUND-THE-WORLD JOURNEY BY CAR

Driving a Metrocab taxi, Jeremy Levine, James Burke, and Mark Aylett (all UK) circumnavigated the world in 19 days 10 hr 10 min. The trio started at Buckingham Palace, London, UK, on June 16 2000 and arrived back on October 11 2000 after a journey of 18,119 miles (29,159 km). This total excludes time spent aboard ships between countries and continents.

The record for the first and fastest circumnavigation of the world by car, under the rules applicable in 1989 and 1991, embracing more than an equator's length of driving (24,901 road miles, or 40,074 km), is held by Mohammed Salahuddin Choudhury and his wife Neena (both India). The journey took 69 days 19 hr 5 min from September 9 to November 17 1989. The couple drove a 1989 Hindustan "Contessa Classic," starting and finishing in Delhi, India.

LONGEST SOLO CYCLE JOURNEY

The greatest mileage amassed in a cycle tour was in excess of 402,000 miles (646,960 km) and was achieved by itinerant lecturer Walter Stolle (Czech Republic) from January 24 1959 to December 12 1976. He visited 159 countries, starting from Romford, Essex, UK.

LONGEST WIND-POWERED LAND JOURNEY

Robert Torline (USA, above) traveled from Brownsville, Texas, USA (Mexican border), to Maida, North Dakota, USA (Canadian border), covering 2,119 miles (3,410 km) on his wind-powered Streetsailor from April 29 to June 16 2001.

LONGEST JOURNEY BY WHEELCHAIR

Rick Hansen (Canada), who was paralyzed from the waist down in 1973 after a car accident, wheeled his wheelchair for 24,901.55 miles (40,075.16 km) through four continents and 34 countries during his "Man in Motion World Tour." The journey started in Vancouver, British Columbia, Canada, on March 21 1985 and finished at the same location on May 22 1987. Hansen undertook his demanding feat in an effort to promote a greater awareness of the potential of disabled people and succeeded in raising $24 million (£14.7 million) for spinal cord injury research.

GREATEST DISTANCE COVERED ON IN-LINE SKATES

Jari Koistinen and V-P Poikonen (both Finland) traveled 1,749 miles (2,815 km) on in-line skates between May 29 and June 22 2000. The pair skated from Helsinki to Utsjoki, Finland, and back, using in-line skates and ski poles, a technique commonly known as "Nordic blading."

FASTEST CROSSING OF THE BERING STRAIT ON SKIS AND BY FOOT

The first and fastest crossing of the Bering Strait by skis and on foot was completed by Dmitry Shparo and his son Matvey (both Russia), when they reached Chariot, Alaska, USA, on March 20 1998. They had begun their journey from Mys Dezhneva (East Cape), Russia, on March 1 that year and traveled a total distance of approximately 180 miles (290 km).

FASTEST CAPE TOWN TO CAIRO RUN

Nicholas Bourne (UK) completed the first and fastest run from Cape Town, South Africa, to Cairo, Egypt. Leaving Cape Town on January 21 1998, Bourne covered more than 7,500 miles (12,069 km), passing through South Africa, Botswana, Zambia, Tanzania, Kenya, Ethiopia, Sudan, and Egypt, arriving at the Great Pyramids, Giza, Cairo, on December 5 1998.

FIRST ANTARCTIC CROSSING

The first ever surface crossing of Antarctica ended at 1:47 pm on March 2 1958, after a 2,158-mile (3,473-km) trek. The journey, from Shackleton Base to Scott Base via the South Pole, lasted 99 days, and began on November 24 1957. The party consisted of 12 people and was led by Vivian Ernest Fuchs (UK).

FASTEST CROSSING OF THE AMERICAS BY MOTORCYCLE

Nick Alcock and Hugh Sinclair (both UK, below) rode a pair of Honda Africa Twin 742-cc motorcycles from Prudhoe Bay, Alaska, USA, to Ushuaia, Argentina, in 47 days 12 hr from August 29 to October 15 2001, a distance of around 15,000 miles (24,000 km). Alcock and Sinclair embarked on the challenge to raise funds for Action Aid.

AMAZING FEATS

LONGEST RIDE WEARING A SUIT OF ARMOR

Dick Brown (UK, above) rode on horseback from Edinburgh Castle, Lothian, UK, to Dumfries, UK – a distance of 208 miles (334.7 km) – wearing a full suit of steel armor, from June 10–14 1989. The suit weighed 68 lb (30.84 kg).

LONGEST MAGGOT BATH

Christine Martin (UK) immersed herself in a bath of maggots for a period of 1.5 hours in April 2002 to raise cash for a trek to Nepal organized by medical charity Action Research. Ten gallons of maggots were poured over Christine as she sat in the tub wearing only a swimsuit. The maggots used in the record attempt were sponsored by The National Bait Company.

LONGEST SIDE-WHEEL CAR DRIVE

Bengt Norberg (Sweden) drove a Mitsubishi Colt GTi-16V on two side wheels nonstop for a distance of 192.873 miles (310.391 km) in 7 hr 15 min 50 sec. Norberg also drove a distance of 27.842 miles (44.808 km) in 1 hour on two side wheels at Rattvik Horse Track, Sweden, on May 24 1989.

LONGEST EGG-AND-SPOON DISTANCE RUN

Dale Lyons (UK), ran the London Marathon, London, UK, (a distance of 26 miles 385 yd, or 42.195 km) while carrying a teaspoon with a fresh egg on it. He completed the marathon in 3 hr 47 min on April 23 1990.

FARTHEST DISTANCE COVERED WALKING BACKWARD IN 24 HOURS

The longest distance covered walking backward for a period of 24 hours is 95.40 miles (153.52 km) by Anthony Thornton (USA) in Minneapolis, Minnesota, USA, from December 31 1988 to January 1 1989. His average speed was 3.9 mph (6.4 km/h).

FASTEST MARATHON RUNNING BACKWARD

Timothy Bud Badyna (USA) completed a marathon (26 miles 385 yd, or 42.195 km) running backward in 3 hr 53 min 17 sec in Toledo, Ohio, USA, on April 24 1994.

FASTEST STAIR CLIMB

The record time for ascending the 1,336 stairs of the world's tallest hotel, the Westin Stamford Hotel, Singapore, is 6 min 55 sec by Balvinder Singh (Singapore). The feat was attained during the hotel's 3rd Annual Vertical Marathon on June 4 1989.

LONGEST NONSTOP CONCERT BY A CHOIR

The longest continuous concert by a choral group lasted 20 hr 23 sec and was performed by the 120 members of the Turtle Creek Chorale (USA), directed by Dr Timothy Seelig (USA). The performance took place at the Lakewood Theater in Dallas, Texas, USA, from August 14–15 1999. The choir was split into four groups. Each group sang for 30 minutes per hour, and they overlapped each other in 15-minute segments.

GREATEST BACKWARD WALKER

Plennie L Wingo (USA) is the greatest exponent of reverse pedestrianism. He completed his 8,000-mile (12,875-km) transcontinental walk from Santa Monica, California, USA, to Istanbul, Turkey, from April 15 1931 to October 24 1932.

LONGEST HANDBELL RINGING SESSION

The longest nonstop handbell ringing by a group of nine players lasted 12 hr 1 min 7 sec and was carried out by the St. Columba Harmony Handbell Ensemble of Durango, Colorado, USA, on June 18 1999 in Durango.

LONGEST MOVIE-WATCHING MARATHON

An audience of 14 people consisting of Chinnawatra Boonrasri, Sirirat Kampongsa, Nuntiya Thammajinda, Nitipol Charoenkool, Pongsakorn Kerdpan, Pongsak Jamonchote, Suwat Kamvisuth, Yuthana Eakpornwut, Wuttichai Leelasvattanakul, Chalee Yongsamith, Sumalee Suwannapatch, Kodchapong Sarobon, Sonravit Eonvonsakun, and Apiradee Phantong (all Thailand) watched 25 films, lasting 50 hr 55 min, at The Grand EGV Cinemas, Bangkok, Thailand, from February 18–20 2000. The audience was allowed to move to a designated room for five minutes between films, and to have a 15-minute eating break after every three movies. The marathon began with 369 film fans, but all except the final 14 subsequently dropped out.

LONGEST VIDEO-WATCHING MARATHON

At an event organized by Court TV, Kevin Keaveny (USA) watched 51 episodes of *NYPD Blue* over 46 hr 30 min 50.91 sec between August 31 and September 2 2001 in New York City, USA.

LONGEST INDIVIDUAL KEYBOARD-PLAYING MARATHON

From March 30 to April 1 2001, Ginés Borges Belza (Spain) played a Yamaha MC-600 electric organ for 49 hr 15 min (including six breaks of 15 minutes) at the Royal Nautical Club of Santa Cruz de Tenerife, Canary Islands, Spain. Belza played a total of 800 individual arrangements, each lasting around three minutes.

LONGEST KISS

Rich Langley and Louisa Almedovar (both USA, above center and right) hold the record for the world's longest kiss, which lasted for 30 hr 59 min 27 sec on December 5 2001 at the TV studios of *Ricki Lake*, New York City, USA.

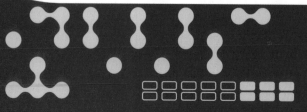

LONGEST IRONING SESSION

Eufemia Stadler (Switzerland) carried out 40 hours of continuously ironing 228 shirts while standing at an ironing board from September 16–18 1999. She was allowed breaks of 15 minutes only every eight hours.

LONGEST TIME SPENT JUGGLING THREE OBJECTS

Terry Cole (UK) juggled three objects, without dropping any of them, for 11 hr 4 min 22 sec in 1995.

LONGEST CARD GAME

Rolando Fasani, Ivano Pancera, Claudio Zanelli, Andrea Zanelli, Mauro Rossi, Armando von Bürer, Eros Zanelli, and Daniele Fiore (all Italy) played the card game "Jass" for 28 hours continuously at the Bellavista Restaurant, Sant'Abbondio, Switzerland, from March 17–18 2001.

LONGEST TIME SPENT ON A BED OF NAILS

The duration record for nonstop lying on a bed of nails (6 in, or 15.2 cm in length and 2 in, or 5 cm apart) is 274 hr 2 min by Inge Wilda Svingen (Norway) on November 3 1984.

The same duration record for a female is 30 hours, set by Geraldine Williams (UK) on May 18–19 1977.

LONGEST TREE SITTING

The official duration record for staying in a tree is 21 years, by Bungkas (Indonesia), who first climbed up into a 55-ft 9.24-in-high (17-m) palm tree in the Indonesian village of Bengkes, in the district of Pakong, in 1970, remaining there until 1991.

LONGEST TIME POLE-SITTING IN A BARREL

Vernon Kruger (South Africa) stayed in a barrel (maximum capacity 150 gal, or 682 liters) at the top of a pole at Dullstroom, Mpumalanga, South Africa, for 67 days 14 min from March 17 to May 23 1997. Kruger's pole was located in the middle of the town square, and tourists often stopped off to see him on their way to the Kruger National Wildlife Park.

LONGEST DURATION SITTING IN A SHACK ON A POLE

Mellissa Sanders (USA) lived in a shack measuring 5 ft 10.8 in x 6 ft 9.6 in (1.8 m x 2.1 m) on top of a pole in Indianapolis, Indiana, USA, from October 26 1986 to March 24 1988, a total of 516 days.

LONGEST WING-WALKING MARATHON

Roy Castle (UK) flew on the wing of a Boeing Stearman biplane for 3 hr 23 min on August 2 1990, taking off from Gatwick, W Sussex, UK, and landing at Le Bourget, near Paris, France. At the time Castle was host of the UK's *Record Breakers* television program.

GREATEST DISTANCE SAILED IN A BATHTUB OVER 24 HOURS

The greatest distance covered by paddling a hand-propelled bathtub on still water in 24 hours is 90.5 miles (145.6 km), by 13 members of Aldington Prison Officers Social Club (UK) on May 28–29 1983.

GREATEST DISTANCE TO DRIBBLE A BASKETBALL

The greatest distance covered in 24 hours while simultaneously dribbling a basketball is 97.37 miles (156.71 km). The feat was carried out by Suresh Joachim (Australia) at Vulkanhallen, Oslo, Norway, from March 30–31 2001.

LONGEST TENNIS BALL-HEADING

Luis Silva (Portugal, below) headed a tennis ball continuously for 59 min 53 sec in Folgosa do Douro, Portugal, on June 10 2001. Silva began training for the record attempt when he was 15 years old, about four years before he successfully achieved his goal.

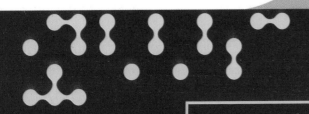

HIGHEST EIGHT-PERSON TIGHTROPE PYRAMID

Circus troupe The Flying Wallendas (USA, above) performed an eight-person pyramid suspended at a height of 25 ft (7.62 m) at Sarasota, Florida, USA, on February 20 2001.

LONGEST DRUMMING MARATHON

Paskaran Sreekaram (Singapore), Selvapandian Shunmuga Sundaram (Singapore), and Mirajkar Nawaz Mohammad (India) banged a set of drums continuously for 27 hr 45 min at Kolam Ayer Community Club, Singapore, from February 2–3 2001.

FASTEST BED-MAKING

The fastest time for making a bed with one blanket, two sheets, an undersheet, an uncased pillow, one pillowcase, one counterpane, and hospital corners is 14 seconds by Sister Sharon Stringer and Nurse Michelle Benkel (both UK) of the Royal Masonic Hospital, London, UK, at Canary Wharf, London, UK, on November 26 1993.

MOST POTATOES PEELED

The greatest quantity of potatoes peeled by five people to a recognized cooking standard and using kitchen knives is 1,064 lb 6 oz (482.8 kg) in 45 minutes by Marj Killian, Terry Anderson, Barbara Pearson, Marilyn Small, and Janene Utkin (all USA) at the 64th Annual Idaho Spud Day celebration. The event took place at Shelley, Idaho, USA, on September 19 1992.

FASTEST CROSSING OF FLORIDA STRAITS BY PADDLEBOARD

The fastest crossing of the 110-mile (180-km) Florida Straits between Havana, Cuba, and Key West, Florida, on a paddleboard, is 19 hr 19 min 52 sec by Michael Lee, Jeff Horn, Derek Levy, and Michael O'Shaughnessey (all USA), paddling in relay, on June 23 2000.

MOST BEER CRATES STACKED IN PYRAMID

On June 21–22 1997 a team of 86 people from Villeroy & Boch Nederland, Anklaarsewg, The Netherlands, stacked 53,955 beer crates to form a pyramid in 15 hr 57 min. The record was achieved in Loo, The Netherlands.

GREATEST DISTANCE TO PUSH A PRAM IN 24 HOURS

A 10-man team from the Royal Marines School of Music, Deal, Kent, UK, pushed a pram containing an adult dressed as a baby a distance of 271.7 miles (437.3 km) in 24 hours from November 22–23 1990.

HEAVIEST WEIGHT PULLED BY A DOG-SLED TEAM

On October 22 2000 in Whitehorse, Yukon, Canada, 210 dogs pulled a sled attached to both a Kenworth tractor and a seven-axle rail trailer combination, the latter with a track mounted drill – adding up to a total weight of 145,302 lb (65,910 kg). The vehicle reached 9 mph (15 km/h) and traveled a distance of six blocks.

FARTHEST DISTANCE TO PUSH A LAWN MOWER IN 24 HOURS

From September 13–14 1997, four members of the Stowmarket and District Round Table, Suffolk, UK, pushed a standard lawn mower 101 miles 429 yd (162.936 km) around a course at Chilton Fields, Suffolk, UK.

GREATEST DISTANCE TO PULL A BOEING 747

A team of 60 British policemen pulled a Boeing 747-400 airplane weighing 451,947 lb (205 tonnes) a distance of 328 ft (100 m) in just 53.33 sec at London Heathrow Airport, London, UK, on September 27 2000.

FARTHEST DISTANCE TO ROLL A BARREL IN 24 HOURS

A team of 10 from Groningen, The Netherlands, rolled a 140-lb (63.5-kg) barrel 163 miles (263.9 km) in 24 hours on November 28–29 1998 at Stadspark, Rotterdam, The Netherlands.

MOST TRAMPOLINE SOMERSAULTS IN ONE HOUR

The most complete somersaults performed in one hour by a team is 7,043 by 10 members of the Kirklees Rebound Trampoline Club, using two trampolines at Huddersfield Sports Centre, Huddersfield, West Yorkshire, UK, on July 24 1999.

HAND-WALKING RELAY

A four-man relay team walking on their hands covered 1 mile (1.6 km) in 24 min 48 sec on March 15 1987 at Knoxville, Tennessee, USA.

FASTEST OPENING OF 300 BEER BOTTLES

The fastest time for opening 300 bottles of beer by a team of three is 1 min 47 sec. The leader of the team was Alois Unertl (Germany) of the German Unertl Brewery in Munich, Germany, on April 2 1999.

MOST CANS STACKED IN A PYRAMID IN 30 MINUTES

A team of Malaysian students constructed a pyramid from 9,455 aluminum cans in 24 minutes on September 23 2000 at Midvalley Mega Mall, Kuala Lumpur, Malaysia. The pyramid had a square base of 30 x 30 cans, measuring 6.5 x 6.5 ft (1.98 x 1.98 m) and reached a height of 11.02 ft (3.36 m).

LONGEST GAME OF HUMAN TABLE FOOTBALL

On August 5 2001 in Ilhavo, Portugal, 360 people took part in a game of human table football (above) that lasted 12 hours. Human table football is played with people tied to huge rotatable poles on a giant football field.

FASTEST THREE-LEGGED MARATHON

Identical twins Nick and Alastair Benbow (UK) set a three-legged running record in the London Marathon, London, UK, with a time of 3 hr 40 min 16 sec on April 26 1998. They were tied together at the wrist and shared a three-legged pair of trousers for the duration of their run.

MOST REVOLUTIONS ON A THRILL SWING

Paavo Lahtinen and Martti Pohjosaho (Finland) completed 212 continuous 360-degree revolutions on a thrill-swing carnival ride measuring 12.46 ft (3.8 m) tall and 9.35 ft (2.85 m) wide on July 7 2000 at Karstula, Finland.

MOST CARS DRIVEN ON TWO WHEELS SIMULTANEOUSLY

A team from Renault drove a continuous line of 16 cars on two wheels simultaneously at a military base at Evreux, France, on November 26 2000. The stunt was filmed for the TV show *L'Émission des Records* that was screened on December 23 2000.

FARTHEST DISTANCE PUSHING A BATHTUB IN 24 HOURS

The greatest distance covered in 24 hours pushing a wheeled bath-tub containing one passenger is 318.96 miles (513.32 km), by 25 people from Tea Tree Gully Baptist Church, Westfield, WA, Australia, on March 11–12 1995.

MOST SHOES SHINED IN EIGHT HOURS

Four teenagers polished off eight hours shining 14,975 shoes at the London Church of Christ at Leicester Square, London, UK, on June 15 1996.

MOST PEOPLE ON A SINGLE PAIR OF SKIS

The greatest number of people to travel on one pair of skis is 64, at the Norwegian Giant Ski Event in Ottawa, Ontario, Canada, on February 4 2001 (below). The participants covered 400 ft (120 m) on the skis, which, at 210 ft (64 m), are the longest pair ever made.

September 5 2001, when the cell phones of 260 people played the same ring tone (cinema advertiser Pearl and Dean's theme tune) simultaneously.

LARGEST WALK

The New Paper Big Walk 2000 had 77,500 participants and started from the National Stadium, Singapore, on May 21 2000. It was organized by The Singapore Press Holdings, The Singapore Amateur Athletic Association and The Singapore Sports Council. The purpose of the walk was to promote healthy living in Singapore.

LARGEST SIMULTANEOUS JUMP

The largest simultaneous jump occurred on September 7 2001 to celebrate the launch of Science Year in the UK. At precisely 11:00 am, 559,493 people began jumping up and down in 2,171 schools all over the UK for one minute. The total number of participants was 569,069. The extra numbers were made up by disabled pupils who contributed to the seismic activity by dropping objects on the ground or hitting the ground with their fists.

LARGEST TWIST

A total of 1,055 people danced the Twist for five minutes at Coquina Beach, Bradenton, Florida, USA, on December 31 1999. The event was organized by the *Manatee Herald Tribune* for the Millennium festivities.

LARGEST GAME OF MUSICAL CHAIRS

On August 5 1989 the largest game of musical chairs began with 8,238 participants at the Anglo-Chinese School in Singapore. Three-and-a-half hours later, the game ended with the lucky 15-year-old winner Xu Chong Wei (Singapore) on the last chair. He won the first prize of a trip for two to Bali.

MOST PEOPLE FLOSSING SIMULTANEOUSLY ON THE SAME LENGTH OF FLOSS

On July 31 2001, 297 people flossed for 45 seconds with a 1,500-ft-long (457.2-m) piece of dental floss to the tune "Eye of the Tiger" at Lake Geneva Youth Camp, Illinois, USA (above). There was a minimum of 2 ft (60 cm) of floss between each person. Dental personnel were on hand to make sure the attempt was executed safely and correctly.

MOST PEOPLE BRUSHING TEETH SIMULTANEOUSLY

On September 9 2001 in "The Great American Brush Off" at Coors Baseball Field in Denver, Colorado, USA, 1,586 baseball fans broke the world record for most people simultaneously brushing their teeth using innovative "eBrushes" supplied by Waterpik Technologies, Inc (USA). The fans were supplied with an eBrush, a tube of toothpaste, a bottle of water, and a spitting receptacle, and each participant brushed for a full minute.

LARGEST CELL PHONE RING

The world's largest cell phone ring took place in Leicester Square, London, UK, on

LARGEST HUG

On October 16 2001 staff and students from the Rocori Area Schools, Minnesota, USA, broke the world record for the largest hug, with 2,903 participants. The circle was continuous, and the participants held the hug for 15 seconds.

LARGEST GAME OF CHINESE WHISPERS

The largest ever game of Chinese Whispers (aka "Telephone") took place at Wembley Conference Centre, London, UK, on May 22 2002. The group of record-breaking whisperers was made up of 296 employees of Procter & Gamble UK and Ireland MDO.

LARGEST IRISH DANCE

A total of 6,971 people danced for five minutes at the Dublin Irish Festival, Dublin, Ohio, USA, on August 1 1998. Professional ceilidh dance callers presided at the event, and Irish bands played traditional jig music.

LARGEST TEA PARTY

The world's largest tea party took place on August 19 2001 at the Fort Canning Park, Singapore.

It was organized by Care Community Services and Dairy Farm Singapore and was attended by 7,121 people. Altogether, 20,700 cups of hot and cold Lipton tea were served on the day, along with 6,500 goodie bags, 20,000 pieces of cake, and 19,500 pieces of fruit. A total of SG$145,000 ($78,985 or £57,535) was raised for charity through ticket sales and individual donations.

LARGEST GATHERING OF CLOWNS

In 1991 at Bognor Regis, Dorset, UK, 850 clowns, including 430 from North America, assembled for their annual convention, which was arranged by Clowns International, the largest and oldest clown organization. The first clown convention was held in 1946.

MOST PEOPLE WEARING GROUCHO MARX GLASSES AT ONE TIME

The largest recorded number of people simultaneously wearing Groucho Marx-style glasses, nose, and moustache at one location is 522 on an enclosed tennis court in Pittsfield, New Hampshire, USA, on July 14 2001.

MOST PEOPLE SKIPPING SIMULTANEOUSLY

On September 24 2000, 1,060 students (above) skipped rope for three minutes at the Tamar Site, Hong Kong, for World Heart Day. The event was organized by The Hong Kong College of Cardiology and the Tung Wah Group of Hospitals.

MOST PEOPLE BLOWING BUBBLES AT ONE TIME

On May 16 1999, 23,680 people blew glycerine bubbles into the air for one full minute prior to West Ham's home Premier League match against Middlesbrough FC at the Boleyn Ground, Upton Park, London, UK. West Ham United FC's anthem is "I'm Forever Blowing Bubbles." The song was inspired by William Murray, who played for West Ham in the 1920s and resembled a child in a Pears' soap advertisement who was pictured blowing bubbles!

LARGEST EASTER EGG HUNT

On April 14 2001 Hershey Canada and Canadian Niagara Hotels, Inc organized the world's largest Easter egg hunt. The event featured 8,200 children aged between six and 12, who hunted for 254,000 eggs in Queen Victoria Park, Niagara Falls, Ontario, Canada. The eggs were made from 25,000 lb (11,340 kg) of chocolate. Laid end to end, they would be two-and-a-half times higher than Mt Everest.

LARGEST MASS BUNGEE JUMP

On September 6 1998, 25 people bungee-jumped simultaneously from a platform suspended 170 ft (52 m) above the ground, in front of the headquarters of Deutsche Bank, Frankfurt, Germany. The event, which was organized by Sanver Bungee on behalf of Frankfurt City Council, was part of a "skyscraper festival" to draw public attention to the city's modern architecture and burgeoning business district.

LARGEST HUMAN LOGO

On July 24 1999 a total of 34,309 people gathered at the National Stadium of Jamor, Lisbon, Portugal, to create the Portuguese logo for Euro 2004, as part of Portugal's successful bid to hold the UEFA football championships in 2004. The event was organized by Realizar Eventos Especiais (Portugal).

MOST COUPLES KISSING SIMULTANEOUSLY

On February 11 2000, 1,588 couples kissed simultaneously for 10 seconds as part of "The Big Kiss" sponsored by Radio Sarnia Lambton, Ontario, Canada.

GREATEST SIMULTANEOUS LEAPFROG

On May 22 2002 at the Wembley Conference Centre, London, UK, 415 employees from Procter & Gamble UK and Ireland MDO broke the world record for most people leapfrogging at one time in one location.

LONGEST DISTANCE LEAP-FROGGED

A team of 14 students from Stanford University, Stanford, California, USA, covered 996.2 miles (1,603.2 km) leapfrogging for 244 hr 43 min in May 1991.

LOUDEST CROWD SCREAM

On July 5 1998 at The Party in the Park, Hyde Park, London, UK, Trevor Lewis (UK) of CEL Instruments Ltd (UK) measured a scream by the crowd at a volume of 126.3 dBA.

MOST NATIONALITIES IN A SAUNA

On March 8 2002 in Halmstad, Sweden, 29 male participants from 29 different countries crammed into the same sauna and shut the door for 10 minutes – setting the record for most nationalities simultaneously in a sauna.

HEAVIEST CAR BALANCED ON THE HEAD
On May 24 1999 former hod-carrier John Evans (UK, above) balanced a gutted Mini car, weighing a total of 352 lb (159.6 kg), on his head for 33 seconds at the London Studios, London, UK.

MOST WATERMELONS CRUSHED
Leonardo D'Andrea (Italy) crushed 16 watermelons with his head in one minute in Madrid, Spain, on October 18 2001. For each melon to count toward the record, it had to be broken into two pieces.

HEAVIEST TRAIN PULLED
Juraj Barbaric (Slovakia) single-handedly pulled a 20 freight-car train weighing 2.2 million lb (1,000 tonnes) a distance of 14 ft 9 in (4.5 m) along a railroad track at Kosice, Slovakia, on June 1 1999.

HEAVIEST WEIGHT LIFTED WITH TEETH
Walter Arfeuille (Belgium) lifted weights totaling 620 lb 10 oz (281.5 kg) a distance of 6.75 in (17 cm) off the ground with his teeth in Paris, France, on March 31 1990.

FASTEST ONE-MILE BARREL ROLL
The record for rolling a full 36-gal (163.6-liter) metal beer barrel over a mile is 8 min 7.2 sec, by Phillip Randle, Steve Hewitt, John Round, Trevor Bradley, Colin Barnes, and Ray Glover (all UK) of Haunchwood Collieries Institute and Social Club, Nuneaton, Warwks, UK, on August 15 1982.

MOST BEER KEGS LIFTED IN SIX HOURS
Tom Gaskin (Ireland) raised a keg of beer weighing 137 lb 8 oz (62.5 kg) above his head 902 times in six hours at Liska House, Newry, Co Down, UK, on October 26 1996.

HIGHEST BEER KEG TOSS
Juha Rasanen (Finland) threw a 27-lb 1.6-oz (12.3-kg) beer keg over a bar that was set at a height of 22 ft 8.76 in (6.93 m) on the set of *El Show de los Récords*, Madrid, Spain, on September 21 2001.

LONGEST WASHING MACHINE THROW
Miguel Ballesteros and José Francisco Dopcio de Pablo (both Spain) managed to throw a washing machine weighing 103 lb 9.8 oz (47 kg) a distance of 20 ft 10.68 in (6.37 m) at the studios of *El Show de los Récords*, Madrid, Spain, on October 23 2001.

HEAVIEST DEADLIFT WITH LITTLE FINGER
The heaviest deadlift with the little finger is 197 lb 8.54 oz (89.6 kg) by Barry Anderson (UK) on October 14 2000 at the Bass Museum, Burton-upon-Trent, Staffs, UK.

HEAVIEST BOAT PULLED
David Huxley (Australia) pulled the 221,785-lb (1,006-tonne) *Delphin*, with a cargo of passengers and 175 cars over 23 ft (7 m) on November 19 1998 in Rostock, Germany.

LONGEST AIRPLANE RESTRAINT
Using ropes looped around his arms, Ilkka Nummisto (Finland) prevented the takeoff of two Cessna planes pulling in opposite directions for 54 seconds at Räyskälä Airport, Finland, on August 1 2001.

FASTEST TIRE-FLIPPING OVER 20 METERS
Flipping a Michelin Radial Steel Cord X26.5R25 (XHA) tire weighing 925 lb 14.4 oz (420 kg), Israel Garrido Sanguinetti (Spain), completed a 20-m (65-ft 7.3-in) course (10 m or 32 ft 9.6 in each way) in 56.3 seconds on *El Show de los Récords*, Madrid, Spain, on December 11 2001.

GREATEST WEIGHT BROKEN ON CHEST WHILE LYING ON BED OF NAILS
On June 23 2001, while lying on a bed of nails, Lee Graber (USA) had concrete blocks weighing a total of 489 lb 9.76 oz (222.07 kg) placed on his chest and then broken with a 14-lb (6.35-kg) sledgehammer. The event took place at Ontario Place, Toronto, Ontario, Canada.

MOST CONCRETE BLOCKS BROKEN USING HAN MOO DO TECHNIQUE
Jani Käkelä (Finland) broke 11 stacked concrete blocks with one blow, using the Han Moo Do technique, in Helsinki, Finland, on October 11 2000. Each block had a minimum density of 40 lb/ft^3 (650 kg/m^3).

MOST BASEBALL BATS BROKEN IN ONE MINUTE
On March 31 2001 in Munich, Germany, Markus Böck (Germany) broke 23 baseball bats with his shin in a minute.

MOST WEIGHT LIFTED WITH EARS, NIPPLES, AND TONGUE
The most weight lifted using ears, tongue, and nipples simultaneously is 29 lb 1.6 oz (13.19 kg) by Joe Hermann (USA), a member of the Jim Rose Circus. He lifted two standard 2-lb 4.8-oz (1.04-kg) steam irons with his earlobes, picked up a 5-lb (2.26-kg) car battery with his tongue, and supported the weight of a 15-lb 11.2-oz (7.12-kg) cinder block from his nipples to earn the record in Los Angeles, California, USA, on September 25 1998.

FASTEST WORLD WIFE-CARRYING CHAMPIONSHIP RUN
The fastest time to complete the annual 771-ft (235-m) obstacle course of the World Wife-Carrying Championships, held in Sonkajärvi, Finland, is 55.5 seconds by Margo Uusorg and Birgit Ulricht (both Estonia, above) on July 1 2000.

FASTEST TIME TO BEND AN IRON BAR AND FIT IT INTO A SUITCASE

The fastest time to bend a 19-ft 7.2-in-long (6-m) iron bar that has a diameter of 0.47 in (12 mm) and fit it into a Samsonite suitcase measuring 19.6 x 27.5 x 7.87 in (50 x 70 x 20 cm) is 44 seconds, by Thomas Bleiker (Switzerland) in Munich, Germany, on January 20 2000. He bent the bar a total of 23 times.

HEAVIEST WEIGHT LIFTED BY A HUMAN BEARD

The heaviest weight lifted by a human beard is 135 lb (61.3 kg) when Antanas Kontrimas lifted Ruta Cekyte (both Lithuania) off the ground for 15 seconds on August 18 2001 at the VIII International Country Festival 2001, Visaginas, Lithuania.

MOST BRICKS LIFTED

Russell Bradley (UK) lifted 31 bricks – laid side-by-side – off a table, raising them to chest height and holding them for two seconds on June 14 1992.

GREATEST WEIGHT OF BRICKS LIFTED

Fred Burton (UK) lifted the greatest weight of bricks ever, when he held 20 bricks, weighing 226 lb 7 oz (102.73 kg) for two seconds on June 5 1998.

HEAVIEST BRICKS BALANCED ON HEAD

John Evans (UK) balanced 101 bricks, weighing a total of 416 lb (188.7 kg), on his head for 10 seconds at the BBC Television Centre, London, UK, on December 24 1997.

MOST WEIGHT ON BODY

The most weight sustained on the body is 3,045 lb (1,381.19 kg) by Master Kahled Dahdouh (USA) on August 13 1999. The weight was made up of cinder blocks measuring 16 x 8 x 8 in (40.6 x 20.3 x 20.3 cm) and three bodybuilders, placed on his chest for five seconds.

MOST CONSECUTIVE ONE-ARM CHIN-UPS

Robert Chisholm (Canada) completed 22 consecutive one-arm chin-ups at Queen's University, Kingston, Ontario, Canada, on December 3 1982.

HEAVIEST TRUCK PULL

The heaviest truck pulled over 100 ft (30.48 m) weighed 54,321 lb (24,640 kg) and was pulled by Kevin Fast (Canada, below) at Cobourg, Ontario, Canada, on June 30 2001.

FASTEST TOMATO KETCHUP DRINKER

Dustin Phillips (USA, above) drank a standard 14-oz (400-g) bottle of Heinz tomato ketchup through a 0.25-in-diameter (0.64-cm) drinking straw in 33 seconds on the set of *Guinness World Records: Primetime* in Los Angeles, California, USA, on September 23 1999. He consumed around 91% of the bottle's contents.

FASTEST BACKWARD RUN FROM LOS ANGELES TO NEW YORK

Between August 18 and December 3 1984 Arvind Pandya (India) ran backward across America from Los Angeles to New York City. His 107-day journey covered around 1,500 miles (2,400 km) at an average of 14 miles (22.5 km) per day.

FASTEST REVERSE DRIVING

Darren Manning (UK) attained a speed of 102.58 mph (165.08 km/h) driving backward in a Caterham 7 Fireblade, at Kemble Airfield, Gloucester, UK, on October 22 2001.

FASTEST BED PUSH

The fastest time for the annual 2.04-mile (3.27-km) Knaresborough Bed Race (established 1966) in North Yorks, UK, is 12 min 9 sec. The record feat was achieved by the Vibroplant team on June 9 1990.

FASTEST WHEELBARROW RACE

The fastest time attained in a 1-mile (1.609-km) wheelbarrow race is 4 min 48.51 sec, by Piet Pitzer and Jaco Erasmus (both South Africa) at Transvalia High School, Vanderbijlpark, South Africa, on October 3 1987. One was running, pushing the barrow, while the other remained seated in the barrow.

FASTEST 50-M 31-LEGGED RACE

Students from the Ogori-minami school in Tokyo, Japan, ran a 31-legged race covering a total of 160.04 ft (50 m) in 9.12 seconds on December 5 1999.

FASTEST HUMAN CALCULATOR

Scott Flansburg (USA) correctly added a randomly selected two-digit number (38) to itself 36 times in 15 seconds without the use of a calculator on April 27 2000.

MOST RICE GRAINS EATEN IN 3 MINUTES

Tae Wah Gooding (South Korea) ate 64 grains of rice, one by one, using chopsticks, in 3 minutes at Peterborough Regional College, Peterborough, Cambs, UK, on November 7 2000.

MOST GRAPES EATEN IN 3 MINUTES

The record for the largest amount of grapes eaten in 3 minutes is held by Mat Hand (UK), who consumed a total of 133 grapes in this time on November 8 2001.

FASTEST RUN UP THE EMPIRE STATE BUILDING

Paul Crake (Australia) ascended the 1,576 steps of the Empire State Building in 9 min 53 sec at the 23rd Annual Empire State Building Run-Up, New York City, USA, on February 23 2000.

Belinda Soszyn (Australia) is the fastest woman to achieve the same feat. In 1996 she completed a run-up in 12 min 19 sec.

MOST SALMONS FILLETED IN 10 MINUTES

Per-Arne Korshag (Sweden) filleted 503.31 lb (228.3 kg) of salmon in 10 minutes on December 13 1998.

MOST OYSTERS OPENED IN ONE MINUTE

Marcel Lesoille (France) opened 29 oysters in one minute on the set of *El Show de los Récords*, Madrid, Spain, on November 15 2001.

FASTEST TIME TO SOLVE A RUBIK CUBE

Vietnamese refugee Minh Thai won the World Rubik Cube Championship in Budapest, Hungary, on June 5 1982.

His winning time was 22.95 seconds. Ernö Rubik's (Hungary) cube, which has 43,252,003,274,489,856,856,000 combinations, was patented in 1977.

FASTEST WINE BOTTLE OPENER

Alain Dorotte (France) opened 13 wine bottles with a "T-handled" corkscrew (non-leverage) in one minute on April 18 2001.

MOST SURGICAL GLOVES INFLATED IN 2 MINUTES

Susanne "Tussen" Formgren (Sweden) inflated three pre-powdered procedure surgical gloves until they burst, in a time of 2 minutes, at the studios of *Guinness Rekord TV*, Stockholm, on February 1 2001.

FASTEST PANTOMIME HORSE

On August 3 1999 at St Andrews School, Cobham, Surrey, UK, Geoff Seale and Stuart Coleman (both UK) won the pantomime horse race, which was run over a distance of 328.08 ft (100 m) in a time of 16.7 seconds. Seven other "horses" competed. The race marked the pair's debut as a pantomime horse.

FASTEST COCONUT HUSKER

Using his teeth, Raman Andiappan (India, above) husked a coconut 18.125-in (46-cm) in circumference and weighing 10 lb 3.66 oz (4.64 kg) in 37.67 seconds on *Guinness World Records: Primetime*, Los Angeles, USA, on March 11 2001.

MOST SAUSAGES EATEN IN ONE MINUTE

The record for the most sausages eaten in one minute is held by Stefan Paladin (New Zealand), who ate eight whole sausages at the Ericsson Stadium, Auckland, New Zealand, on July 22 2001. The sausages were 3.94 in (10 cm) long and 0.79 in (2 cm) wide.

FASTEST TALKER

Steve Woodmore (UK) spoke a total of 595 words in 56.01 seconds – a rate of 637.4 words per minute – on the UK's ITV program *Motor Mouth* on September 22 1990. Most people speak at a rate of about 60 words per minute – around a word a second. In an excited state, a person may reach 120 to 150 words per minute.

FASTEST RAP ARTIST

Rebel XD (USA, real name Seandale Price) beat his own record by rapping 683 syllables in 54.501 seconds on the set of *Guinness World Records: Primetime* in Los Angeles, California, USA, on June 24 1998.

MOST WORDS SPOKEN BACKWARD IN A MINUTE

Sara Jokinen (Finland) spoke 47 words backward in one minute in Helsinki, Finland, on October 19 2001.

FASTEST HAIRCUT

Trevor Mitchell (UK) cut a full head of hair in 1 min 13 sec on November 26 1999 at the Southampton City Guildhall, Hants, UK, as part of BBC TV's *Children in Need* event.

FASTEST TIME TO MAKE 1 LITER OF ICE CREAM

On March 20 2002 Peter Barnham (UK) broke his previous record by making the fastest liter of ice cream in 20.91 seconds. The successful record attempt was carried out on location for the Discovery Channel's *Kitchen Chemistry*, in Maidenhead, Berks, UK.

FASTEST CONSTRUCTION OF A 30-LEVEL JENGA TOWER

The fastest time to build a stable Jenga tower 30 levels high within the rules of the game is 12 min 27 sec by Simon Spalding and Ali Malik (both UK) at Highclere Castle, Hampshire, UK on August 17 1997.

FASTEST MUSIC VIDEO (FILM TO BROADCAST)

The fastest time in which a music video has been filmed and then broadcast is 3 hr 46 min 19 sec. The video, which featured the band Electric Soft Parade (UK), was made using Microsoft Windows XP at HMV, London, UK, on October 25 2001.

FASTEST FURNITURE

"The Casual Lofa," a motorized sofa built by Edd China (UK, below) and David Davenport (UK), has a top speed of 87 mph (140 km/h). Powered by a Mini 1300-cc engine, it is licensed for use on UK roads and is steered by means of turning a medium-sized pizza pan. It has a seating capacity for one driver with two passengers sitting alongside. The car has covered 6,219 miles (10,008.5 km) since it was built.

The fourth-grader's project created an uproar at the time as the therapy she was questioning was being used in over 80 hospitals throughout the USA.

OLDEST FILM DIRECTOR

George Cukor (USA, 1899–1983) made his 50th and final film, *Rich and Famous* (USA,1981) at the age of 81.

YOUNGEST AUTHOR

The youngest commercially published author on record is Dorothy Straight (USA) who wrote *How the World Began* in 1962 at the age of four. It was published in August 1964 by Pantheon Books.

OLDEST MOTORCYCLIST

On May 2 2000 Len Vale Onslow (UK) rode his motorcycle 121 miles (194.9 km) to the gates of Buckingham Palace, London, UK, to receive his congratulatory telegram from HM The Queen on the occasion of his 100th birthday. Len has been riding motorcycles since he was seven years old and still rides regularly.

OLDEST CHORUS LINE MEMBER

The oldest "showgirl" still regularly performing in a chorus line is Beverly Allen (USA, b. November 4 1917). A member of The Fabulous Palm Springs Follies, her jitterbug routine – in which her partner lifts her over his head – is a favorite with audiences.

OLDEST PERSON TO ABSEIL DOWN A BUILDING

On 25 November 2000 Dorothy Williams (UK, b. January 26 1916), successfully abseiled down a 100-ft (30.48-m) building in Flintshire, Wales, UK. The event was sponsored by the North East Wales Search and Rescue Team and raised £2,071 ($3,000) for cancer research. Dorothy plans to become the world's oldest free-fall parachute jumper.

YOUNGEST PUBLISHED COOK

Justin Miller (USA, above, b. 1990) became famous for his cooking prowess at the age of five after appearing on the *David Letterman Show*. Two years later he published his cookbook, *Cooking with Justin: Recipes for Kids (and Parents)*. He now advises the Marriott hotel chain on its children's menus.

YOUNGEST CONSULTANT

On April 15 2000 supermarket chain Tesco announced that it had procured the services of seven-year-old Laurie Sleator (UK), to advise senior executives on the *Pokemon* cartoon craze then sweeping the globe.

YOUNGEST PERSON TO HAVE RESEARCH PUBLISHED

Emily Rosa (USA) became the youngest person to have serious research published in a scientific or medical journal when an article she co-authored at the age of 11 appeared in the *Journal of the American Medical Association* on April 1 1998. The article reported an experiment on Touch Therapy conceived by Emily when she was only eight years old.

OLDEST COMPETITIVE BALLROOM DANCER

The oldest competitive ballroom dancer was Albert J Sylvester (UK, 1889–1989) who retired at the age of 94. In addition to being a record-breaking ballroom dancer, Sylvester was the personal secretary to UK prime minister David Lloyd-George.

OLDEST OPERA SINGER

The Ukrainian bass Mark Reizen (1895–1992) sang the role of Prince Gremin in Tchaikovsky's *Eugene Onegin* at Moscow's Bolshoi Theatre on his 90th birthday in 1985, highlighting his 70-year opera career.

OLDEST PRACTICING BARBER

Born in 1910, Leamon Ward (USA) has been cutting hair professionally since July 1927, when he was 17 – that's over 70 years of continuous barbering. In many cases he has cut the hair of several generations of families.

OLDEST ADOPTION

Paula Louise Daly Winter Dolan (USA, b. 1940) became the oldest person to be adopted on November 5 1998 when, at age 58 years, 5 months and 17 days, she was adopted by her aunt and uncle, John A Winter and Elizabeth R Winter (both USA).

OLDEST MALE PARACHUTIST

Norwegian Bjarne Mæland (b. 1899) made his first tandem parachute jump (in which two parachutists jump at the same time) at the age of 100 years 21 days. He jumped from a height of 10,499 ft (3,200 m) above Stavanger Airport, Sola, Norway, on September 8 1999.

OLDEST WING WALKER

On December 23 1999, 87-year-old Martha Ritchie (South Africa, b. April 5 1912), performed an eight-minute wing walk on a 1942 Boeing Stearman over Port Elizabeth Airport, South Africa.

OLDEST BEST MAN

On August 14 1999, Philip Hicks (UK, b. March 26 1906) served as best man at his daughter's wedding at the age of 93. At the civil ceremony in St Michel de Vax, France, Phillip proudly gave his daughter away before promptly moving to the right to become the best man of his future son-in-law.

YOUNGEST BILLIONAIRE

Taiwan-born Jerry Yang (USA, above), co-founder of internet search engine Yahoo! Inc, became a billionaire in 1997 at age 29. According to *Forbes* magazine, in 2002 Yang's net worth dropped to an estimated $730 million (£520 million).

OLDEST BAREFOOT WATER-SKIER

On February 10 2002, George Blair, (USA, below), successfully water-skied barefoot on Lake Florence, Winter Haven, Florida, USA, at age 87 years 18 days. George had already set the record for the oldest snowboarder on January 22 2001 when he hit the snowy slopes of Steamboat Springs, Colorado, USA, with his snowboard.

OLDEST PERSON TO FLY IN A HOT-AIR BALLOON

Florence Laine (UK, 1894–1999) flew in a hot-air balloon at age 102 years 92 days. The balloon traveled 1.86 miles (3 km) over Cust, New Zealand, on September 26 1996.

OLDEST PILOT

Col Clarence Cornish (USA, 1898–1995) was flying aircraft at the age of 97, the last occasion being when he flew a Cessna 172 on December 4 1995. His first flight had been on May 6 1918, and he made his first solo flight 21 days later. Col Cornish died 18 days after his last flight.

YOUNGEST DJ

Llewellyn Owen (UK, b. February 21 1992), aka "DJ Welly," headlined at London's Warp Club on May 1 2000 at the age of 8 years 70 days. A native Londoner, DJ Welly is paid the same as popular DJs five times his age – approximately £125 ($190) per hour. Since his professional debut, he has headlined at famous clubs such as London's Ministry of Sound and played at the Glastonbury Music Festival.

OLDEST BRIDESMAID

Flossie Bennett (UK, b. August 9 1902) was matron of honor when she was 97 years 6 months old at the wedding of her close friends Leonard and Edna Petchey on February 6 1999 at St Peter's Church, Holton, Suffolk, UK. Len's 12-year-old granddaughter was the other bridesmaid at the service, creating an 85-year age gap between Edna's two bridesmaids.

MOST CHAINSAW JUGGLING ROTATIONS
The greatest number of rotations of three juggled chainsaws is 12 (36 throws) by Karoly Donnert (Hungary, above) on the set of *Guinness Rekord TV*, Stockholm, Sweden on January 30 2001.

FASTEST TIME TO BOIL WATER THROUGH BODY
With electricity passing through his body, Slavisa Pajkic "Biba" (Yugoslavia) was able to heat a 0.5-fl-oz (15-ml) cup of water from 77°F to 206°F (25°C to 97°C) in a time of 1 min 37 sec on November 24 2001.

FARTHEST SPAGHETTI NASAL EJECTION
Kevin Cole (USA) holds the record for the longest spaghetti strand blown out of a nostril in a single blow. On December 16 1998 Cole successfully achieved a record distance of 7.5 in (19 cm) in Los Angeles, California, USA.

LONGEST GRAPE BLOWING
Marianne Gille (Sweden) kept a grape suspended in the air above her mouth for 4.81 seconds in Stockholm, Sweden, on November 29 2001.

LONGEST FRYING PAN SPIN ON FINGER
Anders Björklund (Sweden) was able to spin a frying pan on his finger for 14 minutes on November 29 2001.

HEAVIEST EAR WEIGHTLIFT
The heaviest weight lifted using only the ear is 110 lb 1.6 oz (50 kg) by Li Jian Hua (China) who lifted a column of bricks hanging from a clamp attached to his ear and held the weight for 9.3 seconds on December 17 1998.

MOST TENNIS BALLS HELD IN THE HAND
Roberto Barra-Chicote (Spain) was able to place 16 tennis balls in his hand and hold them for five seconds at the studios of *L'Émission des Records* on November 30 2001.

HIGHEST GOLF BALL STACK
Don Athey (USA) stacked nine golf balls vertically without the use of adhesives on October 4 1998.

MOST FACES SHAVED BY A SAFETY RAZOR
Denny Rowe (UK) shaved 1,994 men in 60 minutes with a safety razor at Herne Bay, Kent, UK, on June 19 1988, taking on average 1.8 second per man and drawing blood four times.

FASTEST UNDERPANTS JUMPER
Matthieu Bommier (France) jumped into and out of a pair of underpants a total of 27 times in one minute on the set of *L'Émission des Records*, Paris, France, on April 18 2001.

MOST BEER BOTTLE CAPS REMOVED WITH TEETH IN ONE MINUTE
José Ivan Hernandez (USA) removed 56 beer bottle caps with his teeth in one minute in the TV studios of *Ricki Lake*, New York City, USA, on December 5 2001.

MOST STORIES IN A HOUSE OF CARDS
On November 6 1999 architecture graduate Bryan Berg (USA) built a free-standing house of standard playing cards that had 131 stories. The house was built to a height of 25 ft 3.48 in (7.71 m) using 91,800 cards in the casino at Potsdammer Platz, Berlin, Germany. The total weight of the 1,765 packs of cards used was 242 lb 8 oz (110 kg). No adhesives of any kind are used on the cards when constructing these creations.

MOST BEER MATS FLIPPED
Dean Gould (UK) flipped a pile of 111 beer mats each 0.05 in (1.2-mm) thick through 180º and caught them at Edinburgh, Lothian, UK, on January 13 1993.

MOST BARRELS JUMPED
The men's record for barrel jumping (circling an ice rink to gain speed, before jumping a row of barrels laid down side by side) is 18 barrels, by Yvon Jolin Junior (Canada) – the first Triple Crown Barrel Jumping Champion in the history of barrel jumping – at Terrebonne, Quebec, Canada on April 12 1980. The distance jumped was 27 ft 8 in (8.43 m). The women's record is a distance of 22 ft 5 in (6.84 m) over 13 barrels, achieved by Marie-Jose Houle (Canada) at Lasalle, Quebec, Canada, on March 1 1987.

FARTHEST FIRE BREATHING DISTANCE
Reg Morris (UK) blew a flame from his mouth to a distance of 31 ft (9.4 m) at The Miner's Rest, Chasetown, Staffs, UK, on October 29 1986.

HIGHEST FIRE BREATHING FLAME
Henrik Segelstrom (Sweden) blew a flame 9 ft 9.6 in (3 m) tall on the set of *Guinness Rekord TV*, Stockholm, Sweden, on November 28 2001.

MOST HULA HOOPING HOOPS
The record for "hula hooping" the most hoops simultaneously is 83, held by Cia Grangér (Finland) in Helsinki, Finland, on October 25 1999. She sustained three full revolutions of the standard size and weight hula hoops between her shoulders and her hips.

BOWLING BALL STACKING
Dave Kremer (USA, above) stacked 10 bowling balls vertically without the use of adhesives on the set of *Guinness World Records: Primetime*, Los Angeles, California, USA, on November 19 1998.

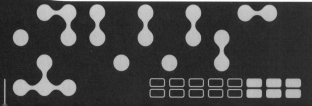

LEAPFROG OVER THE MOST STANDING PEOPLE

In September 2000 Andy Wiltz (USA) leapfrogged over 10 standing people during a local variety show at Seaman High School, Topeka, Kansas, USA. All ten people were over age 16 and over 5 ft (1.53 m) tall. Wiltz did not have a trampoline or any other assistance, but he had a running start before he pushed off the shoulders of the first person in line and flew through the air over all ten of their heads.

MOST CLOTHES PEGS CLIPPED ON A FACE

Pub landlord Garry Turner (UK, left) clipped 133 ordinary wooden clothes pegs on his face at the offices of *Guinness World Records*, London, UK, on August 3 2001.

LONGEST DURATION SITTING IN A GLASS CAGE OF SCORPIONS

Nor Malena Hassan (Malaysia), "Scorpion Queen," sat in a glass cage measuring 130 ft² (12 m²), which contained 2,000 scorpions, for 30 days between July 1–30 2001 in the Kelantan State Museum, Kota Baru, Malaysia. After 19 days she asked for 700 more scorpions to be added to the 2,000. During the attempt she was stung seven times, but only twice seriously.

MOST LIVE RATTLESNAKES HELD IN THE MOUTH
On May 19 2001 Jackie Bibby (USA, above) held eight live rattlesnakes in his mouth by their tails for 12.5 seconds without assistance at the Guinness World Records Experience, Orlando, Florida, USA. Each rattlesnake measured 29 in (74 cm) long.

LONGEST CONTINUOUS SKID ON A BICYCLE
On April 17 2001 James David (USA) performed a continuous 425-ft 3-in (130-m) skid on his bicycle on a flat surface at the Spokane Raceway Park, Washington, USA.

MOST HAIR-CUTTING SCISSORS IN ONE HAND
On January 12 1998 Danny Bar-Gil (Israel), professionally known as Danny Figaro, successfully styled hair using seven pairs of scissors in one hand, controlling each pair independently.

MOST HANDCUFFED MAN
Since 1954 escapologist Nick Janson (UK) has escaped from 1,680 pairs of handcuffs securely locked on his wrists by police officers.

MOST SWORDS SWALLOWED AND TWISTED
Brad Byers (USA), swallowed 10 swords each 27 in (68.5 cm) long and rotated them 180° in his esophagus on August 13 1999 on the set of *Guinness World Records: Primetime* in Los Angeles, California, USA.

MOST SWORDS SWALLOWED BY A WOMAN
The most 14–21-in (35.5–53-cm) swords swallowed by a female is six, by Amy Saunders (UK) on the set of *El Show de los Récords*, Madrid, Spain, on November 27 2001.

LONGEST DURATION FOR A SWORD-TO-SWORD BALANCE
Ali Bandbaz balanced his brother Massoud (both Iran) above his head on the blade tips of two 14.5-in (36.5-cm) steel swords, holding the position for 30 seconds at the studios of *L'Émission des Records*, Paris, France, on October 26 2000.

MOST CARDS HELD IN A FAN
Ralf Laue (Germany) held 326 standard playing cards in a fan in one hand, so that the value and color of each one was visible, at Leipzig, Germany, on March 18 1994.

FASTEST HUMAN CRAB
In the "bridge," or crab position, Agnès Brun (France) covered 65 ft (20 m) in 33.3 seconds. The record was set on *L'Émission des Records*, Paris, France, on November 30 2001.

FARTHEST DISTANCE AN ARROW HAS BEEN SHOT USING THE FEET
The farthest distance an arrow has been shot into a target using feet to control the bow is 18 ft 4.8 in (5.5 m), by Claudia Gomez (Argentina) on the set of *El Show de los Récords*, Madrid, Spain, on November 15 2001.

MOST WATCHES EATEN
On December 18 1998 on the set of *Guinness World Records: Primetime* in Los Angeles, California, USA, Kim Seung Do (South Korea) ate five watches (the entire watch with the exception of the wristband) in a time of 1 hr 34 min 7 sec.

MOST ARROWS CAUGHT BY HAND
Anthony Kelly (Australia) caught 10 arrows in two minutes standing at a distance of 42 ft (13 m) from the archer at the studios of *El Show de los Récords*, Madrid, Spain, on December 5 2001.

MOST CIGAR BOXES BALANCED ON THE CHIN
Terry Cole (UK) balanced 220 unmodified cigar boxes on his chin for nine seconds on April 24 1992.

FARTHEST DISTANCE CARRYING BEER STEINS
On July 10 1992, in a contest at Cadillac, Michigan, USA, Duane Osborn (USA) covered a distance of 50 ft (15 m) in 3.65 seconds with five full steins of beer in each hand.

MOST CHERRY STEMS KNOTTED IN THREE MINUTES
Al Gliniecki (USA) tied 39 cherry stems into knots in three minutes, using his tongue at the Guinness World Records Experience, Orlando, Florida, on January 26 1999.

MOST DOMINOES TOPPLED SINGLE-HANDEDLY
The greatest number of dominoes set up single-handedly and toppled is 281,581 out of 320,236, by Klaus Friedrich (Germany) at Fürth, Germany, on January 27 1984. The dominoes fell in 12 min 57.3 sec, having taken 10 hours a day, for a period of 31 days, to set up.

MOST COINS REGURGITATED ON REQUEST
Stevie Starr (UK) swallowed 11 Spanish 100-peseta pieces, each with a different year of minting, and regurgitated them at will, one by one, on request from 11 different members of the studio audience at *El Show de los Récords*, Madrid, Spain, on December 5 2001.

CAR CRAMMING A VOLKSWAGEN BEETLE
On April 29 2000, 25 people crammed themselves into a standard VW Beetle car (above) in Kremser, Austria. To break this record, all the car windows and doors must be closed, and no body parts can protrude from the car.

LONGEST DURATION SPINNING A FOOTBALL ON THE FOREHEAD

On November 25 2001 Tommy Baker (UK) spun a Nike FIFA-approved football on his forehead for 11.9 seconds after transferring it from his finger on the set of *Guinness Rekord TV*, Stockholm, Sweden.

FULL-BODY ICE CONTACT ENDURANCE

Wearing only swimming trunks, Wim Hof (Netherlands) endured standing in a tube filled with ice cubes for 1 hr 6 min 4 sec on the set of *Tomorrow's World*, at BBC TV Centre, London, UK, on March 13 2002.

HAMBURGER STUFFING

The record for stuffing the most regulation size hamburgers (including buns) in the mouth at one time is three. Johnny Reitz (USA) performed the feat on the set of *Guinness World Records: Primetime* on June 17 1998. The rules require the participant not to swallow any of the hamburger.

MOST FISH CAUGHT WITH ONE HAND IN 30 SECONDS

On March 11 2001 Justin Hall (USA) caught 16 salmon weighing between 4 and 6 lb (1.81 and 2.72 kg) with one hand, which were thrown by Jaison Scott (USA) from a distance of 18 ft (5.48 m).

MOST CANS SCOOPED WHEN SIDE-DRIVING

Sven-Erik Söderman (Sweden) picked up 15 full food cans while driving his car on two wheels, at Mora Siljan Flygplats, Mora, Sweden, on September 12 2001. The rules state that the cans must be set out on opposite sides of a 10-ft-wide (3-m) track, forcing the driver to zig-zag on two wheels.

MOST STRAWS IN THE MOUTH

Marco Hort (Switzerland, below) stuffed 210 drinking straws, each with a diameter of 0.25 in (6.4 mm), into his mouth and held them there for the required 10 seconds on February 21 2002 on the set of *Guinness – Die Show der Rekorde* in Munich, Germany.

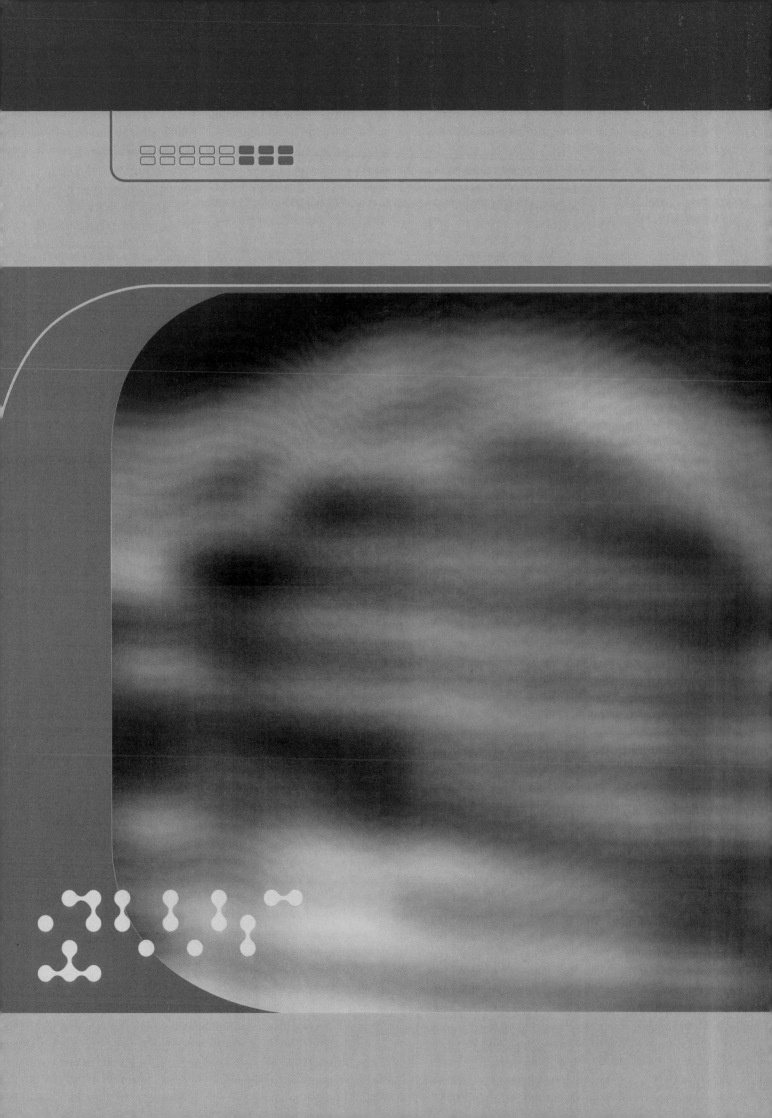

LARGEST HANDS

Somalian-born Hussain Bisad (above), who lives in the UK, has the largest hands of any living person. His hands measure 10.59 in (26.9 cm) from the wrist to the tip of his middle finger. Robert Wadlow (USA), who died in 1940, had the largest hands ever. His hands measured 12.75 in (32.3 cm) from the wrist to the tip of his middle finger. He wore a size 25 ring.

LARGEST NATURAL BREASTS

Annie Hawkins-Turner (USA) has an under-breast measurement of 43 in (1.09 m) and an around-chest-over-nipple measurement of 70 in (1.79 m). She currently wears a US-size 52-I bra, the largest made. These measurements would put her in a 48-V bra, which is not manufactured. She currently lives and works in Washington DC, USA.

MOST VARIABLE STATURE

At the age of 21 in 1920, Adam Rainer (Austria) measured 3 ft 10.5 in (1.18 m). He then had a rapid growth spurt, and by 1931 he had reached 7 ft 1.75 in (2.18 m). As a result of this, he became so weak that he was bedridden for the rest of his life. When he died in 1950, he measured 7 ft 8 in (2.34 m) and remains the only person to have been both a dwarf and a giant.

GREATEST WEIGHT GAIN

The greatest weight gain by a woman was achieved by Doris James (USA) who is said to have gained 328 lb (147 kg) in the 12 months before her death at the age of 38 in August 1965. At her death she weighed 675 lb (306 kg). She was only 5 ft 2 in (1.57 m) tall.

The equivalent weight-gain record for a male is held by Arthur Knorr (USA), who gained 294 lb (133 kg) in 1960 over the last six months of his life.

GREATEST WEIGHT LOSS

The record for weight loss for men is held by Jon Brower Minnoch (USA) with a weight of 1,400 lb (635 kg) – the highest weight ever recorded for a man. He had reduced to 476 lb (216 kg) by July 1979: a weight loss of at least 924 lb (419 kg) over a 16-month period.

Rosalie Bradford (USA) went from a weight of 1,199 lb (544 kg) in January 1987 (the highest weight ever recorded for a woman) to 282 lb (128 kg) in February 1994, a record weight loss of 917 lb (416 kg).

TALLEST WOMAN

When Zeng Jinlian (China) died on February 13 1982, she measured 8 ft 1.75 in (2.48 m). This figure represented her height with assumed normal spinal curvature, as she had severe scoliosis (curvature of the spine) and could not stand up straight. She began to grow abnormally from the age of four months and stood 5 ft 1.5 in (1.56 m) before her fourth birthday and 7 ft 1.5 in (2.17 m) at 13.

Standing 7 ft 7.25 in (2.32 m), Sandy Allen (USA) is currently the tallest living woman. Her abnormal growth began soon after birth, and by the age of 10 she stood an amazing 6 ft 3 in (1.91 m) tall.

LONGEST NOSE

There are accounts that Thomas Wedders (UK) who lived during the 1770s and was a member of a traveling sideshow, had a nose measuring 7.5 in (19 cm) long. The record for the longest nose on a living person belongs to Mehmet Ozyurek (Turkey). His nose was 3.46 in (8.8 cm) long from the bridge to the tip when measured on January 31 2001.

TALLEST TWINS

Non-identical twins Michael and James Lanier (USA) both stand 7 ft 3 in (2.23 m) tall and hold the record for the world's tallest living twins. The tallest identical male twins ever recorded were the Knipe brothers (UK) who both measured 7 ft 2 in (2.18 m). The world's tallest living female identical twins are Heather and Heidi Burge (USA) who are both 6 ft 4.75 in (1.95 m) tall.

LONGEST TONGUE

Umar Alvi (UK) has a tongue (when stuck out) measuring 2.22 in (5.65 cm) from the tip to the center of his closed top lip. The measurement was taken on November 15 2001.

TALLEST MAN

The world's tallest-ever man, Robert Wadlow (USA), stood an amazing 8 ft 11.1 in (2.72 m) when measured before his death at 22 in June 1940.

The tallest living man is Radhouane Charbib (Tunisia) who measured 7 ft 8.9 in (2 m 35.9 cm) as a result of seven measurements taken between April 22 and 23 1999 in Tunis.

OLDEST MAN EVER

Shigechiyo Izumi (Japan) lived to 120 years 237 days. Born on June 29 1865, he is recorded as a six-year-old in Japan's first census in 1871. He died from pneumonia on February 21 1986.

STRONGEST HUMAN BITE

In August 1986 Richard Hofmann (USA) achieved a bite strength of 975 lb (442 kg) for around two seconds in a research test using a gnathodynamometer at the College of Dentistry, University of Florida, Gainesville, USA. This is more than six times the normal human biting strength and is due to his unusually powerful masseter muscles.

OLDEST MAN LIVING

Yukichi Chuganji (b. March 23 1889, above) of Ogori, Fukuoka Prefecture, Japan, became the oldest man in Japan on January 18 2000 and took the world-record title on January 4 2002 at the age of 112 years 288 days.

OLDEST WOMAN

The greatest fully authenticated age to which any human has ever lived is 122 years 164 days. This was achieved by Jeanne Louise Calment (France). She was born on February 21 1875 and died on August 4 1997.

The oldest living woman in the world whose date of birth can be fully authenticated is Kamato Hongo (Japan), born September 16 1887. She took the title at 114 years 183 days on the death of Maude Farris-Luse (USA) who died on March 18 2002.

OLDEST DWARF

Hungarian-born dwarf Susanna Bokonyi (USA) died at the age of 105 on August 24 1984. She was only 3 ft 4 in (1.015 m) tall.

SHORTEST WOMAN

The shortest-ever female was Pauline Musters (Netherlands) who measured 1 ft (30 cm) at her birth in 1876. When she died on March 1 1895, a post-mortem examination showed her to be 2 ft (61 cm) tall (although there was some elongation of her body after death).

LIGHTEST BRAIN

The lightest "normal" or non-atrophied brain on record weighed just 1 lb 8 oz (680 g). It belonged to Daniel Lyon (Ireland), who died in New York, USA, in 1907 at 46. He was just over 5 ft (1.5 m) tall and weighed 145 lb (66 kg).

HEAVIEST BRAIN

The heaviest brain ever recorded weighed 5 lb 1.1 oz (2.3 kg) and had belonged to a 30-year-old male. The record was reported by the Dept of Pathology and Laboratory Medicine at the University of Cincinnati, Ohio, USA, in December 1992.

SHORTEST MAN

The shortest living man is Younis Edwan (Jordan, below) who is believed to be 2 ft 1.5 in (65 cm) tall. The shortest mature man of whom there is independent evidence was Gul Mohammed (India), who measured 1 ft 10.5 in (57 cm) tall. He died in 1997 at 39.

FARTHEST EYEBALL POPPER

Kim Goodman (USA, above) can pop her eyeballs to a protrusion of 0.43 in (11 mm) beyond her eye sockets. Her startling record was set on June 13 1998.

STRETCHIEST SKIN

Apartment landlord Garry Turner (UK) stretched the skin of his stomach a measured length of 6.25 in (15.8 cm) in Los Angeles, California, USA, on October 29 1999. Another bizarre but favorite trick of his is to stretch his neck skin over his mouth to create a "human turtleneck."

OLDEST UNDISCOVERED TWIN

In July 1997, a fetus was discovered in the abdomen of 16-year-old Hisham Ragab (Egypt), who had been complaining of stomach pains. A swollen sac found pressing against his kidneys turned out to be Hisham's identical twin. The fetus, 7 in (18 cm) in length and weighing 4 lb 6 oz (2 kg), had been growing inside Hisham and had lived to the age of 32 or 33 weeks.

LOUDEST SNORING

Kåre Walkert (Sweden) who has the breathing disorder apnea, recorded snoring sound-levels of 93 dBA (about the same noise level as a busy street) on May 24 1993.

MOST FINGERS AND TOES

At an inquest held in London, UK, on September 16 1921, it was reported that a baby boy had 14 fingers and 15 toes. Polydactylism is quite common, with as many as two occurrences in every 1,000 births. Extra digits are usually fleshy bumps without bones but can be complete fingers or toes.

With 10 fingers and two thumbs, Godfrey Hill (UK) has the most fingers on a living person. Godfrey found his hands an advantage at school, topping the class at adding up in the old days when 12 pennies made a shilling.

LARGEST BRAIN TUMOR

Dr Deepak S Kulkarni (India) removed a primary fibrosarcoma tumor weighing 20.1 oz (570 g) from the brain of four-year-old Kaushal Choudhary (India) at Curewell Hospital, Indore, India, on May 25 2000.

LARGEST TUMOR AT BIRTH

The largest tumor at birth weighed 11 oz (0.311 kg) and was pressing against the windpipe of Ryan James Shannon (USA). He was born on January 2 1996 weighing 6 lb 2 oz (2.77 kg), with the tumor weighing 10% of his bodyweight. Nine days after birth, he underwent a four-hour operation to remove the tumor.

LARGEST TUMOR REMOVED INTACT

The largest-ever tumor removed intact was a multicystic mass of the right ovary that had a diameter of 3 ft (1 m) and weighed 303 lb (137.6 kg). The massive growth was removed in its entirety from the abdomen of an unnamed 34-year-old woman in a six-hour operation performed by Prof Katherine O'Hanlan (USA) in October 1991. The patient left the operating room on one stretcher and the cyst on another.

LONGEST LIFE WITH A BULLET IN THE HEAD

Satoru Fushiki (Japan) was accidentally hit in his left eye by an air-gun pellet on January 23 1943 near his home in Kasuga Jinya. He was hospitalized for a month, but the bullet was not removed and he remains blind in that eye as of September 25 2001.

LARGEST TUMOR EVER OPERATED ON

In 1905 Dr Arthur Spohn (USA) had a patient with an ovarian cyst, estimated to weigh a staggering 328 lb (148.7 kg). It was drained during the week prior to the surgical removal of the cyst shell, and after the operation the patient made a full recovery.

LONGEST ATTACK OF HICCUPS

Charles Osborne (USA) started hiccuping in 1922 while trying to weigh a hog before slaughtering it. He was unable to find a cure but led a normal life, had two wives, and fathered eight children. His hiccups continued until they stopped naturally one morning in February 1990.

HAIRIEST FAMILY

Victor "Larry" and Gabriel "Danny" Ramos Gomez (Mexico) are 98% covered with a thick coat of hair. They are two of a family of 19 that spans five generations who all have hypertrichosis, or werewolf syndrome. The women are covered with a light-to-medium coat of hair while the men have thick hair on every inch of their bodies (apart from the palms of their hands and soles of their feet).

MOST KIDNEY STONES PRODUCED

Don Winfield (Canada) produced and passed 3,711 kidney stones between February 20 1986 and June 30 2001.

LONGEST SURVIVAL WITH AN EXPOSED HEART

Christopher Wall (USA), born on August 19 1975, is the longest-known survivor of the condition *ectopia cordis*, where the heart lies outside the body. Most patients die within 48 hours. *Ectopia* occurs in between 5.5 and 7.9 for every one million live births, according to the American Heart Association. He still lives with the condition.

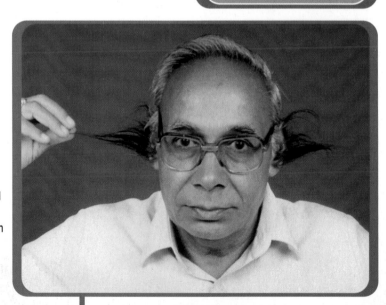

LONGEST EAR HAIR

B D Tyagi (India, above) has hair sprouting from the center of his pinna (outer ear) that measures 4 in (10.2 cm) at its longest point.

LONGEST BEARD ON A FEMALE

American "Bearded Lady" Janice Deveree had a beard that measured 14 in (36 cm) in 1884.

In 1990, Vivian Wheeler (USA) stopped trimming back her unusual facial growth to let her beard grow. She is the current record-holder for the longest beard on a living female, with the longest hair from follicle to tip measuring 11 in (27.9 cm) in 2000.

FEWEST TOES

Some of the Wadomo tribe of the Zambezi Valley, Zimbabwe, and the Kalanga tribe of the eastern Kalahari Desert, Botswana, have only two toes. This syndrome is inherited via a single mutated gene.

MOST ALBINO SIBLINGS

The most albino children in one family is three – Ayonote, Osimo, and Atinuk (UK, below), born to Cynthia and Dixkson Unoarumhi. All have the rare genetic condition, albinism. Both parents, who are black, carry the faulty gene, giving a one-in-four chance that their children would be born with reduced or non-existent pigmentation. All three children have translucent skin, light hazel-green eyes and pale golden hair.

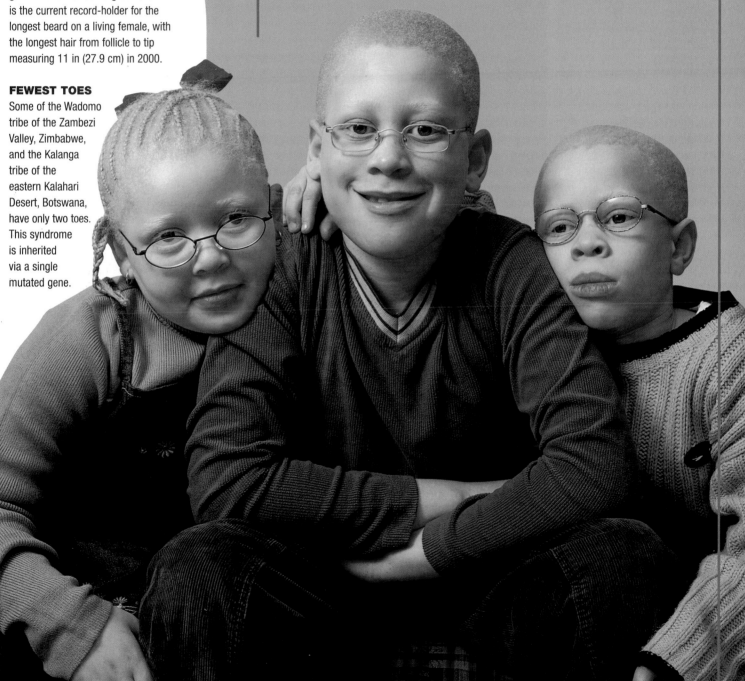

MOST CAESAREAN SECTIONS

Kristina House (USA, above center) gave birth to 11 children by Caesarean section – the baby delivered via an incision in the mother's abdomen – between May 15 1979 and November 20 1998. A woman's body takes over a year to recover from a Caesarean, and it is recommended to have no more than three during a lifetime.

LONGEST SURVIVING KIDNEY TRANSPLANT

Johanna Leanora Rempel (Canada) was given a kidney from her identical twin sister Lana Blatz on December 28 1960. The transplant operation was performed at the Peter Bent Brigham Hospital, Boston, Massachusetts, USA. Both Johanna and her sister have enjoyed excellent health, and both have had healthy children.

RECIPIENT OF MOST BLOOD

When undergoing open-heart surgery at the Michael Reese Hospital, Chicago, Illinois, USA, in December 1970, 50-year-old hemophiliac Warren C Jyrich (USA) required a staggering 2,400 donor units of blood. This is equivalent to 2,282 pints (1,080 liters). On average, the human body contains around 10.56 pints (5 liters) of blood.

LOWEST BODY TEMPERATURE

The lowest authenticated body temperature is 57.5°F (14.2°C), the rectal temperature for two-year-old Karlee Kosolofski (Canada) taken on February 23 1994. Karlee had accidentally been locked out of her home for six hours in a temperature of -8°F (-22°C). The normal human temperature is around 98.6ºF (37ºC) and mild hypothermia sets in under 95°F (35ºC). Despite frostbite leading to the amputation of her left leg she made a full recovery.

HIGHEST BODY TEMPERATURE

Body temperatures above 109ºF (42.7ºC) can prove fatal, but when 52-year-old Willie Jones (USA) was admitted to Grady Memorial Hospital, Atlanta, Georgia, USA, on July 10 1980 with heatstroke, his temperature had reached 115.7ºF (46.5ºC). He was discharged after 24 days.

MOST ARTIFICIAL JOINTS

By the age of 47 Anne Davison (UK) had 12 major joints (elbows, wrists, both shoulders, hips, knees, and ankles) and three knuckles replaced.

Charles Wedde (USA), who has rheumatoid arthritis, also had 12 major joints replaced between 1979 and 1995.

YOUNGEST HEART SURGERY PATIENT

Pioneering surgery to correct a defective heart valve was performed on a 23-week-old fetus by a team of 10 doctors at the Children's Hospital, Boston, Massachusetts, USA. The baby (named Jack) was born six weeks early in November 2001 at Brigham and Women's Hospital, Boston, Massachusetts, USA, with a healthy heart and weighing 5 lb 8 oz (2.49 kg).

YOUNGEST TRANSPLANT PATIENT

On November 8 1996 one-hour-old Cheyenne Pyle (USA) became the youngest-ever transplant patient when she received a donor heart at Jackson Children's Hospital, Miami, Florida, USA. The six-hour operation involved draining Cheyenne's blood and cooling her body to 62.6°F (17°C), the temperature at which organs cease to function. The transplant had to be completed within an hour to prevent damage to her other organs.

LONGEST SURVIVOR OF A PORCINE AORTIC VALVE REPLACEMENT

Harry Driver (UK) received a porcine (pig's) aortic valve replacement on April 12 1978 under surgeon Dr John Keats. It is still in full working order. He is also the oldest living recipient.

HEAVIEST SINGLE BIRTH

Anna Bates (Canada) who stood 7 ft 5.5 in (2.27 m) tall, gave birth to a boy weighing a massive 23 lb 12 oz (10.8 kg) at her home in Seville, Ohio, USA, on January 19 1879. The baby died 11 hours later.

LIGHTEST SINGLE BIRTH

The lowest birthweight recorded for a surviving infant is 10 oz (283 g) for Marian Taggart (UK) in 1938. She was born six weeks prematurely and was fed hourly for the first 30 hours via a fountain pen filled with brandy, glucose, and water. At three weeks she weighed 1 lb 13 oz (821 g), and by her first birthday she was 13 lb 14 oz (6.3 kg).

MOST PREMATURE BABY

James Elgin Gill (Canada) was born 128 days prematurely on May 20 1987, weighing 1 lb 6 oz (624 g); the normal human gestation period is 280 days. James's parents were told that he had no chance of survival. Much of his body was still developing; including his skin, hands and feet, while his eyes were still fused shut. James is now a healthy 15-year-old.

HIGHEST BLOOD SUGAR LEVEL

On November 21 1995, 12-year-old Michael Dougherty (USA) had a blood-sugar level of 2,350 while still conscious. The normal blood-sugar range is between 80–120; this is 19 times above average.

LONGEST DISTANCE BETWEEN PATIENT AND SURGEON

On September 7 2001, a robot removed Madeleine Schaal's (France) gall bladder in Strasbourg, France, while her surgeons (above) operated the robot remotely from New York, USA, a total distance of 3,866 miles (6,222 km) away.

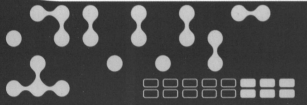

MOST SURVIVING CHILDREN DELIVERED AT A SINGLE BIRTH

A set of septuplets – four boys and three girls – were born to Bobbie McCaughey (USA) on November 19 1997 at University Hospital, Iowa, USA. The babies were conceived by IVF and delivered by Caesarean section at 31 weeks in the space of 16 minutes. They weighed between 2 lb 5 oz and 3 lb 4 oz (1.048 kg and 1.474 kg).

Another set of surviving septuplets (four boys and three girls) were born eight weeks prematurely on January 14 1998 to 40-year-old Hasna Mohammed Humair (Saudi Arabia). The smallest weighed just under 2 lb (907 g).

LONGEST FETAL SURVIVAL OUTSIDE THE WOMB

Triplet Ronan Ingram (UK) survived outside his mother's womb for an amazing 29 weeks. Six weeks after conception, his mother's Fallopian tube ruptured and the rogue fertilized egg attached itself to the exterior wall of her uterus, developing its own placenta while his two sisters developed normally in the womb. The three babies were delivered at 29 weeks by a Caesarean section. Doctors cut 2-lb 4-oz (1.09 kg) baby Ronan free after his two sisters were born. The chances of having two babies in the uterus and another outside are about one in 60–100 million.

EARLIEST BRAIN-CELL TRANSPLANT

The first brain-cell transplant was performed at the University of Pittsburgh Medical Center, Penn, USA, on June 23 1998. The operation aimed to reverse the stroke damage suffered by 62-year-old Alma Cerasini (USA), who had suffered some speech loss and paralysis.

YOUNGEST PERSON TO HAVE A PAIR OF BIONIC ARMS FITTED

Kyle Barton (UK, below) was eight years old when he was fitted with his second bionic arm at the Northern General Hospital, Sheffield, UK, in February 2002. Kyle had to have both his arms and legs amputated after he contracted meningitis in 1998.

EARLIEST DOUBLE ARM TRANSPLANT

In January 2000, Professor Jean-Michel Dubernard (France) headed an international team of 18 surgeons and 32 staff who successfully transplanted two arms just below the elbow on to a 33-year-old French explosives worker who had lost his arms in a rocket accident four years previously.

GREATEST PERCENTAGE OF BURNS TO BODY SURVIVED

David Chapman (UK) survived 90% burns to his body following an accident on July 2 1996. A fuel canister he was holding exploded and turned him into a human fireball. Surgeons at St Andrew's Hospital, Billericay, Essex, UK, spent 36 hours removing his dead skin, and he spent seven hours in the operating room every two days for three weeks. After nine months in a UK hospital undergoing skin grafts donated by members of his family, the 16-year-old flew with his parents to Houston, Texas, USA, on April 14 1997 for treatment by a specialist.

EARLIEST SUCCESSFUL KIDNEY TRANSPLANT

RH Lawler (USA) performed the groundbreaking surgery at Little Company of Mary Hospital, Chicago, Illinois, USA, on June 17 1950.

MOST BODY PIERCINGS IN ONE SESSION

On September 22 2001, American Greg Thompson received a total of 227 new piercings to his body without an anesthetic. All piercings were executed by Beaker Trigg (USA) in one continuous six-hour session at Area 51 Tattoo and Body Piercing, Colorado Springs, Colorado, USA.

LARGEST LIP PLATE

The women of the Surma (above) and Mursi tribes of Ethiopia make lip plates from clay, color them with ochre and charcoal, and fire-bake them. The process of inserting the plates starts about a year before marriage. The final size indicates the number of cattle required from her future husband in return for her hand. The plates can reach up to 6 in (15 cm) in diameter.

MOST BODY PIERCINGS USING SURGICAL NEEDLES

Jerome Abramovitch (Canada) holds the record for most body piercings using surgical needles. On a TV show recorded on October 31 1999, he inserted 200 1.5-in-long (3.81-cm) surgical needles (all 22 gauge) into his chest, neck, and arms.

MOST PIERCED WOMAN

As of August 9 2001, Scottish-born Elaine Davidson (UK) has had her body adorned with a total of 720 piercings. Her record amount of body decoration includes 192 piercings on her ears, forehead, eyebrows, chin, nose, and tongue, and 56 piercings on her stomach, breasts, and hands. Elaine had her first piercing in January 1997.

MOST TATTOOED WOMAN

The world's most tattooed woman is strip artist Krystyne Kolorful (Canada) who has tattoos decorating 95% of her body. They cost approximately CAN$15,000 ($9,486 or £6,667), took 10 years to complete, and are the work of 13 different artists. The largest design on Krystyne's body is a dragon that wraps around her chest and back, and took 40 hours to do.

LONGEST TATTOO SESSION

Kevin Gill (UK) tattooed Dave Sheldrick (UK) for a continuous 27 hr 12 min at Kev's Tattoo Parlour, Welling, Kent, UK, between March 15 and 17 2001.

MOST PIERCED MAN

Antonio Agüero (Cuba) has 230 piercings on his body and head. His face alone holds over 175 rings. It has taken Antonio since 1990 to pierce his ears, cheeks, lips, chin, nostrils, and forehead with the rings, plus the two rods that slide through the bridge of his nose. Agüero charges a nominal fee for photographs of himself in order to help with the upkeep of his large family.

LONGEST BEARD

Norwegian Hans N Langseth's beard measured an impressive 17 ft 6 in (5.33 m) – the longest beard ever recorded – at the time of his burial at Kensett, Iowa, USA, in 1927.

The record for the longest beard on a living male is held by Shamsher Singh (India). By August 18 1997 his beard measured 6 ft (1.83 m) from the end of his chin to its tip.

LONGEST MUSTACHE

The record holder for the world's longest mustache is Kalyan Ramji Sain (India), who has been growing his impressive mustache since 1976. By July 1993 it spanned 11 ft 1 in (3.39 m); the right side is 5 ft 7 in (1.72 m) long and the left side is 5 ft 5 in (1.67 m) long. Dedicated mustache-growers use mustard, oil, butter, and cream to keep their 'taches in top condition.

MOST RHINESTONES TO ADORN A BODY

The record for the most rhinestones to adorn a body was set by Maria Rosa Pons Abad (Spain), who attached 30,361 rhinestones to the body of a model on November 22 2001.

LONGEST TOENAILS

In 1991 the combined length of Louise Hollis's (USA) 10 toenails was 7 ft 3 in (221 cm). Louise was inspired to grow her toenails in 1982 after seeing a TV program featuring the longest fingernails. The mother of 12 rarely wears shoes and keeps all of her broken toenails. Currently, each of her toenails are approximately 6 in (15.24 cm) long.

LONGEST FINGERNAILS

On July 8 1998 the total length of the five nails on the left hand of Shridhar Chillal (India) was a record-breaking 20 ft 2.25 in (6.15 m). He last cut his fingernails in 1952.

The longest fingernails on a female belong to Lee Redmond (USA), who has been growing them for 19 years. Their total length is 21 ft 9 in (6.62 m). The longest nail (on her left thumb) measures 2 ft 3 in (68.58 cm).

LARGEST BICEP

Denis Sester's (USA) right bicep is 30 in (77.8 cm) when cold. He built up his huge muscles by doing arm curls with a 150-lb (68-kg) sand bucket.

MOST BREAST ENLARGEMENTS

The late Lolo Ferrari, aka Eve Valois (France), had a bust measuring 71 in (1.80 m) and a 54-G bra size – the result of 22 enlargements. Her breasts were first increased to 46 in (1.17 m), but she later found an aeronautical engineer who designed 51-inch (1.3-m) molds for her. Lolo's breasts eventually weighed more than 26 lb (11.7 kg).

MOST TATTOOED MAN

Around 99.9% of Tom Leppard's (UK, above) body is tattooed. Tom's tattoo portrays a leopard-skin design – dark spots on a yellow background. He estimates that he has spent over £5,000 ($7,000) on his stunning bodywork.

LONGEST HAIR

The world's longest recorded hair belongs to Hoo Sateow (Thailand) who has not had a haircut in over 70 years, as he believes his hair holds the key to his healing powers. On November 21 1997 it was unraveled and officially measured at 16 ft 11 in (5.15 m).

MOST PLASTIC SURGERY

Since 1979, Cindy Jackson (USA) has spent $99,600 (£69,104) on 28 cosmetic operations. Jackson has had three full facelifts, two nose operations, knee, waist, abdomen and jawline surgery, thigh liposuction, breast reduction and augmentation, and semi-permanent makeup.

MOST WOMEN WITH BOUND FEET

Foot-binding, which began in 10th-century China and was banned in 1911, prevented women's feet from growing over 3.9 in (10 cm). The feet were bound with cloth strips so their shape would resemble lotus flowers. A study in 1997 of 193 women (93 over 80 years old and 100 aged 70–79) in Beijing, China, by the University of California, San Francisco, USA, found that 38% in the over-80 group and 18% of those in the 70–79 group had their feet deformed by the process.

SMALLEST WAIST

The smallest waist recorded on a person of normal stature was 13 in (33 cm), on Ethel Granger (UK), who went from a waist of 22 in (56 cm) to a tiny 13 in (33 cm) between 1929 and 1939. The same size was claimed for French actress Emile Marie Bouchand.

The smallest waist on a living person belongs to Cathie Jung (USA), whose waist measures 15 in (38.1 cm).

The women wore corsets to achieve their records.

LONGEST NECK

The maximum known extension of a human neck is 15.75 in (40 cm), created by the fitting of copper coils, as practiced by women of the Padaung, or Kareni, tribe of Burma (Myanmar) (below) as a sign of beauty. Removal of the coils can prove fatal.

POWERFUL WORLD

DRIEST PLACE ON EARTH

Between 1964 and 2001 the average annual rainfall for the meteorological station in Quillagua (above, situated at lat 21°38'S, long 69°33'W), in the Atacama Desert, Chile, was just 0.02 in (0.5 mm). This discovery was made during the making of the documentary series *Going to Extremes*, by Keo Films in 2001.

HEAVIEST HAILSTONES

The heaviest hailstones ever recorded weighed up to 2 lb 2.4 oz (1 kg) each. They are reported to have killed 92 people when they fell in the Gopalganj district of Bangladesh on April 14 1986.

LARGEST SNOWFLAKE

It is reported that on January 28 1887 at Fort Keogh, Montana, USA, ranch owner Matt Coleman (USA) measured a snowflake that was 15 in (38 cm) wide and 8 in (20 cm) thick, which he later described as being "larger than milk pans."

MOST FREAKISH TEMPERATURE RISE

The freakiest temperature rise was 49°F (27°C) in two minutes, recorded at Spearfish, South Dakota, USA, from -4°F (-20°C) at 7:30 am to 45°F (7°C) at 7: 32 am on January 22 1943.

WARMEST YEAR ON RECORD

The warmest year since records began (in around 1880) was 1998, when it was 1.03°F (0.57°C) warmer than the average global temperature (measured between 1961 and 1990). The 1990s was in fact the warmest decade on record; the six warmest years ever were all in the 1990s.

LEAST SUNSHINE

At the South Pole there is no sunshine for 182 days every year, and at the North Pole the same applies for 176 days per year. This is due to their geographical locations, which means that for half of the year the Sun never rises above the horizon.

MOST POWERFUL NATURAL CLIMATE CHANGE

The El-Niño Southern Oscillation occurs due to cyclic warming of the eastern and central Pacific Ocean. Apart from natural seasonal changes, it is the Earth's most powerful short-term natural climate change. The entire cycle of El Niño and La Niña (its cooler opposite) lasts between three and seven years, causing unusual weather conditions worldwide; notable were the 1982/83 and 1997/98 events.

LONGEST-LASTING RAINBOW

A rainbow over Wetherby, Yorkshire, UK, on March 14 1994 was visible for six hours continuously from 9:00 am to 3:00 pm. Most rainbows last much less than one hour.

OLDEST FOSSILIZED RAINDROPS

On December 15 2001 Chirananda De (India) announced his discovery of the fossilized imprints of raindrops in ancient rocks in the Vindhyan range, Madhya Pradesh, India. These rocks prove that rain fell on Earth at least 1.6 billion years ago.

HOTTEST PLACE ON EARTH

The hottest place on Earth is the air around a lightning strike. For a fraction of a second, the air is heated to an incredible 54,000°F (30,000°C). This is roughly equivalent to five times hotter than the visible surface of the Sun.

EARLIEST IMAGE OF A SPRITE

Sprites are atmospheric electrical phenomena associated with lightning. These unusual flashes shoot upward from the tops of thunderstorms to altitudes of around 60 miles (100 km) above the Earth's surface. Historical reports of these phenomena were not taken seriously until the first image was captured – accidentally – in 1989, when a low-level-light TV camera was pointed above a thunderstorm. Video footage of sprites has been taken from the space shuttle.

LONGEST SEA-LEVEL FOGS

Fogs with visibility under 3,000 ft (900 m) persist for weeks on the Grand Banks, Newfoundland, Canada, with their average durations being more than 120 days per year.

HIGHEST BAROMETRIC PRESSURE

Barometric pressure is the physical pressure exerted by all the air above us, with pressure decreasing as you gain altitude. It is measured in millibars or inches of mercury. The highest ever recorded was 1,083.8 mb (32 in) at Agata, Siberia, Russia, on December 31 1968. This pressure corresponds to being at nearly 2,000 ft (600 m) below sea level, even though Agata is 826 ft (262 m) above sea level.

The lowest barometric pressure was 870 mb (25.69 in) recorded 300 miles (483 km) west of Guam in the Pacific Ocean on October 12 1979.

MOST ROCKETS LAUNCHED BY LIGHTNING

In June 1987, a lightning strike at NASA's launch facility at Wallops Island, Virginia, USA, inadvertently triggered the launch of three unmanned rockets. Two of them began to follow their planned trajectories, while the third rocket splashed into the ocean around 300 ft (90 m) from the launch pad. Ironically, the third rocket was designed to study thunderstorms.

HIGHEST ATMOSPHERIC PHENOMENA

The very highest visible phenomena are the beautiful shimmering lights of the aurorae (above), the lowest of which occur at altitudes of around 60 miles (100 km), while the highest extend up to around 250 miles (400 km).

HIGHEST CLOUDS

The highest clouds in the atmosphere are noctilucent clouds. Best seen in the lower and higher latitudes, these beautiful, tenuous phenomena form above 99.9% of the atmosphere at altitudes of around 50 miles (80 km). They can be seen after sunset, when, due to their high altitude, they are still illuminated by the Sun's rays. They are believed to form from a mixture of ice crystals and dust from meteors.

STRONGEST JET STREAM

Jet streams are narrow, fast-flowing currents of air that exist in the upper atmosphere. The fastest-ever jet stream wind speeds – up to an incredible 310 mph (500 km/h) – have been recorded over Japan during the winter season, when tropical air from northern India flows north-eastward over the islands.

HIGHEST WATERSPOUT

Waterspouts are essentially tornadoes over water. The highest waterspout of which there is a reliable record was one observed on May 16 1898 off Eden, NSW, Australia. A surveyor's reading from the shore gave its height as 5,014 ft (1,528 m) and it was about 10 ft (3 m) in diameter. Waterspouts have been known to suck up fish from the sea and rain them back down on nearby towns.

LONGEST LIGHTNING FLASH

At any one time, about 100 lightning bolts per second hit the Earth. Typically, the actual length of these bolts can be around 5.5 miles (9 km). However, in 1956 meteorologist Myron Ligda (USA) used radar to record a lightning flash that covered a horizontal distance of 93 miles (150 km) inside clouds.

GREATEST DISPLAY OF SOLAR HALOS

On January 11 1999, at least 24 types of solar halo were witnessed by scientists at the geographic South Pole. Solar halos are formed when sunlight is reflected and refracted by ice crystals in the atmosphere, causing rings around the Sun and brightly colored patches in the sky. Atmospheric conditions at the pole are conducive to this type of phenomenon.

LARGEST PIECE OF FALLEN ICE

On August 13 1849 a piece of ice 20 ft (6 m) long was reported to have fallen from the sky in Scotland, UK. The ice was clear but looked as though it was composed of smaller pieces, possibly hailstones (left). An explanation is that the hailstones were fused together by a bolt of lightning. The mass of ice reportedly fell after a crash of thunder.

LONGEST BILL

Bills on Australian pelicans (above, *Pelicanus conspicillatus*) can be up to 18.5 in (47 cm) long. The longest bill, relative to body length, belongs to the sword-billed hummingbird (*Ensifera ensifera*), which has a 4-in (10.2-cm) beak – longer than its body.

MOST FEARLESS MAMMAL

The ratel or honey badger (*Mellivora capensis*) will defend itself against any animal, especially if they disturb its breeding burrow. Its tough skin is impervious to attacks by bees, porcupines, and most snakes, and its skin is so loose that if it is held by the scruff of the neck – for example, by a leopard – it can turn inside its skin and bite its attacker until released.

HIGHEST G-FORCE

Experiments have shown that the beak of the red-headed woodpecker (*Melanerpes erythrocephalus*) hits the bark of a tree with an impact velocity of 13 mph (20.9 km/h). This motion subjects the brain to a deceleration of about 10 G when the head snaps back.

FASTEST BIRD IN LEVEL FLIGHT

The fastest fliers in level flight are found among ducks and geese (Anatidae). Some powerful species such as the red-breasted merganser (*Mergus serrator*), the eider (*Somateria mollissima*), the canvasback (*Aythya valisineria*), and the spur-winged goose (*Plectropterus gambensis*) can, on rare occasions, reach 56–62 mph (90–100 km/h).

BEST ANIMAL REGENERATION

Sponges (Porifera) have the most remarkable powers of regeneration of any animal. If they lose a segment of their body, it grows right back. If a sponge is forced through a fine-meshed silk gauze, the separate fragments can re-form into a full-size sponge.

FASTEST CREATURES ON LAND

When measured over a short distance, the cheetah (*Acinonyx jubatus*) can maintain a record-breaking steady maximum speed of around 62 mph (100 km/h) on level ground. That's nearly the highway speed limit in the USA!

The American antelope (*Antilocapra americana*), found in parts of the western USA, southwestern Canada and parts of northern Mexico, is the fastest land animal when measured steadily over a long distance. The antelope has been witnessed traveling continuously at 35 mph (56 km/h) for as far as 4 miles (6 km).

The fastest bird on land is the ostrich, which, although it cannot fly, can run at a speed of up to 45 mph (72 km/h) when necessary. The ostrich also holds the record for the longest stride, which may exceed 23 ft (7 m) in length when sprinting.

OLDEST ELEPHANT

Lakshmikutty (1913–1997), a female elephant donated to the Guruvayur Sri Krishna temple, Mathrubhami, India, on November 17 1923, lived to be 84 years old. Standing at 9 ft (2.76 m) tall, she was crowned "Elephant Queen" in 1983.

HIGHEST FREQUENCY HEARING

Due to their ultrasonic echolocation (sensory perception by which they orientate themselves), bats have the most acute hearing of any terrestrial animal. Most species use frequencies in the 20–80 kHz range, although some can hear frequencies as high as 120–250 kHz, compared with a limit of 20 kHz for humans.

GREATEST DISTANCE FLOWN BY A BIRD

A common tern (*Sterna hirundo*), banded as a juvenile on June 30 1996 in central Finland, flew a record 16,250 miles (26,000 km) before being recaptured alive at Rotamah Island, Vic, Australia, in January 1997. To have reached there, the bird must have flown an exhausting 124 miles (200 km) per day.

LARGEST LAND MAMMAL

The male African bush elephant (*Loxodonta africana*) has an average shoulder-height of 9 ft 10 in –12 ft 2 in (3–3.7 m) and an average weight of 8,800–15,400 lb (4–7 tonnes). The heaviest recorded specimen was shot in Angola, Africa, on November 7 1974. Its projected standing height was 13 ft (3.96 m) and weighed a massive 26,984 lb (12.24 tonnes).

FASTEST WING BEAT

The horned sungem (*Heliactin cornuta*), a hummingbird from tropical South America, has the fastest wing beat at 90 beats/sec. The wings move so fast that you can barely see them.

GREATEST TREE-CLIMBING FISH

The climbing perch (*Anabas testudineus*) from south Asia is remarkable for its ability to walk on land and climb palm trees. It will even walk to search for better habitat. The species has special gills that allow it to absorb atmospheric oxygen. Mudskippers (Perciformes) can also live out of water for short periods and climb trees using their pectoral fins.

NOISIEST LAND MAMMAL

Male howler monkeys (*Alouatta*, above) of Central and South America have an enlarged bony structure at the top of their windpipe that amplifies their shouts. Their noisy calls can be heard over distances of up to 3 miles (4.8 km) away.

SMALLEST OWL

The elf owl (*Micrathene whitneyi*) from southwest USA and Mexico is usually quoted as the smallest owl, averaging a tiny 4.75–5.5 in (12–14 cm) in length and weighing less than 1.75 oz (50 g).

HIGHEST-FLYING BIRDS

The highest altitude recorded for a bird is 37,000 ft (11,300 m) for a Ruppell's vulture (*Gyps rueppellii*), which collided with a commercial aircraft over Abidjan, Côte d'Ivoire, on November 29 1973. The impact shut down one of the aircraft's engines, but it landed safely. Enough feathers were recovered to make a positive identification of this high-flier, which is rarely seen above 20,000 ft (6,000 m).

LARGEST ANTLERS

The record antler spread, or "rack," of any living species is 6 ft 6.5 in (1.99 m) on a moose (*Alces alces*) killed near the Stewart River, Yukon, Canada, in October 1897. The rack is on display in Chicago's Field Museum, Illinois, USA.

LARGEST MAMMAL EYES

The Pygmy tarsier (*Tarsius pumilus*) from southeast Asia, which has a head and body length of 3.3– 6.3 in (8.5–16 cm) has huge forward-pointing eyes with a diameter of 0.6 in (1.6 cm). This eye-size is equivalent to humans having eyes the size of grapefruits. Tarsiers are the only primates that can move their heads 180 degrees to the left and right.

LARGEST WINGSPAN

The largest wingspan of any living species of bird was that of a male wandering albatross (*Diomedea exulans*) of the southern oceans, with a wingspan of 11 ft 11 in (3.63 m). It was caught by crew of the Antarctic research ship USNS *Eltanin* in the Tasman Sea on September 18 1965.

KEENEST VISION

It has been calculated that large birds of prey have the keenest vision. They can detect a target object at a distance three or more times farther than that achieved by humans. Under ideal conditions a peregrine falcon (*Falco peregrinus*) can spot a pigeon at a range of over 5 miles (8 km).

LARGEST BIRD EGG

The largest egg on record was an ostrich egg weighing 5 lb 2 oz (2.35 kg), laid in June 1997 at Datong Xinda ostrich farm, Shanxi, China. An ostrich egg normally weighs 2.2–3.9 lb (1.0–1.78 kg) equal to 24 hen's eggs in volume. Although only 0.06 in (1.5 mm) thick, the shell can support the weight of an adult human.

SMALLEST MAMMAL

The world's smallest mammal is the bumblebee bat or Kitti's hog-nosed bat (*Craseonycteris thonglongyai*), which has a body no bigger than a large bumblebee. It has a head–body length of only 1.14–1.30 in (29–33 mm), and a wingspan of approximately 5.1–5.7 in (130–145 mm). It can only be found in the limestone caves on the Kwae Noi River, Thailand.

LARGEST BIRD'S NEST

A nest built by a pair of bald eagles (*Haliaeetus leucocephalus*), near St Petersburg, Florida, USA, measured 9 ft 6 in (2.9 m) wide and 20 ft (6 m) deep. Examined in 1963, it was estimated to weigh more than 4,400 lb (2 tonnes).

GREEDIEST ANIMAL

The larva of the polyphemus moth (*Antheraea polyphemus*, above) of North America eats an amount equal to 86,000 times its own birthweight in its first 56 days. In human terms, this would be the same as a 7-lb (3.17-kg) baby taking on a staggering 602,000 lb (273 tonnes) of nourishment.

MOST INTELLIGENT PARROT

The world's most intelligent parrot, an African grey (*Psittacus erithacus*) called Alex (above), knows the words for more than 35 objects and seven colors. He also has a functional use of phrases and can distinguish between shapes with three, four, five, or six sides.

Another contender is a parrot called Smudge, owned by Mark Steiger (Switzerland), who managed to remove 10 keys from an S-shaped keyring on November 30 2001.

BIRD WITH THE LARGEST VOCABULARY

The bird with the most extensive vocabulary was a budgerigar called Puck, owned by Camille Jordan (USA). Puck knew an estimated 1,728 words by the time of its death in 1994.

LONGEST DOG SWIM

On September 2 1995, two black Labradors named Kai and Gypsy swam the "Maui Channel Swim" from Lanai to Maui Island in Hawaii, USA – a distance of 9.5 miles (15.2 km) – in 6 hr 3 min 42 sec. The dogs' owner, Steve Fisher (USA), swam along with them the entire time. Kai and Gypsy are also talented windsurfers and often accompany Steve on his large, modified surfboard.

DOG WITH THE LARGEST REPERTOIRE OF TRICKS

Toy poodle Chanda-Leah, owned and trained by Sharon Robinson (Canada), can perform a repertoire of 469 tricks including playing the piano, knowing her three, four, and five times tables, and riding a skateboard.

HIGHEST JUMP BY A DOG

On September 27 1993 an 18-month-old lurcher dog named Stag broke the canine high-jump record for a leap-and-scramble over a smooth wooden wall without any climbing aids. The dog, which is owned by Mr and Mrs PR Matthews of Redruth, Cornwall, UK, cleared 12 ft 2.5 in (3.72 m) at the annual Cotswold Country Fair in Cirencester, Glos, UK.

FARTHEST CANINE TREK

In 1979, Jimpa, a Labrador/boxer cross, turned up at his home in Pimpinio, Vic, Australia, after walking 2,000 miles (3,220 km) across the continent. Jimpa's owner, Warren Dumesney (Australia), had taken the dog with him 14 months earlier when he went to work on a farm at Nyabing, WA, Australia. During his extraordinary trek, the dog negotiated the almost waterless Nullarbor Plain, South Australia.

MOST CELEBRATED CANINE RESCUER

The most famous canine rescuer of all time is a St Bernard dog called Barry, who rescued more than 40 people during a 12-year career on the Swiss Alps. His numerous successful rescues included that of a boy who was lying half-frozen under an avalanche in which his mother had perished. Barry spread himself across the boy's body to warm him and licked his face until he succeeded in waking him up. He then carried the youngster back to the nearest dwelling.

MOST NUMERATE CHIMPANZEE

Ai is the first chimpanzee to be able to count from one to nine. She is also able to remember five of these numbers chosen at random and can put them into ascending order in a fraction of a second. Ai was born in west Africa in 1976 and was brought to the Primate Research Institute, Kyoto University, Japan, in December 1977. There, she was nurtured by Prof Tetsuro Matsuzawa (Japan) and her numeracy skills blossomed.

LONGEST SCENT-TRACKING

In 1925 a Doberman pinscher called Sauer, who was trained by Det Sgt Herbert Kruger (South Africa), tracked a stock thief for 100 miles (160 km) over the arid Great Karroo plateau, South Africa, by scent alone.

HIGHEST-ALTITUDE SKYDIVE BY A DOG

On May 20 1997, Brutus, the Skydiving Dog, jumped from a large twin-engine plane at 15,000 ft (4,572 m) above sea level, flying high above the town of Lake Elsinore, California, USA, and set a new world record. His owner,

Ron Sirull (USA), first began to take Brutus along on his skydives to prevent the dog from chasing his plane down the runway. Brutus, a miniature dachshund, currently boasts 71 separate skydives in his career and has his own custom-made goggles.

ONLY CANONIZED DOG

Guinefort, a French greyhound who was killed while saving a child from a snake, was later made a saint for his brave act. In the 13th century, healing miracles were performed on sickly children at his tomb until Dominican monks quashed the cult.

MOST PROFICIENT SIGNING GORILLA

In 1972, Koko – a gorilla born at San Francisco Zoo – was taught Ameslan (American Sign Language for the Deaf) by Dr Francine Patterson (USA). By 2000 Koko had a working vocabulary of over 1,000 signs and understood around 2,000 words of spoken English. She can refer to the past and future, argue, joke, and lie. When Koko was asked by Dr Patterson whether she was an animal or a person, she replied, "Fine animal gorilla."

FIRST DOG IN SPACE

A dog called Laika (above) became the first animal in space in November 1957 when she went into orbit on *Sputnik 2*. Sadly, her vehicle was not designed to return to Earth and Laika (meaning "barker" in Russian) died after a few days.

MOST SUCCESSFUL SNIFFER DOG

Snag, a US Customs Labrador retriever trained and partnered by Jeff Weitzmann (USA), has made 118 drug seizures, worth a canine record $810 million (£580 million).

LONGEST SURVIVING HEADLESS CHICKEN

On September 10 1945 a Wyandotte chicken called Mike was decapitated but went on to survive for 18 months. The cut had missed the jugular vein and much of the brain stem had been left intact. His owner, Lloyd Olsen (USA), fed and watered the headless chicken directly into his gullet with the aid of an eyedropper. Mike eventually choked to death in an Arizona motel.

FIRST CHIMPANZEE TO OPERATE A COMPUTER

In 1972, Lana the chimpanzee was trained to read and write Yerkish, a language of words represented by abstract symbols on a computer keyboard, at the Yerkes Primate Research Center in Atlanta, Georgia, USA. After three years she had acquired a vocabulary of 120 words and could ask for a cup of coffee in 23 different ways.

LONGEST-SERVING MILITARY MULE

The unit mascot for the 853 AT Coy ASC (MA Mules) was a Spanish mule called Pedongi, who was on active service with the Indian Army from May 4 1965 until her death at the age of 37 on March 5 1998. Her name was derived from the first battle area she was sent to, at Pedong in north-east India.

BRAVEST DONKEY

On May 19 1997, an Australian Army donkey called Murphy, was posthumously awarded the RSPCA Australia Purple Cross on behalf of all the donkeys in the 1915–16 Gallipoli campaign. Murphy carried thousands of wounded soldiers to field hospitals.

OLDEST PRIMATE

Cheeta the chimpanzee, who appeared in the Tarzan films of the 1930s and 1940s starring Johnny Weissmuller and Maureen O'Sullivan (both USA), is the world's oldest living primate. He had reached the age of 69 years and one month by April 2001. Cheeta has been enshrined in the Palm Springs Walk of Stars in Palm Springs, California, USA, and is involved in the promotion of the chimp foundation CHEETA (the Committee to Help Enhance the Environment of Threatened Apes).

LONGEST SURVIVAL BY A SHEEP

On March 24 1978, Alex Maclennan (UK) found one ewe still alive after he had dug 16 dead sheep out of a snowdrift. The flock was buried for 50 days in Sutherland, Highland, UK, following the great blizzard in January 1978. The sheep's hot breath created air holes in the snow, and the animal had gnawed its own wool for protein.

FASTEST SNAIL

The World Snail Racing Championships have been held outside St Andrew's church in Congham, Norfolk, UK, every July since 1970. Around 150 participants enter each year, racing against each other from the center of a 13-in (33-cm) circular course to its perimeter. The all-time record holder is Archie, a young snail trained by Carl Bramham (UK), whose record-breaking sprint to the winning post in 1995 took 2 min 20 sec.

MOST SUCCESSFUL POLICE DOG

Police dogs (above) are a vital aid to law enforcement. Although many canine breeds are used in this line of work, the world's top police dog is a golden retriever – Trepp – who is credited with more than 100 arrests (up to 1979) and the recovery of over $63 million (£28.6 million) worth of narcotics.

SOCIETY AND POLITICS

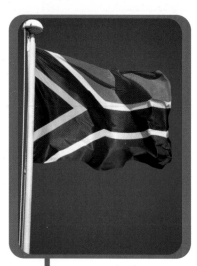

MOST OFFICIAL LANGUAGES

The Republic of South Africa (the RSA flag flies above) has 11 official languages. These are: Afrikaans, English, Ndebele, North Sotho, South Sotho, Swazi, Tsonga, Tswana, Venda, Xhosa, and Zulu. South Africa has a population of 43,840,000.

MOST LAND BOUNDARIES

China and Russia share the land boundary record, both having 14. China's are: Afghanistan, Bhutan, India, Kazakhstan, Kyrgyzstan, Laos, Mongolia, Myanmar (Burma), Nepal, North Korea, Pakistan, Russia, Tajikistan, and Vietnam. Russia's boundaries are with: Azerbaijan, Belarus, China, Estonia, Finland, Georgia, Kazakhstan, Latvia Lithuania, Mongolia, North Korea, Norway, Poland, and Ukraine.

OLDEST CAPITAL CITY

The oldest capital city in the world is Damascus (also known as Dimishq), Syria. It has been continuously inhabited since around 2500 BC. In 1998 it had an estimated population of 1,431,821.

NORTHERNMOST CAPITAL CITY

The world's northernmost city, (and also the northernmost national capital), is Reykjavik, Iceland (64º08'N). The most northerly capital of a dependency is Nuuk (formerly Godthåb), Greenland (64º15'N).

SOUTHERNMOST CAPITAL CITY

Wellington, New Zealand, is the southernmost capital city of an independent country (41º17'S). The world's southernmost capital of a dependent territory is Port Stanley, Falkland Islands (51º43'S), with a population of 1,600 (excluding service personnel) in 1999.

LARGEST COUNTRY

Russia takes up 11.5% of the world's surface, with a total area of 6,592,848 miles^2 (17,075,400 km^2). This vast country is 70 times as large as the UK, but with a population of 147,231,000 in 1997, it is only 2.5 times as populated.

MOST DENSELY & SPARSELY POPULATED COUNTRIES

Of those countries with an area over 965 miles^2 (2,500 km^2), the most densely populated is Bangladesh. In 2000, it had a population of 129,194,000 living in 56,977 miles^2 (147,570 km^2) at a density of roughly 2,267 people per mile^2 (875 per km^2).

The most sparsely populated sovereign country is Mongolia, with a population of 2,440,000 (in 1999) in an area of 603,908 miles^2 (1,564,116 km^2). This equates to a density of roughly four people per mile^2 (1.6 per km^2).

MOST POPULOUS ISLAND

Java, Indonesia, has a population (in 1997) of 118,700,000 living in an area of 51,037 miles^2 (132,186 km^2), or 2,325 people per mile^2 (897 per km^2).

OLDEST AND YOUNGEST POPULATIONS

In the Marshall Islands in the Pacific Ocean, 49.29% of the population is under the age of 15. In July 2001, out of a total population of 70,822, about 34,909 were aged between 0 and 14 years. In the Gaza Strip (under Palestinian authority), 48.89% of the population is aged under 15. By contrast, in Monaco, 10.8% of the population was age 75 and over in 1995.

MOST SPARSELY POPULATED CONTINENT

Although there are no native people here, Antarctica has been permanently occupied by relays of scientists since 1943. The seasonal population varies and can reach 4,000. Antarctica is also the coldest, highest, windiest, and most remote continent.

MOST DENSELY POPULATED ISLAND

Ap Lei Chau, off the south-west side of Hong Kong, China, has a population of 80,000 living in an area measuring a tiny 0.5 mile^2 (1.3 km^2). The actual population density is a very cramped 160,000 per mile^2 (60,000 per km^2).

MOST IMMIGRANTS

The country that regularly receives the most legal immigrants is the USA. Records show that between 1820 and 1996 the USA received 63,140,227 official immigrants. In 1996, the illegal alien population was 5 million of which 2.7 million were Mexican.

OLDEST TOWN

The town of Dolní Vêstonice in the Czech Republic has been dated to the prehistoric Gravettian culture of 27,000 BC – during the upper Paleolithic age.

LONGEST MARITIME BOUNDARY

The longest maritime boundary is that between the Danish dependent territory of Greenland and Canada at 1,676 miles (2,697 km).

HIGHEST PRISON POPULATION

According to Amnesty International, the prison population in the USA had topped 2 million prisoners by February 2000. This accounts for 25% of the world's prison population, yet the USA accounts for only 5% of the world's population.

LEAST POPULOUS COUNTRY

Vatican City (above), the world's smallest country, is also the least populous, with just 890 inhabitants in 2001. Situated in Rome, the Vatican City comprises St Peter's Church, St Peter's Square, the Vatican, and the Vatican Gardens.

HIGHEST & LOWEST LIFE EXPECTANCY

Japan is the country with the highest life expectancy at birth. The average for the total population is 80.5 years. For males, the life expectancy stands at 77.3 years and for females 83.9 years.

Sierra Leone has the world's lowest life expectancy at birth. The average for the total population is 37.3 years. For males, the life expectancy stands at 35.9 years, and for females 39.8 years.

MOST PLASTIC SURGEONS

The country with the most plastic surgeons in the world is the USA with an approximate total of 5,965 according to The International Confederation for Plastic, Reconstructive and Aesthetic Surgery.

LARGEST SHORTAGE OF WOMEN

With a male population of 66%, men most outnumber women in Qatar.

LARGEST SHORTAGE OF MEN

In Ukraine, 53.7% of the population is female. Worldwide, it is estimated that there are currently 1,015 males for every 1,000 females.

HIGHEST & LOWEST GNI

According to World Bank 2000 figures (using data from 206 countries), the country with the highest GNI (Gross National Income, formerly GNP or Gross National Product) per capita was Luxembourg, with a GNI of $44,340 (£29,302). For the same period, the UK's GNI was $24,500 (£16,191) and the USA's $34,260 (£22,641). GNI is the total value of goods and services produced by a country in one year divided by its population. These figures indicate the proportion of GNI each person would receive if it were divided equally. Second is Liechtenstein, then Switzerland. For 2000, Ethiopia had the world's lowest GNI per capita of $100 (£66).

LOWEST LITERACY RATE

In Niger, only 15% of the total adult population (aged over 15) is literate, and only 6.6% of the adult female population is literate. The literacy rate for females in Afghanistan was 15% in 1999, but the country is now thought to have a similar rate to Niger. The rate of adult female literacy in Afghanistan was set to fall as the fundamentalist Taliban regime banned the education of females. The Taliban fell in 2001, but it is not known how this will affect the literacy rate.

MOST POPULOUS COUNTRY

China is the world's most populated country, with an estimated 1,265,207,000 people in 2000 (Chinese children shown below). The annual rate of increase was 1.3%, or over 16 million people, between 1997 and 1998. Its population is more than that of the whole world 150 years ago. By 2025 it is estimated that China's population will exceed 1.48 billion.

MOST POPULAR POLITICAL CAT

Socks (above), a stray cat rescued by a neighbor of Bill and Hillary Clinton (both USA) when they lived in Little Rock, Arkansas, USA, was adopted by the future First Family in 1991. During his eight-year stint in the White House, Socks was said to receive 75,000 letters and parcels a week. The popular kitty answered his fan mail with help from his personal correspondence staff.

OLDEST ROYAL

HM Queen Elizabeth the Queen Mother (UK, 1900-2002) was the oldest member of the British royal family. She married Prince Albert (UK, later George VI) on April 26 1923, and on his coronation became the first British-born Queen Consort since Tudor times as well as the Last Empress of India. She died on March 30 2002, at the age of 101.

MOST PRESIDENTIAL PALACES

Saddam Hussein, President of Iraq since 1979, has eight principal palaces, plus other minor residences throughout Iraq. In Babylon, Saddam has a palace that was built alongside the remains of the palace of Nebuchadnezzar II (620–562 BC). Every brick is stamped with the legend "The Leader, Saddam Hussein, Victor of Allah."

MOST STATE ROLES HELD BY A MODERN ROYAL

Cambodia's King Norodom Sihanouk was king from 1941 to 1955, prime minister from 1955 to 1966, head of state from 1960 to 1970, head of the government-in-exile in 1970, president in 1976, president-in-exile from 1982 to 1988, head of the government-in-exile from 1989 to 1991, president of the National Council in 1991, and head of state from 1991 to 1993. In 1993 he was restored as king.

LARGEST POLITICAL PARTY MEMBERSHIP

The Chinese Communist Party, formed in 1920, had a membership of around 59 million in April 2000.

LARGEST PRESIDENTIAL ENTOURAGE

US President Bill Clinton's official visit to China in June 1998 involved an entourage of 1,200 people. They included 200 secret service agents, 150 military personnel, 30 senior delegates, 375 reporters, four TV crews, 150 support staff, and 70 senior advisers. Four passenger planes, including Air Force One, were used, and military transport planes flew in 10 armored limousines, two communication vans, a mobile hospital, and a bullet-proof lectern. In comparison, when US President Richard Nixon visited China in 1972, he was accompanied by just 300 people.

LARGEST THEFT FROM A GOVERNMENT

On April 23 1986 the Philippine government announced that it had finally identified the $860.8 million (£569.5 million) salted away by the former President Ferdinand Marcos and his wife, Imelda. The total national loss from November 1965 on was thought to be a staggering $5–$10 billion (£3.4–£6.8 billion).

LARGEST GATHERING OF WORLD LEADERS

The 55th session of the United Nations' General Assembly brought together 144 kings, heads of states, prime ministers, and presidents for the Millennium Summit held in New York City, USA, from September 6 to 8 2000. There were over 1,300 official cars at the event, thousands of secret service agents, up to 6,000 police officers, and more than 2,500 members of the international media.

HEAVIEST MONARCH

The world's heaviest monarch was the 6-ft 3-in-tall (1.90-m) King Taufa'ahau Tupou IV of Tonga, who in September 1976 recorded a weight of 462 lb (209.5 kg). By 1993 he was reported to have slimmed down to 280 lb (127 kg), and by 1998 had lost even more weight as a result of a fitness program.

OLDEST TREATY

The oldest treaty still in force is the Anglo-Portuguese Treaty, which was signed in London over 625 years ago on June 16 1373, making Portugal the UK's oldest ally.

MOST HANDSHAKES BY A NATIONAL POLITICAL FIGURE

On August 22 1998, US House Speaker Newt Gingrich (USA) shook hands with 3,609 people at the King County Republican Picnic on Vashon Island, Washington, USA. Speaker Gingrich began shaking hands during a photo opportunity at 10:30 am and finished at 3:30 pm.

HIGHEST-PAID PRIME MINISTER

The former Prime Minister of Japan, Yoshiro Mori, who served from April 5 2000 to April 26 2001, had an annual salary of ¥69,290,000 ($676,000 or £470,700), including monthly allowances and bonuses.

MONARCH APPEARING ON MOST COINAGE

The image of Her Majesty Queen Elizabeth II (UK) appears on the coinage of at least 35 different countries – more countries than any other living monarch. Elizabeth II has been Queen of the UK and head of the Commonwealth since the death of her father, George VI, in 1952. She celebrated her Golden Jubilee in 2002.

MOST MONEY SPENT PER VOTE IN AN ELECTION

Michael R Bloomberg (USA, above), the Republican candidate in the 2001 mayoral election in New York City, USA, spent $68,968,185 (£49,962,464) on his successful campaign. This equates to $92.60 (£63.65) for each of the 744,757 votes he won.

LONGEST REIGN IN EUROPE

The longest-reigning European monarch was Afonso I Henrique of Portugal, who ascended the throne on April 30 1112 and died on December 6 1185 after reigning for 73 years 220 days, first as count and then (after July 25 1139) as king.

MOST VOTES FOR A CHIMPANZEE

In the 1988 mayoral election campaign in Rio de Janeiro, Brazil, the anti-establishment Brazilian Banana Party presented a chimp called Tião as their candidate. The chimp came third out of twelve candidates, receiving over 400,000 votes. The campaign slogan was "Vote monkey – get monkey."

LONGEST-SERVING FEMALE PRIME MINISTER

Sirimavo Bandaranaike (Sri Lanka) was prime minister of Sri Lanka for a total of 17 years 208 days: July 21 1960 to March 25 1965; May 29 1970 to July 22 1977, and November 12 1994 to August 10 2000.

LARGEST ROYAL FAMILY

There are more than 4,200 royal princes and more than 40,000 other relatives in the Saudi royal family.

RICHEST MONARCH

In April 2002, it was estimated that the personal wealth of Prince Alwaleed Bin Talal Alsaud of Saudi Arabia stood at $20 billion (£13.9 billion). King Fahd remains the technical ruler of Saudi Arabia, but the stroke he suffered in 1995 means his half-brother Prince Abdullah rules de facto.

Queen Beatrix of The Netherlands, who ascended the throne in 1980, has an estimated net worth of around $3.46 billion (£2.43 billion), making her the world's wealthiest modern queen. In comparison, Queen Elizabeth II (UK) is worth only $330 million (£230 million).

MOST ACCESSIBLE PRIME MINISTER

With the exception of the leaders of some of the world's micro-states, the most accessible premier was the Danish Prime Minister Poul Nyrup Rasmussen (who served from 1993 to 2001), whose home telephone number was in the public domain. Rasmussen was known to answer telephone queries from Danish citizens personally.

LONGEST-SERVING PRESIDENT TODAY

Omar Bongo has been president of the oil-rich central West African republic of Gabon since December 2 1967. He was re-elected unopposed at presidential elections every seven years under a single-party system until 1993, when he was returned with a narrow majority following the restoration of a multi-party system.

MOST HIT RECORDS BY A ROYAL

Princess Stephanie of Monaco, the younger daughter of Prince Rainier III and Princess Grace, is the only royal to have had pop music hits in Europe. Her album *Rendez-Vous,* recorded with the record label Success, made it into the German Top 10 and Dutch Top 40, as well as the Italian and French charts.

YOUNGEST LEADER OF THE LABOUR PARTY

In 1994, at the age of 41, Tony Blair (UK, below) became the youngest-ever leader of the British Labour Party. After the UK's 1997 general election, 44-year-old Mr Blair became the youngest British prime minister of the 20th century.

LARGEST GAY AND LESBIAN RIGHTS MARCH

On April 25 1993, 300,000 people gathered in support of the "March on Washington for Gay, Lesbian and Bi-equal Rights" (above). The event, near the Washington Memorial in Washington DC, USA, was to support legislation granting equal rights for homosexuals in America, including anti-discrimination regulations based on sexual orientation and an end to the ban on homosexuals in the military.

HIGHEST TAXES

In Denmark the highest rate of personal income tax is 63%, with the basic rate starting at 44%. In return for these high taxes, the Danes receive a wide range of governmental benefits, including free health assistance, free higher education, and an extensive system of similar social services.

MOST EXPENSIVE MATCHMAKER

Orly the Matchmaker of Beverly Hills, California, USA, has been running an upscale international introductions company for the last 25 years – the most expensive service of its kind in the world. Run by a former model, Orly's world-renowned, old-fashioned matchmaking skills are available for a membership fee that can cost up to $100,000 (£70,000).

MOST BEER CONSUMED

The Czech Republic is the world's leading beer consumer per capita, with each person drinking an average of 42.7 gal (160 liters) in 1998. The population as a whole consumed 436.68 million gal (1,653 million liters) during 1998. The USA consumed the greatest volume of beer in the world in the same year, disposing of some 6.439 million gal (24,376 million liters) – which works out at an average of 23.5 gal (89 liters) per person.

MOST COFFEE CONSUMED

The country that consumes the most coffee per capita is Finland where 24.91 lb (11.3 kg) of coffee per person was consumed in 1998. The total amount of coffee consumed in the country in 1998 was 127.8 million lb (58,000 tonnes). In the same year, the USA consumed the greatest amount of coffee in the world with a total of 2.5 billion lb (1.148 million tonnes) – around 646 cups per person (4.2 kg per capita).

GREATEST ELECTRICITY CONSUMPTION

The USA used 3,235.9 billion kW per hour in 1999 – which is almost a quarter of the total net electricity consumption used by the entire world (12,832.7 billion kW per hour). The greatest consumers of electricity per capita are the Norwegians, who used 26,956 kW per hour per person in 1995 compared to 12,663 kW per hour per capita in the USA.

HEAVIEST SMOKERS

South Korea has the highest per capita consumption of cigarettes in the world, at 4,153 cigarettes per capita per annum. Japan is second with 2,739 and Hungary third with 2,689. An estimated 4.6 trillion cigarettes were smoked in 1999. If you laid them end to end, they would reach to the Sun and back.

HIGHEST COST OF LIVING

According to *The Economist* Intelligence Unit's bi-annual survey, Tokyo and Osaka/Kobe (both Japan) are the most expensive cities to live in the world, jointly holding the top spot for the first time in nine years (previously Tokyo has held the title alone). After them, the list reads: Hong Kong, Libreville (in Gabon), Oslo, London, New York City and Zurich (jointly), Singapore, Taipei and Tel Aviv (jointly).

HIGHEST BIRTH RATE

In 1998, the highest estimated birth rate for the central African country of Niger was 52 births per 1,000 people. This compares to the United Kingdom, which had 13 births per 1,000 people in 1980 and 12 births per 1,000 people in 1998.

HIGHEST DEATH RATE

The current highest estimated death rate is 25 per 1,000 people for Sierra Leone (the former French colony in western Africa) in 1998. This compares to the UK's rate of 12 deaths per 1,000 people in 1980 and 11 deaths per 1,000 in 1998.

LARGEST HUMAN RIGHTS ORGANIZATION

Amnesty International, which was first launched in the UK in 1961, now has in excess of 1.2 million members and subscribers in more than 100 countries, national offices in more than 50 countries, and more than 4,200 local groups situated on every continent. The human rights organization operates independently of any government, political ideology, economic interest or religion. It believes in releasing prisoners of conscience regardless of their origin, providing fair trials for all political prisoners, abolishing the death penalty, torture, and other cruel treatment of prisoners as well as eliminating all types of politically motivated killings and "disappearances."

LARGEST EMPLOYER

The world's largest commercial or utility employer is Indian Railways, which had an amazing 1,583,614 regular employees when it was last measured in March 1997. The Indian Railways' wage bill for the period 1996-97 worked out as a massive 105,145,000,000 rupees ($2.1 billion or £1.5 billion).

HIGHEST ANNUAL RACING CLUB BETTING TURNOVER

The total betting turnover of the Hong Kong Jockey Club (stadium, above) for the 1997/98 season was $12.1 billion (£7.3 billion). Approximately one third of Hong Kong's adult population is reported to regularly bet on horse racing.

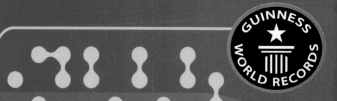

HIGHEST AND LOWEST UNEMPLOYMENT

In 1996, Bosnia-Herzegovina had the highest rate of unemployment, with 75% of the labor force not in paid employment.

Liechtenstein had the lowest recorded unemployment of any world state in 1997, with 97.3% of its labor force in work.

MOST VALUABLE FOOTBALL CLUB

Manchester United Football Club, who play in the English Premiership, had a market capitalization of more than £1 billion ($1.59 billion) on March 8 2000, becoming the first football club ever to reach that milestone.

MOST PUBS VISITED

Bruce Masters (UK) has visited 31,751 pubs and 1,974 other drinking establishments since 1960, sampling the local brew in each case where available, making a total of 33,725 bar visits by the end of 2000. His busiest year was 1974, when he frequented 3,016 pubs. From his own statistics, the most popular name for a pub is the Red Lion, of which he has visited 480.

LARGEST LOTTERY WINS

The Big Game Lottery, which is composed of seven different states in the US (Georgia, Illinois, Maryland, Massachusetts, Michigan, New Jersey and Virginia) reached a sky-high jackpot of $350 million (£220 million) on the day it was due to be drawn, May 9 2000. The winnings were split between two ticket holders.

The largest individual lottery win is $197 million (£122 million) by Maria Grasso (USA) for the Big Game Lottery draw on April 13 1999.

MOST EXPENSIVE OFFICE LOCATION

As of March 2002, London, UK (below), is the world's most expensive location for office space. Cost per 11 ft^2 (1 m^2), including rent, taxes, and service charges, is $1,525 (£1,074). Tokyo, Japan, is second with $1,070 (£754) per 11 ft^2 (1 m^2).

LARGEST SPACE FUNERAL

The ashes of 24 space pioneers and enthusiasts, including *Star Trek* creator Gene Roddenberry (USA) and former Nazi rocket scientist Krafft Ehricke (Germany), went into orbit on April 21 1997, on board Spain's *Pegasus* rocket, at a cost of $4,300 (£3,000) each. In lipstick-sized capsules (above) inscribed with a name and a personal message, the ashes will orbit for between 18 months and 10 years.

LARGEST MASS CREMATION

In December 1997, at a temple in Smut Scom province, Thailand, 21,347 skulls and thousands of tons of bones were cremated to mark the end of urban burials in the overcrowded Thai capital, Bangkok. The bones and skulls represented remains that had been left unclaimed from a former Chinese cemetery in Bangkok.

LONGEST MARRIAGE

China-born William Wen Lung Hsieh (b. 1899) and his wife Woo Fung Siu (b. 1900, both USA) married on March 17 1917 and their marriage lasted 84 years 6 months 15 days until William's death on October 1 2001.

MOST CHILDREN WITH THE SAME BIRTH DATE

The only verified record of a family producing five single children with the same date of birth is that of Catherine (1952), Carol (1953), Charles (1956), Claudia (1961), and Cecilia (1966), born to Carolyn and Ralph Cummins (both USA), all on February 20.

The three children of the Henriksen family (Norway) – Heidi (1960), Olav (1964), and Lief-Martin (1968) – all celebrate infrequent birthdays: they fall on Leap Year Day – February 29.

OLDEST BRIDE

The oldest recorded bride is Minnie Munro (Australia), aged 102, who married Dudley Reid (Australia), at the advanced age of 83, at Point Clare, NSW, Australia, on May 31 1991.

GREATEST HEIGHT DIFFERENTIAL BETWEEN HUSBAND AND WIFE

Fabien Pretou (France), who stands 6 ft 2 in (1.885 m) tall, married Natalie Lucius (France) who was 3 ft 1 in (94 cm) tall, at Seyssinet-Pariset, France, on April 14 1990 – a height difference of 37 in (94.5 cm). Fabien has to take things easy around the home as it's all adapted for Natalie's size. If he wants to cook her dinner, he has to sit down to be at the right height for the stove.

MOST PROLIFIC MOTHER

The greatest officially recorded number of children born to one mother is an incredible 69, born to the wife of Feodor Vassilyev, an 18th-century Russian peasant. In 27 confinements she gave birth to 16 pairs of twins, seven sets of triplets, and four sets of quadruplets. Her husband had 18 more children with a second wife.

LARGEST SINGLE TOMB

The Mount Li tomb, the burial place of China's first emperor, Qin Shi Huangdi, is situated 25 miles (40 km) east of Xian, China. The two walls surrounding the grave measure 7,129 x 3,195 ft (2,173 x 974 m) and 2,247 x 1,896 ft (685 x 578 m). The site has become world famous for its army of terracotta soldiers, which were arranged in formation in four pits around the emperor's tomb.

LARGEST TV AUDIENCE FOR A LIVE BROADCAST

The worldwide TV audience for the funeral of Diana, Princess of Wales (UK), at Westminster Abbey, London, UK, on September 6 1997, was estimated at 2.5 billion. An estimated 750 million had watched her wedding to HRH Prince Charles on TV in 1981.

EARLIEST SIAMESE TWINS

Conjoined twins derive the name Siamese from Chang and Eng Bunker ("left" and "right" in Thai) born on May 11 1811 to Chinese parents. The boys were joined by a cartilaginous band at the chest. In April 1843 they married Sarah and Adelaide Yates (both USA) and fathered 10 and 12 children respectively. The twins died within three hours of each other on January 17 1874, at the age of 62.

MOST MARRIAGES

The most monogamous marriages undertaken by one person is 28, by former Baptist minister Glynn "Scotty" Wolfe (USA), who first married in 1927. He believed he had a total of 41 children.

The most monogamous marriages by a woman is 22. Linda Essex (USA), has had 15 different husbands since 1957. Her most recent marriage, in October 1991, also ended in divorce.

MOST VALUABLE PIECE OF WEDDING CAKE

A box containing a piece of the Duke and Duchess of Windsor's (UK) wedding cake from June 1937 sold at Sotheby's, New York City, USA, on February 27 1998 for a massive $29,900 (then £18,040). It was bought by Benjamin and Amanda Yin (both USA). The lot was originally estimated at $500–$1,000 (£300–£600). Proceeds from the sale were donated to charity.

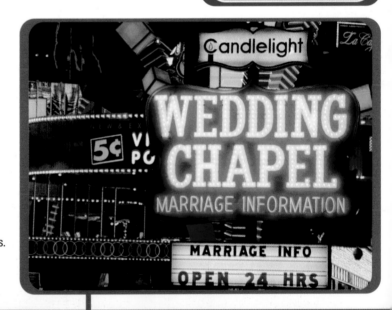

CITY WITH THE MOST WEDDINGS

Regarded as the world's "wedding capital," Las Vegas, Nevada, USA (above), has over 100 chapels performing about 8,400 marriages a month – 280 daily or one wedding every 5 min 17 sec. Foreign couples make up 12% of this total.

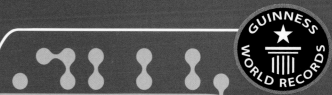

MOST TIMES MARRIED

Lauren Lubeck Blair and David E Hough Blair (both USA) married each other for the 61st time on April 19 2001, at London's Hard Rock Cafe, UK. The Blairs have married each other a total of 59 times since they first got hitched in 1984; all the wedding ceremonies have been in separate locations. In 2000, the Blairs got married 21 times. Their favorite wedding was in Gretna Green, Scotland, UK.

LARGEST CEMETERY

The 990-acre (400-ha) Ohlsdorf Cemetery, Hamburg, Germany, has handled 982,117 burials and 413,589 cremations as of December 31 1996. It has been in continuous use since 1877.

LARGEST MASS SUICIDE

As reported by 1st-century historian Flavius Josephus (Israel), 960 Jewish zealots committed suicide by cutting each others' throats at Masada, Israel, in 73 AD, as the fortress was being besieged by Romans.

The greatest mass suicide of modern times occurred on November 18 1978, when 913 members of the People's Temple cult died of cyanide poisoning at Jonestown, Guyana.

TALLEST CEMETERY

The permanently illuminated Memorial Necrópole Ecumônica, in Santos, near Saõ Paulo, Brazil, is 10 stories high and occupies an area of 4.4 acres (1.8 ha). Begun in March 1983, the first burial was held there on July 28 1984.

OLDEST COUPLE TO MARRY

On February 1 2002, French couple Francois Frenandez (b. April 17 1906) and Madeleine Francineau (b. July 15 1907) married at their rest home in Clapiers, France, at the ages of 95 and 94 respectively.

MOST EXPENSIVE WEDDING

The wedding of Mohammed, son of Sheik Rashid Bin Saeed Al Maktoum, to Princess Salama (both UEA) in Dubai in May 1981 lasted seven days and cost around $44.5 million (£22 million). It was held in a specially built stadium for 20,000 people.

MOST COUPLES MARRIED SIMULTANEOUSLY

On August 25 1995, some 35,000 couples were married (right) in the Olympic Stadium in Seoul, South Korea, in a ceremony officiated over by Sun Myung Moon of the Holy Spirit Association for the Unification of World Christianity. In addition, 325,000 more couples around the world took part in the ceremony through a satellite link.

LARGEST PAPAL CROWD

On January 15 1995, during his visit to the Philippines, Pope John Paul II (above, center right) offered Mass to a crowd estimated at between 4 and 5 million people. The Mass took place at Luneta Park, Manila.

LONGEST-SERVING ALTAR BOY

Tommy Kinsella (Ireland) began to serve at Mass in the Church of the Holy Redeemer, Bray, Co Wicklow, Ireland, in April 1917, at the age of 11. He continued working for the same church for 81 years until his death on April 1 1999.

LARGEST RELIGION

Christianity is the world's predominant religion. In 2000 it had approximately 2 billion followers, or one third of the world's entire population.

FASTEST-GROWING RELIGION

Islam is the world's fastest-growing religion. In 1990, 935 million people were Muslims and this figure had escalated to around 1.2 billion by 2000, meaning that around one in five people follow Islam. Although the religion began in Arabia, by 2002 80% of all believers in Islam lived outside the Arab world. In the period 1990–2000, approximately 12.5 million more people converted to Islam than to Christianity.

LARGEST RELIGIOUS BUILDINGS

The largest religious structure is Angkor Wat (City Temple), enclosing 17,502,118.3 ft² (1,626,000 m²) in Cambodia (formerly Kampuchea), built during the period 1113–50. Its external wall measures 4,200 ft (1,280 m), and its population – before it was abandoned in 1432 – stood at 80,000. The whole complex of 72 major monuments extends over 15.4 miles (24.8 km).

The largest synagogue in the world is Temple Emanu-El on Fifth Avenue at E 65th Street, New York City, USA, which has an area of 37,922 ft² (3,523 m²). The main sanctuary can accommodate 2,500 people, and the adjoining Beth-El Chapel seats 350. When these and the temple's other three sanctuaries are in use, 5,500 people can fit inside the synagogue.

Srirangam Temple, at Tiruchirappalli, Tamil Nadu, India, is the world's largest Hindu temple. Dedicated to the Hindu god Vishnu, it covers an area of 6,792,027 ft² (631,000 m²) and has a 32,592-ft (9,934-m) perimeter. The temple comprises seven concentric enclosures around the inner sanctum, the highest of which rises to 230 ft (70.1 m).

The world's largest Buddhist temple is Borobudur, Central Java, Indonesia, which was built between 750 and 842 AD. The 2,118,880-ft³ (60,000-m³) stone structure is 113 ft (34.5 m) in height, and its base measures 403 x 403 ft (123 x 123 m).

The largest mosque complex in the world is Shah Faisal Mosque, near Islamabad, Pakistan. The total area of the complex is 2,041,913 ft² (189,700 m²), with the covered area of the prayer hall measuring 51,666 ft² (4,800 m²). The complex

LARGEST DONATION OF HAIR

Every pilgrim to the Tirupati temple in Andhra Pradesh, India, donates a tonsure of their hair. An estimated 6.5 million people make such donations and over $2.2 million (£1.4 million) is raised in funds through the annual auction of hair. The temple attracts an average of 30,000 visitors per day and 600 barbers are employed to shave the pilgrims' hair 24 hours a day.

can accommodate 100,000 worshipers in the prayer hall and courtyard and 200,000 more people in the adjacent grounds.

The Cathedral Church of St John the Divine, New York City, USA, is the largest Anglican cathedral. The Gothic Revival building has a floor area of 120,986 ft² (11,240 m²) and a volume of 16,822,141 ft³ (476,350 m³). At 601 ft (183.2 m), the nave is also longer than that of any other church.

The world's largest church is the Basilica of Our Lady of Peace (Notre Dame de la Paix) at Yamoussoukro, the Côte d'Ivoire's administrative and legal capital. Completed in 1989 at a cost of $164 million (£93.5 million), it has a total area of 322,917 ft² (30,000 m²), with seating for 7,000 people. Including its gold cross, the church is 518 ft (158 m) high.

SMALLEST CHURCH

The world's smallest church is that of Santa Isabel de Hungría in Colomares Castle, Benalmádena, Spain. The church was consecrated on April 7 1990 and stands as a monument to the Italian explorer Christopher Columbus. Mass is held there only on special occasions, and, with a total floor area of 21.09 ft² (1.96 m²), only one person can fit in to pray at a time.

MOST PROLIFIC CRYING STATUE

On 14 days between 2 February and 17 March 1995, a 40-cm (15.75-in) plaster statue of the Virgin Mary, standing at the Marian shrine at Medjugorje, Bosnia-Herzegovina, apparently wept tears of blood. One such manifestation was witnessed by the diocesan bishop. Most reports of weeping statues do not receive any form of recognition from the Roman Catholic Church.

LARGEST MONKEY BUFFET

The Kala Temple in Lopburi province, north of Bangkok, Thailand, provides an annual spread of tropical fruit and vegetables weighing 6,613.86 lb (3,000 kg) for around 2,000 local monkeys (above). The buffet is now a major tourist attraction.

LARGEST ROSARY

In January 2001, teachers and students at St Joseph School in Cairo, Illinois, USA, made the world's largest rosary. It measured 173 ft 9 in (52.9 m).

LARGEST UNDERGROUND TEMPLE

The world's largest underground temple has been excavated over a period of 16 years by members of the 800-strong Damanhur religious community living in Baldissero, near Turin, Italy. The temple was excavated from the side of a hill and takes up a total volume of 211,888 ft³ (6,000 m³). The community has carved out its temple – the "Temple of Humankind" – using only pickaxes and buckets.

LARGEST PILGRIMAGE CENTRES

The House of the Virgin Mary at Loretto, Italy, receives 3.5 million pilgrims (as opposed to tourists) a year, more than three times the number that visit Lourdes, France. Traditionally the Holy House of Loretto was said to have been transported by angels from Palestine to Italy.

The annual pilgrimage (or *hajj*) to Mecca, Saudi Arabia, attracts an average attendance of 2 million people, more than that to any other Islamic holy place.

MOST RECENTLY FOUND BUDDHIST RELIC

The Buddha's ashes were divided into eight lots and sent for safekeeping to various parts of Asia. In 1981, one of the eight boxes was found at Yunju 46 miles (75 km) from Beijing, China.

OLDEST COMPLETE STAINED GLASS

The oldest intact stained glass in the world depicts the prophets and can be found in a window of the Cathedral of Augsburg, in Germany. It dates from the second half of the 11th century.

OLDEST BIBLE PUBLISHER

The oldest publisher of bibles is Cambridge University Press. Its first bible was the Geneva version of 1591.

MOST EXPENSIVE SACRED OBJECT

The 15th-century gold Buddha in Wat Trimitr Temple, Bangkok, Thailand, has a higher intrinsic value than any other sacred object. It is 10 ft (3 m) tall and weighs around 127,867 lb (58 tonnes). At $370 (£260) per fine ounce (April 1996 prices), the Buddha was valued at $46 million (£32.7 million), or $53.7 million (£37.1 million) in 2001. The gold under the statue's plaster exterior was only found in 1954.

LARGEST RELIGIOUS CROWD

Around 20 million people gathered for the Hindu festival of Ardh Kumbha Mela (below) at Allahabad (Prayag), Uttar Pradesh, India. on January 30 1995. The site of the gathering was the confluence of the rivers Yamuna, Ganges, and the subterranean river Saraswati. Allahabad is one of four different sites between which the festival is rotated every three years.

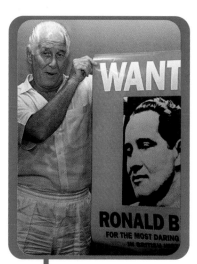

GREATEST TRAIN ROBBERY
Between 3:03 am and 3:27 am on August 8 1963, a General Post Office mail train was ambushed at Sears Crossing, Bucks, UK, and robbed at nearby Bridego Bridge. The gang, which included Ronnie Biggs (UK, above), escaped with around 120 mailbags, containing £2,631,784 (then $7,369,784) in banknotes heading for London to be destroyed. Only £343,448 (then $961,757) was ever recovered.

MOST PROLIFIC CANNIBAL
During the 19th century, Ratu Udre Udre, a cannibalistic Fijian chief, reportedly ate between 872 and 999 people. The chief had kept a stone to record each body that he had consumed, and these were placed along his tomb in Rakiraki, northern Viti Levu, Fiji.

COUNTRY WITH THE FEWEST PRISONERS
According to the International Center for Prison Studies, as of 2001 the country with the fewest prisoners is Indonesia, which has approximately 162,886 prison inmates out of an estimated national population of 214.8 million. Indonesian prisoners represent only 29 out of every 100,000 of the country's population.

COUNTRY WITH THE MOST MURDERS
In 1997, the USA had an estimated 25,000 cases of homicide. The offense rate for homicide was 8.2 per 100,000 of the population.

GREATEST ART ROBBERY
On April 14 1991, 20 paintings, estimated to be worth $500 million (then £280 million), were stolen from the Van Gogh Museum in Amsterdam, The Netherlands. Only 35 minutes later, they were found in an abandoned car near the museum.

MOST VALUABLE OBJECT EVER STOLEN
Though its price has not been officially calculated, the *Mona Lisa* is arguably the most valuable object ever stolen. The painting vanished from the Louvre, Paris, France, on August 21 1911 and was discovered in Florence, Italy, in 1913. Vincenzo Perugia (Italy), a former Louvre employee, was later charged with the theft of the famous work of art.

LARGEST JEWEL ROBBERY
On August 11 1994 at the Carlton Hotel, Cannes, France, a three-man gang carrying machine guns made off with FF250 million ($45 million or £29.1 million) worth of gems from the hotel's jewelry shop.

GREATEST MODERN KIDNAP RANSOM
Two Hong Kong businessmen, Walter Kwok and Victor Li, paid off gangster Cheung Tze-keung, ("Big Spender"), a record total ransom of $206 million (£144 million) in exchange for their freedom after they were kidnapped in 1996 and 1997, respectively.

SURVIVOR OF MOST HANGING ATTEMPTS
The survivor of the greatest number of legal hanging attempts is Joseph Samuel (Australia), a 22-year-old who was sentenced to death for murder in Sydney, NSW, Australia. On September 26 1803, the first attempt at execution failed when the hangman's rope broke. Another attempt was made, but this was also abandoned, after the rope stretched so much that Samuel's feet touched the ground. At the third attempt, the rope broke again. Samuel was then reprieved.

LARGEST SPEEDING FINE
Anssi Vanjoki (Finland) was fined €116,000 ($104,000 or £71,600) for driving his Harley Davidson motorcycle at 46.6 mph (75 km/h) in a 31 mph (50 km/h) zone in Helsinki, Finland, on October 2001. In keeping with Finnish law, by which speeding offenders are fined according to their annual incomes, Vanjoki, a director of telecommunications company Nokia, was ordered to pay the equivalent of 14 days of his 1999 income of approximately €14 million ($12.5 million or £8.6 million).

LARGEST JAIL BREAK
On February 11 1979, an Iranian employee of the Electronic Data Systems Corporation (EDS) led a mob into Ghasr prison, Tehran, Iran, in an attempt to rescue two American colleagues. The mastermind of the plan was EDS owner and future presidential candidate H Ross Perot. Around 11,000 other prisoners took advantage of the confusion to stage history's largest jail break.

MOST ARRESTED PERSON
By 1998, Tommy Johns (Australia), had been arrested nearly 3,000 times for being drunk and disorderly in a public place.

MOST PEOPLE KILLED IN A TERRORIST ACT
The greatest number of individuals killed in a terrorist act is 2,800 (624 positively identified bodies), in the attack on the World Trade Center, New York City, USA, on September 11 2001. The figure includes those killed in the Center's two towers, 157 aboard the two Boeing 767s that struck them and 479 staff from emergency services. The final toll may never accurately be known.

LARGEST PRISON SYSTEM
The state of California has the biggest prison system in the industrialized world. The state holds more inmates in its jails and prisons than France, Great Britain, Germany, Japan, Singapore, and The Netherlands combined.

MOST PROLIFIC MURDER PARTNERSHIP

The sisters Delfina and María de Jesús Gonzáles (Mexico), who abducted girls to work in their brothel, are known to have murdered at least 90 prostitutes, as well as some of the girls' clients. The two women were sentenced to 40 years imprisonment in 1964.

LARGEST DAMAGES FOR SEXUAL HARASSMENT

The record individual award in a sexual harassment case was $50 million (£32 million), made to Peggy Kimzey (USA), a former employee of Wal-Mart, the largest retail chain in the United States, on June 28 1995.

LONGEST-SERVING POLITICAL PRISONER

Kim Sung-myun (South Korea) was imprisoned for 43 years 10 months in Seoul, South Korea, for supporting Communist North Korea. He was freed in August 1995 at the age of 70.

COUNTRY WITH THE MOST EXECUTIONS

According to figures released by Amnesty International in March 2001, China executes more people than the rest of the world combined. During 1999 China executed 1,077 people, while the figure for the rest of the world totaled 736. In 2000, the limited records available to Amnesty International revealed that at least 1,511 death sentences had been passed in China and at least 1,000 executions had been carried out. These are believed to be only a fraction of the true figures.

US STATE WITH THE MOST EXECUTIONS

As of April 2001, Texas had carried out more executions than any other state in the US. Since 1974, Texas has executed 244 convicted criminals, followed by Virginia, with 82, and Florida, with 51.

MOST PROLIFIC MURDERER

It emerged at his trial that Behram, aka the "Indian Thug," strangled at least 931 victims with his yellow-and-white cloth strip, or *ruhmal*, in Oudh (now in Uttar Pradesh, India) from 1790–1840.

LONGEST PRISON SENTENCE FOR MURDER

Andrew Aston (UK), who clubbed two senior citizens to death during a series of robberies, was given 26 life sentences on February 20 2002, during his trial at Birmingham Crown Court, West Midlands, UK. Aston battered 24 other elderly victims in their homes over three months in 2001, posing as a policeman to gain entry and then attacking them for money to feed his cocaine habit.

LARGEST DRUG SEIZURES BY WEIGHT

On September 29 1989 in Sylmar, California, USA, officers from the Drug Enforcement Administration (DEA) in Alexandria, Virginia, seized 47,554 lb (21,570 kg) of cocaine.

According to figures from the DEA, the largest ever heroin seizure took place in Bangkok, Thailand, on February 11 1988, when officers impounded 2,816 lb (1,277 kg) of the drug.

LARGEST MINT

The US Treasury, constructed in 1965–69 in Philadelphia, Penn, USA, covers 11.5 acres (4.7 ha). In 2001 it produced 9.5 billion coins – nearly 38 million daily. The Graebner Press, a high-speed stamping machine, can produce coins at a rate of 42,000 per hour, with a record production of 12,647,096,000 coins in 2000. A mint in Denver, Colorado, USA, set a new record for coin production by a single facility in 2000, producing over 15.4 billion coins.

GREATEST BANKNOTE FORGERY

The German Third Reich's Operation Bernhard during World War II aimed to ruin the British economy with a flood of fake notes. Over nine million counterfeit British notes valued at £130 million ($520 million) were forged by 140 Jewish prisoners at Sachsenhausen concentration camp, Germany. The notes were sent to Nazi-occupied or neutral countries to pay agents or to be exchanged for other currencies.

EARLIEST PAPER MONEY

The earliest recorded use of paper currency can be traced back to the Song dynasty (960–1279) in China. It was utilized by a group of wealthy merchants and businessmen in Szechuan, where the art of printing also originated.

SMALLEST PAPER MONEY BY SIZE

The smallest national note ever issued, in terms of physical size, was the 10-bani note of the Ministry of Finance of Romania in 1917. Its printed area measured 1.08 x 1.49 in (27.5 x 38 mm). This is roughly one tenth the size of a $1 bill.

OLDEST COIN

The earliest coins recorded are not stamped with a date but were made during the reign of King Gyges of Lydia, Turkey, around 630 BC. They were composed of electrum, a naturally occurring amalgam of gold and silver.

EARLIEST DATED COINS

A Samian silver tetradrachm struck in Zankle (now Messina), Sicily, Italy, is dated year 1 (494 BC). The date is indicated by the letter "A" on one side of the coin. The earliest-known dated coins from the Christian era are the Danish "Bishop of Roskilde" coins, of which six are known. The coins bear the inscription MCCXXXIIII, standing for the year 1234.

LARGEST CHECK BY VALUE

The greatest amount paid by a single check in the history of banking was $3,971,821,324 (£2,474,655,000). It was issued on March 30 1995 and signed by Nicholas Morris, Company Secretary of Glaxo plc, UK. The check represented a payment by Glaxo plc to Wellcome Trust Nominees Limited in respect of the Trust's share in Wellcome plc. The Lloyds Bank Registrars' computer system could not generate a check this large, so it was completed by a Lloyds employee using a typewriter. The typist was so overawed by the responsibility of the task that it took her three attempts to type out the check for this massive amount.

LARGEST RETURN OF CASH

In May 1994, Howard Jenkins (USA), a 31-year-old roofing engineer, discovered that a mystery $88 million (£62 million) had been transferred mistakenly into his bank account. Although he initially withdrew $4 million (£2.8 million), his conscience got the better of him shortly afterward, and he returned the $88 million in full.

MOST EXPENSIVE GOLD BAR

The largest known transaction for a single numismatic item took place on November 7 2001, when an 80-lb (30-kg) pioneer gold assay bar (dubbed the "Eureka"), retrieved from the 1857 shipwreck SS *Central America*, was bought for $8 million (£5.5 million) by an anonymous buyer.

LONGEST CONTINUOUS ISSUER OF BANKNOTES

The longest continuous issuer of banknotes in the world is the Bank of England, UK. It has been issuing banknotes without interruption since 1694, when it was first established to raise money for King William III's war against the French.

HIGHEST-VALUE BANKNOTES

The highest-value banknote ever issued by the US Federal Reserve System is a $100,000 note, bearing the head of US president Woodrow Wilson, which is used only for transactions between the Federal Reserve and the Treasury Department.

The highest-value notes in circulation were printed when the US Federal Reserve released $10,000 banknotes bearing the head of 19th-century US Supreme Court Chief Justice Salmon P Chase. It was announced in 1969 that no additional notes higher than $100 would be issued. Only 200 $10,000 bills remain in circulation or "unretired."

TALLEST COIN COLUMN

The tallest single column of coins ever stacked on the edge of a coin was built by Dipak Syal (India) on May 3 1991 and made up of 253 Indian one-rupee pieces on top of a vertical five-rupee coin. He also balanced 10 one-rupee coins and 10 10-paise coins alternately horizontally and vertically in a single column on May 1 1991.

LARGEST CORPORATE BANKRUPTCY

In terms of assets, the largest corporate bankruptcy amounted to $63.3 billion (£44.4 billion) filed by US energy-trading company Enron (above) on December 2 2001. Until this date, Enron had been America's seventh-largest company.

HEAVIEST HOARD OF COINS

The largest-ever hoard of coins in terms of weight was a 96,320-lb (43-tonne) haul of gold (worth $23.8 million or £5 million). It was recovered from the White Star Liner HMS *Laurentic*, which sank after it struck a mine in waters 132 ft (40 m) deep off Malin Head, Donegal, Ireland, on January 25 1917.

SMALLEST MINT

The single-press mint of the Sovereign Military Order of Malta, in Rome, Italy, is housed in one room and has issued proof coins since 1961.

LARGEST GOLD RESERVES

The US Treasury held approximately 262 million fine ounces of gold during 1996, equivalent to $100 billion (£65 billion) at the June 1996 price of $382 (£249) per fine ounce.

HIGHEST-DENOMINATION BANKNOTE

The Hungarian 100 million B-pengo (100,000,000,000,000,000,000 pengo), issued in 1946, is the highest denomination banknote, though the figure was not printed on it. It was worth around $0.20 (£0.05) at the time.

BANKNOTE WITH THE MOST ZEROS

The Yugoslavian 500-billion dinar note (equivalent to £0.70 or $1), issued in 1993, had 11 zeros printed on it.

MOST CORPORATE DEBT FAILURES

A record 211 companies defaulted on $115.4 billion (£79.5 billion) of debt in 2001 – a record in both number of defaults and total amount. This is an increase of more than 120% from 2000, when 132 companies defaulted on $42.3 billion (£39.1 billion) of debt.

LARGEST CURRENCY INTRODUCTION

On January 1 2002, 15 billion euro banknotes and 50 billion euro coins (with a value of over €664 billion – £407 billion or $592 billion) were put into circulation in Austria, Belgium, Finland, France, Germany, Greece, Ireland, Italy, Luxembourg, The Netherlands, Portugal, and Spain, affecting 290 million people. Put end to end, the new euro banknotes would stretch to the Moon and back two-and-a-half times.

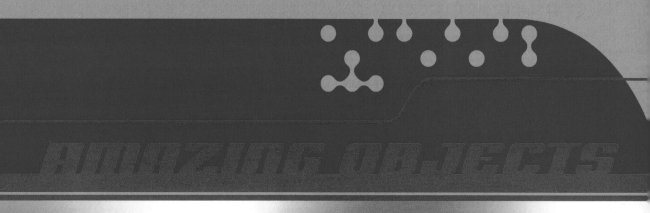

AMAZING OBJECTS

HIGHEST-HEELED SHOES

The highest-heeled shoes that are commercially available (above) boast 11-in (27.9-cm) platforms and 16-in (40.6-cm) heels. Available in red or black leather, these Vertigo shoes sell for $1,092 (£725). The company that manufactures the shoes, LadyBWear (UK), warns that it is not responsible for anyone who falls while they are wearing the staggering heels.

LARGEST BRA

In September 1990, the company Triumph International Japan Ltd produced a brassiere with an underbust measurement of 78 ft 8 in (24 m) and a bust measurement of 91 ft 10 in (28 m).

LARGEST CHRISTMAS TREE MADE FROM LIGHTS

A Christmas tree made entirely from lights was assembled in the garden of Pietro Cucchi (Italy) in Milan, Italy, on November 23 1998. The tree was 167 ft 3.8 in (51 m) tall and 68 ft 10.8 in (21 m) at its widest point; it consisted of 77,300 bulbs. The tree remained illuminated until it was dismantled on January 18 1999.

LARGEST CHANDELIER

The world's largest set of chandeliers was created by the Kookje Lighting Co Ltd of Seoul, South Korea. It is 39 ft (12 m) high, weighs 23,523 lb (10.67 tonnes), and features 700 bulbs. The colossal chandelier was completed in November 1988 and occupies three floors of the Lotte Chamshil department store in Seoul.

LARGEST ADVENT CALENDAR

The Coca-Cola BlowUP Media Advent calendar was 177 ft 1.9 in (54 m) long and 56 ft 9 in (17.3 m) high. It was unveiled by schoolchildren outside Birmingham Town Hall, Birmingham, UK, on November 30 2001.

LARGEST BOUQUETS

The world's largest bouquet measured 77 ft (23.4 m) in length. Completed on August 26 2001 by a team led by Ashrita Furman (USA), it was shown in the town of Jamaica, New York, USA.

The largest bouquet sold by a florist (in one order) featured 518 stems, had a diameter of 3 ft 9 in (1.2 m), and weighed 62 lb 11.3 oz (28.49 kg). The record-breaking bouquet was ordered from Flores do Liz, Leiria, Portugal, and delivered on July 29 2001.

LARGEST BUCKET OF MAPLE SYRUP

Rapid Duct Supply (Canada) made the world's largest maple syrup bucket, measuring 3 ft (0.91 m) in height and 3 ft 2 in (0.96 m) in diameter, with a capacity of 133 gal (605 liters) for the annual Elmira Maple Syrup Festival, Ontario, Canada, held on April 1 2000.

HEAVIEST CARROT

British-born John Evans grew a carrot that weighed an astonishing 18 lb 13 oz (8.61 kg) when measured at the 1998 Alaska State Fair.

LARGEST GLASS SCULPTURE

The Bellagio in Las Vegas, USA, is the most expensive hotel ever built and can also boast the largest glass sculpture ever created. The floral-design chandelier stretches above the hotel's foyer and measures 29 ft 6 in x 65 ft 7 in (9 x 20 m). It was produced by glass artist Dale Chihuly (USA). Titled *Fiori di Como*, the work comprises 10,000 lb (4,535 kg) of steel and 140,000 lb (8,143 kg) of hand-blown glass.

LARGEST BANANA BUNCH

Kabana SA and Tecorone SL (Spain) grew a gigantic bunch of bananas that contained 473 individual fruits on the island of El Hierro, Canary Islands, Spain. When the bunch was measured on July 11 2001 it weighed in at an impressive 287 lb (130 kg).

LARGEST PUMPKIN

Gerry Checkon (USA) grew a pumpkin that measured 1,131 lb (513 kg) when weighed at the Pennsylvania Pumpkin Bowl, Altoona, PA, USA, on October 2 1999. Altoona's Pumpkin Bowl is the official Great Pumpkin Commonwealth weigh-off site.

LARGEST SHIRT

The world's largest shirt, the Tide Shirt, was 148 ft 11.4 in (45.4 m) long, with a chest of 162 ft 8.7 in (49.6 m) and sleeves of 29 ft 6.3 in x 49 ft 2.5 in (9 x 15 m). It was made for Procter & Gamble Romania, makers of Tide detergent and measured in Bucharest, Romania, on September 27 2001.

LARGEST FOOTBALL SHIRT

The world's largest ever football shirt measured 118 x 113 ft (35.9 x 34.4 m). It bore the national colors of Trinidad and Tobago and was shown around the two islands in July 2001 as part of the run-up to the FIFA Under-17 World Championships.

LARGEST LEATHER BOOT

Handmade by Pasquale Tramonta (Italy), the world's largest leather boot measures 13 ft 7.7 in (4.16 m) high, 8 ft 10.2 in (2.7 m) long, and 31 in (80 cm) wide. Five years of work went into making it, at a cost of 25 million lire ($11,416 or £7,896). The boot, which weighs 617 lb (280 kg) and was made from 40 leather hides, can accommodate at least three people.

LONGEST GARLIC STRING

The world's longest string of garlic bulbs (above) measured an incredible 364 ft 1.6 in (110.99 m) and was made by Somerfield Stores Ltd (UK). It was displayed at Greenwich Park, London, UK, in November 2001.

LARGEST CONTAINER OF BODY CREAM

The largest body cream container was 6 ft 6.7 in (2 m) in diameter, 1 ft 8.8 in (53 cm) high, and held 247.4 gal (1,124,490 ml) of NIVEA Creme. Made by Beiersdorf Hellas, it was unveiled in Athens, Greece, on December 15 2001. The giant cosmetic was created for NIVEA'S 90th anniversary and was 16,327 times larger than the original.

LARGEST CHRISTMAS CRACKER

The largest functional Christmas cracker ever constructed was 181 ft 11 in (55.45 m) long and 11 ft 9 in (3.6 m) in diameter. It was built by ex-international rugby league player Ray Price (Australia), for Australian company Markson Sparks! and pulled in the parking lot at Westfield Shopping Town, Chatswood, Sydney, NSW, Australia, on December 16 1998.

LARGEST SWIMMING POOL

The world's largest swimming pool is the seawater Orthlieb Pool, Casablanca, Morocco. It is 1,574 ft (480 m) long, 246 ft (75 m) wide, and has an area of 8.9 acres (3.6 ha).

The largest land-locked pool currently in use is Willow Lake at Warren, Ohio, USA, which is 600 x 150 ft (183 x 46 m) in size.

LARGEST ACOUSTIC GUITAR

The largest playable acoustic guitar in the world measures 59 ft 11 in (16.75 m) long, 24 ft 10 in (7.57 m) wide and 8 ft 9 in (2.67 m) deep. Built by a team of more than 50 people from Realizarevents, Porto, Portugal, it weighs a massive 28,818 lb (4.064 tonnes).

LARGEST ELECTRIC GUITAR

The largest playable electric guitar in the world is 43 ft 7.5 in (13.29 m) tall, 16 ft 5.5 in (5.01 m) wide, and weighs 2,000 lb (907 kg). Modeled on a 1967 Gibson Flying V and built to a scale of 1:12, it was made by students from Conroe Independent School District Academy of Science and Technology, Conroe, Texas, USA, at a cost of $3,000 (£1,975). Construction of the guitar began in October 1999 and the instrument was played for the first time at the Cynthia Woods Mitchell Pavilion on June 6 2000, when the opening chord of The Beatles' song "A Hard Day's Night" was strummed.

LARGEST GRILLED SANDWICH

Cabot Creamery of Vermont, USA, created the world's largest grilled cheese sandwich on November 4 2000 at the 2nd Annual Everglades Cheese & (Florida) Cracker Festival, Everglades City, Florida, USA. After it had been cooked, the sandwich measured 5 ft x 10 ft 0.5 in x 2.5 in (1.52 m x 3.05 m x 6.35 cm) and 11 ft 2.75 in (3.42 m) across the diagonal.

TALLEST SAND SCULPTURE

On July 12 2001, the Holland Sand Sculpture company (Netherlands) created a sand sculpture of a fairy castle (left) measuring 68 ft 7.2 in (20.91 m) in height.

MOST VALUABLE SCULPTURE BY A LIVING ARTIST

On May 15 2001 *Michael Jackson and Bubbles* (above), a porcelain sculpture created in 1988 by Jeff Koons (USA), sold for $5,616,750 (£3,945,344) at Sotheby's, New York City, USA. It measures 42 x 70.5 x 32.5 in (106.7 x 179.1 x 82.6 cm).

MOST EXPENSIVE MAGAZINE

Visionaire magazine, created by Stephan Gan (USA), is sold at a starting price of $175 (£120) per issue. However, collectors are said to pay up to $5,000 (£3,500) for hard-to-find issues such as No. 18, which came in its own Louis Vuitton portfolio case.

MOST VALUABLE CIGARS

On November 16 1997 at Christie's, London, UK, an Asian buyer paid a record £9,980 ($16,349) for 25 Trinidad cigars made by the Cuban National Factory.

MOST VALUABLE COMIC

A first edition copy of *Action Comics*, from June 1938, sold for $100,000 (£68,771) in 1997. Featuring the first appearance of "Superman," it is now thought to be worth an astonishing $185,000 (£115,625).

MOST VALUABLE DIAMOND, PER CARAT

The highest price paid for a diamond, per carat, is $926,315.79 (£555,678), for a 0.95-carat fancy purple-red stone sold at Christie's, New York City, USA, on April 28 1987.

MOST VALUABLE JEWELRY BOX

A Cartier jeweled vanity case, set with a fragment of ancient Egyptian steel, was sold at Christie's, New York City, USA, for $189,000 (£127,651) on November 17 1993.

MOST EXPENSIVE WALLET

A platinum-cornered, diamond-studded crocodile creation made by Louis Quatorze of Paris and Mikimoto of Tokyo, sold in September 1984 for $74,816 (£56,000).

MOST EXPENSIVE COMMERCIALLY AVAILABLE WRISTWATCH

In 1999 Gianni Vivé Sulman of London, UK (once makers of the world's most expensive perfume), produced a watch costing more than $520,000 (£325,000) plus taxes. Only five are to be made every year.

MOST VALUABLE PEN

A Japanese collector paid a record price of FF1.3 million ($218,007 or £122,677) in February 1988 for the "Anémone" fountain pen made by Réden, France. It was encrusted with 600 different precious stones, including emeralds, amethysts, rubies, sapphires, and onyx, and took craftsmen more than a year to make.

MOST EXPENSIVE PEN

The world's most expensive pen is "La Modernista Diamonds," made by Caran d'Ache, Geneva, Switzerland, which was on sale in Harrods, London, UK, for £169,000 ($265,000) from September to December 1999.

MOST EXPENSIVE CREDIT CARD

The American Express Centurion credit card, also known as the "Black Card," has an annual fee of $1,000 (£700) and is open only to those with a minimum income of $215,000 (£150,000) per annum. The Black Card has no spending limits and is offered by invitation only to selected individuals who travel frequently, entertain a great deal, and expect exceptional service.

MOST EXPENSIVE MOBILE PHONE

A mobile phone designed by David Morris International of London, UK, was sold for £66,629 ($104,050) in 1996. Made entirely from 18-carat gold, the unique phone had a keypad encrusted with pink and white diamonds.

MOST EXPENSIVE PAIR OF JEANS

Gucci "genius jeans" – complete with African beading, tribal feathers, strategically placed rips, and silver buttons and rivets – were sold in Gucci stores for $3,134 (£1,840) after their launch in Milan, Italy, in October 1998.

MOST EXPENSIVE SINGLE PURCHASE OF WHISKY

On November 16 2000 Turkey-based businessman Norman Shelley (UK), purchased a collection of 76 bottles of Macallan malt whisky at the current value of £231,417.90 ($341,154). The oldest bottle dated from 1856.

MOST EXPENSIVE SPIRIT

A bottle of 60-year-old Macallan malt whisky sold for £11,000 ($15,663) at Fortnum & Mason, London, UK, in February 2000.

MOST VALUABLE WINE BOTTLE

A record £105,000 ($151,840) was paid for a bottle of 1787 Château Lafite claret, sold to Christopher Forbes (USA) at Christie's, London, UK, on December 5 1985.

MOST VALUABLE FURNITURE

The highest price paid for a single piece of furniture is £8.58 million ($15.1 million) at Christie's, London, UK, on July 5 1990. This was the auction price for the 18th-century Italian Badminton cabinet owned by the Duke of Beaufort (UK).

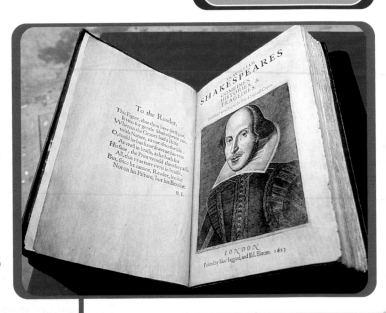

MOST VALUABLE WORK OF SHAKESPEARE

One of only five copies of William Shakespeare's (UK) First Folio, dated 1623, was sold at Christie's, New York City, USA, on October 8 2001 for $6,166,000 (£4,156,947). This is the highest price ever paid for a 17th-century book.

MOST EXPENSIVE GLASS OF WINE

A somewhat sobering FF8,600 ($1,382.80 or £982) was paid for the first glass of 1993 Beaujolais Nouveau released in Beaune (from Maison Jaffelin), in the wine region of Burgundy, France. It was bought by Robert Denby (UK) at Pickwick's, a British-themed pub in Beaune, on November 18 1993.

MOST VALUABLE FISH

The high cost of the eggs from the Russian sturgeon (*Huso huso*) make it the world's most expensive fish. One 2,706-lb (1,227-kg) female caught in the Tikhaya Sosna River, Russia, in 1924, yielded 540 lb (245 kg) of best quality caviar, worth nearly $289,000 (£203,000) in today's market.

MOST VALUABLE ILLUSTRATED MANUSCRIPT

Leonardo da Vinci's (Italy) illustrated manuscript known as the *Codex Hammer*, in which he predicted the invention of the submarine and the steam engine, sold for a record $30.8 million (£19,388,141) at Christie's, New York City, USA, on November 11 1994. The only Leonardo manuscript now in private hands, it was bought by Microsoft boss Bill Gates (USA).

GEMSTONE MOST IN DEMAND

Global sales from the world's largest diamond trading center in Antwerp, Belgium, totaled $25.8 billion (£17.2 billion) in 2000, a record since trading began in the 15th century. A recent diamond record-breaker was the most valuable piece of jewelry made for a film, a necklace (right) – with 1,308 diamonds – worn by Nicole Kidman (Australia) in the film *Moulin Rouge* (AUS/USA, 2001), valued at $1 million (£660,000).

MOST VALUABLE SCULPTURE SOLD AT AUCTION

The most valuable sculpture sold at auction is Alberto Giacometti's (Italy) *Grande femme debout I*, conceived in 1960 and cast in 1962, which was sold at Christie's, New York City, USA, on November 8 2000 for $14,306,000 (£10,004,196).

MOST VALUABLE CELLO

The highest ever auction price for a cello is £682,000 ($1,213,278) paid at Sotheby's, London, on June 22 1988 for a Stradivarius known as the "Cholmondeley." The instrument was made in Cremona, Italy, in about 1698.

MOST VALUABLE JAZZ INSTRUMENT

A saxophone once owned by Charlie Parker (USA) sold for £93,500 ($144,500) at Christie's London, UK, on September 7 1994.

MOST VALUABLE VIOLIN

A violin made by Guarneri del Gesu (Italy) in 1742 and owned by the late Yehudi Menuhin (USA), was sold for an undisclosed amount to an anonymous collector in Zurich, Switzerland, on 29 October 1999. Swiss dealer Musik Hug would not disclose the price but said it was "approximately $1.25 million (£781,250) above what had ever been paid for a violin" – which was £947,500 ($1,360,927) in 1998.

MOST EXPENSIVE PERFUME

"Parfum VI" designed by perfumer Arthur Burnham (UK), which comes in a 4-in (10-cm) bottle (made with platinum, 24-carat gold, rubies, and diamonds), was launched in June 2000 at a cost of £47,500 ($71,380). Inspired by the Phantom VI Rolls-Royce, only 173 were made.

BUILDINGS AND STRUCTURES

TALLEST OFFICE BUILDING

In March 1996, the Petronas Towers in Kuala Lumpur, Malaysia, overtook the Sears Tower's record as the world's tallest office building. Stainless-steel pinnacles 241 ft (73.5 m) long placed on top of the 88-story towers brought their height to 1,482 ft 8 in (451.9 m). The Sears Tower has 110 stories and is 1,453 ft 6 in (443 m) tall.

TALLEST TOTEM POLE

A totem pole 180 ft 3 in (54.94 m) tall, called "Spirit of Lekwammen" (land of the winds), was raised on August 4 1994 at Victoria, British Columbia, Canada, prior to the Commonwealth Games held there that year.

TALLEST CATHEDRAL SPIRE

The world's tallest cathedral spire is that of the Protestant cathedral of Ulm in Germany. Work on the building began in 1377, but the tower in the center of the west façade, which is 528 ft (160.9 m) high, was not completed until 1890.

TALLEST MINARET

The tallest minaret in the world is that of the Great Hassan II Mosque, Casablanca, Morocco, which is 656 ft (200 m) high. The cost of the mosque's construction was 5 billion dirhams ($513.5 million or £360 million). Among minarets of earlier centuries the tallest is the Qutb Minar, south of New Delhi, India, built in 1194 to a height of 238 ft (72.54 m).

TALLEST CHIMNEY

The coal powerplant No 2 stack at Ekibastuz, Kazakhstan, completed in 1987, is 1,378 ft (420 m) tall. Its diameter tapers from 144 ft (44 m) at the base to 46 ft 7 in (14.2 m) at the top, and it weighs 132,277,200 lb (60,000 tonnes). The stack is on a par with the world's fourth-tallest office building, Shanghai's Jin Mao Tower, which is 1,381 ft (421 m) tall.

TALLEST BUILDING

The tallest free-standing tower in the world is the $63-million (£28-million) CN Tower in Toronto, Canada, which rises to 1,815 ft 5 in (553.34 m). Excavation for the erection of the 286,600,600-lb (130,000-tonne) reinforced, post-tensioned concrete tower began on February 12 1973, and the structure was "topped out" on April 2 1975. A 416-seat restaurant revolves in the tower's Sky Pod at a height of 1,150 ft (351 m), and visibility can extend to hills 75 miles (120 km) away.

TALLEST MONUMENT

The world's tallest monument is the stainless-steel Gateway to the West arch in St Louis, Missouri, USA, which was completed on October 28 1965. The monument was erected to mark the westward expansion in the USA following the Louisiana Purchase of 1803, in which the United States bought the state of Louisiana from France. The Gateway is a sweeping arch spanning 630 ft (192 m) and rising to the same height. Designed in 1947 by the Finnish-American architect Eero Saarinen, it cost $29 million (£7 million) at the time.

TALLEST FLAGPOLE

The tallest flagpole in the world is at Panmunjon, North Korea, near the border with South Korea. It is 525 ft (160 m) high and flies a flag 98.5 ft (30 m) long. The flagpole is the result of a propaganda war between the two countries, and was reportedly built in response to a tall flagpole erected in a nearby South Korean village.

TALLEST STATUE

A bronze statue of Buddha measuring 394 ft (120 m) high, was completed in Tokyo, Japan, in January 1993. A joint Japanese-Taiwanese project, which took seven years to complete, it is 115 ft (35 m) wide and weighs 22,204,600 lb (1,000 tonnes).

TALLEST LIGHTHOUSE

The steel "Marine Tower" lighthouse at Yamashita Park in Yokohama, Japan, stands 348 ft (106 m) high. It has a power of 600,000 candelas (a basic unit of luminous intensity), a visibility range of 20 miles (32 km) and an observatory 328 ft (100 m) above the ground. It was built to mark the 100th anniversary of the first recorded trade between Yokohama and the West, in 1854.

TALLEST RESIDENTIAL BUILDING

The Trump World Tower (above) in New York City, USA, is the world's tallest purely residential building, standing 861 ft (262.5 m) high. The tower has 72 stories, although the luxuriously lofty ceilings make it taller than most other buildings with a similar number of floors.

TALLEST OBSERVATION WHEEL

The "British Airways London Eye," designed by architects David Marks and Julia Barfield (both UK), has a diameter and height of 443 ft (135 m) and made its first "flight" on February 1 2000. It is the fourth-tallest structure in London, UK, and can carry up to 800 passengers.

TALLEST CINEMA

The world's tallest cinema complex is the UGC Cinema, Glasgow, Strathclyde, UK, with an overall height of 203 ft 4.9 in (62 m). It holds 18 screens, has a seating capacity of 4,277 and is 12 stories high. The complex opened on September 21 2001.

TALLEST OPERA HOUSE

The Civic Opera House at 20 North Wacker Drive in Chicago, Illinois, USA, is an imposing 45-story skyscraper made from limestone and is able to accommodate 3,563 people. The building opened in 1929.

TALLEST FULLY ROTATING TOWER

The Glasgow Tower (above) at the Glasgow Science Centre, Glasgow, Strathclyde, UK, is 416 ft (127 m) tall and is the tallest tower in the world capable of fully rotating through 360 degrees from base to top. It opened in spring 2001.

TALLEST FOUNTAIN

At its full pressure of 375 lb/in^2 (26.3 kg/cm^2) and a rate of 5,850 gal/min (26,500 liters/min), the fountain at Fountain Hills, Arizona, USA, produces a column of water that reaches a height of 562 ft (171.2 m).

TALLEST FREE-STANDING STRUCTURE

The tallest free-standing structure on Earth is the Petronius oil and gas drilling platform, which stands 1,870 ft (570 m) above the ocean floor in the Gulf of Mexico. Operated by Texaco, it began production on July 21 2000. The highest point on the platform, the vent boom, is over 2,000 ft (610 m) above the ocean floor, making it more than 165 ft (50 m) taller than Toronto's CN Tower.

TALLEST STRUCTURE EVER

The all-time height record for any structure is the guyed Warszawa Radio mast at Konstantynow, 60 miles (96 km) northwest of the capital of Poland. The mast was designed by Jan Polak and, prior to its fall during renovation work on August 10 1991, it towered at 2,120 ft 8 in (646.38 m) in height and weighed 1,212,500 lb (550 tonnes). It was completed on July 18 1974 and put into operation on July 22 1974.

The tallest structure in the world today is a stayed television transmitting tower 2,063 ft (629 m) tall, between Fargo and Blanchard, North Dakota, USA. It was built for KTHI-TV, Channel 11 in 30 days (from October 2 to November 1 1963) by 11 men from Hamilton Erection, Inc (USA). From that time until the completion of the Warszawa Radio mast, the tower was the tallest structure in the world, a title that it regained following the collapse of the Warszawa mast.

HIGHEST HABITABLE FLOOR IN A SKYSCRAPER

Chicago's Sears Tower (below) has the highest habitable floor of any skyscraper. Its 110 stories rise to 1,454 ft (443 m). Although the Petronas Towers in Kuala Lumpur is the world's tallest office building, its top floor (the 88th) is around 200 ft (60 m) lower.

FARTHEST DISTANCE TO MOVE A LIGHTHOUSE

To save the Cape Hatteras Lighthouse (above) in North Carolina, USA, from a receding shoreline, the National Park Service (NPS) decided to move it about 0.5 mile (0.8 km) farther inland. After replacing its granite base with steel supports and hydraulic jacks on rollers, engineers began moving the 208-ft-high (63-m) lighthouse along a specially designed track on June 17 1999. It reached its destination, about 2,900 ft (883 m) from its original location, on July 9 1999.

DEEPEST ROAD TUNNEL

The Hitra Tunnel in Norway, linking the mainland to the island of Hitra, reaches a depth of 866 ft (264 m) below sea level. The tunnel is 3.8 miles (5.6 km) long, with three lanes, and was opened in December 1994. It is so deep that if you were to use its floor as the foundation for a building, you would need to build a 66-story tower before reaching the surface of the sea above.

LARGEST ROAD TUNNEL

The road tunnel with the largest diameter in the world is the one that runs through Yerba Buena Island, San Francisco, California, USA. It is 79 ft (24 m) wide, 56 ft (17 m) high, and 541 ft (165 m) long.

More than 280,000 vehicles pass along the tunnel's two decks each day. It carries five lanes of traffic on each of its two decks and is so large that a four-story house could be pulled through it.

LONGEST ROAD TUNNEL

The tunnel on the main road between Bergen and Oslo, Norway, which cuts through the high range of mountains dividing west and east Norway, is 15.2 miles (24.5 km) long. The two-lane Lærdal Tunnel opened in 2001 and reportedly cost $113.1 million (£80.7 million) to construct.

LONGEST BRIDGE-TUNNEL

The Chesapeake Bay bridge-tunnel, which opened to traffic on April 15 1964, extends 17.65 miles (28.4 km) from the Eastern Shore region of the Virginia Peninsula to Virginia Beach, Virginia, USA. The longest bridged section is Trestle C, at 4.56 miles (7.34 km), while the longest tunnel section is the Thimble Shoal Channel Tunnel, at 1.09 miles (1.75 km).

LARGEST RESERVOIR

The most voluminous man-made reservoir is the Bratskoye Reservoir on the river Angara in Russia. It has a volume of 40.6 miles^3 (169.3 km^3) and an area of 2,112 miles^2 (5,470 km^2), which means that the largest of the Egyptian pyramids at Giza would fit into it nearly 70,000 times. Built between 1961 and 1967, the reservoir is the power source for a sizeable hydroelectric power plant.

HIGHEST CAUSEWAY

In the mid-1990s, a causeway (raised road) was built to replace Bailey Bridge, which spanned Khardungla Pass, Ladakh, India. The bridge had been built in August 1982 and at one time stood at a higher altitude (18,380 ft or 5,602 m) than any other road bridge in the world.

HIGHEST BRIDGE

The world's highest bridge is suspended 1,053 ft (321 m) above the Royal Gorge of the Arkansas River in Colorado, USA. A suspension bridge with a main span of 880 ft (268 m), the structure took six months to build and opened to the public on December 6 1929.

HEAVIEST BUILDING RELOCATION

The Cudecom Building, an eight-story apartment building in Bogotá, Colombia, weighing 16.9 million lb (7,700 tonnes) was moved intact 95 ft (28.95 m) by the company Antonio Paez-Restrepo Cia, Sociedad en Comandita, on October 6 1974, in order to make way for a road.

OLDEST BRIDGE

The oldest datable bridge still in use today is the slab-stone single-arch bridge over the Meles River in Izmir (formerly Smyrna), Turkey. The bridge is thought to have been constructed in around 850 BC.

Remnants of Mycenaean bridges over the Havos River, dating back to around 1600 BC, exist in Mycenae, Greece.

LONGEST STEEL-ARCH BRIDGE

The New River Gorge Bridge, near Fayetteville, West Virginia, USA, which was completed in 1977, has a record span of 1,700 ft (518 m).

GREATEST DISTANCE A BRIDGE HAS BEEN MOVED

Unable to handle increasing volumes of traffic, London Bridge was auctioned in 1962 and bought for $2,460,000 (then £876,068) by Robert McCulloch (USA). The bridge was dismantled and moved brick-by-brick to Lake Havasu City, Arizona, USA – a total distance of 5,300 miles (8,530 km) – where it was reassembled and opened in 1971. It later transpired that McCulloch bought the wrong bridge – he had presumed that he was buying Tower Bridge.

LIGHTS WITH THE GREATEST RANGE

The lights 1,089 ft (332 m) above the ground on the Empire State Building, New York City, USA, have the greatest range of any lights. Each of the four-arc mercury bulbs is visible 80 miles (130 km) away on the ground and 300 miles (490 km) away in an aircraft.

LARGEST MAN-MADE FLOATING ISLAND

On August 10 1999, the Mega-Float island (above) opened in Tokyo's Yokosuka Port, Japan. It is 3,280 ft 10 in (1,000 m) long, 396 ft 11.7 in (121 m) wide, and 9 ft 10 in (3 m) deep, and is used to simulate disasters and test new aircraft.

LONGEST CABLE-SUSPENSION BRIDGE

The main span of the Akashi-Kaikyo road bridge – which links the Japanese islands of Honshu and Shikoku – is 1.23 miles (1,990.8 m) long. The bridge's overall suspended length, including side spans, totals 2.43 miles (3,911.1 m). Its two towers rise 974 ft 5 in (297 m) above water level, and the two main supporting cables are 44 in (1.12 m) in diameter, making both the tower height and the cable diameter world records. Work on the bridge began in 1988, and it opened to traffic on April 5 1998.

LONGEST WALL

The Great Wall of China is the longest wall in the world. It was first built to repel marauding tribes of Mongol raiders from the north. The main part of the wall is 2,150 miles (3,460 km) long, nearly three times the length of Great Britain, and the structure also features 2,195 miles (3,530 km) of branches and spurs. Construction of the wall began in the reign of Qin Shi Huangdi (221–210 BC), but it did not take on its present-day form until the Ming dynasty (1368–1644). The height of the wall varies from 15 ft to 39 ft (4.5 m to 12 m), and it is up to 32 ft (9.8 m) thick. It runs from Shanhaiguan, on the Gulf of Bohai, west to Yumenguan and Yangguan and was was kept in repair up until the 16th century. Around 32 miles (51.5 km) of the wall have been destroyed since 1966.

WIDEST ROAD
The toll plaza for the San Francisco-Oakland Bay Bridge (below) features 23 traffic lanes – 17 of which are westbound and serve the bridge in Oakland, California, USA.

LARGEST INHABITED CASTLE

The royal residence at Windsor Castle (above) at Windsor, Berks, UK, is built in the form of a parallelogram measuring 1,890 x 540 ft (576 x 164 m). It was constructed mainly in the 12th century under Henry II.

HIGHEST RESIDENTIAL APARTMENTS

The John Hancock Center in Chicago, Illinois, USA, contains the highest residential apartments in the world. It stands 1,127 ft (343.5 m) high and comprises 100 stories. Although the building is mixed-use, floors 44 to 92 are residential. The building was completed in 1970 and remodeled in 1995.

LARGEST NON-PALATIAL RESIDENCE

St Emmeram Castle in Regensburg, Germany, has 517 rooms and a floor area of 231,000 ft² (21,460 m²). It belonged to the late Prince Johannes von Thurn und Taxis, whose family use only 95 of the rooms. The castle is valued at over DM336 million ($178 million or £122 million).

OLDEST HOTEL

The Hoshi Ryokan in the village of Awazu, Japan, is reputedly the oldest hotel in the world. It dates back to 717 AD, when Taicho Daishi built an inn near a hot-water spring that was reputed to have miraculous healing powers. The waters are still celebrated to this day for their recuperative effects. The Ryokan currently has 100 bedrooms.

TALLEST HOTEL

The all-suite Burj Al Arab – The Arabian Tower – located 9 miles (15 km) south of Dubai, United Arab Emirates, is the world's tallest hotel. Measured on October 26 1999, it stood 1,052 ft (320.94 m) high from ground level to the top of its mast. The hotel, which is built on a man-made island and is shaped like a sail, has 202 suites, 28 "double-height" stories, and has a floor area of 1.2 million ft² (111,480 m²).

MOST EXPENSIVE HOTEL APARTMENT

The 10-room Bridge Suite at the Royal Towers of Atlantis in the Bahamas can be rented for $25,000 (£15,084) per night. This price includes a bar lounge, two entertainment centers, a baby grand piano, and a dining room with a 22-carat gold chandelier.

HIGHEST DENSITY OF HOTEL ROOMS

Las Vegas, Nevada, USA, boasts an incredible 120,000 hotel and motel rooms, nearly one for every four of its 456,000 inhabitants. The city single-handedly accounts for around 3.33% of all hotel rooms in the USA.

HIGHEST CONCENTRATION OF THEME HOTELS

There are more than 16 theme hotels on the Strip in Las Vegas, Nevada, USA. The *Luxor* has a sphinx, a black pyramid, and an obelisk; *New York New York* features a one-third-scale New York skyline; and *Paris* has a half-scale Eiffel Tower. Other themes include Treasure Island and Venice.

LARGEST HOTEL

The MGM Grand Hotel/Casino in Las Vegas, Nevada, USA, consists of four 30-story towers on a site covering 112 acres (45.3 ha). The hotel has 5,005 rooms, with suites of up to 6,000 ft² (560 m²) in area, a 15,200-seat arena, and a 33-acre (13.3-ha) theme park.

HIGHEST-ALTITUDE HOTEL

The Hotel Everest View above Namche, Nepal – the village closest to Everest base camp – stands at a record height of 13,000 ft (3,962 m).

LARGEST ICE HOTEL

Sweden's Ice Hotel in Jukkasjärvi, has a total floor area of 13,124 ft² (4,000 m²), comprising 15 suites and 32 bedrooms. Lying 120 miles (200 km) north of the Arctic Circle, the hotel has been rebuilt and expanded every December since 1990. It features ice sculptures, a cinema, saunas, colonnaded halls, a bar made out of ice, and an ice chapel. The hotel currently has 120 ice beds, which are covered with thick reindeer pelts. The inside temperature hovers around the 20°F (-6°C) mark.

LARGEST WOODEN BUILDING

Built in 1912, Woolloomooloo Bay Wharf, Sydney, NSW, Australia is 1,312 ft (400 m) long and 206 ft (63 m) wide; it stands on 3,600 piles. The building on the wharf is five stories high, 1,150 ft (350.5 m) long and 141 ft (43 m) wide, with a total floor area of 688,890 ft² (64,000 m²). It has been converted into a hotel, apartments, and a marina complex.

LARGEST FORT

Fort George near Ardersier, Highland, UK, is 2,100 ft (640 m) long and has an average width of 620 ft (189 m) on a site 42 acres (17.2 ha) in area. It was built from 1748 to 1769.

LARGEST PALACE

Situated in the center of Beijing, China, the Imperial Palace covers a rectangular area measuring 3,150 x 2,460 ft (960 x 750 m) over an area of 178 acres (72 ha). Its outline survives from an original construction dating back to the rule of Yongle, the third Ming emperor, in the 15th century. Due to reconstruction work, however, most of the palatial buildings (five halls and 17 palaces) date back only to the 18th century.

LARGEST GARDEN

In the late 17th century, Andre le Notre (France) created a magnificent garden (above) for Louis XIV at Versailles, France. The gardens and parkland take up over 15,000 acres (6,070 ha), of which the formal garden covers 247 acres (100 ha).

HIGHEST HOTEL

China's Grand Hyatt Shanghai in Pudong is the highest hotel in the world. It occupies floors 53 to 87 of the 88-story Jin Mao Tower, China's tallest building, and – at 1,377.9 ft (420 m) – one of the world's tallest buildings. The hotel opened for business on March 18 1999, and offers spectacular views over the Bund financial center and the adjacent Huang Pu River.

LARGEST TEPEE

Dr Michael Doss (USA) of the Crow Indian Reservation, Montana, USA, is the creator of the world's largest tepee. It stands 42 ft (12.8 m) high, has a 252-ft (76.8-m) circumference and a 50-ft (15.2-m) diameter.

MOST DURABLE RESIDENT

Virginia Hopkins Phillips of Onancock, Virginia, USA, lived in the same house from the time of her birth in 1891 until just after her 102nd birthday in 1993.

MOST EXPENSIVE HOUSE SALE

Businessman Eric Hotung's house at 6–10 Black's Link, Hong Kong, sold for HK$778.88 million ($101,909,312 or £62,767,500) on May 12 1997.

LARGEST RESIDENTIAL PALACE

The Istana Nurul Iman, the palace of HM the Sultan of Brunei in the capital Bandar Seri Begawan, was completed in January 1984 at a reported cost of $422 million (£300 million).

The palace is the largest residence in the world, with a total floor space of 2,152,780 ft² (200,000 m²), 1,788 rooms, and 257 lavatories. The underground garage houses the Sultan's 153 cars.

LARGEST HOLLYWOOD HOME

Hollywood's largest home is the house at 594 Mapleton Drive, Hollywood, California, USA. It occupies 56,550 ft² (5,253 m²) and was extended to 123 rooms by its owner, TV producer Aaron Spelling (USA). The house is valued at $37 million (£26.4 million) and includes a gym, bowling alley, swimming pool, and skating rink.

MOST EXPENSIVE ISLAND SOLD

The most expensive island ever sold was Palmyra Island (USA), 960 miles (1,545 km) southwest of Honolulu. In 2000 the island was bought by The Nature Conservancy for $30 million (£21 million) from the Fullard-Leos family. Palmyra is unique in that no settlers have ever colonized it.

MOST EXPENSIVE NON-PALATIAL HOUSE BUILT

Hearst Castle (below), at San Simeon, California, USA, was built between the years 1922 and 1939 for the newspaper tycoon William Randolph Hearst (USA), at a cost of more than $30 million (£6.5 million), the equivalent of over $350 million (£250 million) today. The house has more than 100 rooms, a 104-ft-long (32-m) heated swimming pool, an 83-ft-long (25-m) assembly hall, and a garage that can accommodate 25 limousines. The house required 60 servants to maintain it. Today, guided tours of Hearst Castle take place throughout the year.

HIGHEST CAPACITY AIRLINER

The jet airliner with the highest capacity is a custom-built Boeing 747-400 (above), which entered service with Northwest Airlines (USA) in January 1989. The plane has a wingspan of 213 ft (64.9 m), a range of 8,290 miles (13,340 km) and can carry 566 passengers.

LONGEST-DURATION FLIGHT BY A MODEL AIRCRAFT

The longest-duration flight by a powered model aircraft is 33 hr 39 min 15 sec by Maynard Hill (USA), on October 1 and 2 1992.

MOST EXPENSIVE PRIVATE JET

At an amazing price of $45 million (£31 million), the Gulfstream V-SP is the most expensive private jet ever made. It has a range of 7,800 miles (12,500 km) at long-range cruise speeds and is capable of flying 5,750 miles (9,260 km) at Mach 0.87. It has Rolls-Royce BR-710 engines and airframe drag reduction.

FASTEST PASSENGER AIRLINER

Russia's Tupolev Tu-144, first flown on December 31 1968, is reported to have reached Mach 2.4 (1,600 mph or 2,587 km/h), although its normal cruising speed was Mach 2.2.

MOST POWERFUL JET ENGINE

A prototype General Electric GE90-115B turbofan engine achieved steady-state thrust of 123,000 lb (55,800 kg) during flight tests in December 2001 – almost twice as much as each of the four engines used by the Boeing 747-400. The engine will eventually be put to use on Boeing 777s, due to enter service in 2003, and will be certified at 115,000 lb (52,160 kg).

SMALLEST JET AIRCRAFT

The smallest jet is *Silver Bullet*, which was built by Bob and Mary Ellen Bishop (USA) in 1976. It is 3.7 m (12 ft) long, has a 17-ft (5.2-m) wingspan, weighs 437 lb (198 kg), and can fly at 300 mph (483 km/h).

SMALLEST MONOPLANE AIRCRAFT

The smallest monoplane is the *Baby Bird*, designed and built by Donald R Stits (USA). It is 11 ft (3.35 m) long, with a wingspan of 6.25 ft (1.91 m), and weighs 252 lb (114.3 kg) when empty. It is powered by a 55-hp (41.25-kW) two-cylinder Hirth engine, giving a top speed of 110 mph (177 km/h). It was first flown by Harold Nemer (USA) on August 4 1984, at Camarillo, California, USA.

HIGHEST ALTITUDE IN AN AUTOGYRO

On July 20 1982, over Boscombe Down, Wilts, UK, Wing Commander Kenneth H Wallis (UK) reached an altitude of 18,516 ft (5,643.7 m) in a WA-121/Mc gyrocopter.

AIR-SPEED RECORD

The highest officially recorded air speed is 2,193.17 mph (3,529.56 km/h), by Capt Eldon W Joersz and Maj George T Morgan Jr (both USA), achieved in a Lockheed SR-71A Blackbird near Beale Air Force Base, California, USA, over a 158-mile (250-km) course on July 28 1976.

LONGEST JOURNEY BY POWERED PARAGLIDER

Bob Holloway (USA) flew his powered paraglider a distance of 1,500 miles (2,400 km), from close to the Canadian border in Washington, USA, to the Mexican border in Arizona, USA, between June 15 and 26 2001.

FASTEST SPEED IN A HELICOPTER

Under Fédération Aéronautique Internationale (FAI) regulations, the world speed record for helicopters was set by John Eggington and his co-pilot Derek J Clews (both UK), who averaged a remarkable 249.09 mph (400.87 km/h) when in flight over Glastonbury, Somerset, UK, in a Westland Lynx demonstrator helicopter on August 11 1986.

WORST SINGLE-AIRCRAFT INCIDENT

The worst single-aircraft accident occured on August 12 1985, when JAL Boeing 747 Flight 123 crashed into Mount Osutaka near Tokyo, Japan, killing 520 of the 524 passengers and crew on board.

HIGHEST-FLYING PROPELLER-DRIVEN AIRCRAFT

The highest altitude reached by a propeller-driven aircraft is 96,500 ft (29,413 m), when the unmanned solar-powered *Helios* prototype flew over the Hawaiian island of Kauai on August 13 2001. *Helios* is one of a new breed of high-altitude aircraft that could provide an alternative to communications satellites.

MOST WIDELY USED AIRLINER

Launched in 1965, the Boeing 737 has become the world's most widely used airliner. Over 2,800 units are in use worldwide, and in January 2000 it became the first airliner to clock up more than 100 million flight hours.

FASTEST SPEED IN AN AUTOGYRO

Wing Commander Kenneth H Wallis (UK, above) flew a WA-116/F/S gyrocopter with unpowered rotors, to a speed of 120.3 mph (193.6 km/h) over a 1.86-mile (3-km) course in Norfolk, UK, on September 18 1986.

LONGEST PERIOD SPENT AIRBORNE

Robert Timm and John Cooke (both USA) kept their Cessna 172 Hacienda aloft for 64 days 22 hr 19 min 5 sec from December 4 1958 to February 7 1959. They took off at McCarran Airfield, Las Vegas, Nevada, USA, and landed at the same place after covering a distance equivalent to six times round the world, with refueling taking place in the air.

LONGEST FLIGHT BY POWERED PARACHUTE

The official FAI record for the longest distance flown in a single hop by a powered parachute is 400 miles (644 km), by Juan Ramon Morillas Salmeron (Spain), from Almonte, Huelva, Spain, to Minuesa, Teruel, Spain, on June 21 1998.

LONGEST DISTANCE FLOWN BY A PAPER AIRCRAFT

The greatest distance flown by a paper aircraft is 193 ft (58.82 m), by Tony Felch (USA), set indoors at La Crosse, Wisconsin, USA, on May 21 1985.

LONGEST FLIGHT BY AN UNMANNED AIRCRAFT

The longest flight by a full-scale unmanned conventional aircraft is 8,600 miles (13,840 km) by a USAF Northrop Grumman Global Hawk *Southern Cross II* (above) on April 22 2001. The journey from Edwards Air Force Base, California, USA, to RAAF Base Edinburgh, SA, Australia, took 23 hr 23 min.

LARGEST PASSENGER AIRCRAFT (STILL IN DEVELOPMENT)

The Airbus A380, which was launched in December 2000 and is expected to enter service by 2007, will have a wingspan of 261 ft 10 in (79.8 m) and a length of 239 ft 6 in (73 m). It will be able to carry 555 passengers in considerable comfort and will have a maximum takeoff weight of 1,234,587 lb (560 tonnes).

FASTEST RADIO-CONTROLLED MODEL AIRCRAFT

Leonid Lipinski (USSR) flew a model aircraft at 245.94 mph (395.64 km/h) on December 6 1971.

LARGEST AIRLINE AIRCRAFT FLEET

The airline with the most aircraft is American Airlines (USA), which, in September 2001, operated a fleet of nearly 700 planes. Its nearest two rivals were United and Delta (both USA), with close to 600 planes. The largest non-US airline was British Airways (UK), with 357 aircraft.

LARGEST AIRSHIP

The world's largest airships were the 471,568-lb (213.9-tonne) *Hindenburg* (LZ 129) and the *Graf Zeppelin II* (LZ 130), each of which had a length of 803 ft 10 in (245 m) and a hydrogen gas capacity of 7,062,100 ft^3 (200,000 m^3). The *Hindenburg* was launched in 1936, while the *Graf Zeppelin II* made its first flight in the following year. Both airships were built in Germany.

LARGEST AEROSPACE COMPANY

In 2000 Boeing, who are based in Seattle, Washington, USA, made $51.321 billion (£34.381 billion), earning profits of $2.128 billion (£1.425 billion). Boeing's workforce at the time totaled 198,100.

EARLIEST HELICOPTER FLIGHT

In 1935 the Breguet-Dorand Laboratory Gyroplane (France) became the first helicopter to be fully controllable and fly successfully.

LONGEST DURATION FLIGHT IN HUMAN-POWERED VEHICLE

Kanellos Kanellopoulos (Greece) kept his Daedalus 88 aircraft aloft for 3 hr 54 min 59 sec when pedaling the 71.93 miles (114.11 km) between two Greek islands on April 23 1988.

MILITARY SERVICE

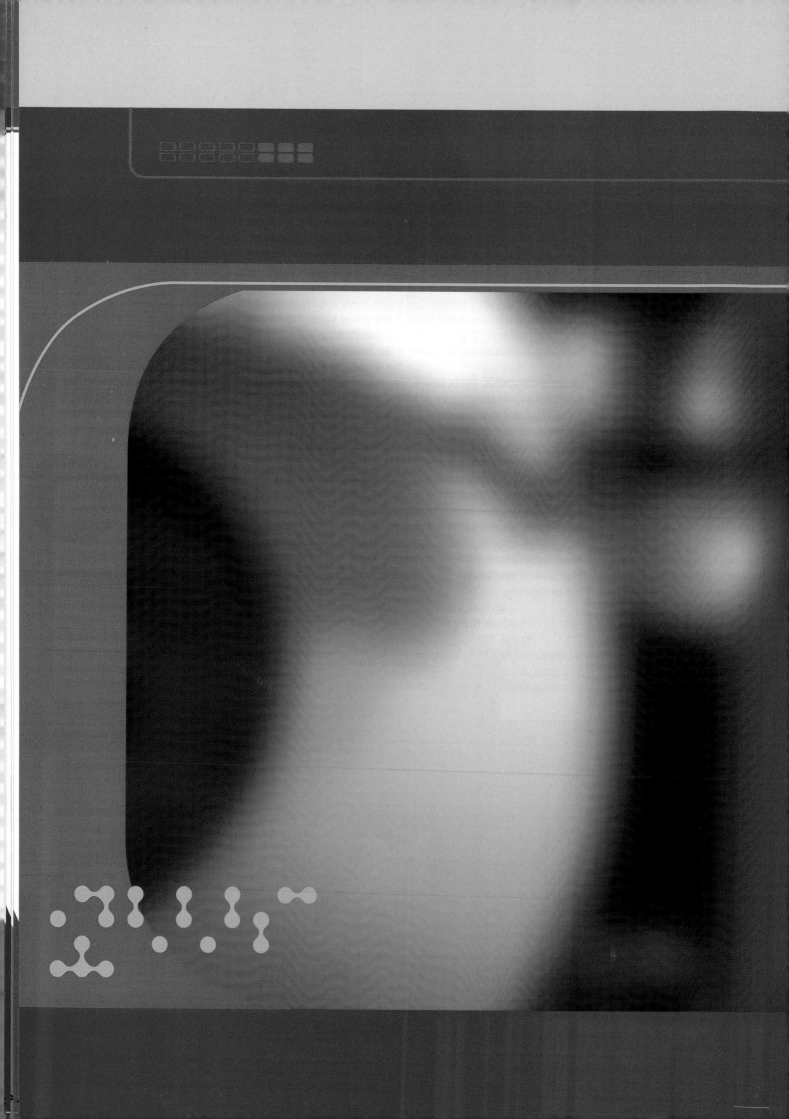

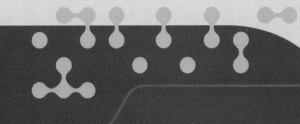

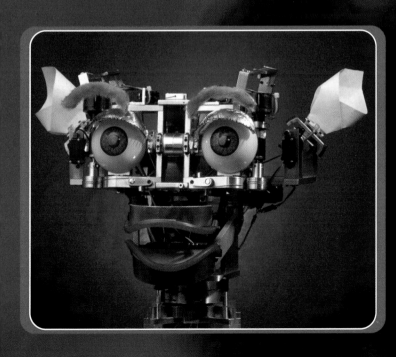

EARLIEST E-MAIL

In 1971, the first-ever e-mail was sent by Ray Tomlinson (USA), an engineer working at the computer company Bolt, Beranek & Newman in Cambridge, Massachusetts, USA. The e-mail was initially designed as an experiment by Ray to see if he was able to get two computers to exchange a message. He was also responsible for choosing to use the @ symbol to separate the recipient's name from their location. The first e-mail message was "QWERTYUIOP."

HIGHEST NUMBER OF TELEPHONES PER CAPITA

The principality of Monaco holds the record for the most telephones per head of population, with 1,994 for every 1,000 people.

COSTLIEST E-MAIL

In 1997, a subsidiary of US-based petroleum company Chevron Corp paid $2.2 million (£1.3 million) to settle a sexual harassment lawsuit filed against it by four female employees. Evidence presented by the women's lawyers included e-mail records listing 25 reasons why beer is supposedly better than women. In settling, Chevron denied the women's allegations.

FIRST POLE-TO-POLE TELEPHONE CALL

On April 28 1999, at 10:30 am (GMT), the first phone call between people at the North and the South Poles took place, lasting 45 minutes. Taking part were: George Morrow, Tom Carlson, Joel Michalski, Vince Hurley, Mike Comberiate, Ron Ruhlman, and Claire Parkinson (all USA). The day before, the same team had carried out the first Internet link and webcast from the North Pole.

BUSIEST INTERNATIONAL TELEPHONE ROUTE

The busiest international telephone route is between the USA and Canada. In 2001 there were approximately 10.4 billion minutes of two-way traffic between the two countries.

LARGEST SWITCHBOARD

The world's biggest switchboard is the one in the Pentagon, Arlington, Virginia, USA, which has 34,500 lines that handle nearly one million calls per day through about 100,000 miles (160,934 km) of telephone cable. Its busiest day was June 6 1994 – the 50th anniversary of D-Day – when it took 1,502,415 calls.

LARGEST TELECOMMUNICATIONS COMPANY

The Nippon Telegraph and Telephone Corporation (NTT), Tokyo, Japan, is the world's largest telecommunications company. In 2001, NTT had revenues of $97,956 million (£69,163 million) and profits totaling $2,821 million (£1,991 million). The company had a workforce of 224,000 employees.

LARGEST HOLDER OF DOMAIN NAMES

The US company Namezero holds 1,307,300 domain names, more than any other company in the world.

LARGEST DIGITAL SATELLITE RADIO BROADCASTER

From its two geosynchronous satellites (which orbit the Earth while staying above a fixed point on its surface), WorldSpace broadcasts digital radio channels to Africa, Asia and Europe with a total surface area (or "footprint") of 30.8 million miles^2 (80 million km^2). Its first satellite, AfriStar, began broadcasting in October 1999 and AsiaStar began after its launch in March 2000.

MOST COMPREHENSIVE CYBERSPACE MAP

Working from the Bell Laboratories, New Jersey, USA, researchers Bill Cheswick and Hal Burch (both USA) created a map of cyberspace (above) featuring 88,000 endpoints. The pair used colors to represent different Internet Service Providers (ISPs). To create the map, Cheswick sent out electronic tracers from his New Jersey-based computer, which died on reaching a terminal destination. At their point of expiry, the messages sent back a "death notice," which enabled Burch's program to create the map.

FASTEST AROUND-THE-WORLD TEXT MESSAGE

On February 20 2002 at the 3GSM World Congress in Cannes, France, Logica sent a text message around the world by forwarding it to cell phones in six countries in six continents, and finally back to the original phone in Cannes. The message was received back in France only 3 min 17.53 sec after the original sender began typing in the message.

OLDEST COMPUTER

The first fully automated, software-driven computer was designed and run by Tom Kilburn and Freddie Williams (both UK) on June 21 1948. The pair used a 17-instruction program on a machine called "Baby," which calculated the highest factor of 2 to the power of 18.

COUNTRY WITH THE MOST CELL PHONES

The country with the greatest number of cellular telephone users is the USA, with a grand total of 69.209 million subscribers in 1998.

LARGEST HOST OF INTERNATIONAL TELEPHONE CALLS

In 2000, US company WorldCom (CEO and president Bernard J Ebbers, above right) was recognized as the world's largest carrier of international telephone calls, in terms of outgoing traffic, with 12.4 billion minutes of communications.

MOST NEW COMPUTER VIRUSES IN A MONTH

The greatest number of new computer viruses to appear in any one month was approximately 16,000, in January 1999. The same year also saw the highest ever number of new computer viruses, with 26,193 entering "the wild." The majority of these new viruses were a direct consequence of the circulation on the internet of a new construction kit for viruses.

LONGEST TELEPHONE CABLE

The world's longest submarine telephone cable is FLAG (Fiber-optic Link Around the Globe), which runs for 16,800 miles (27,000 km) from Japan to the United Kingdom. It links three continents (Europe, Africa, and Asia) and 11 countries, and is capable of supporting 600,000 simultaneous telephone calls.

SMALLEST COMPUTER VIRUS

The smallest computer virus to date is the TrivialOW.13 virus. With a size of just 13 bytes, this DOS-based virus overwrites data in the files it infects. It was first detected in January 1998 and is no longer active.

MOST POPULAR COUNTRY LEVEL DOMAIN

According to NetNames Ltd, as of March 2001, the most popular country level domain is *.uk* (Britain), with over 2 million domain registrations. Britain is closely followed by Germany. The USA has the most internet sites, but few of them use *.us* in their URL.

MOST POPULAR TOP-LEVEL DOMAIN NAME (TLD)

Of the 35.3 million domain names in existence worldwide (as of April 2001), the most popular is *.com*, which is used by 22.3 million hosts.

LARGEST INTERNET SEARCH ENGINE

Google, with around 2.215 billion pages, has the largest continually refreshed web page index of any search engine in the world. Founded by Larry Page (below left) and Sergey Brin (below right, both USA), Google's first office was a garage in Menlo Park, California, USA, which opened in September 1998 with a staff of four people.

FASTEST COMPUTER

The NEC Earth Simulator (above) at the Yokohama Institute for Earth Sciences in Japan is capable of carrying out 35.6 trillion calculations per second – approximately five times the speed of the previous record holder. Built by HNSX Supercomputers, a division of NEC, the computer is designed to simulate Earth's complex climate in order to predict climate change and global warming, both of which have serious implications for Japan. Its 5,104 processors are housed in cabinets that cover an area equivalent to four tennis courts.

MOST HUMAN-LIKE COMPUTER PROGRAM

A computer program called ALICE, created by Richard Wallace (USA), is the most human-like computer program, and it won the annual 2001 Loebner Prize. A bronze medal is awarded each year to the program that wins the highest score from a panel of expert judges, who attempt to converse with the competing programs via a keyboard. The silver medal will be awarded to the program that convinces half the judges that it is a human, and a gold medal will be awarded once half the judges are convinced by a program conversing with speech rather than text. Neither the silver nor the gold medal have yet been awarded.

SHORTEST INSTRUCTION MANUAL FOR A COMPUTER

The Apple iMac personal computer comes with an instruction manual that consists of just six pictures and 36 words. The computer therefore certainly lives up to its sales pitch, which states that a user can simply take it out of the box and plug it in.

MOST WIDELY USED INDUSTRIAL ROBOT

Puma (Programmable Universal Machine for Assembly), designed by Vic Scheinman in the 1970s and made by Swiss company Staubli Unimation, is the most commonly used robot in university laboratories and automated assembly lines.

FASTEST-SELLING ENTERTAINMENT ROBOT

Sony Corporation's AIBO Entertainment Robot ERS-110, a robotic pet puppy, retailed for $2,066 (£1,289) when it first went on sale on May 31 1999, and 3,000 were sold within 20 minutes. AIBO is 11 in (27.9 cm) tall and can recognize its surroundings using a built-in sensor. ("Aibo" means "pal" or "partner" in Japanese.) It can be programmed to perform tricks or to "play" on its own. On June 1 1999, 2,000 AIBOs became available over the internet in America; the initial rush to buy the robot caused web servers to crash. The latest model, the ERS-220, features enhanced touch sensors and word recognition, as well as a motion sensor surveillance mode.

SMALLEST CASSETTE

The NT digital cassette made by the Sony Corporation of Japan for use in dictating machines is just 1.18 x 0.82 x 0.19 in (30 x 21 x 5 mm).

LARGEST PLASMA SCREEN

Plasma technology is the latest revolution in high-quality computer screens. It features charged gas between two layers of glass, which operate under the same principles as fluorescent lights and neon tubes. The result is a perfectly flat and uniformly focused high-quality image on a slim screen. The largest plasma screen produced to date measures 63 in (160 cm) diagonally and is manufactured by Samsung.

SMALLEST GPS WATCH

The Casio PAT2GP-1V watch measures 2.3 x 2 x 0.8 in (58.5 x 51.5 x 21.0 mm). It receives data from the fleet of Global Positioning System (GPS) satellites to pinpoint the location of the wearer to within 33 ft (10 m), anywhere on Earth. It can be connected to a home computer to plan map routes, which can be stored in the watch itself.

HIGHEST-JUMPING ROBOT

Sandia National Laboratories, USA, have developed experimental robots that use combustion-driven pistons to jump to heights of 30 ft (9 m). The diminutive robots have potential applications in planetary exploration, where several "hopper" robots could be released by a lander to survey the surrounding landscape.

HIGHEST RESOLUTION MONITOR

The T220, made by IBM, has a higher resolution than any other monitor in the world. With a liquid crystal display (LCD) screen size of 22.2 in (55.5 cm) and a resolution of 3,840 x 2,800 pixels, the T220 has a total of 9.4 million pixels. Its technological superiority enables it to provide around 12 times higher detail than most conventional monitors.

SMALLEST BLACK BOX RECORDER

The smallest "black box" recorder is the Accu-counter, a device fitted to firearms that records the number and exact time of each shot fired from that weapon. It is typically 1 in (2.5 cm) long, 0.5 in (1.3 cm) wide, and 0.25 in (0.6 cm) thick. Made by Accu-counter, Inc (USA), it is expected to be adopted by law enforcement agencies and the military to monitor firearm use.

FASTEST-GROWING ENTERTAINMENT PRODUCT

Since the DVD player launched in 1997 over 627 million DVDs have been sold, according to research and consultancy company Understanding & Solutions. After the launch of CD players in 1983, 256 million CDs sold over the same period.

MOST THERAPEUTIC ROBOT
PARO, a robotic seal designed by Takanori Shibata of the Intelligent Systems Institute (Japan) as a therapeutic robot, can respond to human touch and sound. During a six-week trial, from May to July 2001 in a day care center for the elderly, tests demonstrated a marked improvement in the levels of stress among patients after interaction with the robot.

images of the Earth's surface at a resolution of 24 in (61 cm) per pixel. QuickBird can also take multispectral images at 8 ft (2.44 m) per pixel. (Multispectral images use different parts of the spectrum, as opposed to monochrome images.)

MOST INTELLIGENT PEN AND PAPER
The Swedish company Anoto has created a digital pen that allows the user to digitally store up to 50 written pages in its memory. This information can then be transferred directly to a nearby computer or – via Bluetooth technology – to any computer in the

world over the Internet. (Bluetooth technology uses short-range radio as a replacement for physical wires, enabling wire-free communications between computers, cell phones, PDAs, and the internet.) The pen writes on special digital paper that enables the pen to know exactly where on the paper it is. The paper is divided into a grid with squares 0.08 x 0.08 in (2 x 2 mm). Inside each square is a pattern of dots that varies according to which area of the paper the user is looking at.

MOST EMOTIONALLY RESPONSIVE ROBOT
Kismet (below), created by Cynthia Breazeal (USA) at Massachusetts Institute of Technology (MIT), is a robotic head powered by 21 motors and 15 networked computers. It is designed to recognize different emotions while interacting with humans, and to respond to them. Nine of the computers are used to control Kismet's vision alone.

LARGEST ROBOT DOG
The Roboscience (UK) RS-01 Robodog, is 32 x 26 x 14 in (82 x 67 x 37 cm). Strong enough to lift a five-year-old child, the RS-01 is far larger and more powerful than its nearest rivals.

HIGHEST-RESOLUTION COMMERCIALLY AVAILABLE SATELLITE IMAGES
DigitalGlobe's QuickBird Satellite is capable of taking images with a higher resolution than that of any other commercially available satellite images. Launched on October 18 2001 on a Boeing Delta 2 rocket, QuickBird can take black-and-white

MOST ADVANCED CYBERNETIC LIMB IMPLANT
Prof Kevin Warwick (UK) had a second silicon chip implanted into his arm on March 14 2002. Linked directly to nerve fibers in his wrist, this tiny device enables him to interact with some objects without touching them. The chip measures his nerve impulses, then transmits them to a computer, which in turn translates them into commands.

SPECIES WITH THE MOST CHROMOSOMES

The plant species with the most chromosomes per cell discovered to date is adder's tongue fern (*Ophioglossum reticulatum*, above), which has 630 pairs of chromosomes per cell.

LARGEST CLONED ANIMAL

On January 6 2000, Xiangzhong Yang (China), from the University of Connecticut, USA, and scientists from the Kagoshima Prefectural Cattle Breeding Development Institute, Japan, announced that they had successfully cloned six calves from skin cells taken from a bull's ear. Some of the calves have now reached adulthood.

EARLIEST CLONED PRIMATE

Two monkeys were cloned in August 1996 at the Primate Research Center, Beaverton, Oregon, USA. The pair were created from embryos rather than from an adult animal, which means that the monkeys are not genetically identical to any existing animal. The embryos were implanted into the wombs of host mothers using IVF.

LARGEST MOLECULE IN THE CELL

DNA, the double helix-shaped molecule discovered in 1953 by James Watson (UK) and Francis Crick (USA), contains all the genetic code needed to build an individual. Each of the ten trillion cells in the human body contains this code. If a DNA molecule was unwound and stretched out, it would be around 6 ft (2 m) long. If all the DNA in the human body could be stretched out end-to-end, it would reach to the Sun and back more than 600 times.

EARLIEST CLONED KIDNEYS

In January 2001, scientists from Advanced Cell Technologies, Mass, USA, revealed that they had successfully grown kidneys using cloning technology for the first time. The technique took a DNA-containing nucleus from a single cow skin cell and fused it with a host egg. The egg multiplied into an embryo rich in stem cells. These cells were then chemically manipulated to grow into kidney cells, using an artificial kidney-shaped scaffold. Several of these miniature kidneys were grown in this way and transplanted back into the cow, where they began to produce urine. Each of the kidneys was a couple of inches (several centimeters) long.

OLDEST NATURAL CLONES

Darwinulidae, a family of ostracod (crustaceans around 0.04 in or 1 mm long) reproduce asexually. Fossil records show that this has been happening for at least 100 million years. So every individual alive today is an almost exact clone of an individual from the Cretaceous Period. The only genetic differences are due to genetic mutations in the intervening period and, therefore, their evolution has been extremely slow.

FARTHEST TRACED DESCENDANT BY DNA

History teacher Adrian Targett (UK) can genetically trace his family back farther than any other person. He is a direct descendant, on his mother's side, of "Cheddar Man," a 9,000-year-old skeleton found in a cave in Cheddar Gorge, Somerset, UK. Scientists took a DNA sample from one of Cheddar Man's molars and found a near perfect match in Targett, who lives less than half a mile away.

MOST COMPATIBLE ANIMALS FOR ORGAN TRANSPLANTATION INTO HUMANS

Although they share about 95% of their DNA with us, compared to 98.9% for the pygmy chimp, pigs are considered to be the most compatible animals for potential organ transplants into humans. This is because pig organs are more similar in size to human organs, and there is also a risk of contracting AIDS from primate organs. There are also ethical problems with the use of primates compared to pigs – in the West, for example, we raise pigs for food, but not monkeys.

OLDEST EXTRACTED HUMAN DNA

In January 2000, it was announced that scientists had extracted DNA from a bone belonging to a 60,000-year-old ancestor of modern humans. The skeleton, nicknamed "Mungo Man," was unearthed at Lake Mungo, NSW, Australia, in 1974 and was dated (between 56,000 and 68,000 years old) in 1999. Mungo Man's DNA challenges the "Out of Africa" theory of evolution, which holds that we are all descended from a common ancestor (*Homo erectus*) in Africa. Mungo Man has a skeleton that is anatomically the same as ours, but its DNA appears to have no links with *Homo erectus*.

ANIMALS MOST GENETICALLY SIMILAR TO HUMANS

Bonobos (primates similar to chimpanzees), which live only in the rainforests of central Democratic Republic of Congo, share 98.9% of their DNA with humans. This species, often called the "pygmy chimpanzee," numbers no more than a few tens of thousands of individuals. Chimps share around 98.5% of DNA with humans.

MOST GENETICALLY DIVERSE PEOPLE ON EARTH

For some genetic traits, Pygmies and African bushmen (above) have up to 17 genetic variations, whereas most people on Earth have two or three. They may represent the survivors of the original human population.

MOST ADVANCED CLONED HUMAN EMBRYO

In October 2001, a team of scientists at Advanced Cell Technologies, Mass, USA, led by Dr Jose Cibelli (USA), created the first cloned human embryos, using a cumulus cell from a mature human egg. One of these embryos managed to divide into six cells before growth ceased after around five days. The research aims to eventually produce cloned stem cells for use in curing disease.

MOST SUCCESSFUL PLANT-TO-ANIMAL GENE TRANSFER

In January 2002, scientists led by Akira Iritani (Japan) announced that they had successfully implanted genetic vegetable material into an animal. The genetically modified pigs contain a spinach gene that will reportedly make pork meat less fatty and thus more healthy to eat. The pigs were born in mid-1998, and no health problems have been reported.

LONGEST-LIVED HUMAN CELLS

Cells from Henrietta Lacks (USA) are still alive and being grown worldwide in laboratories decades after her death in 1951. Cells from her cervical cancer were removed and subsequently found to lack chromosome 11 – now known as the "tumor suppressor." As a result of this error, these cells can divide indefinitely and are essential tools in biomedical research.

LARGEST HUMAN CHROMOSOME SEQUENCED

On December 20 2001, scientists at the Sanger Centre (UK) announced their completion of the sequence of chromosome 20. This chromosome has nearly 60 million DNA letters and more than 720 genes (about 2% of the three billion letters that make up the human genetic code). Thirty two of the genes are linked to genetic disorders and disorders of the immune system. The smallest human chromosome sequenced is chromosome 21, also mapped at the Sanger Centre (UK) in 1999.

RAREST ANIMAL TO BE SUCCESSFULLY CLONED

On October 1 2001, scientists announced that a European Mouflon lamb had been cloned and had survived. This rare breed of sheep, found on Cyprus, Sardinia, and Corsica, represents the first-ever successful cloning of an endangered species. A European team led by the University of Teramo, Abruzzo, Italy, created the clone. There are fewer than 1,000 Mouflon sheep surviving in the wild.

OLDEST CLONED ANIMAL

Dolly (left), a Finn Dorset sheep cloned from the breast cell of an adult ewe, was born at Edinburgh's Roslin Institute, Midlothian, UK, in July 1996. Her arrival prompted a debate on the ethics of cloning. Named after the US country singer Dolly Parton, she was mated naturally with a Welsh mountain ram in 1997 and gave birth to a healthy lamb called Bonnie on April 13 1998.

MOST COMMON ELEMENT

Hydrogen is the most common element in both the universe (in which it represents over 90% of all elements) and the solar system (in which it makes up 70.68% of all elements). Iron is the most common element on Earth, making up 36% of its mass, and molecular nitrogen (N_2) is the most common element in the atmosphere at 75.52% by mass or 78.08% by volume. The picture above, taken by the Hubble space telescope, shows large formations of interstellar dust and molecular hydrogen in the Eagle Nebula.

OLDEST NUCLEAR CHAIN REACTION

On June 2 1972 French scientists analyzing uranium ore in Gabon, west Africa, found tiny anomalies in the ratio of isotopes in the samples. This led to the discovery of the Oklo natural fossil reactors. About 2 billion years ago, these were active underground nuclear fission reactors, powered by uranium ore that had been concentrated by geological processes and cooled by ground water. Seventeen such sites have been discovered in Gabon.

HARDEST ELEMENT

The diamond allotrope of carbon (C) has value of 10 on Moh's scale of hardness. Diamonds have historically been mined principally in India, Brazil, South Africa, and Russia.

RAREST ELEMENT ON EARTH

The element astatine is the rarest element found in the Earth's crust, with around 0.9 oz (25 g) of the element occurring naturally.

FASTEST SPEED POSSIBLE

The fastest speed possible in the universe is the speed of light. This is achieved only by light and other forms of electromagnetic radiation, such as radio waves, X-rays, and infrared radiation. The speed of light varies according to what the light is traveling through. Light moves most rapidly in a vacuum. In such conditions it achieves a velocity of 983,571,056.4 ft/sec (299,792,458 m/sec). As a result, the light we see from the Sun left it around 8.3 minutes beforehand, and the light from the Moon takes about 1.3 seconds to reach Earth.

LARGEST MICROBE

The largest known protozoans (forms of minute invertebrates) in terms of volume are the extinct calcareous Foraminifera (Foraminiferida) of the genus *Nummulites*. Individuals up to 6 in (150 mm) wide were found in rocks in Turkey that dated back to the Middle Eocene geological period. (The Eocene era lasted from around 55–38 million years ago.)

LARGEST KNOWN PROTEIN

The largest known single-chain protein is found in muscle cells and is referred to by two different names: titin and connectin. A molecule of titin can reach a length of one micron (0.00004 in or 0.000001 m) and may be larger than some cells.

STRONGEST FORCE IN THE UNIVERSE

There are four fundamental forces in the universe that account for all interactions between matter and energy. They are known as the strong nuclear, weak nuclear, electromagnetic, and gravitational forces. The most powerful of these four is the strong nuclear force, which is 100 times stronger than the next strongest – electromagnetic force. The strong nuclear force operates exclusively within the nucleus of an atom.

WEAKEST FORCE IN THE UNIVERSE

The four fundamental forces in the universe are given relative strength values, with electromagnetic force given the value of 1. Gravitational force, the weakest of the four, has a strength of 10^{-40}, relative to electromagnetism. An illustration of how much weaker gravity is when compared to electromagnetism, for instance, is demonstrated by the fact that it is easy for a toy magnet to pick up a nail, despite the fact that the whole of Earth's gravity is working to pull it back down.

SMALLEST UNIT OF LENGTH

The smallest possible size for anything in the universe is the Planck length. At 1.6×10^{-35} m, it is equivalent to around one millionth of a billionth of a billionth of a billionth of a centimeter across (a decimal point followed by thirty-four zeroes and a one), this is the scale at which quantum foam is believed to exist. (The laws of quantum physics cause minute wormholes to open and close constantly, giving space a rapidly changing, foam-like structure.) Quantum foam is potentially a tremendous source of energy: the power in one cubic centimeter of empty space would be enough to boil all the Earth's oceans.

OLDEST HOMINID FOOTPRINTS

The oldest known human-like footprints were discovered in Laetoli, northern Tanzania, in 1978. They belong to two or three hominids who walked upright on the ashy plains of the area approximately 3.6 million years ago. The trackway consists of approximately 70 footprints in two parallel trails of around 100 ft (30 m) in length.

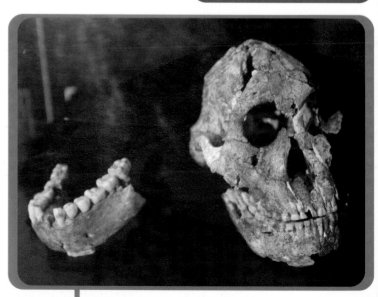

EARLIEST KNOWN HUMAN ANCESTOR

In December 2000 scientists on the Kenya Paleontology Expedition announced the discovery of 6-million-year-old fossilized hominid remains. *Orrorin tugenensis* (above) walked on two legs and was similar in size to an adult female chimp.

LARGEST KNOWN PRIME NUMBER

Michael Cameron (Canada), a participant in the Great Internet Mersenne Prime Search (GIMPS) announced the discovery of the largest known prime number on December 5 2001. It is $2^{13,466,917}-1$. Written out in full, the number would have 4,053,946 digits. A reward of $100,000 (£68,568) is offered to the person who discovers the first 10-million-digit prime number.

LOWEST POSSIBLE TEMPERATURE

The temperature of a substance is determined by the speed at which the atoms or molecules that make up that substance vibrate. Theoretically, the coldest that any substance can be is when there is no such vibration at all, resulting in absolute zero – "0K" (zero Kelvin) or -273.15°C. This has never been achieved in a laboratory on Earth, and even in the coldest parts of deep space, the temperature is slightly above absolute zero.

FASTEST MICROBE

By means of a polar flagellum (a whip-like outgrowth) rotating 100 times per second, the rod-shaped bacillus *Bdellovibrio bacteriovorus* can travel 50 times its own length of 0.2 micrometers per second. This would be the equivalent of a human sprinter reaching 200 mph (320 km/h), or a swimmer covering 20 miles (32 km) in six minutes.

MOST POWERFUL REACTION

When matter reacts with antimatter, both are annihilated and all of the mass converts to energy. Less than 3.5 oz (100 g) of antimatter would produce energies similar to the power of a hydrogen bomb (below), if annihilated with matter.

MOST PROLIFIC ANTIMATTER PRODUCER

The laboratory Fermilab, in Batavia, Illinois, USA, produces around 100 billion protons of antimatter every hour. This amounts to around one billionth of a gram each year. Antimatter is similar to normal matter, but the charges on the subatomic particles are reversed. For example, an anti-electron, also known as a positron, is the same as an electron but with a positive rather than a negative charge.

FASTEST ATOMIC CLOCK

A team of physicists at the National Institute of Standards and Technology in Boulder, Colorado, USA, have developed an atomic clock (above), which ticks nearly a quadrillion (million billion) times per second. It is hoped that this clock will eventually be accurate to one second in 100 million years.

LOWEST MAN-MADE TEMPERATURE

In 1995 a team of scientists led by Eric Cornell and Carl Wieman (both USA) cooled atoms of rubidium to a record low temperature of less than 170 billionths of a degree above absolute zero – the coldest temperature possible.

HIGHEST MAN-MADE TEMPERATURE

The highest temperature ever created by man is 5.2×10^8 Kelvin, which works out as almost 30 times the temperature you will find at the center of the Sun. It was achieved on July 19 1996 by scientists who were working at the Naka Fusion Research Establishment in Nakamachi, Ibaraki, Japan.

SMALLEST LASER SCULPTURE

In August 2001 researchers at Osaka University, Osaka, Japan, used lasers to create a 3D model of a bull that measured 0.00027 x 0.00039 inches (seven thousandths of a millimeter high and ten thousandths of a millimeter long) – the same size as a single red blood cell. It is so small that 30 could fit inside the period at the end of this sentence.

SLOWEST LIGHT

In January 2001 scientists in Cambridge, Massachusetts, USA, were able to slow down light itself to a complete halt. Light usually travels at the speed of 186,000 miles/sec (300,000 km/s), but naturally slows when it passes through a denser medium such as water or glass.

MOST DENSE MATTER

Scientists at the Brookhaven National Laboratory, Long Island, New York, USA, have created matter 20 times more dense than the nucleus of an atom. By smashing the nuclei of gold atoms together at close to the speed of light, they created subatomic particles that existed for a fraction of a second. Matter this dense may not have existed in the universe since its creation in the "Big Bang," which physicists believe occurred between 12 and 15 billion years ago.

DEEPEST OPERATING NEUTRINO OBSERVATORY

The Sudbury Neutrino Observatory is located 6,800 ft (2,072 m) below ground in the INCO Creighton Mine, Ontario, Canada. The observatory consists of a 39-ft (12-m) diameter vessel containing around 900 tonnes of heavy water. It is designed to detect neutrinos – neutral elementary particles produced by nuclear fusion in the Sun – and its depth allows it to detect only these particles.

LONGEST RUNNING LAB EXPERIMENT

Since 1930 the University of Queensland, Brisbane, Australia, has been conducting an experiment into the viscosity of black pitch. The pitch was placed in a funnel, out of which it slowly drips. In late 2000 the eighth drop fell, demonstrating that pitch is about 100 billion times more viscous than water. The experiment is expected to continue for at least another 100 years.

LARGEST VAN DE GRAAFF GENERATOR

The largest Van de Graaff generator was built in 1931 by scientists at Cambridge's Massachusetts Institute of Technology, USA. It consists of two columns, each with a 15-ft (4.57-m) hollow aluminum sphere at the top. The two spheres are oppositely charged, causing discharges of 5 million volts. The machine was originally used to smash atoms and research high-energy X-rays. It is currently grounded and on permanent display at the Thomson Theater of Electricity at the Boston Museum of Science, Boston, Massachusetts, USA.

HIGHEST ARCHAEOLOGICAL SITE

Dr Johan Reinhard (USA) and a team sponsored by the National Geographic Society discovered three Inca mummies while exploring the Andes mountain range at Salta, Argentina. The mummies, the frozen remains of children sacrificed an estimated 500 years ago, were found at the peak of the Llullaillaco mountain, at an altitude of 22,000 ft (6,706 m).

MOST NOBEL PRIZES FOR CHEMISTRY AND PHYSICS

American scientists have a total of 51 outright or shared winners of the Nobel prize for chemistry and an additional 52 prizes for physics.

LONGEST RECORDED DREAM

Dream sleep is characterized by rapid eye movements known as REM. The longest recorded period of REM is one of 3 hr 8 min registered by volunteer David Powell (USA) in an experiment at the Puget Sound Sleep Disorder Center, Seattle, Washington, USA, on April 29 1994. Dream sleep usually lasts around 20 minutes.

MOST SYSTEMATIC STUDY INTO "HAUNTED" LOCATIONS

In 2001 Dr Richard Wiseman (UK, above) measured the reactions of 250 people to haunted locations. The data should provide insights into the effects of factors such as magnetic fields, light levels, temperature, and low-frequency sound on the mind.

MOST LEAD TURNED TO GOLD

In 1980 Glenn Seaborg (USA) used nuclear physics to turn several thousand atoms of lead into gold at the Lawrence Berkeley Laboratory, Berkeley, California, USA. However, the experimental technique is far too expensive to enable the routine manufacturing of gold from lead.

MOST DETAILED HUMAN DISSECTION

The world's most detailed dissection, the "Visible Human Project," took place at the University of Colorado, Boulder, USA, from November 1994 to November 1995. A male cadaver was divided into 1,878 slices, 0.03 in (1 mm) thick, and a female cadaver was cut into 5,189 slices, 0.01 in (0.33 mm) thick. Every slice was then photographed by a digital camera to create a virtual anatomy "text book" for students to experiment upon.

MOST NOBEL PRIZE WINNERS FROM A SINGLE LABORATORY

Eleven researchers have received Nobel prizes for work done while they were based at Bell Laboratories, New Jersey, USA. The first was in 1927, and the most recent came in 1998.

LEAST DENSE SOLID

The solid substance with the lowest density is aerogel – tiny spheres of bonded silicon and oxygen atoms joined into long strands separated by pockets of air. The latest versions of this substance weigh just 3 mg/cm^3, and are produced by the Jet Propulsion Laboratory in Pasadena, California, USA.

SMELLIEST SUBSTANCES

The smelliest substances on Earth are "US Government Standard Bathroom Malodor" and "Who-Me," two man-made chemicals with five and eight chemical ingredients respectively. "Bathroom Malodor" smells primarily of human feces and is incredibly repellent to people at two parts per million. The smelliest molecules are ethyl mercaptan and butyl seleno-mercaptan, which smell of a combination of rotting cabbage, garlic, onions, burned toast, and sewers.

SHORTEST FLASH OF LIGHT

The shortest flash of light was a burst recorded at 650 billion-billionths of a second (0.00000000000000065 sec) in 2001 by scientists led by Ferenc Krausz (Austria) at the Vienna Institute of Technology, Vienna, Austria. The technique will be used to study the behavior of electrons.

MOST ELEMENTS DISCOVERED

Since Albert Ghiorso (USA) began his scientific career in 1942, he has discovered or co-discovered a record 12 different chemical elements.

STRONGEST MAGNETIC FIELD

In June 2000 the Hybrid Magnet at the National High Magnetic Field Laboratory, Tallahassee, Florida, USA, achieved a DC magnetic field strength of 45T – about 1.5 million times stronger than that of the Earth's magnetic field. The amount of electricity needed to run the magnet at its full field, 27 mW, could supply 1,500 houses.

STRONGEST ACID

Normal solutions of strong acids and alkalis tend toward pH values of 0 and 14 respectively, but this scale is inadequate for superacids, the strongest of which is an 80% solution of antimony pentafluoride in hydrofluoric acid (fluoro-antimonic acid). The acidity function of this solution has not been measured, but even a weaker 50% solution is 1,018 times more powerful than concentrated sulphuric acid.

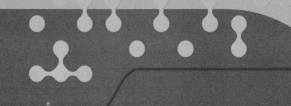

ENTERTAINMENT

BIGGEST RECORD DEAL

In April 2001 Virgin/EMI paid the singer Mariah Carey (USA, above) a "signing-on bonus" of $21 million (£14.73 million) when she agreed to a four-album deal reported to be worth between $80–$100 million (£56–£70 million). At the time, Virgin/EMI claimed that she was the "biggest-selling female artist of all time" with worldwide sales of more than 150 million and 15 US No.1 singles. Carey had also spent longer in the US No.1 spot (61 weeks) than any other female. In January 2002 after releasing one album, *Glitter*, Virgin/EMI paid her $29 million (£20.34 million) to end the deal.

BEST-SELLING HIP-HOP ALBUM IN THE USA

The best-selling rap/R&B album ever released in the USA is *CrazySexyCool* by TLC (USA), which has reached sales of 11 million, surpassing MC Hammer's (USA) 10 million-selling *Please Hammer, Don't Hurt 'Em*. One member of the all-female TLC, Lisa "Left Eye" Lopes was tragically killed in a car accident in April 2002.

BEST-SELLING REGGAE ALBUM

Legend by Bob Marley (Jamaica), released posthumously after Marley died in 1981, is reggae's best-selling album of all time. In the UK, where it topped the charts in 1984, *Legend* has had certified sales of 1.8 million, and although it did not hit the Top 40 in the USA, it has still sold more than 10 million copies.

BEST-SELLING ALBUM

The best-selling album of all time is *Thriller* by Michael Jackson (USA), with global sales since its release in 1982 of more than 47 million copies.

EARLIEST GOLD DISC MUSIC AWARD

The first actual gold disc was sprayed by RCA Victor for presentation to the US trombonist and band-leader Alton "Glenn" Miller for his "Chattanooga Choo Choo" on February 10 1942.

MOST CHARTED ARTIST ON UK SINGLES CHART

Elvis Presley's (USA) releases spent a cumulative total of 1,173 weeks on the UK singles chart since "Heartbreak Hotel" debuted on May 11 1956. Presley's last UK No.1 was "Way Down" in 1977, the year he died.

MOST CONCERTS PERFORMED IN 12 HOURS

The Bus Station Loonies (UK) played 25 gigs in 12 hours in and around Plymouth, Devon, UK, on September 29 2001. The four-piece band played 15-minute sets at each spot, were supported by two road crews, and raised £1,200 ($1,800) for charity.

MOST CONSECUTIVE NO.1 SINGLES

The KinKi Kids (Japan) have had 13 consecutive singles debut at No.1 on the Japanese charts between July 28 1997 and November 20 2001.

MOST EXPENSIVE MUSIC VIDEO

The promotional video for "Scream," the hit single by siblings Michael and Janet Jackson (both USA), cost about $7 million (£4.4 million) to make in 1995. Directed by Mark Romanek (USA), "Scream" won the MTV Music Video Award for Dance in 1995 and the Grammy for Music Video Short Form in 1996 and was shot on seven different sound stages. In 1995 "Scream" became the first single to enter the US chart inside the top five.

MOST CONSECUTIVE WEEKS AT NO.1 ON US SINGLES CHART

"One Sweet Day" by Mariah Carey and Boyz II Men (USA), topped the US chart for 16 weeks in 1995 and 1996.

MOST GRAMMY AWARDS WON BY A FEMALE ARTIST

Aretha Franklin (USA) has won 15 Grammys since she received her first award in 1967 for Best R&B Vocal Performance with "Respect." She has also won the most Grammys for R&B Female Vocal Performances, claiming 11 awards between 1967 and 1987.

MOST SUCCESSFUL MALE COUNTRY ARTIST

Garth Brooks (USA) is the most successful country music recording artist of all time. Since his debut in 1989, Brooks has registered album sales of more than 100 million.

YOUNGEST SOLO ARTIST AT NO.1 ON US ALBUM CHART

Stevie Wonder (USA) was just 13 years 3 months old when *Little Stevie Wonder – The Twelve Year Old Genius*, released in 1963, topped the US charts. In 1976 Wonder, who has been blind since just after his birth, signed a contract with the world-famous Motown record label worth $13 million (£7.3 million), which at the time was the largest ever deal made in music industry history.

LONGEST STAY ON A US SINGLES CHART

"How Do I Live" by country singer LeAnn Rimes (USA) entered the Top 25 US Country Singles Sales Chart on June 21 1997 and was still there a massive 250 weeks later in April 2002, having sold more than 3 million copies – a record for a country single.

OLDEST ARTIST TO SELL A MILLION ALBUMS

Compay Segundo (Cuba, above) has sold more than one million albums worldwide since he turned 88 in 1995. Segundo first recorded in the 1930s and found fame with the late-1990s Latin superband Buena Vista Social Club.

LARGEST RAP GROUP

Hip-hop outfit Minority Militia (USA) is the world's largest rap group, with a remarkable 124 members. Each member of the crew plays a full and active part in their recordings, either rapping, singing, playing an instrument, or producing on their 2001 album *The People's Army*, released on Lowtown records.

OLDEST RECORDS

The BBC record library contains more than one million records. The oldest records in the library are white wax cylinders dating from 1888. The earliest commercial disc recording was manufactured in 1895.

EARLIEST MILLION-SELLING CD

The first CD to sell one million copies worldwide was UK band Dire Straits' 1986 album *Brother in Arms*, which topped the charts in 22 countries.

MOST MULTI-PLATINUM RIAA CERTIFICATES

Elvis Presley (USA) has 35 multi-platinum Recording Industry Association of America (RIAA) certificates, for singles and albums with more than 2 million sales.

MOST NO.1 SINGLES ON UK CHART

The Beatles (UK) and Elvis Presley (USA) both hold the record for the most No.1 singles on the UK charts, with 17 each. The Beatles (right, clockwise from far left – George Harrison, John Lennon, Ringo Starr, and Paul McCartney), scored their successes in the period between 1963 and 1969, while Presley's were spread over 20 years from 1957 to 1977.

BEST-SELLING DVD SINGLE

Madonna's (USA) "What It Feels Like For A Girl" sold 6,200 copies in its first week of release in May 2001 – the greatest ever registered week's sale for any single released on the DVD format. The previous record was also held by Madonna – full name Madonna Ciccone – with 4,200 sales for "Music," which was set when it was released in September 2000.

MOST BRIT AWARDS

British band Blur hold the record for winning the most BRIT (British Record Industry Trust) Awards in a year, with four presented to them in 1995.

HIGHEST ANNUAL EARNINGS BY A RAP ARTIST

Rap mogul Dr Dre (USA, above) earned $31.5 million (£21.1 million) in 2000, according to the *Forbes* Celebrity 100 List of 2001. Dre has sold millions of copies of his solo material as well as producing Snoop Dogg and Eminem (both USA).

MOST PERFORMERS ON ONE SINGLE

The greatest number of people to sing on one hit single is 275,000 on British band S Club 7's "Have You Ever." The single was released on November 19 2001 as part of the BBC's Children in Need appeal and features contributions from children at 3,616 UK schools.

FASTEST-SELLING ALBUM

The Beatles' *1*, a compilation of all the British band's No.1 singles in the USA and UK, sold 3.6 million on its first day, November 13 2000, and 13.5 million copies around the world in its first month in the stores.

BEST-SELLING ALBUM BY A TEENAGE SOLO ARTIST

Released in 1999 *Baby One More Time* by Britney Spears (USA) sold 13 million copies in the USA alone in less than two years.

BEST-SELLING US ALBUM BY A FEMALE SOLO ARTIST

Canadian country singer Shania Twain's album *Come On Over* has sold a total of 19 million copies in the USA and 30 million worldwide since its release on November 4 1997.

BEST-SELLING ALBUM ON UK CHART

The album to have sold the most copies in the UK is *Sgt Pepper's Lonely Hearts Club Band* by The Beatles, with a reported 4.5 million sales since its release in June 1967. Music critics often vote the album as one of the best ever recorded.

BEST-SELLING GROUP OF ALL TIME

The Beatles have amassed the greatest sales for any group. All-time worldwide sales have been estimated by EMI at more than one billion discs and tapes to date. Up to 2001 the band were certified for album sales of 163.5 million in the USA alone.

BEST-SELLING SINGLE

The biggest selling single of the rock era is Elton John's (UK) "Candle In The Wind 1997"/"Something About The Way You Look Tonight." It was released in September 1997 and sold 33 million copies worldwide in just three months. The song, originally written about US actress Marilyn Monroe, was re-recorded in tribute to the late Diana, Princess of Wales, after her death in 1997.

HIGHEST ANNUAL TOUR EARNINGS BY A COUNTRY MUSIC ARTIST

Shania Twain's 1999 US tours grossed $36.6 million (£23.2 million). This amount was more than any other country music performer, and $3.1 million (£2 million) more than she earned on the road in 1998.

BEST-SELLING RAP ARTIST

US rap legend 2Pac (born Tupac Shakur) has certified US album sales of 33.5 million up to the end of 2001, and has had more hits after his death (at the age of 25 in September 1996) than he amassed while he was alive. The hits include two US No.1 albums, *The Don Killuminati* (1997) and *Until The End Of Time* (2001) and a dozen US R&B chart singles.

HIGHEST ANNUAL EARNINGS BY A BAND

Despite breaking up in 1970, The Beatles were still the highest-earning band in 2000. The group earned a total of $150 million (£100.5 million) according to the *Forbes* Celebrity 100 List released in 2001. Surviving members Paul McCartney and Ringo Starr (both UK) are among the richest musicians in the world.

LONGEST MUSIC VIDEO

American pop star Michael Jackson's part-feature film, part-music video *Ghosts* (1996) is 35 minutes long and was based on a concept by horror writer Stephen King (USA).

HIGHEST ANNUAL EARNINGS BY A FEMALE SINGER

Britney Spears earned $38.5 million (£25.5 million) in 2000, according to the *Forbes* Celebrity 100 List of 2001.

LARGEST ATTENDANCE AT A FREE ROCK CONCERT

British singer Rod Stewart's free concert held at Copacabana Beach, Rio de Janeiro, Brazil, on New Year's Eve 1994, reportedly attracted a total audience of 3.5 million.

MOST AWARDS WON BY A MALE CANTONESE POP ARTIST

As of April 2000, Hong Kong's Andy Lau has won 292 awards for a singing career that began in 1988. Since 1992 Lau has appeared in concert 179 times. He has also featured in 101 movies since 1981.

BEST-SELLING TEENAGE ARTIST

Before she turned 20 years old on December 2 2001, Britney Spears had sold 37 million records around the world – the best ever sales figures for a solo teenage artist.

MOST SUCCESSFUL VIRTUAL BAND

Gorillaz (above) are the world's most successful virtual band, with global sales of 3 million for their eponymous debut album. The animated band was created by Blur frontman Damon Albarn and cartoonist Jamie Hewlett (both UK).

MOST
BRIT AWARDS

Robbie Williams (UK), has won 13 BRIT (British Record Industry Trust) Awards during his career – more than any other artist or act. His most recent win was for Best British Male Solo Artist, at the ceremony on February 20 2001. Singer Williams was in the hugely successful British band Take That before he launched his own stellar solo career.

MOST CHARTS
TOPPED WORLDWIDE
BY ONE ALBUM

Since November 13 2000, the album *1* by The Beatles has topped the music charts in 35 different countries.

MOST PSEUDONYMS
USED BY A POP STAR

John Lennon (UK), one of the founder members of The Beatles, recorded and produced music under 15 different names until his murder in New York City, USA, in 1980.

MOST WEEKS AT NO.1 IN
THE US SINGLES CHART

Elvis Presley's 18 No.1 records have occupied the top of the charts for a combined total of 80 weeks. US singer Presley holds a total of 14 Guinness World Records.

FASTEST-SELLING POP
ALBUM IN THE USA

The record for the greatest first-week sales of an album in the USA is held by US pop group *NSYNC who sold 2.41 million copies of their album *No Strings Attached* when released on March 21 2000. The album sold one million copies on the first day, shipped 7 million copies in the first two weeks, and sold more than 100,000 copies a week for a world record 26 successive weeks.

HIGHEST-EARNING SOLO AUSTRALIAN POP PERFORMER

Kylie Minogue (below) sold 200,000 tickets and grossed £3.52 million ($5 million) for a 16-date Australian tour in 2001 – a record for an Australian solo act. The singer played nine sold-out nights in Sydney, NSW, and another seven in Melbourne, Victoria.

MOST TONY AWARDS FOR A MUSICAL

The Producers (above), written by American comedian Mel Brooks, was nominated for a record 15 Tony Awards on May 7 2001, winning 12 of them. It beat the previous record of 10 awards won by *Hello Dolly!* in 1964. The Tony Awards, named after US actress Antoinette Perry, are one of theater's most coveted accolades.

LARGEST CONTRA LINE

An amazing 806 people danced a contra for more than five minutes on September 6 1998 in Ann Arbor, Michigan, USA, to the dance "Only in Arbor," played to the tune of "Reel Beatrice."

LARGEST TAP DANCE

The most tap dancers in a single routine were the 6,951 who gathered at the City Square in Stuttgart, Germany, on May 24 1998. Their display lasted 2 min 15 sec.

LARGEST LOCOMOTION DANCE

At the Darlington Railway Centre and Museum, Durham, UK, 374 people were able to "do the locomotion" dance for 15 minutes on October 1 2000. The participants danced around *Locomotion No 1*, the world's first passenger steam train, which was built by George Stephenson (UK) in 1825.

LARGEST CHORUS LINE

On September 28 1997, 593 people from the Roy Castle Foundation (UK), performed for the finale of the *Roy Castle Record-Breaking Extravaganza* at the Royal Liverpool Philharmonic Hall, Liverpool, Merseyside, UK.

LARGEST SPECIALLY BUILT THEATER

The specially built theater with the greatest capacity is the Perth Entertainment Centre, WA, Australia, with 8,500 seats and a main stage measuring 70 x 45 ft (21.3 x 13.7 m). It was opened on December 26 1974 and was the first venue for HM Queen Elizabeth II's 1976 Australian tour.

FASTEST FLAMENCO

Sandro Guerrero Toril (Spain) recorded a world's best 507 taps in one minute in Munich, Germany on November 6 2000.

The record for most taps per second is 16 heel taps by Solero de Jérez (Australia), set in September 1967 in Brisbane, Queensland, Australia.

LONGEST RUNNING ONE-MAN WEST END SHOW

An Evening with Tommy Steele opened at the Prince of Wales Theatre, London, UK, on October 11 1979 and closed on November 29 1980 having run for 414 days. Steele, a British singer and actor, then took the show to Australia and Sweden.

OLDEST WORKING MIME ARTIST

Born on January 13 1914, Arnold Jones (USA) is still working as a mime artist six hours a day, five days a week entertaining crowds in Hollywood, California, USA. He has been a professional mime artist for more than 70 years, starting at 14 as "The Mechanical Man" at fairs throughout America's Midwest.

MOST EXPENSIVE STAGE PRODUCTION

The stage adaptation of Disney's 1994 film *The Lion King* is the most expensive theatrical production ever. The show opened in November 1997 on Broadway, New York City, USA, and cost around $15 million (then £9.3 million). The British production, which opened in London on October 19 1999, was not much cheaper, costing more than £6 million ($9.6 million).

LONGEST RUNNING ANNUAL THEATER REVUE

The longest running annual revue, a theatrical production of comic sketches and songs based around star performers, were *The Ziegfeld Follies*, which went through 25 editions between 1907 and 1957 at numerous venues in the USA.

LARGEST COUNTRY DANCE

A total of 1,914 people gathered in Edinburgh, Lothian, UK, to dance the world's largest "strip the willow" on December 30 2000. The display was organized by Unique Events Ltd (UK) as part of the city's "Night Afore Fiesta" Hogmanay celebrations.

MOST ONE-MAN SHOW PERFORMANCES

The longest run of one-man performances is 849, by Victor Borge (Denmark) in *Comedy in Music* from October 2 1953 to January 21 1956 at the Golden Theater on Broadway, New York City, USA.

OLDEST INDOOR THEATER

The oldest indoor theater in the world is the Teatro Olimpico in Vicenza, Italy. Designed by Italian architect Andrea di Pietro, it was begun three months before his death in 1580 and completed by his pupil Vicenzo Scamozzi (Italy) in 1583. The venue is preserved today in its original form.

LONGEST DANCE MARATHON

Mike Ritof and Edith Boudreaux (both USA) logged 5,152 hr 48 min to win $2,000 (£411) at the Merry Garden Ballroom, Chicago, Illinois, USA, between August 29 1930 and April 1 1931. Such marathon ballroom dances were extremely popular in America during the Great Depression of the early 1930s, when hundreds of people would dance for days for cash prizes.

LARGEST ARTS FESTIVAL

The world's largest arts festival, the Edinburgh Fringe Festival (above) held annually in Edinburgh, Lothian, UK, began in 1947. In its record year of 1998, a total of 9,810 artists gave 16,141 performances of 1,309 different shows.

LONGEST SHAKESPEARE PLAY

Hamlet is the longest of British playwright William Shakespeare's 37 plays. Written in 1604, the play consists of 4,042 lines of 29,551 words. *Hamlet* also contains the longest of any of Shakespeare's 1,277 speaking parts, with Hamlet, the Prince of Denmark, having 1,569 lines of 11,610 words.

LONGEST TIME SPENT IN BED TOGETHER BY A STAGE COUPLE

Jessica Tandy and Hume Cronyn (both USA) have the distinction of having spent more time in bed together than any other stage couple. In October 1951 they opened at the Ethel Barrymore Theater, New York City, USA, in Jan de Hartog's (Netherlands) *The Fourposter* and continued to play the parts for two years.

FASTEST TAP DANCER

James Devine (Ireland) recorded the fastest rate ever measured for tap dancing, producing 38 taps per second in a display in Sydney, NSW, Australia, on May 25 1998.

MOST STAGE FLIGHTS

Ichikawa Ennosuke (Japan) has flown across the stage more than 5,000 times since April 1968 while performing a Japanese stunt called *chunori*. Accomplished through pulleys and a safety belt, *chunori* has been a popular Japanese stage trick for nearly three centuries.

LONGEST RUNNING WEST END MUSICAL

The longest running musical still playing in the West End is *Les Misérables* (below), which opened at the Palace Theatre, London, UK, on December 4 1985. The longest running musical in history is *Cats*, which closed in May 2002 after 8,538 UK performances.

LONGEST RUNNING TV DRAMA

ITV's *Coronation Street* (UK, Jean Alexander as Hilda Ogden shown above), made by Granada, ran twice weekly from December 9 1960 until October 20 1989. It is now aired four times a week. As of March 6 2002, 5,226 episodes have been shown. William Roache (UK) has played Ken Barlow without a break since the outset – a record 42 years.

LONGEST RUNNING TV QUIZ SHOW

University Challenge (UK) has been broadcast for 33 years. The first edition was broadcast on September 21 1962, but the show stopped in 1987 for a seven-year break. It re-started in 1994 and is still running, currently once a week on BBC2.

LONGEST RUNNING PRIME-TIME ANIMATED SERIES

Matt Groening's (USA) *The Simpsons* has had 282 episodes aired on the Fox (USA) network as of March 10 2002. *The Simpsons* originally featured as a 30-second spot on *The Tracey Ullman Show* in 1987. After 50 cartoons were aired, Groening was offered his own series, first seen as a Christmas special on December 17 1989 and then as a regular series from January 14 1990. It is the longest running prime-time series still releasing new episodes, and it holds the record for the most celebrities featured in a cartoon TV series, with 256 cameos to date.

LARGEST TV PHONE VOTE

During the final of Thames Television and 19 Television's (both UK) *Pop Idol*, broadcast on ITV on February 9 2002, the communications firm, Telescope (UK), registered 8.7 million votes over a 2-hr 15-min period. During the course of the show British Telecom (UK) received a massive 94 million call attempts to the voting lines as viewers tried to get through.

MOST EXPENSIVE TV DOCUMENTARY PER MINUTE

The BBC's (UK) documentary series *Walking with Dinosaurs*, which showed how dinosaurs lived, reproduced, and became extinct, cost over £37,654 ($61,112) per minute to produce. It took more than two years to make the six 27-minute episodes at a total cost of £6.1 million ($9.9 million).

MOST EXPENSIVE TV PROGRAM

In January 1998 Warner Brothers (USA), makers of the hospital drama *ER*, the USA's No. 1 show with a then weekly audience of 33 million, agreed to a three-year deal with NBC (USA), earning $857.6 million (£536 million) for 22 episodes at $13.1 million (£8.2 million) per one-hour episode. In April 2000, NBC paid $640 million (£400 million) for three more series until 2004, which works out at $9.6 million (£6 million) an episode.

HIGHEST PAID TV DRAMA ACTOR PER EPISODE

In August 1998 actor Anthony Edwards (USA), *ER*'s Dr Mark Greene, saw his salary increase from $125,000 (£77,160) per episode to $400,000 (£246,900) an episode in a four-year, $35-million (£21.6-million) deal.

HIGHEST CURRENT ANNUAL EARNINGS BY A TV ACTRESS

Jennifer Aniston, Lisa Kudrow, and Courteney Cox Arquette (all USA) – the female leads in NBC's *Friends* since 1994 – earned $1 million (£703,334) each per episode of the 2002 season. With around 24 episodes per season, each of the actresses will earn $24 million (£16.8 million) for the ninth series. In 1994 they each earned $40,000 (£26,000) per episode.

HIGHEST PAID TV COMEDY ACTOR PER EPISODE

Kelsey Grammer (USA) is to be paid a salary of $1.6 million (£1.1 million) per show for playing psychoanalyst Frasier Crane in the 2002 and 2003 series of *Frasier*.

LONGEST RUNNING POP SHOW

The first edition of the BBC's *Top of the Pops* was aired on January 1 1964. Artists appearing included Dusty Springfield, The Rolling Stones, The Dave Clark Five, and The Hollies. The Beatles and Cliff Richard and The Shadows (all UK) were shown on film.

LONGEST RUNNING TV SHOW

NBC's *Meet the Press*, first transmitted on November 6 1947, was subsequently shown weekly from September 12 1948, and has had 2,708 shows aired as of March 24 2002.

LARGEST ANNUAL RADIO AUDIENCE

Surveys in over 100 countries show that the global estimated audience for the BBC World Service (UK), which is broadcast in 41 languages, was 140 million regular listeners in 1995.

MOST RADIO STATIONS

The USA has over 10,000 authorized radio stations, more than any other country in the world.

MOST EXPENSIVE TV ADVERTISING CAMPAIGN

The $8.1-million (£5.7-million) new ads for Pepsi Cola (USA) equate to a spending of $89,700 (£63,000) per second. They were first aired during the Superbowl, at the Louisiana Superdome, New Orleans, USA, on February 3 2002. The commercials starred pop singer Britney Spears (USA).

LARGEST TV AUDIENCE FOR A REALITY SHOW

On August 24 2000, for the final episode of CBS's *Survivor* program in the USA, about 51 million people, or 41% of America's viewing public, watched Richard Hatch (USA, above left) win the $1-million (£660,000) prize money.

LONGEST RUNNING RADIO PROGRAM

Rambling with Gambling, aired six days a week on WOR radio in New York City, USA, was first broadcast in March 1925 and was continued by three generations of the Gambling family. The final broadcast by the latest family member, John Gambling (USA), was on September 11 2000; thus the show ran for more than 75 years.

RADIO DJ MARATHON

DJ Kristian Bartos's (Sweden) broadcast on WOW 105.5 radio, Stockholm, Sweden, lasted for 103 hr 30 min. Beginning at 6:40 am on October 8 2001 he finally closed his program at 2:10 pm on October 12 2001.

The longest radio talk show was one of 33 hours on BBC Three Counties (UK). The show ran from 5:00 am on November 16 until 2:00 pm on November 17 2001. Presented by Nick Lawrence (UK), the show was in aid of the BBC's Children in Need.

LONGEST RUNNING RADIO DRAMA

BBC Radio 4's *The Archers,* created by Godfrey Baseley (UK), was first broadcast on January 1 1951. Actor Norman Painting (UK) appeared in the first episode as the character Philip Archer and holds the record for the longest career as a radio actor in the same role.

EARLIEST BROADCAST

The first advertised broadcast was made on December 24 1906 by Prof Reginald Aubrey Fessenden (Canada) from the mast of the National Electric Signalling Company at Brant Rock, Mass, USA. The transmission included Handel's *Largo*.

HIGHEST EARNINGS FOR A TV CHILD ACTOR

Twins Mary-Kate and Ashley Olsen (USA, below) began their TV careers at the age of nine months when they starred in *Full House*. By the age of nine they earned a combined total of $79,000 (£56,000) per episode. Now 15, they star in Fox Family Channel's *So Little Time*. Their merchandise empire generates around $1 billion (£696 million) annually, and they are said to be the most powerful girls in Hollywood.

EARLIEST ALPHABET
The earliest example of alphabetic writing is that found on clay tablets (similar to the above) showing the 32 cuneiform (wedge-shaped) letters of the Ugaritic alphabet, a now-extinct Semitic language of Syria. The tablets were found in 1929 at Ugarit (now Ras Shamra), Syria and were dated to around 1450 BC.

LARGEST ADVANCE FOR FICTION
It was reported in August 1992 that publishing house Berkeley Putnam (USA) had paid $14 million (then £7.3 million) for the North American rights to the novel *Without Remorse* by Tom Clancy (USA).

MOST OVERDUE LIBRARY BOOK
A German book about the Archbishop of Bremen, published in 1609, was borrowed from Sidney Sussex College, Cambridge, UK, by Colonel Robert Walpole (UK) between 1667 and 1668. Prof Sir John Plumb (UK) found the book 288 years later in the library of the then Marquess of Cholmondeley (UK) at Houghton Hall, Norfolk, UK. No fine was exacted when he returned it.

BEST-SELLING AUTHOR
The world's best-selling fiction writer is the late Dame Agatha Christie (UK), whose 78 crime novels have sold an estimated 2 billion copies in 44 languages. Agatha Christie also wrote 19 plays and, under the pseudonym Mary Westmacott, six romantic novels. Annual royalty earnings from her works are estimated to be worth millions.

BEST-SELLING NON-FICTION BOOK
Although it is impossible to obtain exact figures, there is little doubt that the Bible is the world's best-selling and most widely distributed book. A survey by the Bible Society concluded that around 2.5 billion copies were printed between 1815 and 1975, but more recent estimates put the number at more than 5 billion.

BEST-SELLING CHILDREN'S BOOKS
The 80 titles in the *Goosebumps* series by RL Stine (USA) have sold 220 million copies worldwide since the first book, *Welcome to Dead House*, was published in 1992.

LARGEST DICTIONARY
Deutsches Wörterbuch consists of 34,519 pages and 33 volumes. It was started in 1854 by Jacob and Wilhelm Grimm (both Germany) – best known for their collection of fairy tales – and was completed in 1971.

LARGEST ENGLISH LANGUAGE DICTIONARY
The printed version of the second edition (1989) of the *Oxford English Dictionary* (also available on CD-ROM), contains 21,543 pages in 20 volumes, comprising over 231,000 main entries. In 1993 a series of Additions Volumes, containing entries for additional vocabulary, began to appear: around 4,000 new entries are produced annually.

LARGEST LIBRARY BOOK FINE PAID
On December 15 1959, Art Ogg (USA) borrowed a copy of *Snow Dog* by Jim Kjelgaard (USA) from the Prairie Creek Library in Dwight, Illinois, USA. In 1999 he discovered the book in his mother's attic and returned it on the 40th anniversary of the due date, December 29 1999, paying an overdue fine of $292.20 (£180).

HIGHEST ANNUAL EARNINGS BY AN AUTHOR
According to the *Sunday Times* Rich List 2002, *Harry Potter* author JK Rowling's (UK) net worth increased from £65 million ($93 million) in 2001 to £226 million ($325 million) in 2002, largely due to royalties from the hit film *Harry Potter and the Sorcerer's Stone* (UK, 2001).

HIGHEST ADVANCE FOR A FIRST NOVEL
In 1999 *Sunday Times* journalist Paul Eddy (UK) was reported to have been paid a record $2.8 million (£1.7 million) by British and American publishers for his first novel, *Flint*, and its unwritten (at that time) sequel.

LARGEST MAGAZINE
A 100-page special edition of the March 2002 Paris Gallery magazine, measuring 26.3 x 38.5 in (67 x 98 cm) and weighing 22 lb (10 kg), was produced for the 2002 Dubai (UAE) Shopping Festival. Around 150 high-quality big copies were printed, identical to the normal-sized version.

MOST PULITZER PRIZE WINS BY A FICTION WRITER
Three American writers have twice won the Pulitzer Prize for fiction: Booth Tarkington (*The Magnificent Ambersons* in 1919 and *Alice Adams* in 1922); William Faulkner (*A Fable* in 1955 and *The Reivers* in 1963) and John Updike (*Rabbit is Rich* in 1982 and *Rabbit at Rest* in 1991).

MOST BOOKER PRIZE WINS BY A WRITER
JM Coetzee (South Africa) and Peter Carey (Australia) have both won the Booker Prize twice. Coetzee won with his novels *Disgrace* (1999) and *Life & Times of Michael K* (1983). Carey first won in 1989 with *Oscar and Lucinda*, and again in 2001 with *True History of the Kelly Gang*.

LARGEST ADVANCE FOR NON-FICTION
Former US President Bill Clinton (USA, above) agreed to sell the worldwide rights to his memoirs to Alfred A Knopf Inc (USA) for an advance of more than $10 million (£7.1 million). The book is scheduled for publication in 2003.

LARGEST CIRCULATION FOR A MAGAZINE

Parade, a syndicated color magazine, is distributed with 330 newspapers across the USA every Sunday and currently has a circulation of around 35.9 million, the highest in the world for any magazine. It has a readership of 77.6 million and in 2001 had advertising revenues of around $570 million (£400 million).

HIGHEST CURRENT DAILY NEWSPAPER CIRCULATION

Yomiuri Shimbun (founded 1874) published in Tokyo, Japan, had a combined morning and evening circulation of 14,323,781 in January 2002.

HIGHEST EVER DAILY NEWSPAPER CIRCULATION

Komsomolskaya Pravda (founded 1925), the youth paper of the former Soviet Communist Party, reached a peak daily circulation of 21,975,000 copies in May 1990. Its name means "Young Communist League Truth."

LARGEST ATTENDANCE FOR A BOOK READING

British author JK Rowling, author of the record-breaking *Harry Potter* series, was one of three authors who read excerpts from their works to an audience of 20,264 at the SkyDome Stadium, Toronto, Ontario, Canada, on October 24 2000, as part of The Harbourfront Centre's International Festival of Authors. Canadian author Kenneth Oppel read from his novel *Silverwing*, while his compatriot Tim Wynne-Jones presented an excerpt from *The Boy in the Burning House*. Rowling's reading came from the fourth Harry Potter novel, *Harry Potter and the Goblet of Fire*.

MOST VALUABLE TYPEWRITER

Ian Fleming (UK), former spy and creator of fictional British agent James Bond 007, commissioned a gold-plated typewriter in 1952, which was custom made in New York City, USA, and cost the author $174 (then £62). On May 5 1995 it was sold for £56,250 ($89,229) at Christie's, London, UK. Fleming wrote all but his very first novel (*Casino Royale*) on this typewriter.

MOST SYNDICATED COMIC STRIP

Garfield, created by Jim Davis (USA) and circulated by Universal Press Syndicate (USA), is the world's most syndicated comic strip, appearing in 2,570 papers worldwide.

LONGEST RUNNING COMIC BOOK

The Dandy has been published continuously by DC Thomson & Co of Dundee, UK, since its first edition of December 4 1937. The weekly comic's best-known character is Desperate Dan, an unshaven cowboy from Cactusville, whose favorite food is cow pie cooked in a dustbin lid.

BEST-SELLING BOOK OF ALL TIME

Excluding non-copyright works such as the Bible and the Qu'ran, the world's all-time best-selling book is *Guinness World Records* (formerly *The Guinness Book of Records*). Since it was first published in October 1955, global sales in 37 languages have exceeded a massive 91,941,000 (to June 2001).

SMALLEST PRINTED BOOK REPRODUCTION

A tiny version of the Bible (left) was made by Massachusetts Institute of Technology (MIT) scientists Pawan Sinha, Pamela R Lipson, and Keith R Kluender (all USA) in 2001. Using microlithography, a process similar to that used in the manufacturing of computer microchips, they reprinted the full New Testament text of the King James Bible in 24-carat gold on a crystalline silicon tablet measuring just 0.196 x 0.196 in (5 x 5 mm).

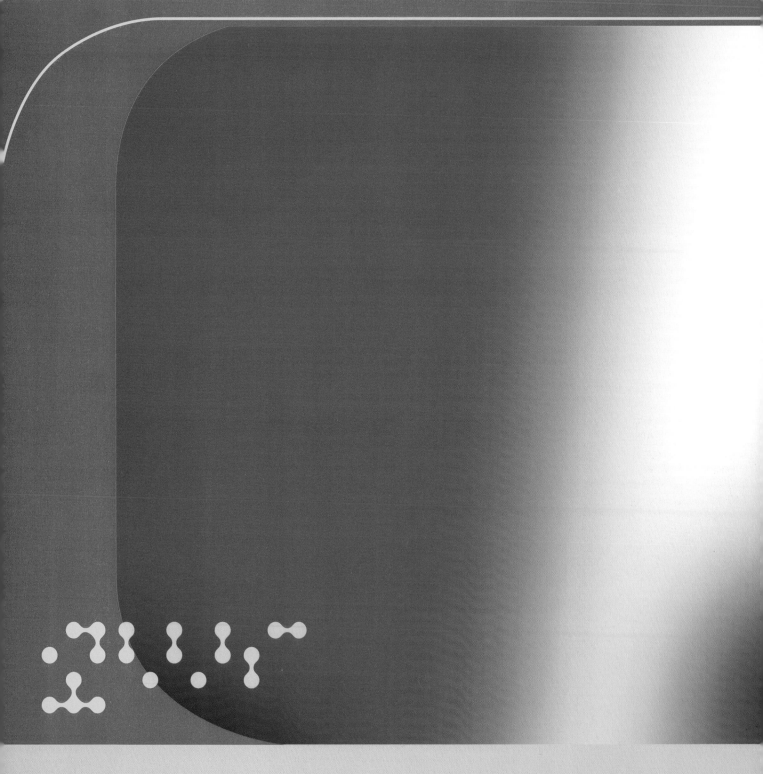

MOST RUNS IN CAREER

The most runs scored in a Major League career is 2,248 by Rickey Henderson (USA, above) up to the end of the 2001 season. To date, Henderson has played 23 seasons for seven franchises, and he also holds the record for most stolen bases in a career, with 1,380. Henderson, who was born on Christmas Day 1958, played for the Boston Red Sox in 2002.

BASEBALL

LONGEST HOME RUN

The longest measured home run in a Major League game is 193 m (634 ft) by Mickey Mantle (USA), when playing for the New York Yankees against the Detroit Tigers at Briggs Stadium, Detroit, Michigan, USA, on September 10 1960.

MOST HOME RUNS IN CAREER

Hank Aaron (USA), who played for Milwaukee (later the Atlanta Braves), scored a record 755 home runs between 1954 and 1976. Aaron, from Mobile, Indiana, was one of the first black players to play Major League baseball. When he scored the home run that set the new record on April 8 1974 the game had to be suspended for 15 minutes while the crowd celebrated.

MOST HOME RUNS IN ONE GAME

The most home runs scored in a Major League game is four, first achieved by Robert "Bobby" Lowe (USA) for Boston against Cincinnati on May 30 1894. The feat has been equalled 11 times since then.

MOST HOME RUNS IN CONSECUTIVE GAMES

Three players have hit home runs in eight consecutive Major League games; Richard Dale Long (USA) for the Pittsburgh Pirates in May 1956; Donald Arthur Mattingly (USA) for the New York Yankees in July 1987, and Ken Griffey Jr (USA) for the Seattle Mariners in July 1993.

MOST HOME RUNS IN ONE WEEK

The most home runs hit in a week is 10, scored in six consecutive games by Frank Howard (USA) for the Washington Senators in May 1968.

MOST HOME RUNS IN ONE MONTH

Sammy Sosa (Dominican Republic) of the Chicago Cubs holds the record for the most home runs in one month, after he smashed 20 in 22 games in June 1998.

MOST CONSECUTIVE HITS

The most consecutive hits in the Major League is 12. The record is shared by two players and first to achieve the feat was Michael Franklin "Pinky" Higgins (USA) of the Boston Red Sox in June 1938. He was followed by Walter "Moose" Dropo (USA), playing for the Detroit Tigers in July 1952.

HITS IN MOST CONSECUTIVE GAMES

Joe DiMaggio (USA) connected in 56 successive games for the New York Yankees in 1941; he was 223 times at bat, with 91 hits, scoring 16 doubles, four triples, and 15 homers. DiMaggio is considered to be one of the finest players to have picked up a bat; he also found fame through his 1954 marriage to American actress and pin-up Marilyn Monroe.

MOST STRIKEOUTS IN A WORLD SERIES MATCH

The record for most strikeouts in a World Series match is 17 and was set on October 2 1968 by the St Louis Cardinals pitcher Robert Gibson (USA). Gibson's World Series records include seven successive complete-game victories. He was such a skilled sportsman that he even played for legendary basketball team, the Harlem Globetrotters.

MOST STRIKEOUTS IN CAREER

Nolan Ryan (USA) pitched 5,714 strikeouts during his Major League career with the New York Mets, the California Angels, the Houston Astros, and the Texas Rangers from 1966 to 1993. In 1979 Ryan became the first player in Major League history to sign a contract worth $1 million when he joined the Houston Astros.

HIGHEST ATTENDANCE AT WORLD SERIES

The record attendance for the World Series is 420,784 over the six-match series between the Los Angeles Dodgers and the Chicago White Sox from October 1 to 8 1959, which the Dodgers won 4-2.

The single game record is 92,706 for the fifth game of the series, at the Memorial Coliseum in Los Angeles, California, USA, on October 6 1959.

MOST GAMES PITCHED IN CAREER

In a career that saw him play for six different teams, California-born Jesse Orosco (USA, above turning out for the Baltimore Orioles) pitched a record total of 1,093 games from his first season in 1979 until April 2000.

LONGEST GAME

The Chicago White Sox and the Milwaukee Brewers played a game that lasted 8 hr 6 min on May 9 1984. The White Sox eventually won 7-6 in the 25th innings of the match.

MOST CONSECUTIVE GAMES WON BY A PITCHER

Carl Owen Hubbell (USA) won 24 consecutive games for the New York Giants in 1936 and 1937.

MOST VALUABLE CATCHER

In 1998 Mike Piazza (USA) signed a contract with the New York Mets that made him the world's most valuable catcher. He will earn a total salary of $91 million (£56.2 million) over seven years, and has the use of a luxury box for all home games and a hotel suite while on the road.

MOST GAMES PLAYED IN CAREER

Peter Rose (USA) played in a record 3,562 games and had a record 14,053 at bats in a career that spanned two decades, mostly for the Cincinnati Reds.

MOST CONSECUTIVE GAMES PLAYED

Cal Ripken Jr (USA), who made his debut in 1981, featured in 2,632 consecutive Major League games for the Baltimore Orioles from May 30 1982 to September 19 1998.

MOST BASE HITS IN A SEASON

Ohio-born George Harold Sisler (USA) made a record 257 base hits in one Major League season while playing for the St Louis Cardinals in 1920.

MOST HOME RUNS IN A SEASON

The most home runs scored in a season is 73 by Barry Bonds (USA, below) of the San Francisco Giants in 2001. Bonds has also won more Most Valuable Player awards than anyone else in baseball, with four. He won his fourth for his achievements with the Giants in 2001.

MOST HITS IN A ROOKIE SEASON

The most hits by a rookie in a Major League season is 242 by the prodigious Ichiro Suzuki (Japan, above) playing for the Seattle Mariners in 2001. In doing so, Suzuki broke the 90-year record set by "Shoeless" Joe Jackson (USA) for the Cleveland Naps (later the Cleveland Indians) in 1911.

OLDEST WORLD SERIES PLAYER

Jack Quinn was 47 years 91 days when he pitched in the World Series for the Philadelphia Athletics on October 4 1930. Quinn is also the oldest player to hit a home run in the Major League, which he did at 47.

OLDEST PLAYER

Leroy "Satchel" Paige (USA) was 59 years 80 days old when he pitched for Kansas City As in his final match on September 25 1965.

YOUNGEST PLAYER

The youngest Major League player was the Cincinnati Reds pitcher Joseph Nuxhall (USA), who played his first game at 15 years 314 days in June 1944. He did not play again in the National League until 1952.

MOST AT BATS IN A SEASON

Playing for the Kansas City Royals in 1980, Willie Wilson (USA) made a record 705 at bats in one season.

PITCHING PERFECT GAME

A perfect nine-innings game, in which the pitcher allows the opposition no hits, no runs, and no man to reach first base, was first achieved by John Lee Richmond (USA), playing for Worcester against Cleveland in the National League on June 12 1880. There have been 13 subsequent perfect games over nine innings, but no pitcher has achieved this feat more than once.

LARGEST REPLICA BAT

The world's largest replica baseball bat is 120 ft (36.5 m) high and weighs 68,000 lb (30,844 kg). The giant bat was made by Hillerich & Bradsby, in Louisville, Kentucky, USA, and can be found outside the Louisville Slugger Museum.

MOST FREE THROWS IN AN NBA SEASON

Jerry West (USA, above right) scored 840 free throws for the Los Angeles Lakers during the 1965/66 National Basketball Association (NBA) season. Nicknamed "Mr Clutch," a reference to his knack of being able to pull his team through tight matches, West's image is immortalized in the current NBA logo.

BASKETBALL

LONGEST GAME

Members of the Suncoast Clippers played out a 24-hour epic basketball game at Maroochydore Eagles Basketball Stadium, Queensland, Australia, on November 21–22 1998.

TALLEST PLAYER

Suleiman Ali Nashnush (Libya) was reputedly 8 ft 0.25 in (2.45 m) when he played for his country in 1962.

TALLEST NBA PLAYERS

Two men tie for the title of tallest players ever to turn out for a team in the NBA: Gheorghe Muresan (Romania), who currently plays for the Washington Bullets, and

Manute Bol (Sudan), who also played for the Bullets, among other teams. Both players are 7 ft 7 in (2.31 m) tall.

The tallest player to be selected for an NBA team was 7-ft-8-in (2.33-m) Yasutak Okayamo (Japan), who was picked by the Golden State Warriors in 1981 but never played in the NBA.

MOST INDIVIDUAL POINTS IN NBA MATCH

When playing for the Philadelphia 76ers against the New York Knicks on March 2 1962, Wilt "The Stilt" Chamberlain (USA) scored a record 100 points.

LONGEST GOAL THROWN

Christopher Eddy (USA) scored a field goal from a distance of 90 ft 2.25 in (27.49 m) for Fairview High School against Iroquois High School at Erie, Pennsylvania, USA, on February 25 1989. The shot came in overtime and the last-ditch long-range effort won the game for Fairview, 51–50.

OLDEST NBA PLAYER

Robert Parish (USA) was 43 years 231 days old when he played his last game for the Chicago Bulls on April 19 1997.

HIGHEST POINTS AVERAGE IN NBA CAREER

Michael Jordan (USA, below) holds the highest point-scoring average for players who have registered over 10,000 NBA points. His average of 31 came from almost 30,000 points in just under 1,000 games for the Chicago Bulls from 1984 to 1998 and the Washington Wizards in 2001/02.

MOST WINS IN NBA SEASON

The greatest number of wins in an NBA season is 72 by the Chicago Bulls in the 1995/96 season.

MOST POINTS IN NBA SEASON

Wilt Chamberlain (USA) scored 4,029 points for the Philadelphia Warriors in the 1961/62 season.

MOST NBA TITLES

The Boston Celtics have won more NBA Championship titles than any other team. They took the title in 1957, 1959 to 1966, 1968, 1969, 1974, 1976, 1981, 1984, and 1986.

HIGHEST TEAM SCORE IN NBA MATCH

On December 13 1983 the Detroit Pirates beat the Denver Nuggets 186–184 in Denver, Colorado, USA, a record for the highest score ever achieved by a team in an NBA game.

MOST MINUTES PLAYED IN NBA CAREER

Kareem Abdul-Jabbar (USA) was on court for 57,446 minutes in the course of his career. He played for the Milwaukee Bucks from 1969–75 and the Los Angeles Lakers from 1975–89.

MOST CONSECUTIVE FREE THROWS IN NBA SEASON

Between March 24 and November 9 1993 Mike Williams (USA) racked up 97 consecutive free throws for the Minnesota Timberwolves.

MOST NBA PLAY-OFF APPEARANCES

Kareem Abdul-Jabbar (USA), took part in a record-breaking 237 NBA play-off games in his career.

HIGHEST AVERAGE POINTS IN NBA PLAY-OFFS

The highest points-scoring average in play-off games is 33.4 points by Michael Jordan (USA), who scored 5,987 points in 179 games as a member of the Chicago Bulls.

MOST FOULS IN NBA CAREER

Kareem Abdul-Jabbar (USA) notched up 4,657 fouls over 1,560 games between 1969 and 1989.

MOST WINS IN MEN'S WORLD CHAMPIONSHIP

The men's basketball World Championship was instituted in 1950. The most successful nation in the tournament is Yugoslavia with four titles in 1970, 1978, 1990, and 1998.

MOST MEN'S PARALYMPIC TITLES

The USA has won a record five men's Paralympic basketball titles. Their wins came in 1960, 1964, 1972, 1976, and 1988.

MOST WOMEN'S PARALYMPIC TITLES

The greatest number of women's Paralympic basketball titles won by one country is three by Canada in 1992, 1996, and 2000.

MOST FREE THROWS IN 10 MINUTES

On March 6 2001 Jeff Liles (USA) scored 285 free throws out of a total of 326 attempts in 10 minutes at Prairie High School, New Raymer, Colorado, USA.

HIGHEST SCORE IN COLLEGE BASKETBALL

The National Collegiate Athletic Association (NCAA) aggregate record for the highest score in a college basketball match is 399. The record total was reached when Troy State beat De Vry Institute, Atlanta, 258–141 at Troy, Alabama, USA, on January 12 1992. Troy's score represents the highest individual team points total in a match.

YOUNGEST PLAYER TO START AN NBA MATCH

The youngest player to start an NBA game is Kobe Bryant (USA, above right), who was 18 years 158 days old when he played for the Los Angeles Lakers against the Dallas Mavericks on January 28 1997.

MOST BASKETBALLS DRIBBLED BY ONE PERSON

Joseph Odhiambo (USA) dribbled six basketballs simultaneously at his home in Mesa, Arizona, USA, on August 15 2000.

GREATEST NUMBER OF PEOPLE DRIBBLING BASKETBALLS AT ONCE

On March 10 2001, 50 basketball fans set the world record for the most people to dribble basketballs at one time in Nashville, Tennessee, USA. Led by ex-Washington Bullets and Chicago Bulls star Charles Davis (USA), each participant dribbled his basketball constantly for a period of five minutes.

MOST BASKETBALLS SPUN SIMULTANEOUSLY

The greatest number of basketballs spun simultaneously is 28 by Michael Kettman (USA) on May 25 1999 on the set of *Guinness World Records* in London, UK. The balls were Franklin Hardcourt No. 1 regulation basketballs, and Kettman spun them on a specially designed frame for five seconds.

MOST LAY-UPS WHILE JUGGLING THREE BASKETBALLS

Joseph Odhiambo (USA) achieved 38 lay-ups in one minute while juggling three basketballs at Rehoboth Christian High School, Gallup, New Mexico, USA, on June 8 2001.

MOST THREE-POINT SHOTS BY A TEAM IN ONE MATCH

The greatest number of three-point shots made in one game by a team is 32 by the Garrett Falcons Varsity Boys Basketball team, Garrett Academy of Technology, North Charleston, South Carolina, USA, in their game against Bowman Academy on January 2 1998.

MOST POINTS IN NBA CAREER

The most points scored in a career in the NBA is 38,387 (at an average of 24.6 per game) by Kareem Abdul-Jabbar (USA, above center) from 1969 to 1989, first as a member of the Milwaukee Bucks and then with the Los Angeles Lakers.

ICE HOCKEY

HIGHEST SCORE
Australia beat New Zealand 58–0 in a world championship match at Perth, WA, Australia, on March 15 1987.

LONGEST MATCH
A match featuring players from the Labatt's Ice Cats women's team, at Powell River, British Columbia, Canada, on September 29 and 30 2001, lasted for 26 hr 2 min 14 sec.

MOST ASSISTS IN STANLEY CUP GAME
The most assists by a player in a Stanley Cup game is six and is shared by Mikko Leinonen (Finland) for the New York Rangers v. the Philadelphia Flyers on April 8 1982, and by Wayne Gretzky (Canada) for the Edmonton Oilers versus the Los Angeles Kings on April 9 1987.

MOST GOALS IN STANLEY CUP GAME BY ONE PLAYER
Five players have scored five goals in a Stanley Cup game: Newsy Lalonde for Montreal Canadiens v. Ottawa Senators on March 1 1919; Maurice Richard in Montreal Canadiens' 5–1 win over Toronto Maple Leafs on March 23 1944; Darryl Glen Sittler for Toronto Maple Leafs against Philadelphia Flyers (8–5) on April 22 1976; Reggie Leach for Philadelphia Flyers against Boston Bruins (6–3) on May 6 1976 and Mario Lemieux for Pittsburgh Penguins against Philadelphia Flyers (10–7) on April 25 1989. To date, only Canadian players have achieved this feat.

MOST TEAM GOALS IN NHL SEASON
The Edmonton Oilers scored 446 goals in the 1983/84 NHL season. The Oilers also achieved a record 1,182 scoring points in that season.

MOST GOALS BY PLAYER IN NHL MATCH
The greatest number of goals scored by one individual in an NHL game is seven by Joe Malone for the Quebec Bulldogs in their game against the Toronto St Patricks in Quebec City, Canada, on January 31 1920.

MOST GOALS BY PLAYER IN NHL SEASON
The most goals scored in an NHL season is 92 by Wayne Gretzky (Canada) for the Edmonton Oilers in the 1981/82 season.

MOST GOALS BY ROOKIE IN NHL SEASON
Teemu Selanne (Finland) scored a total of 76 goals as a rookie for the Winnipeg Jets in the 1992/93 season.

MOST GOAL ASSISTS BY INDIVIDUAL IN NHL GAME
The record for the greatest number of goal assists by an individual in an NHL game is seven and is shared by two players. Billy Taylor (Canada) achieved this feat for the Detroit Red Wings against Chicago Blackhawks on March 16 1947. Wayne Gretzky (Canada) achieved the same record three times with the Edmonton Oilers:

against the Washington Capitals on February 15 1980, against the Chicago Blackhawks on December 11 1985, and against the Quebec Nordiques on February 14 1986.

MOST SHUT-OUTS IN NHL CAREER
The most goaltending shutouts in an NHL career is 103 by Terry Sawchuk (USA) for Detroit Red Wings, Boston Bruins, Toronto Maple Leafs, Los Angeles Kings, and New York Rangers between 1949 and 1970. Sawchuk also holds the record for the greatest number of appearances by a goaltender – 971.

MOST INDIVIDUAL WINS IN NHL SEASON
The greatest number of individual wins in an NHL season is 47 by Bernie Parent (Canada) for the Philadelphia Flyers in the 1973/74 season.

MOST POINTS IN NHL CAREER
The greatest number of points scored in an NHL career is 2,857 by Wayne Gretzky (Canada), who played for four teams – the Edmonton Oilers, the Los Angeles Kings, the St Louis Blues, and the New York Rangers – between

1979 and 1999. Gretzky's points total comprises 894 goals and 1,963 assists achieved in 1,487 games.

Wayne Gretzky also holds the record for the most points scored in an NHL season – 215 for the Edmonton Oilers in the 1985/86 season. Included in the points total are 163 assists, another record.

In his professional hockey career, Gretzky scored a record 1,072 goals. In addition to his 894 NHL regular season goals and 122 Stanley Cup goals, he scored another 56 times in the World Hockey Association (WHA) in the 1978/79 season.

MOST STANLEY CUPS
The most Stanley Cup wins by a team is 24 by the Montreal Canadiens who won the cup in 1916, 1924, 1930, 1931, 1944, 1946, 1953, 1956 through 1960, 1965 1966, 1968, 1969, 1971, 1973, 1976 to 1979, 1986, and 1993. Their 32 appearances in the final is also a record.

MOST INDIVIDUAL STANLEY CUP WINS
Henri Richard (Canada) achieved a total of 11 Stanley Cup wins with the Montreal Canadiens between 1956 and 1975, the year in which he retired.

MOST WINS IN NHL SEASON
The most wins in an NHL season is 62 by the Detroit Red Wings in the 1995/6 season.

HIGHEST PERCENTAGE OF WINS PER MATCHES
The highest percentage of wins to games in an NHL season is the 87.5% achieved by the Boston Bruins, who amassed a total of 38 wins from 44 games in 1929/30.

MOST WOMEN'S TEAM OLYMPIC GOLD MEDALS
Women's ice hockey was first contested at the 1998 Nagano Olympics in Japan. The winner was the USA (US goalkeeper Sara DeCosta pictured above) who defeated Canada 3–1 in the final.

MOST HAT TRICKS IN NHL CAREER

The greatest number of hat tricks scored in an NHL career is 50, by Wayne Gretzky (Canada, above). Gretzky played for the Edmonton Oilers, the Los Angeles Kings, the St Louis Blues, and the New York Rangers between 1979 and 1999.

FASTEST GOAL

The record time for the quickest goal scored in an NHL match after the opening whistle is five seconds. It is shared by Doug Smail (Canada) for the Winnipeg Jets against St Louis Blues at Winnipeg, Canada, on December 20 1981, Bryan John Trottier (Canada) for the New York Islanders *v.* Boston Bruins at Boston, Massachusetts, USA, on March 22 1984, and Alexander Mogilny (Russia) for the Buffalo Sabres against Toronto Maple Leafs at Toronto, Canada, on December 21 1991.

MOST NHL CAREER WINS BY GOALTENDER

Patrick Roy (Canada), goaltender for the Colorado Avalanche, had logged 516 NHL wins up to the end of

April 2002. The record was set on October 17 2000 in a game against the Washington Capitals.

MOST MATCHES IN CAREER

Gordon "Gordie" Howe (Canada) played professionally in 2,421 games. He achieved his record over 26 seasons between 1946 and 1979.

MOST POINTS BY INDIVIDUAL IN ONE MATCH

The record for the greatest number of points scored by an individual in a professional ice hockey game is 10 and is shared by Jim Harrison (Canada) with three goals and seven assists for Alberta – later the Edmonton Oilers – in a WHA match at Edmonton, Canada, on January 30 1973, and by Darryl Sittler (Canada), who managed six goals and four assists for the Toronto Maple Leafs against the Boston Bruins in an NHL match at Toronto, Canada, on February 7 1976.

MOST MEN'S INDIVIDUAL OLYMPIC GOLD MEDALS

The greatest number of gold medals won by any player is three, achieved by Soviet players Vitaliy Semyenovich Davydov, Anatoliy Vasilyevich Firsov, Viktor Grigoryevich Kuzkin, and Aleksandr Pavlovich Ragulin in 1964, 1968, and 1972, Vladislav Aleksandrovich Tretyak in 1972, 1976 and 1984, and Andrey Khomutov in 1984, 1988 and 1992.

MOST MEN'S TEAM OLYMPIC GOLD MEDALS

Ice hockey was first contested at the Olympic Games in 1920. The most wins is eight by the USSR, in 1956, 1964, 1968, 1972, 1976, 1984, 1988 and 1992. In 1992 the team competed as the CIS, or Commonwealth of Independent States, although all the players were Russian.

LONGEST MEN'S OLYMPIC CAREER

The longest Olympic career is that of Richard Torriani (Switzerland) between 1928 and 1948. He competed in 1928, 1936, and 1948, winning bronze medals in 1928 and 1948.

MOST MEN'S WORLD CHAMPIONSHIP TITLES

The World Championship was first held for amateurs in 1920 in tandem with the Olympic Games, which were also regarded as the World Championship until 1968.

From 1976 the World Championship has been open to professionals. The USSR took 22 world titles from 1954 to 1990 (and won as Russia in 1993), including the Olympic titles of 1956, 1964, and 1968.

MOST WOMEN'S WORLD CHAMPIONSHIP TITLES

The women's World Championship has been held since 1990, and has been won each time by Canada, in 1990, 1992, 1994, 1997, 1999, 2000 and 2001. In winning seven straight titles, Canada have not lost one game.

MOST PENALTY MINUTES

Dave "Tiger" Williams (Canada) amassed 3,966 penalty minutes in 17 seasons from 1971 to 1988. He played for the Toronto Maple Leafs, the Vancouver Canucks, the Detroit Red Wings, the Los Angeles Kings, and the Hartford Whalers.

MOST POINTS BY PLAYER IN STANLEY CUP MATCH

The most points scored by a player in a Stanley Cup game is eight, shared by Patrik Sundström (Sweden), with three goals and five assists in New Jersey Devils' 10–4 win over Washington Capitals on April 22 1988, and Mario Lemieux (Canada, below), with five goals and three assists for Pittsburgh Penguins v Philadelphia Flyers on April 25 1989.

FOOTBALL

MOST EXPENSIVE FOOTBALL PLAYER

The highest reported transfer is the $68 million (£47 million) that took France's Zinedine Zidane (below) from Juventus (Italy) to Real Madrid (Spain) in July 2001. Manchester United (UK) paid Lazio (Italy) a UK record £24.7 million ($34.6 million) for midfielder Juan Sebastian Veron (Argentina) in the same month.

MOST WORLD CUPS

The World Cup was initiated by the Fédération Internationale de Football Association (FIFA) and held for the first time in July 1930. It is contested every four years and Brazil has won the most tournaments, lifting the trophy four times – in 1958, 1962, 1970, and 1994.

A women's competition has been held every four years since 1991. The USA won in 1991 and 1999, and Norway was the winner in 1995.

YOUNGEST AND OLDEST PLAYER IN WORLD CUP

Norman Whiteside (UK) played for Northern Ireland against Yugoslavia on June 17 1982 when he was 17 years 41 days.

Roger Milla (Cameroon) played and scored for Cameroon against Russia on June 28 1994, at a given age of 42 years 39 days, although some records suggest he was even older.

MOST WORLD CUP APPEARANCES

Antonio Carbajal (Mexico) appeared in five World Cup finals tournaments, keeping goal for Mexico in every competition between 1950 and 1966. He played 11 games in all.

This was equalled by Lothar Matthäus (Germany) who played in 1982, 1986, 1990, 1994, and 1998 taking part in a record 25 games.

YOUNGEST WORLD CUP SCORER

Edson Arantes do Nascimento (Brazil), better known as Pelé, was 17 years 239 days when he scored for Brazil against Wales on June 19 1958 in Gothenburg, Sweden.

FASTEST WORLD CUP GOAL

The quickest goal scored in a World Cup finals match came 15 seconds after kick-off from Vaclav Masek of Czechoslovakia (now Czech Republic) against Mexico in Veña del Mar, Chile, on June 7 1962.

In qualification matches, Davide Gualtieri of San Marino scored after just seven seconds against England in Bologna, Italy, on November 17 1993.

HIGHEST INTERNATIONAL SCORE

The highest score in an international match is Australia's 31–0 defeat of American Samoa in a World Cup qualifier at Coffs Harbour, NSW, Australia, on April 11 2001. Striker Archie Thompson's 13 goals for Australia in the game is also an international scoring record.

MOST EUROPEAN CHAMPIONSHIPS

The European Championship, which was first held in 1960 and takes place every four years, has been won a record three times by Germany – in 1972, 1980, and 1996 (on the first two occasions as West Germany).

A women's tournament was inaugurated in 1984 and has been won four times by Germany – in 1989, 1991, 1995, and 1997.

MOST MEN'S OLYMPIC TITLES

Great Britain has won a record three Olympic titles – in 1900 (an unofficial competition), 1908, and 1912. Hungary has also won the competition three times – in 1952, 1964, and 1968.

MOST COPA AMERICAS

The Copa América, the South American national championship, has been won 15 times by Argentina between 1910 and 1993.

MOST CONCACAF CHAMPIONSHIPS

Costa Rica have won the CONCACAF (Confederation Of North, Central And Caribbean Association Football) Championship (now Gold Cup) on 10 occasions between 1941 and 1989.

MOST ASIAN CUPS

Iran in 1968, 1972, and 1976 and Saudi Arabia in 1984, 1988, and 1997 have both won three Asian Cups.

MOST INTERNATIONAL CAPS

The most international appearances is 160 by Hossam Hassan (Egypt) from 1985 to March 2002.

The women's record for international appearances is 225 by Kristine Lilly (USA) between 1987 and 2000.

MOST GOALS SCORED BY A GOALKEEPER

Paraguayan goalkeeper José Luis Chilavert (above) scored a hat trick of penalties for Vélez Sarsfield in their 6–1 defeat of Ferro Carril Oeste in the Argentine league.

Chilavert scored a record 54 league and international goals between July 1992 and October 2000, largely from penalties and free kicks. He is the only keeper to have scored in a World Cup qualifying game (against Argentina in 1997).

MOST APPEARANCES

Goalkeeper Peter Shilton (UK) made 1,389 appearances, including a record 1,005 League appearances – 286 for Leicester City (1966–74); 110 for Stoke City (1974–77); 202 for Nottingham Forest (1977–82); 188 for Southampton (1982–87); 175 for Derby County (1987–92); 34 for Plymouth Argyle (1992–94); one for Bolton Wanderers (1995) and nine for Leyton Orient (1996–97); 125 internationals; 13 under-23 internationals; 86 FA Cup; 102 League Cup; one League play-off; four Football League XI, and 53 other European and club competitions.

MOST CONSECUTIVE PREMIERSHIP MATCHES SCORED IN

Ruud Van Nistelrooy (Netherlands) scored in eight consecutive English Premiership matches for Manchester United (UK) during the 2001/2002 season. In doing so, he bettered the efforts of Mark Stein (UK), Thierry Henry (France), and Alan Shearer (UK), who had all managed seven.

MOST GOALS IN ONE SEASON

William "Dixie" Dean (UK) scored 60 goals in 39 matches for Everton in 1927/28. With three more in cup ties and 19 in representative matches, Dean's total was 82.

The Scottish League record is 66 in 38 games by James Smith (UK) of Ayr United, also in 1927/28.

YOUNGEST HAT TRICK SCORER IN BRITISH FOOTBALL

The youngest scorer of three goals in a single game in British football is Trevor Francis (UK), who was 16 years 307 days old when he scored four goals in the old Second Division for Birmingham City against Bolton Wanderers on February 20 1971.

The youngest hat trick scorer in England's top division is Alan Shearer (UK), who was 17 years 240 days old when he scored three goals for Southampton against Arsenal on April 9 1988.

Since the formation of the English Premiership in 1992, the youngest hat trick scorer is the Liverpool and England striker Michael Owen (UK), who was 18 years 62 days old when he netted three times while playing for Liverpool against Sheffield Wednesday on February 14 1998.

Ian Dickson (UK) was 18 years 215 days old when he scored the youngest hat trick in the Scottish League. Remarkably, it came on Dickson's debut for Montrose against Third Lanark on October 22 1966.

MOST CONSECUTIVE HAT TRICKS

Masashi Nakayama (Japan) scored hat tricks in four successive matches when playing for Jubilo Iwata in the J-League. His scoring spree began with five goals against Cerezo Osaka on April 15 1998 and ended with a hat trick against Consadole Sapporo on April 29 1998. In total, he scored 16 goals in the four games.

HIGHEST WOMEN'S SCORE

The highest score in a women's match is Willenhall Town Ladies 57–0 victory over Burton Brewers Ladies at Willenhall, West Midlands, UK, on March 4 2001.

MOST SEASON TICKETS SOLD

Every year Spanish club Barcelona sell around 98,000 season tickets (the total capacity) for their home ground, the Nou Camp, making it the football stadium with the greatest number of season-ticket holders.

HIGHEST ATTENDANCE

The greatest recorded crowd at any match was 199,854 at the Brazil v. Uruguay World Cup match in the Maracanã Municipal Stadium, Rio de Janeiro, Brazil, on July 16 1950.

The official British record is 149,547 at the Scotland-England international at Hampden Park, Glasgow, Strathclyde, UK, on April 17 1937.

The Scottish Cup final at Hampden in 1937 attracted a non-international official record 146,433, but the UK's largest estimated attendance was at the FA Cup final between West Ham United and Bolton Wanderers at Wembley Stadium in London, UK, on April 28 1923, where there were serious congestion problems. Thousands gatecrashed and although official admissions were 126,047, it is estimated that as many as 160,000 to 200,000 people were at the game.

MOST PITCHES

The National Sports Center in Blaines, Minnesota, USA, has 57 pitches – 55 of which can be used at any one time – making it the largest such soccer complex in the world.

MOST FEDERATIONS IN WORLD CUP QUALIFIERS

A record 198 federations registered to play the FIFA qualifiers for the 2002 World Cup, which was played in South Korea and Japan. Supporting the fun were the tournament's trio of mascots, Nic, Ato, and Kaz (above, from left).

MOST PENALTIES MISSED IN A SOCCER INTERNATIONAL

Martín Palermo (above) has the unfortunate record of missing three penalties in one international, while playing for Argentina against Colombia in the 1999 Copa América held in Paraguay. Palermo first hit the bar, put the second into the crowd, and the third was saved. Not surprisingly, Argentina lost.

MOST EUROPEAN CUPS

Spanish club Real Madrid have won a record nine European Cups. The tournament, now known as the Champions League and considered to be the most prestigious in European football, was first held in 1956. Real Madrid won the first five between 1956 and 1960 and also won the cup in 1966, 1998, 2000, and 2002.

MOST EUROPEAN CUP-WINNERS CUPS

Until it was disbanded in 1999, the European Cup-Winners Cup was contested annually by the winners of Europe's national cups. The trophy was won a record four times by Spain's Barcelona in 1979, 1982, 1989, and 1997.

MOST SUCCESSIVE NATIONAL LEAGUE TITLES

The record number of successive national league championships is 11 by the Al-Ansar Sporting Club of Lebanon between 1988 and 1999.

MOST FA CUP MEDALS

Three players have won five FA Cup winners' medals – James Henry Forrest (UK) with Blackburn Rovers in 1884, 1885, 1886, 1890, and 1891; the Hon Sir Arthur Fitzgerald Kinnaird (UK) with the Wanderers in 1873, 1877, and 1878 and Old Etonians in 1879 and 1882; and Charles Harold Wollaston (UK) with the Wanderers in 1872, 1873, 1876, 1877, and 1878.

The most Scottish FA Cup winners' medals won is eight by Charles Campbell (UK) for Queen's Park in 1874, 1875, 1876, 1880, 1881, 1882, 1884, and 1886.

LONGEST BRITISH UNBEATEN RUN

Nottingham Forest went undefeated for 42 consecutive English First Division matches from November 20 1977 to December 9 1978.

In Scotland, Celtic went undefeated for 62 successive matches from November 13 1915 to April 21 1917.

HIGHEST SCORE IN A NATIONAL CUP FINAL

In 1935 Lausanne-Sports beat Nordstern Basel 10–0 in the Swiss Cup Final and two years later suffered defeat by the same margin at the hands of Grasshopper of Zurich.

BIGGEST TOURNAMENT

The second Bangkok League Seven-a-side Competition, which was held from January 9 to April 25 1999, was contested by 5,098 teams (35,686 players), a world record for a football competition.

LONGEST GOALKEEPING CLEAN SHEET

The longest time that a keeper has succeeded in preventing a goal from being scored past him in first-class competition is 1,275 minutes (just over 14 matches) by Abel Resino (Spain) for Atlético Madrid in 1991.

The record in international matches is 1,142 minutes (nearly 13 matches) by Dino Zoff (Italy) from September 1972 to June 1974.

The British record is 1,196 minutes by Chris Woods (UK), playing for Glasgow Rangers from November 26 1986 to January 31 1987.

MOST VALUABLE MEDAL

A record £124,750 ($177,280) was paid for England goalkeeper Gordon Banks's (UK) 1966 World Cup winner's medal at Christie's, London, UK, on March 23 2001.

MOST LUCRATIVE SHIRT SPONSORSHIP

In 2000 American sportswear giant Nike agreed to pay Manchester United, who play in the English Premiership, a record $431.9 million (£302.9 million) to become the club's official shirt supplier.

MOST EXPENSIVE GOALKEEPER

In July 2001 Gianluigi Buffon (Italy) moved from Serie A club Parma to Juventus for a reported transfer fee of $46.8 million (£32.6 million).

HEAVIEST GOALKEEPER

England international Willie "Fatty" Foulke (UK) stood 6 ft 3 in (1.90 m) and weighed 311 lb (141 kg). His final games in the early 1900s were for Bradford City, by which time he had ballooned to 364 lb (165 kg). Foulke once halted a game by snapping the crossbar.

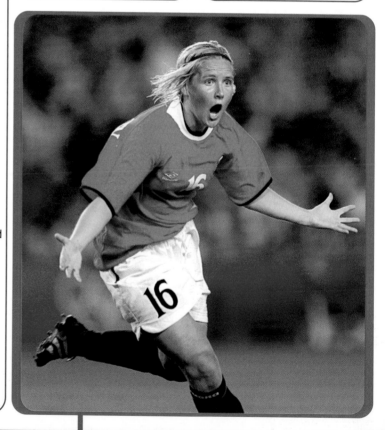

MOST WOMEN'S SOCCER OLYMPIC TITLES

Women's football was introduced to the Olympic Games in 1996. The winner in 1996 was the USA, while in Sydney in 2000 Norway (goalscorer Ragnhild Gulbrandsen pictured above) beat the USA 3–2 in the final to claim the title.

MOST PREMIERSHIP GOALS

The most goals scored in the English Premiership is 204 by Alan Shearer (UK, below). Shearer began his goal-scoring career with Southampton, before moving to Blackburn Rovers and then to Newcastle United in July 1996, for a then British record transfer fee of £15.6 million ($22.4 million). Shearer, an England captain, was also top scorer in the 1996 European Championship.

GREATEST DISTANCE TRAVELED BY TEAMS

The greatest distance traveled between two clubs in the top division of a national league is 2,979 miles (4,766 km). The journey is between the home grounds of LA Galaxy and New England, based on the West and East coasts of the United States respectively, in the US Major League.

EARLIEST COMPETITION

The oldest trophy is the Youdan Cup, won in 1867 by Hallam FC in Sheffield, South Yorkshire, UK. The trophy was sponsored by local enthusiast Thomas Youdan (UK), and was contested on only one occasion.

MOST UNDISCIPLINED MATCH

In the local cup match between Tongham Youth Club, Surrey, UK and Hawley, Hampshire, UK, on November 3 1969 the referee booked all 22 players, including one who went to hospital and one of the linesmen. The match, which was won by Tongham 2–0, was described by a participating player as a "good hard game."

All 11 players and two substitutes of Glencraig United from Faifley, near Clydebank, UK, were booked in the dressing room before a 2–2 draw with Goldenhill Boys' Club on February 2 1975. The official, who had refereed Glencraig before, took offense to a crude chant that greeted his arrival and decided to take appropriate action.

MOST AFRICAN CUP OF NATIONS TITLES

Three countries have won the title on four occasions – Ghana in 1963, 1965, 1978, and 1982; Egypt in 1957, 1959, 1986, and 1998 and Cameroon (Salomon Olembe pictured above, center) in 1984, 1988, 2000, and 2002.

LONGEST PENALTY SHOOT-OUT

In a West Riding Amateur League Cup tie between Littletown FC and Storthes Hall at Heckmondwike, W Yorkshire, UK, on December 29 2001, a total of 34 penalties were taken when the match ended 1–1 after extra time. All 34 penalties were scored – 17 apiece – until the match was abandoned due to the failing light.

LONGEST TIME SPINNING A FOOTBALL ON ONE FINGER

Raphael Harris (Israel) spun a regulation-size football continuously on one finger for 4 min 21 sec on October 27 2000 in Jerusalem, Israel.

FARTHEST DISTANCE TRAVELED WHILE CONTROLLING A BALL

Jan Skorkovsky (Czech Republic) juggled a football for 26.219 miles (42.195 km) while completing the Prague Marathon in a time of 7 hr 18 min 55 sec on July 8 1990.

OLDEST PLAYER

The oldest English League player was Neil McBain (UK), who played for New Brighton at 51 years 120 days in a Third Division North match against Hartlepool on March 15 1947. McBain played as goalkeeper because of injuries to other players.

LONGEST WOMEN'S CONTROL OF A FOOTBALL

Cláudia Martini (Brazil) juggled a ball for 7 hr 5 min 25 sec using her feet, legs, and head at Caxias do Sul, Brazil, on July 12 1996.

LONGEST CONTROL OF A FOOTBALL WITH HEAD

Goderdzi Makharadze (Georgia) kept a football aloft with his head for 8 hr 12 min 25 sec in a record display of control at the Boris Paichadze National Stadium, Tbilisi, Georgia, on May 26 1996.

HIGHEST BEACH VOLLEYBALL CAREER EARNINGS

Karch Kiraly (USA, above) won a record $2,841,065 (£1,995,770) in official Association of Volleyball Professionals (AVP) Tour earnings up to the end of the 1999 season. His 141 AVP Tour titles in his career is also a record.

VOLLEYBALL

MOST MEN'S TEAM OLYMPIC TITLES

The USSR won three men's Olympic titles – in 1964, 1968, and 1980. The men's team failed to win a medal only once, in 1992, when they entered as the Commonwealth of Independent States (CIS).

MOST WOMEN'S TEAM OLYMPIC TITLES

The USSR won four women's team titles in Olympic volleyball – in 1968, 1972, 1980, and 1988.

MOST MEN'S OLYMPIC MEDALS

Three players have three Olympic medals – Yuriy Poyarkov (USSR) won gold medals in 1964 and 1968 and a bronze in 1972; Katsutoshi Nekoda (Japan) won gold in 1972, silver in 1968 and bronze in 1964, and Steve Timmons (USA) won gold in 1984 and 1988 and bronze in 1992.

LARGEST AMOUNT OF PRIZE MONEY WORLD CHAMPIONSHIP

In 1998, $2.2 million (£1.6 million) was awarded in prize money, which at the time was a record in the world championships of any team sport. A total of $1 million (£710,000) for individuals and $1.2 million (£850,000) for teams was at stake.

MOST MEN'S WORLD CHAMPIONSHIP TITLES

The first men's World Championship was held in Prague, Czechoslovakia (now Czech Republic), in 1949 and was won by the USSR, which has taken five more titles since – in 1952, 1960, 1962, 1978, and 1982.

MOST WOMEN'S WORLD CHAMPIONSHIP TITLES

The USSR have dominated the women's World Championship, winning the title on five occasions – in 1952 (the year the women's tournament was introduced), 1956, 1960, 1970, and 1990.

NETBALL

MOST WORLD CHAMPIONSHIP TITLES

Australia has won the Netball World Championship (instituted in 1963) eight times – in 1963, 1971, 1975, 1979, 1983, 1991, 1995, and 1999.

LONGEST MATCH

Members of Sasol Netball Club, Evander, South Africa, played a game of netball for 50 hours from March 30 to April 1 2001.

HIGHEST SCORE IN WORLD CHAMPIONSHIP MATCH

On July 9 1991 the Cook Islands defeated Vanuatu 120–38 during the Netball World Championship at Sydney, NSW, Australia.

ROLLER HOCKEY

MOST WORLD CHAMPIONSHIP TITLES

England won the first roller hockey World Championship and took all the titles from 1936 to 1939. Since then, Portugal has won the most titles, with 14 between 1947 and 1993. Portugal remains the world leader in this sport today, having joined the Fédération Internationale de Patinage à Roulettes (FIPR) in 1946.

KORFBALL

LARGEST TOURNAMENT

Invented by Nico Broekhuysen, a Dutch teacher, korfball was first played in the Netherlands in 1901. Similar to netball and basketball (*korf* is Dutch for "basket"), the sport can be played by mixed-sex teams.

On June 12 1999, 1,796 competitors played in the Kom Keukens/Ten Donck international youth korfball tournament in Ridderkerk, The Netherlands.

HIGHEST TEAM SCORE IN WORLD CHAMPIONSHIP FINAL

The highest team score in the final of the World Championship is The Netherlands' 23–11 defeat of Belgium in 1999, in Adelaide, SA, Australia. The margin of victory, 12, is also the greatest ever attained in the final.

MOST POINTS AT NETBALL WORLD CHAMPIONSHIPS

The most points scored by one player at the Netball World Championship is 543 by Irene van Dyk (South Africa, above) in 1995. Van Dyk is pictured in a New Zealand shirt, who she played for after leaving South Africa in 2000.

LACROSSE

HIGHEST MEN'S INTERNATIONAL SCORE
The highest score ever achieved in a World Cup match is Scotland's 34–3 win over Germany in Manchester, UK, on July 25 1994.

In the World Cup Premier Division, the record score is the USA's 33–2 win over Japan, also in Manchester, UK, on July 21 1994.

HIGHEST WOMEN'S INTERNATIONAL SCORE
Great Britain and Ireland defeated Long Island 40–0 during their 1967 tour of the USA.

MOST MEN'S WORLD CHAMPIONSHIP TITLES
The USA has won seven of the eight World Lacrosse Championships – in 1967, 1974, 1982, 1986, 1990, 1994, and 1998. After what was the first drawn international match, Canada won the world title in 1978, beating the USA 17–16 in overtime.

MOST WOMEN'S WORLD CHAMPIONSHIP TITLES
The first Lacrosse World Cup was held in 1982, replacing the World Championship, which had been held three times since 1969. Including both competitions, the USA won six times, in 1974, 1982, 1989, 1993, 1997, and 2001.

MOST WOMEN'S INTERNATIONAL APPEARANCES
Vivien Jones (UK) played in a record 97 international matches – 85 games for Wales, nine for the Celts, and three for Great Britain – from 1977 to 2001. Her club career was with Putney and St Mary's College.

HOCKEY

FASTEST INTERNATIONAL GOAL
John French (UK) scored seven seconds after the face-off for England against West Germany at Nottingham, UK, on April 25 1971.

MOST INTERNATIONAL GOALS
Paul Litjens (Netherlands) scored 267 goals in 177 international games.

HIGHEST SCORE IN MEN'S INTERNATIONAL
The record international score is India's 24–1 defeat of USA in Los Angeles, California, USA, in 1932.

HIGHEST SCORE IN WOMEN'S INTERNATIONAL
The highest score in a women's international match occurred when England beat France 23–0 in Merton, London, UK, on February 3 1923.

MOST MEN'S WORLD CUP TITLES
Pakistan has won the Fédération Internationale de Hockey (FIH) World Cup four times, in 1971, 1978, 1982, and 1994. The men's cup was inaugurated in 1971.

MOST WOMEN'S WORLD CUP TITLES
The Netherlands has won the FIH World Cup five times, in 1974, 1978, 1983, 1986, and 1990. The women's cup was first held in 1974.

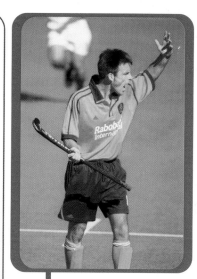

MOST MEN'S INTERNATIONAL HOCKEY APPEARANCES
By January 2001 Jacques Brinkman (above) had represented The Netherlands 337 times since his international debut in 1985.

LARGEST ATTENDANCE
A record number of 65,165 spectators watched England play the United States in an international fixture held at Wembley Stadium, London, UK, on March 11 1978.

MOST WOMEN'S OLYMPIC TITLES
A women's hockey tournament was added to the Moscow Olympics in 1980. Australia has won Olympic hockey titles in 1988 and 1996.

MOST HOCKEY OLYMPICS UMPIRED
Graham Dennis Nash (UK) umpired in five successive Olympic Games from 1976 to 1992 and officiated 144 international hockey games.

GAELIC FOOTBALL

MOST ALL-IRELAND CHAMPIONSHIP TITLES
The greatest number of All-Ireland Championships won by one team is 31 by Kerry between 1903 and 1997. The greatest number of successive wins is four by Wexford (1915–18).

HIGHEST ATTENDANCE
The Down v. Offaly final at Croke Park, Dublin, Ireland, in 1961 was watched by a record crowd of 90,556.

HURLING

MOST ALL-IRELAND CHAMPIONSHIP TITLES
The most All-Ireland Championships won by one team is 28 by Cork between 1890 and 1999.

HIGHEST ATTENDANCE
In 1954, 84,865 spectators attended the All-Ireland Final between Cork and Wexford at Croke Park, Dublin, Ireland.

LOWEST ALL-IRELAND FINAL SCORE
The lowest score in an All-Ireland Final was in the first championship at Birr, Ireland, in 1887, when Tipperary (1 goal, 1 point) beat Galway (0).

HANDBALL

HIGHEST INTERNATIONAL SCORE
The highest international score was USSR's 86-2 defeat of Afghanistan in the Friendly Army Tournament at Miskolc, Hungary, in August 1981.

MOST MEN'S WORLD CHAMPIONSHIP TITLES
For the dominant indoor version of the game, the most men's titles is four by Romania in 1961, 1964, 1970, and 1974, and Sweden in 1954, 1958, 1990, and 1999. However, West Germany won the outdoor title five times between 1938 and 1966, and have won the indoor title twice, in 1938 and 1978.

MOST WOMEN'S WORLD CHAMPIONSHIP TITLES
Three women's titles have been won by Romania in 1956, 1960 (both outdoor), and 1962 (indoor); West Germany in 1971, 1975, and 1978 (all outdoor), and the USSR in 1982, 1986, and 1990 (all outdoor).

CROQUET

MOST HOOPS SCORED IN 24 HOURS
The most hoops scored in 24 hours is 819 in the 24-hour challenge match between Orange City and Bathurst City Croquet Clubs at Orange, NSW, Australia, on January 26 and 27 2001. Orange won by 413 hoops to 406.

JAI-ALAI

FASTEST SPORT
The fastest speed a projectile moves in any ball game is around 188 mph (302 km/h) in jai-alai, a sport that originates from the Basque areas of Spain and France. The jai-alai ball is three-quarters the size of a baseball and harder than a golf ball. The speed at which it is hurled compares to the electronically measured 170 mph (273 km/h) of a golf drive.

SHINTY

MOST CHALLENGE CUPS
Newtonmore, Highland, UK, has won the Camanachd Association Challenge Cup (instituted in 1896) a record 28 times between 1907 and 1986. Shinty, a game similar to Ireland's hurling, is a sport that is played almost exclusively in Scotland.

FOOTBAG

MOST PARTICIPANTS
A record 946 people formed one circle of footbag or hacky sack – a small, soft ball or beanbag that is juggled in the air by foot – at the Cornerstone Festival, Bushnell, Illinois, USA, on July 6 2001.

BEST MEN'S CONTROL
The record for keeping a footbag airborne is 63,326 consecutive kicks in 8 hr 50 min 42 sec by Ted Martin (USA). Martin set this record at Lions Park, Mount Prospect, Illinois, USA, on June 14 1997.

BEST WOMEN'S CONTROL
The women's record for keeping a footbag in the air is 24,713 kicks in 4 hr 9 min 27 sec, achieved by Constance Constable (USA). She set the record in a display at the California Athletic Club, Monterey, California, USA, on April 18 1998.

TENPIN BOWLING

MOST WOMEN'S PROFESSIONAL BOWLING TITLES
As of December 31 1999 Shinobu Saito (Japan) holds a record 67 professional bowling titles.

MOST TITLES
Earl Roderick Anthony (USA) won a career record 41 PBA titles and was the first player to earn $1 million (£600,000) in tenpin bowling.

MOST WORLD CUP TITLES
Paeng Nepomuceno (Philippines) has won the annual World Cup four times – in 1976, 1980, 1992, and 1996. He won his first world title at 19 years old, also a record.

HIGHEST SCORE OVER 24 HOURS
A team of six tenpin bowlers scored 251,630 at Eastways Lanes, Erie, Pennsylvania, USA on July 25–26 1997. During this attempt a member of the team, Cory Bithell (USA), set an individual record of 59,702.

LONGEST BOWLING SESSION
The longest tenpin bowling session is 37 hr 8 min by Steve Taylor (UK) at the Sutton Superbowl, London, UK, on September 17–19 2001.

HIGHEST HURLING ALL-IRELAND FINAL SCORE
In 1989 Tipperary beat Antrim 41 (4 goals, 29 points) to 18 (3 goals, 9 points) to win the final (above). The aggregate record was when Cork 39 (6 goals, 21 points) defeated Wexford 25 (5 goals, 10 points) in the 1970 final.

LONGEST BOWLS MARATHON

Six members of Durie Hill Bowling Club, Wanganui, New Zealand (above), played outdoor bowls for a record 40 hr 8 min from April 13 to 14 2001. The attempt was hampered by torrential rain, but a pump kept the surface playable.

BOWLS

MOST OUTDOOR TEAM WORLD CHAMPIONSHIP TITLES

Instituted in 1966, the Leonard Trophy has been won four times by Scotland in 1972, 1984, 1992, and 1996.

MOST CONSECUTIVE CHAMPIONSHIPS

The Herrington Workmen's Flat Green Bowling Club of the Sunderland and District Bowling Association, Co Durham, UK, won the Swan Cup 25 times in a row from 1967 to 1991.

MOST OUTDOOR INDIVIDUAL WORLD CHAMPIONSHIP TITLES

David Bryant (UK) won a record three singles titles in 1966, 1980, and 1988. With the triples in 1980, and the Leonard Trophy in 1980 and 1988, he won a total of six World Championship gold medals. Bryant also won the English indoor singles a record nine times between 1964 and 1983, and claimed five gold medals in the Commonwealth Games between 1962 and 1978.

HIGHEST OUTDOOR SCORE

The highest score in a fours match of 21 ends – played by teams of four – is Sorrento Bowling Club's 67-5 win over Sportsmans at Duncraig, WA, Australia, on March 14 1998.

HIGHEST OUTDOOR INTERNATIONAL SCORE

During the World Championships at Melbourne, Victoria, Australia, on January 16 1980, Swaziland beat Japan by a record 63-1. The World Championships were first held in 1966 in Sydney, NSW, Australia.

HIGHEST INDOOR SCORE

The highest total in fours is 64-0 by Durbanville against George Lee Park during the 1997 South African Women's Bowling Association National Championships in Cape Town, South Africa, on March 10 1997.

OLDEST LAWN GREEN PLAYER

Ron Buchan (New Zealand, b. 1907), began playing lawn green bowls in 1926. He was national singles champion in 1964 and 1965, and fours champion in 1957.

AFL

MOST CAREER GOALS

The most goals scored in an Australian Football League (AFL) career is 1,357 by Tony Lockett (Australia) from 1983 to 1999.

HIGHEST TEAM SCORE

The highest Australian Football League (AFL) score by one team is 239 (37-17) by Geelong against Brisbane on May 3 1992. Australian Rules Football dates back to 1858. The earliest games featured 40 players on each side and goalposts that were 1 mile (1.6 km) apart.

MOST MATCHES

Michael Tuck (Australia) played 426 AFL matches between 1972 and 1991. He was only the second league player to reach the 400-game milestone before retiring in 1991.

MOST AFL TITLES

Australia has three major football leagues – the Australian Football League, the South Australian National Football League, and the Western Australian Football League. The AFL is the biggest and has been won by the Carlton Blues (Justin Murphy pictured below) a record 16 times between 1906 and 1995.

WOMEN'S POLE VAULT

Stacy Dragila (USA, below) holds the record for the women's pole vault after she cleared 15 ft 9 in (4.81 m) at a meet in Palo Alto, California, USA, on June 9 2001. California-born Dragila started her pole-vaulting career in 1993. Her nickname, "The Goat Roper," derives from the rodeo goat-tying competitions she took part in when she was growing up.

MOST WORLD RECORDS IN ONE DAY

Jesse Owens (USA) set six world records in 45 minutes at Ann Arbor, Michigan, USA, on May 25 1935 with a 9.4-sec 100-yd race at 3:15 pm; a 26-ft 8.25-in (8.13-m) long jump at 3:25 pm; a 20.3-sec 220-yd race (which also included a record for the 200 m) at 3:45 pm; and a 22.6-sec 220-yd low hurdles (which included the 200-m hurdles record) at 4 pm. Owens's four gold medals at the 1936 "Hitler Olympics" in Berlin, Germany, are a legendary moment in sport, as the success of the African-American athlete visibly annoyed Germany's Nazi leader Adolf Hitler, who believed in white supremacy and had hoped the Games would be dominated by white or Aryan athletes.

OLDEST TRACK AND FIELD RECORD HOLDER

Gerhard Weidner (West Germany) set a 20-mile walk record on May 25 1974 when he was 41 years 71 days old. This makes him the oldest person to set an official world record in an event open to all ages and recognized by an international governing sporting body.

The women's record is held by Marina Styepanova (USSR), who was 36 years 139 days old when she completed the 400-m hurdles in a time of 52.94 sec at Tashkent, Uzbekistan, on September 17 1986.

YOUNGEST TRACK AND FIELD RECORD HOLDER

The youngest man to set an official world record is Thomas Ray (UK), at 17 years 198 days, when he pole-vaulted a height of 11 ft 2.75 in (3.42 m) on September 19 1879.

Wang Yan (China) set a women's 5,000-m walk record at the age of 14 years 334 days with a time of 21 min 33.8 sec at Jian, China, on March 9 1986, making her the youngest woman to hold a record in an individual event.

MOST SUCCESSIVE WINS IN ONE WORLD CHAMPIONSHIPS EVENT

The International Association of Athletics Federations (IAAF) World Championships have been held biennially since 1983 and come second only to the Olympic Games.

From the inaugural games until 1997, Ukrainian pole-vaulter Sergei Bubka was dominant in his event, winning it seven times in a row.

The greatest dominance on the track is shared by Michael Johnson (USA) in the 400 m and Haile Gebrselassie (Ethiopia) at 10,000 m. Both won their events at four consecutive championships from 1993–99.

Astrid Kumbernuss (Germany) holds the women's record, with three wins in a row in the shot from 1995–99.

MOST WORLD CHAMPIONSHIPS GOLD MEDALS

Michael Johnson (USA) has won nine World Championships gold medals in his career: in the 200 m of 1991 and 1995, the 400 m in 1993, 1995, 1997, and 1999, and in the 4 x 400-m relay in 1993, 1995, and 1999.

The women's record is five medals, held by Gail Devers (USA). Her wins were in the 100 m of 1993, the 100-m hurdles in 1993, 1995, 1999 and the 4 x 100-m relay in 1997.

MEN'S 5,000 M, 10,000 M AND INDOOR 5,000 M

Distance runner Haile Gebrselassie (Ethiopia, above) is the first man to hold world records in both 5,000 m and 10,000 m since 1978 and set his indoor world record for 5,000 m within one week of running his first indoor race.

WOMEN'S 1,000 M

Mozambique's Maria Mutola (above) holds the 1,000-m record with a run of 2:30.94 in Stockholm, Sweden, on February 25 1999. Between 1992 and 1995 Mutola had a remarkable run of winning all of the 42 races she entered.

MOST WORLD CHAMPIONSHIPS MEDALS

Merlene Ottey (Jamaica) has won a staggering 14 medals in the IAAF World Championships, which is more than any other athlete has achieved. The sprinter claimed three gold, four silver, and seven bronze medals between 1983 and 1997.

The most medals won by a man is 10 by the formidable Carl Lewis (USA). He won eight golds – 100 m, long jump and 4 x 100-m relay in 1983; 100 m, long jump and 4 x 100-m relay in 1987; 100 m and 4 x 100-m relay in 1991 – a silver in the 1981 long jump, and a bronze in the 200 m in 1993. Lewis also won nine Olympic gold medals in his career, including four at the 1984 Games in Los Angeles, USA, thus emulating his hero, the American athlete Jesse Owens.

MOST MEDALS IN WORLD INDOOR CHAMPIONSHIPS

The most medals won at the World Indoor Championships in individual events is six by Merlene Ottey (Jamaica). The sprinter claimed three gold medals (60 m in 1995; 200 m in 1989 and 1991), two silver medals (60 m in 1991 and 200 m in 1987), and one bronze medal (60 m in 1989).

The men's record is five medals by Ivan Pedroso (Cuba) in the long jump, who took golds in 1993, 1995, 1997, 1999, and 2001, and Javier Sotomayor (Cuba) in the high jump, who took gold in 1989, 1993, 1995, and 1999 and bronze in 1991.

LONGEST TRACK AND FIELD WINNING SEQUENCES

Iolanda Balas (Romania) won a record 150 successive competitions at the high jump from 1956 to 1967.

The record for a track event is held by Ed Moses (USA), who won 122 400-m hurdles races in a row from August 16 1977 to June 4 1987. His domination of the event was so complete that at one time he held the 13 fastest times ever recorded.

WOMEN'S OUTDOOR WORLD RECORDS

100 m 10.49
Florence Griffith-Joyner (USA)
Indianapolis, Indiana, USA
July 16 1998
200 m 21.34
Florence Griffith-Joyner (USA)
Seoul, South Korea
September 29 1988
400 m 47.60
Marita Koch (East Germany)
Canberra, ACT, Australia
October 6 1985
800 m 1:53.28
Jarmila Kratochvílová (Czechoslovakia)
Munich, Germany
July 26 1983

1,000 m 2:28.98
Svetlana Masterkova (Russia)
Brussels, Belgium
August 23 1996
1,500 m 3:50.46
Qu Yunxia (China)
Beijing, China
September 11 1993
1 mile 4:12.56
Svetlana Masterkova (Russia)
Zurich, Switzerland
August 14 1996
2,000 m 5:25.36
Sonia O'Sullivan (Ireland)
Edinburgh, Lothian, UK
July 8 1994
3,000 m 8:06.11
Wang Junxia (China)
Beijing, China
September 13 1993
5,000 m 14:28.09
Jiang Bo (China)
Beijing, China
October 23 1997
10,000 m 29:31.78
Wang Junxia (China)
Beijing, China
September 8 1993
20,000 m 1:05:26.6
Tegla Loroupe (Kenya)
Borgholtzhausen, Germany
September 3 2000
25,000 m 1:29:29.2
Karolina Szabó (Hungary)
Stara Sagora, Bulgaria
April 23 1988
30,000 m 1:47:05.6
Karolina Szabó (Hungary)
Gothenburg, Sweden
April 23 1988
One hour distance 18,340 m
Tegla Loroupe (Kenya)
Borgholtzhausen, Germany
August 7 1998
100-m hurdles 12.21
Yordanka Donkova (Bulgaria)
Stara Sagora, Bulgaria
August 20 1988
400-m hurdles 52.61
Kim Batten (USA)
Gothenburg, Sweden
August 11 1995
3,000-m steeplechase 9:25.31
Justyna Bak (Poland)
Nice, France
July 9 2001
4 x 100-m relay 41.37
East Germany
(Silke Gladisch, Sabine Rieger,
Ingrid Auerswald and Marlies Gohr)
Canberra, ACT, Australia
October 6 1985

4 x 200-m relay 1:27.46
United States 'Blue' (LaTasha Jenkins, Chryste Gaines, Nanceen Perry and Torri Edwards)
Philadelphia, Pennsylvania, USA
April 29 2000
4 x 400-m relay 3:15.17
USSR (Tatyana Ledovskaya, Olga Nazarova, Maria Pinigina, and Olga Bryzgina)
Seoul, South Korea
October 1 1988
4 x 800-m relay 7:50.17
USSR (Nadezhda Olizarenko, Lyubov Gurina, Lyudmila Borisova, and Irina Podyalovskaya)
Moscow, Russia
August 5 1984
High jump 6 ft 10.25 in (2.09 m)
Stefka Kostadinova (Bulgaria)
Rome, Italy
August 30 1987
Pole vault 15 ft 9 in (4.81 m)
Stacy Dragila (USA)
Palo Alto, California, USA
June 9 2001
Long jump 24 ft 8.25 in (7.52 m)
Galina Chistyakova (USSR)
St Petersburg, Russia
June 11 1988
Triple jump 50 ft 10.25 in (15.50 m)
Inessa Kravets (Ukraine)
Gothenburg, Sweden
August 10 1995
Shot 74 ft 3 in (22.63 m)
Natalya Lisovskaya (USSR)
Moscow, Russia
June 7 1987
Discus 252 ft (76.80 m)
Gabriele Reinsch (East Germany)
Neubrandenburg, Germany
July 9 1988
Javelin 234 ft 8 in (71.54 m)
Osleidys Menédez (Cuba)
Réthymno, Crete, Greece
July 1 2001
Hammer 249 ft 6 in (76.07 m)
Mihaela Melinte (Romania)
Rudlingen, Germany
August 29 1999
Heptathlon 7,291 points
Jacqueline Joyner-Kersee (USA)
Seoul, South Korea
September 23–24 1988.
Day 1: 100-m h: 12.69; HJ: 6 ft 1.25 in (1.86 m); Shot: 51 ft 10 in (15.80 m); 200 m 22.56
Day 2: LJ: 23 ft 10.25 in (7.27 m); Javelin: 149 ft 10 in (45.66 m); 800 m: 2:08.51

WINTER OLYMPICS

MOST INDIVIDUAL OLYMPIC GOLD MEDALS

Bjørn Dæhlie (Norway) won eight Olympic gold medals in Nordic skiing between 1992 and 1998.

The women's record is six by Lidya Skoblikova (USSR) in speed skating from 1960 to 1964, and Lyubov Yegerova (Russia) in Nordic skiing from 1992–94.

MOST MEN'S ALPINE SKIING OLYMPIC GOLD MEDALS

Four skiers have won three gold medals in the Winter Olympics – Anton "Toni" Sailer (Austria) in the downhill, slalom, and giant slalom races of 1956; Jean-Claude Killy (France) in the downhill, slalom, and giant slalom in 1968; Alberto Tomba (Italy) in the slalom and giant slalom in 1988 and in 1992's giant slalom, and Kjetil André Aamodt (Norway) in the super-giant slalom in 1992 and 2002 as well as the combined event in 2002.

MOST WOMEN'S ALPINE SKIING OLYMPIC MEDALS

The most medals won at the Winter Games is five – by Switzerland's Vreni Schneider, who in addition to golds in the 1988 giant slalom and the 1988 and 1994 slaloms, won silver in the combined and bronze in the giant slalom in 1994. Katja Seizinger (Germany) also has five – bronze in the 1992 and 1998 super-giant slaloms and golds in the downhills of 1994 and 1998 and the combined in 1998.

MOST INDIVIDUAL OLYMPIC MEDALS

Norway's Bjørn Dæhlie won 12 medals in Nordic skiing between 1992 and 1998. The women's best is 10 by Raisa Smetanina (USSR/Russia) in Nordic skiing from 1976 to 1992.

MOST NATIONAL TOTAL OLYMPIC GOLD MEDALS

Norway has won 94 gold medals in the Winter Olympics between 1924 and 2002. Norway also has the most medals won overall, with 263 medals in 78 years.

MOST NATIONAL OLYMPIC GOLD MEDALS AT ONE GAMES

The USSR won 13 gold medals in 1976 at the Innsbruck Winter Olympic Games, in Austria.

MOST MEN'S ALPINE SKIING OLYMPIC MEDALS

Kjetil André Aamodt (Norway, below) has won the most men's Alpine Olympic medals. In addition to his record three gold medals, he has won two silver (downhill, combined 1994) and two bronze (giant slalom 1992, super-giant slalom 1994).

MOST NATIONAL OLYMPIC MEDALS IN ONE GAMES

The most medals won by a single country at a Winter Olympic Games is 35 by Germany at the Winter Games that were held at Salt Lake City, Utah, USA, in 2002.

OLDEST WINTER OLYMPIC COMPETITOR

The oldest competitor in the history of the Winter Olympic Games is British participant James Coates, who came seventh in the skeleton event at St Moritz, Switzerland, in 1948, at age 53 years 328 days.

Anne Abernathy (US Virgin Islands) was 48 years 307 days when she took part in the luge event at the 2002 Salt Lake City Games in Utah, USA, making her the oldest female competitor in Winter Olympic history.

MOST WOMEN'S ALPINE SKIING GOLD MEDALS

The most Olympic gold medals won by a woman is three, a feat achieved by four competitors: Vreni Schneider (Switzerland), Katja Seizinger (Germany), Deborah Campagnoni (Italy), and Janica Kostelic (Croatia, above).

MOST FREESTYLE SKIING OLYMPIC MEDALS

Since freestyle skiing was introduced to the Games in 1992, no skier has won more than one gold in the discipline. However, six skiers have won two medals (either gold, silver, or bronze): Edgar Grospiron (France), Janne Lahtela (Finland, above), Elizaveta Kozhevnikova (Russia), Stine Lise Hattestad (Norway), Kari Traa (Norway), and Tae Satoya (Japan).

YOUNGEST WINTER OLYMPIC COMPETITOR

Britain's Magdalena Cecilia Colledge was just 11 years 74 days old when she took part in the figure skating competition at the Winter Games of 1932, held at Lake Placid, New York, USA.

The youngest male competitor is Jan Hoffman (East Germany), who was 12 years 113 days old when he competed in the figure skating competition at the Calgary Winter Olympics, Alberta, Canada, in 1988.

MOST COUNTRIES TO WIN OLYMPIC MEDALS

Medals were won by a record 25 different countries at the most recent Winter Games, held at Salt Lake City, Utah, USA, in 2002.

MOST OLYMPIC COMPETITORS

The 2002 Winter Olympic Games at Salt Lake City, Utah, USA, involved competitors from a record number of 77 different countries.

PARALYMPIC GAMES

MOST PARALYMPIC MEDALS

Since the first Winter Paralympics, held in 1976 at Örnsköldsvik, Sweden, the most medals have been won by Austria, with a total of 301.

MOST INDIVIDUAL PARALYMPIC GOLD MEDALS

Between 1988 and 2002, Norway's Ragnhild Myklebust won 17 gold medals in the Winter Paralympics. The record for men is 12, held by Frank Hoefle (Germany), also between 1988 and 2002.

MOST INDIVIDUAL PARALYMPIC MEDALS

The most medals won by an individual at the Winter Paralympic Games is 19 by Frank Hoefle (Germany), who took 12 gold, four silver, and three bronze in biathlon and Nordic skiing between 1988 and 2002. The women's record is 18 by Ragnhild Myklebust (Norway), who won 17 gold and one bronze in the biathlon and Nordic skiing disciplines between 1988 and 2002.

MOST NATIONAL PARALYMPIC GOLD MEDALS

Norway has won the most overall gold medals, with a total of 118.

MOST PARALYMPIC MEDAL-WINNING NATIONS

The most nations to win a medal at the Paralympics is 22 in the 2002 Games at Salt Lake City, Utah, USA.

MOST ALPINE SKIING PARALYMPIC GOLD MEDALS

Reinhild Moeller (Germany) and Sarah Will (USA) share the record for most gold Alpine skiing medals, with 12 apiece. The men's record is 11 by Rolf Heinzmann (Switzerland).

MOST BIATHLON PARALYMPIC MEDALS

The most medals won in biathlon is four by Frank Hoefle (Germany) from 1992–2002. The women's record is three, held by Ragnhild Myklebust (Norway) in events between 1994 and 2002, and Marjorie Van de Bunt (Netherlands) from 1994 to 2002.

MOST BIATHLON PARALYMPIC GOLD MEDALS

The most gold medals won is three by Frank Hoefle (Germany) between 1992 and 1998. The women's record is two by Ragnhild Myklebust (Norway), Marjorie Van de Bunt (Netherlands), and Verena Bentele (Germany).

MOST NORDIC SKIING PARALYMPIC GOLD MEDALS

The most gold medals won in Nordic skiing is 15 by Ragnhild Myklebust (Norway) from 1988 to 2002. The men's record is nine, shared by Terje Loevaas (Norway) between 1984 and 1994 and Frank Hoefle (Germany) between 1988 and 2002.

MOST NORDIC SKIING PARALYMPIC MEDALS

The most medals won in Nordic skiing is 15 by Ragnhild Myklebust (Norway), all gold, between 1988 and 2002, and Frank Hoefle (Germany), who won nine gold, four silver, and two bronze between 1988 and 2002.

SKIING

GREATEST DISTANCE SKIED EVERY DAY FOR ONE YEAR

In 1994 Arnie Wilson and Lucy Dicker (both UK) skied every day in a round-the-world expedition. They covered 3,678 miles (5,919 km) at 237 resorts in 13 countries on five continents. Dicker tragically died in an avalanche in the French Alps soon after completing the expedition.

MOST ALPINE SKIING PARALYMPIC MEDALS

Switzerland's Hans Burn (above) holds the record for most Alpine skiing medals at the Winter Paralympics. He won 14 medals between 1988 and 2002 – six gold, five silver, and three bronze.

MOST MEN'S OLYMPIC BIATHLON TITLES

Ole Einar Bjorndalen (Norway, above) has won a record four individual titles in his Olympic career – the 10 km in 1998 and the 10 km, 20 km, and pursuit in 2002. He also won a relay gold medal in the 4 x 7.5 km in 2002.

SKIING

MOST MEN'S BIATHLON WORLD CHAMPIONSHIPS TITLES

Frank Ullrich (West Germany) won a record six individual world titles, four at 10 km from 1978 to 1981 (including the 1980 Olympics) and two at 20 km in 1982 and 1983.

Biathlete Alexander Tikhonov was in 10 successful Soviet relay teams between 1968 and 1980 and also won four individual titles.

MOST WOMEN'S BIATHLON OLYMPIC GOLD MEDALS

A women's competition was first held in 1992, and five people have two titles – Anfissa Restzova (Russia),

Myriam Bédard (Canada), Uschi Disl (Germany), Katrin Apel (Germany), and Andrea Henkel (Germany).

MOST WOMEN'S BIATHLON WORLD CHAMPIONSHIPS TITLES

The first World Championships were held in 1984, and the most titles won by an individual is four, by Petra Schaaf (Germany). She won the 5 km in 1988 and the 15 km in 1989, 1991, and 1993. Kaya Parve (USSR) has won six titles, but four of these were in relay events and only two were individual.

MOST MEN'S ALPINE SKIING WORLD CHAMPIONSHIPS TITLES

The World Alpine Championships were first held in 1931. Anton "Toni" Sailer (Austria) has won seven titles: all four – giant slalom, slalom, downhill, and the non-Olympic Alpine combination – in 1956, and also the downhill, giant slalom, and combined in 1958.

The women's record is held by Christl Cranz (Germany). She won seven individual events and five combined from 1934–39.

MOST WOMEN'S NORDIC SKIING TITLES

The first World Nordic Skiing Championships were at the 1924 Winter Olympics in Chamonix, France. The most titles won by a woman is 17 by Yelena Välbe (USSR and Russia) from 1989–98, made up of 10 individual and seven relay. She has 14 World Championships gold medals and 41 World Cup victories.

MOST WOMEN'S NORDIC SKIING OLYMPIC MEDALS

Raisa Smetanina (USSR, CIS in 1992) has won 10 Olympic medals – four gold, five silver, and one bronze – from 1980–92.

MOST WOMEN'S NORDIC SKIING OLYMPIC GOLD MEDALS

Lyubov Yegorova (Russia) has won six Olympic gold medals: three in 1992 (for CIS) and three in 1994.

MOST NORDIC SKI-JUMPING WORLD CHAMPIONSHIP TITLES

Norway's Birger Ruud won five Nordic ski-jump titles between 1931 and 1935. He is the only person to win Olympic events in each of the Alpine and Nordic disciplines.

MOST MEN'S WORLD CUP WINS

Introduced for Alpine events in 1967, the most individual event World Cup wins is 86 (46 giant slalom and 40 slalom from a total of 287 races) by Ingemar Stenmark (Sweden) in 1974–89. This included a men's record 13 wins in one season in 1978/79, 10 of which were part of a record 14 successive giant slalom victories between March 18 1978 and January 21 1980.

MOST WOMEN'S WORLD CUP WINS

Annemarie Moser (Austria) won a women's record 62 individual events from 1970 to 1979. She had a record 11 consecutive downhill wins from December 1972 to January 1974.

MOST WORLDLOPPET MASTERS TITLES

The most times an individual has qualified as a Worldloppet Gold Master is nine by Jan Jasiewicz (Switzerland) up to the end of the 2001 season. To qualify as a Gold Master a skier must complete 10 cross-country skiing marathons in the Worldloppet series, all in different countries and over at least two continents.

MOST NORDIC COMBINED OLYMPIC GOLD MEDALS

The most Nordic combined gold Olympic medals won is three by Samppa Lajunen (Finland, above) in the individual, sprint and relay of 2002, and Ulrich Wehling (East Germany) in the individual events of 1972, 1976, and 1980.

MOST "VERTICAL FEET" SKIED BY MEN

On April 29 1998 Edi Podivinsky, Luke Sauder, Chris Kent (all Canada), and Dominique Perret (Switzerland) skied 353,600 ft (107,777 m) in a time of 14 hr 30 min on a slope at Blue River, British Columbia, Canada.

MOST "VERTICAL FEET" SKIED BY WOMEN

Jennifer Hughes (USA) skied a total of 305,525 ft (93,124 m) for almost 15 hours at Atlin, British Columbia, Canada, on April 20 1998. Hughes was accompanied by snowboarder Tammy McMinn (Canada). They were lifted from the bottom of the run to the top by helicopter.

LONGEST MEN'S COMPETITIVE SKI-JUMP

Andreas Goldberger (Austria) leapt a staggering 738 ft (225 m) in a ski-jump competition held at Planica, Slovenia, on March 18 2000.

LONGEST WOMEN'S SKI-JUMP

The women's ski-jumping record is 367 ft (112 m), held by Eva Ganster (Austria) at Bischofshofen, Austria, on 7 January 1994.

LONGEST SKI-JUMP ON A DRY-SKI SLOPE

On June 30 1981 Hubert Schwarz (West Germany) jumped 302 ft (92 m) at Berchtesgarten, Germany.

MOST SNOW-BOARDING OLYMPIC MEDALS

Karine Ruby (France) has won two Olympic Games snowboarding medals – gold in the 1998 parallel giant slalom and silver in the same event in 2002. Ross Powers (USA, above) also has two medals – the half-pipe gold in 2002 and the bronze in 1998.

MOST FREESTYLE WORLD CHAMPIONSHIPS TITLES

Since the first World Championships in Tignes, France, in 1986, Edgar Grospiron (France) has won three titles – in the moguls in 1989 and 1991, and the aerials in 1995. He also won an Olympic title in 1992.

The most world titles won by a woman is also three, held by Candice Gilg (France). She won the moguls in 1993, 1995, and 1997.

MOST MEN'S FREESTYLE WORLD CUP TITLES

The Freestyle World Cup, instituted in 1980, has been won five times by France's Eric Laboureix, in 1986, 1987, 1988, 1990, and 1991.

MOST WOMEN'S FREESTYLE WORLD CUP TITLES

Connie Kissling (Switzerland) won a record 10 Freestyle World Cup titles between 1983 and 1992.

MOST SOMERSAULTS AND TWISTS IN A FREESTYLE AERIAL JUMP

Matt Chojnacki (USA) managed a remarkable quadruple-twisting quadruple back flip during a freestyle jump at the Winter Park Resort in Colorado, USA, on April 4 2001.

LONGEST DOWNHILL RACE

"The Inferno" in Switzerland is 9.8 miles (15.8 km) from the top of the Schilthorn to Lauterbrunnen.

FASTEST SKIER

The highest recorded speed for a skier is 154.165 mph (248.105 km/h) by Austrian Harry Egger at Les Arcs, France, on May 2 1999.

The fastest female skier is Karine Dubouchet (France), who reached 145.728 mph (234.528 km/h) at Les Arcs, France, on May 2 1999.

SNOWBOARDING

MOST WORLD CUP TITLES

Karine Ruby (France) won 16 World Cup titles from 1995 to 2002 in four disciplines. Mathieu Bozzetto (France) has won the most men's titles – six.

MOST WORLD TITLES

The most titles won (including Olympic titles) is three by Karine Ruby (France). She took the giant slalom in 1996, the snowboard cross in 1997, and the 1998 Olympic title.

FASTEST SNOWBOARDER

Darren Powell (Australia) recorded a highest ever snowboarding speed of 125.459 mph (201.907 km/h) at Les Arcs, France, on May 2 1999.

MOST WOMEN'S BIATHLON OLYMPIC MEDALS

Uschi Disl (Germany, above) has won eight Olympic biathlon medals: two gold, four silver, and two bronze.

FASTEST MEN'S SPEED SKATING 1,000 M

Gerard van Velde (Netherlands, above) skated 1,000 m in a time of 1:07.16 at Salt Lake City, Utah, USA, on February 16 2002.

SPEED SKATING

MOST MEN'S OLYMPIC GOLD MEDALS

Two skaters have secured five golds in this sport – Clas Thunberg (Finland) in 1924 and 1928 (one of which was a tied gold) and Eric Arthur Heiden (USA), who uniquely won all his golds at just one Olympic Games at Lake Placid, New York, USA, in 1980.

MOST WOMEN'S OLYMPIC GOLD MEDALS

Lidya Pavlovna Skoblikova (USSR) won six Olympic speed skating gold medals: two in 1960 and four more in 1964.

MOST MEN'S OLYMPIC MEDALS

In addition to his record five gold medals, Clas Thunberg (Finland) won a silver and one tied bronze, giving him seven Olympic medals in total. This record is shared with Norwegian Ivar Ballangrud, who won four gold, two silver, and a bronze between 1928 and 1936.

MOST WOMEN'S SHORT-TRACK OLYMPIC MEDALS

The most Olympic medals won by a woman in short-track speed skating is five by Chun Lee-kyung (South Korea) with four gold and one bronze, and Yang Yang (China), who has four silvers and one bronze medal.

MOST WOMEN'S OLYMPIC MEDALS

Karin Kania (East Germany) won three golds, four silvers, and a bronze from 1980–88.

MOST SHORT-TRACK SPEED-SKATING OLYMPIC MEDALS

The greatest number of Olympic medals won by a man in short-track speed skating is five by Marc Gagnon (Canada, below). He won three gold and two bronze medals between 1994 and 2002.

FASTEST MEN'S 500 M

Hiroyasu Shimizu (Japan) skated 500 m in 34.32 at Salt Lake City, Utah, USA, on March 10 2001. This record was set at the traditional long-track distance, in which skaters race in pairs against the clock counter-clockwise on a standard oval course that measures 1,312 ft (400 m).

FASTEST WOMEN'S 500 M

Catriona LeMay Doan (Canada) skated 500 m in 37.22 at Calgary, Alberta, Canada, on December 9 2001.

FASTEST WOMEN'S 1,000 M

Christine Witty (USA) skated 1,000 m in 1:13.83 at Salt Lake City, Utah, USA, on February 17 2002.

FASTEST MEN'S 1,500 M

Derek Parra (USA) skated 1,500 m in a record 1:43.59 at the 2002 Winter Olympics in Salt Lake City, Utah, USA, on February 19 2002.

FASTEST MEN'S 3,000 M

Gianni Romme (Netherlands) skated 3,000 m in 3:42.75 at Calgary, Alberta, Canada, on August 11 2000.

FASTEST WOMEN'S 3,000 M

Claudia Pechstein (Germany) skated 3,000 m in 3:57.70 at Salt Lake City, Utah, USA, on February 10 2002.

FASTEST MEN'S 5,000 M

Jochem Uytdehaage (Netherlands) skated 5,000 m in a record time of 6:14.66 at Salt Lake City, Utah, USA, on February 9 2002.

FASTEST WOMEN'S 5,000 M

Claudia Pechstein (Germany) skated 5,000 m in 6:46.91 at Salt Lake City, Utah, USA, on February 23 2002.

FASTEST MEN'S 10,000 M

Jochem Uytdehaage (Netherlands) skated 10,000 m in 12:58.92 at Salt Lake City, Utah, USA, on February 22 2002.

FASTEST MEN'S SHORT-TRACK 500 M

Jeffrey Scholten (Canada) skated a short-track 500 m in a record time of 41.514 at Calgary, Alberta, Canada, on October 13 2001. Short-track differs from long-track in that it is a race between two opposing skaters rather than against the clock.

FASTEST WOMEN'S SHORT-TRACK 500 M

Evgenia Radanova (Bulgaria) skated a short-track 500 m in a world record time of 43.671 at Calgary, Alberta, Canada, on October 19 2001.

FASTEST MEN'S SHORT-TRACK 1,000 M
Steve Robillard (Canada) skated a short-track 1,000 m in a record time of 1:25.985 in Calgary, Alberta, Canada, on October 14 2001.

FASTEST WOMEN'S SHORT-TRACK 1,000 M
Yang Yang (China) skated a short-track 1,000 m in a record time of 1:31.871 in Calgary, Alberta, Canada, on October 20 2001.

FASTEST MEN'S SHORT-TRACK 1,500 M
Steve Robillard (Canada) skated a short-track 1,500 m in 2:15.383 at Calgary, Alberta, Canada, on October 12 2001.

FASTEST WOMEN'S SHORT-TRACK 1,500 M
Choi Eun-kyung (South Korea) skated a short-track 1,500 m in a record time of 2:21.069 at Salt Lake City, Utah, USA, on 13 February 2002.

FASTEST MEN'S SHORT-TRACK 3,000 M
Kim Dong-sung (South Korea) skated a short-track 3,000 m in 4:46.727 at Szekesfehervar, Hungary, on 8 November 1998.

FASTEST WOMEN'S SHORT-TRACK 3,000 M
Choi Eun-kyung (South Korea) skated a short-track 3,000 m in 5:01.976 at Calgary, Alberta, Canada, on October 22 2000.

FASTEST WOMEN'S SHORT-TRACK 3,000-M RELAY
A South Korea team consisting of Park Hye-won, Joo Min-jin, Choi Min-kyung, and Choi Eun-kyung skated a short-track 3,000-m relay in 4:12.793 at Salt Lake City, Utah, USA, on February 20 2002.

FASTEST MEN'S SHORT-TRACK 5,000-M RELAY
A Canada team of Eric Bédard, Marc Gagnon, Jean-Francois Monette, and Mathieu Turcotte skated a short-track 5,000-m relay in 6:43.730 at Calgary, Alberta, Canada, on October 14 2001.

FIGURE SKATING

MOST GRAND SLAMS
The greatest number of figure skating grand slams – victory in the European, World, and Olympic titles in the same year – ever achieved by a man is the two claimed by Karl Schäfer (Austria) in 1932 and 1936.

YOUNGEST FIGURE SKATING WORLD CHAMPION
The youngest winner of a world title is Tara Lipinski (USA, above), who was just 14 years 286 days old when she won the individual figure skating World Championship on March 22 1997 in Lausanne, Switzerland.

Two women have achieved the same feat – Sonja Henie (Norway) in 1932 and 1936, and Katarina Witt (West Germany) in 1984 and 1988. Witt won two Olympic gold medals before retiring in 1988.

MOST MEN'S OLYMPIC GOLD MEDALS
Sweden's Gillis Grafström won three figure skating golds in successive Olympic Games from 1920 to 1928. He also won the World Championship three times – the last in 1929 – and a fourth Olympic medal, a silver, in 1932, after which he retired. The Grafström spin is named after him.

MOST WOMEN'S OLYMPIC GOLD MEDALS
Sonja Henie (Norway) won three Olympic figure skating gold medals at the Games of 1928, 1932, and 1936. Henie, the "Pavlova of ice," was trained by Gillis Grafström (Sweden), who won three figure skating Olympic gold medals himself before his retirement in 1932.

MOST MEN'S WORLD CHAMPIONSHIP TITLES
Ulrich Salchow (Sweden) won a record 10 figure skating world titles from 1901 to 1905 and 1907 to 1911. His contribution to the sport is forever commemorated by the Salchow jump, which is named after him.

MOST WOMEN'S WORLD CHAMPIONSHIP TITLES
The most individual figure skating World Championship titles won by a woman is 10 by Sonja Henie (Norway) between 1927 and 1936.

MOST ICE-SKATING CONTINUOUS SPINS
The most continuous spins made on one foot is 60 by Neil Wilson (UK) at the Spectrum Centre, Guildford, Surrey, UK, on July 1 1997.

FASTEST WOMEN'S 1,500 M
Anni Friesinger (Germany, above) skated 1,500 m in 1:54.02 at Salt Lake City, Utah, USA, on February 20 2002. In so doing, she broke her own record of 1:54.38 over the same distance, which she had set 11 months earlier.

MOST WOMEN'S BOBSLEIGH WORLD CHAMPIONSHIP MEDALS

The most medals won by an individual is two: Susi-Lisa Erdmann (Germany) won bronze in 2001 and 2002 (with Nicole Herschmann, both above), Jean Racine and Jennifer Davidson (USA) took silver in 2000 and 2001, and Swiss pair Francoise Burdet and Katharine Sutter won gold in 2001 and bronze in 2000.

BOBSLEIGH

MOST WOMEN'S WORLD CHAMPIONSHIP AND OLYMPIC TITLES

A women's World Championship was introduced in 2000 and debuted at the 2002 Winter Olympic Games. The winners have so far been Germany, Switzerland, and the USA, with no country winning more than once.

MOST WORLD CHAMPIONSHIP TITLES

The most individual world titles won is 11 by Eugenio Monti (Italy) from 1957–68. The most successful bobsleigher of all time, he won eight two-man and three four-man titles.

MOST OLYMPIC GOLD MEDALS

East Germany's Meinhard Nehmer and Bernhard Germeshausen both won three gold medals – in the 1976 two-man event and the 1976 and 1980 four-man races.

MOST OLYMPIC MEDALS

Between 1980 and 1992 Bogdan Musiol (East Germany and Germany after 1990) won seven bobsleigh medals – one gold, five silver, and one bronze – the most ever won by any bobsleigher at the Olympics. Musiol took part in four Games and never came home without a medal.

MOST FOUR-MAN WORLD CHAMPIONSHIP AND OLYMPIC TITLES

The world four-man bobsleigh title, instituted in 1924, has been won 20 times by Switzerland, including a record five Olympic victories (1924, 1936, 1956, 1972, and 1988).

YOUNGEST OLYMPIC BOBSLEIGH CHAMPION

William Guy Fiske (USA) was 16 years 260 days old when he won the gold medal with the five-man bobsleigh team during the 1928 Winter Olympics held at St Moritz, Switzerland.

OLDEST OLYMPIC BOBSLEIGH CHAMPION

Jay O'Brien (USA) was 47 years 357 days old when he won the gold medal with the four-man bobsleigh team during the 1932 Winter Olympics held at Lake Placid, New York, USA.

SKELETON

MOST WORLD TITLES

Skeleton features riders on sleds, negotiating a winding course on their stomachs. Alex Coomber (UK) has won a record four world titles – the World Cups of 2000, 2001, 2002, and the 2000 World Championships.

FASTEST CRESTA RUN COMPLETION TIME

The Cresta Run in St Moritz, Switzerland, dates from 1884. It is a 3,977-ft (1,212-m-long) ice run with a drop of 514 ft (157 m) and a gradient of between 1:2.8 to 1:8.7. Carved from ice, the run uses natural contours to form its curves. The racers lie head-first on skeleton toboggans, hurtling down the track only inches above the ground, and steer with their shoulders. The fastest time is 50.09 seconds (an average of 54.13 mph or 87.11 km/h) by James Sunley (UK) on February 13 1999.

OLDEST CRESTA RUN RIDER

Prince Constantin von Liechtenstein (b. December 23 1911), successfully completed the Cresta Run on February 15 2000 at the incredible age of 88 years 54 days.

MOST CRESTA RUN WINS

The greatest number of wins in the Cresta Run Curzon Cup competition (instituted 1910) is eight by the 1948 Olympic champion Nino Bibbia (Italy) between 1950 and 1969; and by Franco Gansser (Switzerland) in 1981, 1983–86, 1988–89, and 1991.

LUGE

MOST WOMEN'S OLYMPIC GOLD MEDALS

Luge is similar to skeleton, but the riders lie on their backs and negotiate the curves using their legs to steer. The most women's Olympic gold luge medals won is two, by Steffi Walter (East Germany) with victories in the women's single-seater luge event in 1984 and 1988.

MOST MEN'S WORLD CHAMPIONSHIP AND OLYMPIC TITLES

The most luge World Championship titles won is six by Georg Hackl in the single-seater bob in 1989 and 1990 (for East Germany) and 1992, 1994, 1997, and 1998 (for Germany). Stefan Krausse and Jan Behrendt (East Germany/Germany) won six titles in the two-seater bob, one lying on top of the other, from 1989–98.

MOST WOMEN'S WORLD CHAMPIONSHIP TITLES

Margit Schumann (East Germany) won the World Championship four times between 1973 and 1977. She won the Olympic bronze in 1972, the World Championships in 1973–75 and 1977, and the 1976 Olympic title.

MOST TWO-MAN BOBSLEIGH WORLD CHAMPIONSHIP AND OLYMPIC TITLES

Switzerland (above) has won the two-man bobsleigh World Championships 17 times and has a record four Olympic golds (1948, 1980, 1992, and 1994).

SALT LAKE 2002

SALT LAKE 2002

MOST CURLING OLYMPIC GOLD MEDALS

The ancient Scottish sport of curling was introduced to the Winter Olympic Games as a medal sport in 1998, and no country has picked up more than one gold medal. In 1998 the first winners were Switzerland (men) and Canada (women). In 2002, Norway (men, above) and Great Britain (women) were triumphant.

FASTEST SPEED

Tony Benshoof (USA) reached a speed of 86.6 mph (139.39 km/h) on the 2002 Olympic luge track at Park City, Utah, USA, on October 16 2001. The speed was reached during training for the 2001 Luge World Cup Series. Benshoof was a member of the USA 2001/02 Luge Team and participated at the 2002 Olympics in Salt Lake City. The run was timed by a "speed trap" consisting of timing lights spaced 16 ft 5 in (5 m) apart.

CURLING

FASTEST GAME

Eight curlers from the Burlington Golf and Country Club, Ontario, Canada, curled an eight-end game in a time

of 47 min 24 sec, with penalties of 5 min 30 sec on April 4 1986, using rules agreed with the Ontario Curling Association. Originally introduced to Canada by Scottish immigrants, curling is a competitive sport between two teams of four players each. The intention is to propel a 44-lb (20-kg) object called a stone down a sheet of ice toward a target ring of concentric circles.

MOST MEN'S WORLD CHAMPIONSHIPS

Canada has won the men's World Championship on 27 occasions between 1959 and 2002. The tournament was first held in 1959.

MOST WOMEN'S WORLD CHAMPIONSHIPS

The Canadian women's team have won a record 12 World Championships between 1980 and 2001. The first women's curling club was founded in 1895, but the World Championships were not held until 1979.

LONGEST THROW

The longest throw of a curling stone was an impressive 576 ft 4 in (175.66 m) by Eddie Kulbacki (Canada) at Park Lake, Neepawa, Manitoba, Canada, on January 29 1989. The attempt took place on a specially prepared sheet of curling ice that was itself a record 1,200 ft (365.76 m) in length.

ICE SLEDGE HOCKEY

MOST PARALYMPIC ASSISTS

Ice sledge hockey is contested at the Winter Paralympic Games. Athletes move on sledges with two blades that allow the puck to pass beneath and have picks to propel themselves and move the puck across the ice. Each team has five players and a goaltender. The most assists in the sport at the Paralympic Games is 15 by Helge Bjoernstad (Norway). His total of 10 in 2002 is a record for a single Games.

MOST PARALYMPIC GOALS

Jens Kask (Sweden) has scored 16 goals in three Paralympic ice sledge hockey tournaments between 1994

and 2002. The most goals scored in a single Games is 11 by Sylvester Flis (USA) in 2002.

MOST PARALYMPIC POINTS

Since the introduction of the sport to the Winter Paralympic Games in 1994, the most points scored by an individual player is 26 by Helge Bjoernstad (Norway).

The most ice sledge hockey points scored at a single Paralympic Winter Games by an individual player is 18 (11 goals, 7 assists) by Sylvester Flis (USA) in 2002.

MOST ICE SLEDGE HOCKEY PARALYMPIC MEDALS

Since its introduction in 1994, no country has won the Paralympic ice sledge hockey title more than once. The winners have been Sweden (1994), Norway (1998), and the USA (2002, left). Norway was second in both 1994 and 2002, and Sweden won the bronze in 1998 and 2002.

FORMULA 1

MOST F1 TITLES
Juan Manuel Fangio (Argentina) first became F1 World Champion in 1951 and then went on to win the title every year from 1954 to 1957 – a record five in total. Fangio retired in 1958, having won 24 Grand Prix races (two shared) from 51 starts.

MOST GRAND PRIX WINS
Michael Schumacher (Germany) has accumulated a record 53 wins from the 162 races he has taken part in up to the end of the 2001 F1 season.

MOST GRAND PRIX RACES
Ricardo Patrese (Italy) has started the most Grand Prix races – 256 between 1977 and 1993.

MOST TITLES BY A MANUFACTURER
Ferrari, the Italian manufacturer of the famous red racing car (below), holds the record for Formula 1 constructors' championships, with 11 titles between 1961 and 2001. Ferrari's total of 145 wins in Grand Prix races up to the end of the 2001 season is also the best achieved by any manufacturer.

MOST GRAND PRIX RACES WITHOUT WINNING
Andrea de Cesaris (Italy) took part in 208 races over 14 years for 10 different racing teams without managing to record a single victory.

CLOSEST RACE
The smallest winning margin for a Grand Prix was when Peter Gethin (UK) beat Ronnie Peterson (Sweden) by 0.01 sec in the Italian Grand Prix at Monza, Italy, on September 5 1971. Since 1982 timing for all races has been to thousandths of a second, and on April 13 1986 Ayrton Senna (Brazil) beat Nigel Mansell (UK) by just 0.014 sec in the Spanish Grand Prix at Jerez, Spain.

MOST POLE POSITIONS
The most pole positions a driver has registered in their career is 65 by Ayrton Senna (Brazil), coming from a total of 161 races (41 wins) when driving for the Toleman, Lotus, McLaren, and Williams teams. Senna's career was tragically cut short when he was killed in an accident on May 1 1994 while qualifying for the San Marino Grand Prix in Imola, Italy.

MOST CONSECUTIVE POLE POSITIONS
French driver Alain Prost recorded seven consecutive F1 pole positions in the 1993 season when driving for the Williams-Renault team. Prost finished the year as World Champion.

MOST POLE POSITIONS IN ONE SEASON
Driving for the Williams-Renault team in 1992, Nigel Mansell (UK) started a record 14 races in pole position on the grid. That year, Mansell won the World Championship. He went on to compete in American IndyCars the following year and won the 1993 IndyCar Series at the first attempt.

MOST POINTS BY A MANUFACTURER IN A SEASON
In the 1988 F1 season, the McLaren team scored a massive 199 points. The team's drivers that year were Ayrton Senna (Brazil) and Alain Prost (France), who between them won 15 out of the 16 races, also a record for a constructor. Senna took eight wins and three second places, and Prost seven wins and seven second places.

MOST GRAND PRIX WINS IN A SEASON
The most Grand Prix victories in a year is nine, a record shared by both Nigel Mansell (UK) in 1992, and by Michael Schumacher (Germany), three times in 1995, 2000, and 2001.

MOST CONSECUTIVE WINS OF A GRAND PRIX
Ayrton Senna (Brazil) dominated the Monaco Grand Prix in Monte Carlo, Monaco, winning the race five times in a row from 1989 to 1993.

GREATEST NUMBER OF FASTEST LAPS IN SEASON

Mika Hakkinen (Finland, above) recorded the greatest number of fastest laps in one F1 season with nine in 2000, while competing for the McLaren-Mercedes team. Despite this success, Hakkinen ended the year in second place with 89 points, behind German driver Michael Schumacher, who amassed 108 points for his team, Ferrari.

YOUNGEST AND OLDEST GRAND PRIX WINNERS

The youngest Grand Prix winner was Bruce McLaren (New Zealand), who won the US Grand Prix at Sebring, Florida, USA, on December 12 1959 when he was 22 years 104 days old.

Troy Ruttman (USA) was 22 years 80 days when he took first place in the Indianapolis 500, Indiana, USA, on May 30 1952, which was part of the World Championship at the time.

The oldest winner of a Grand Prix race (before 1950, when the F1 World Championship was instigated) was the legendary Italian racing driver Tazio Giorgio Nuvolari, who won the Albi Grand Prix held at Albi, France, on July 14 1946 when he was 53 years 240 days old.

YOUNGEST CHAMPION

The youngest F1 World Champion is Brazilian driver Emerson Fittipaldi, who was first crowned World Champion on September 10 1972 at the age of 25 years 273 days.

YOUNGEST AND OLDEST GRAND PRIX DRIVERS

The youngest driver to qualify for a Grand Prix was Michael Thackwell (New Zealand), who drove in the Canadian Grand Prix in Montreal, Quebec, Canada, on September 28 1980 at 19 years 182 days.

Louis Alexandre Chiron (Monaco) was a record age of 55 years 291 days when he finished sixth in the Monaco Grand Prix in Monte Carlo, Monaco, on May 22 1955.

INDYCAR

MOST CHAMPIONSHIP TITLES

IndyCar racing has existed for more than 30 years and has undergone a number of different guises in this time. Formerly known as the AAA (American Automobile Association, 1956–78), USAC (US Auto Club, 1956–78), CART (Championship Auto Racing Teams, 1979–91), IndyCar

(1992–97), and currently the Fed-Ex Series Championship, the most titles claimed by one driver is seven by AJ Foyt Jr (USA); 1960, 1961, 1963, 1964, 1967, 1975, and 1979.

MOST RACE WINS IN CAREER

AJ Foyt Jr (USA) won a record 67 IndyCar races in his career, which spanned from 1958 to 1993. Among those wins is the Indy 500, held in Indianapolis, Indiana, USA, which Foyt won five times. He also won the Le Mans 24-Hour Endurance race and the Daytona 24-Hour race.

MOST POLE POSITIONS

Italy-born US-based Mario Andretti was in pole position for a record 67 IndyCar races from 1965–94.

FASTEST INDY 500 QUALIFICATION

The fastest qualification, taken as an average speed over four laps, for the Indy 500, Indianapolis, Indiana, USA, was achieved by Arie Luyendyk (Netherlands) driving a Reynard-Ford-Cosworth on May 12 1996. His average speed of 236.986 mph (381.392 km/h) includes a single-lap world record speed of 237.498 mph (382.216 km/h).

LE MANS

MOST LE MANS 24-HOUR ENDURANCE RACE WINS

The most wins by an individual at the Le Mans 24-Hour Endurance race, held in Le Mans, France, is six by Jacky Ickx (Belgium) in 1969, 1975, 1976, 1977, 1981, and 1982.

MOST LE MANS 24-HOUR ENDURANCE TEAM WINS

Porsche, founded in Stuttgart, Germany, has won the most Le Mans 24-Hour races in history. Its cars have won the race 15 times – in 1970, 1971, 1976, 1977, 1981–1987, 1993, 1996, 1997, and 1998.

NASCAR

MOST CHAMPIONSHIP TITLES

Since the competition was first held in 1949, drivers Richard Petty and Dale Earnhardt (both USA) have won seven titles each in the NASCAR (National Association for Stock Car Auto Racing) championship. Petty's seven successes came in 1964, 1967, 1971, 1972, 1974, 1975, and 1979, while Earnhardt was victorious in 1980, 1986, 1987, 1990, 1991, 1993, and 1994.

HIGHEST CAREER EARNINGS

The highest earnings in a NASCAR career is $41,445,551 (£29,011,885) by Dale Earnhardt (USA) between 1975 and 2001.

MOST RACE VICTORIES

Richard Petty (USA) won a record 200 NASCAR races in his racing career from 1958 to 1992.

FASTEST TIME TO COMPLETE INDY 500 RACE

Arie Luyendyk (Netherlands, above) completed the world-famous Indy 500, which was first held in 1911 in Indianapolis, Indiana, USA, in a record time of 2 hr 41 min 18.404 sec driving a Lola-Chevrolet on May 27 1990.

ISLE OF MAN TT SERIES

OLDEST MOTORCYCLE RACE
The oldest annually contested motorcycle race in the world is the Auto-Cycle Union Tourist Trophy (TT) or Isle of Man TT series. It was first held on the 15.81-mile (25.44-km) Peel (St. John's) course on the Isle of Man, UK, on May 28 1907 and is now run on the island's Mountain circuit.

LONGEST CIRCUIT
The 37.73-mile (60.72-km) Mountain circuit on the Isle of Man, UK, on which the principal TT races have taken place since 1911 (with minor changes in 1920), has 264 curves and corners and is the longest-used circuit for any motorcycle race.

MOST RACES WON IN A CAREER
The most Isle of Man TT race wins in a career is 26 by Joey Dunlop (Ireland, above) from 1977–2000. Dunlop has a remarkable record in TT racing; including his first in 1977, he won a record 19 titles – including the Formula 1 title five times in a row between 1982 and 1986. Dunlop was tragically killed while racing in Estonia in 2000.

MOST SUCCESSIVE WINS IN TWO EVENTS
The first rider to win three consecutive TT titles in two different disciplines was James A. Redman (Rhodesia, now Zimbabwe). He won both the 250-cc and 350-cc races in 1963, 1964, and 1965.

MOST EVENTS WON IN A YEAR
The most different classes won in one year is four (Formula 1, Junior, Senior, and Production) by Phillip McCallen (Ireland) in 1996.

FASTEST RACE
David Jefferies (UK) registered an average speed of 121.94 mph (196.24 km/h) to set a race speed record time of 1 hr 51 min 22.8 sec to win the 2000 Senior TT on a Yamaha R1 on June 9 2000.

In the same race, Jeffries also set a record TT lap speed of 125.68 mph (207.27 km/h).

WORLD MOTORCYCLE CHAMPIONSHIPS

MOST TITLES
The World Motorcycle Championships were started in 1949 by the Fédération Internationale de Motocyclisme (FIM). The most titles won in a career is 15 by Giacomo Agostini (Italy). Agostini won seven successive 350-cc titles from 1968 to 1974, and eight 500-cc titles, consecutively from 1966 to 1972 and in 1975. Agostini retired from competitive racing in 1976.

MOST 250-CC TITLES
The most 250-cc World Motorcycle Championship titles won by a rider is four by Phil Read (UK) in 1964, 1965, 1968, and 1971. Read also won the 125-cc title in 1968 and two additional 500-cc titles.

YOUNGEST WORLD MOTORCYCLE CHAMPION
Loris Capirossi (Italy, below) is the youngest rider to win a World Championship title. He was 17 years 165 days old when he clinched the 125-cc title on a Honda on September 16 1990.

MOST 125-CC TITLES
Angel Roldán Nieto (Spain) won seven 125-cc titles in 1971, 1972, 1979, 1981, 1982, 1983, and 1984.

Nieto also holds the record for most 50-cc World Championship titles, having taken six from 1969 to 1977.

MOST RACES WON IN A CAREER
The most career race wins in the World Motorcycle Championships is 122 – 68 at 500-cc class and 54 at 350-cc class – by Giacomo Agostini (Italy) between 1965 and 1977.

MOST RACES WON IN A SEASON
The most races won in a World Motorcycle Championships season is 19, shared by Giacomo Agostini (Italy) in the 1970 season and Mike Hailwood (UK) in 1966.

MOST SINGLE CLASS WINS IN A CAREER

The most wins in a single racing class in a career is 79, set by Rolf Biland (Switzerland). Biland was racing in the sidecar class.

MOST SINGLE CLASS WINS IN A SEASON

The most wins in a single class in one season was achieved by Australian Michael Doohan, who had 12 wins in the 500-cc class during the 1997 season. Doohan's victory on October 4 1998 at his home Australian Grand Prix in Brisbane, Queensland, Australia, provided him with his fifth successive 500-cc World Motorcycle Championship title.

MOST TITLES WON BY A MANUFACTURER

Honda, the Japanese company founded by Soichiro Honda in 1948, has won the most World Motorcycle Championships, taking 48 titles in all classes between 1961 and 1999.

OLDEST WORLD CHAMPION

The oldest competitor to win a world title in any class is West Germany's Hermann-Peter Muller, who won the 250-cc title in 1955 at the age of 46.

WORLD SUPERBIKE CHAMPIONSHIP

MOST TITLES

The World Superbike Championship was first held in 1988, and the most titles won by a rider is four, by Carl Fogarty (UK) in 1994, 1995, 1998, and 1999. He claimed all the titles while riding for Ducati.

Fogarty started his career in TT and won the Isle of Man Formula 1 title in 1990. He also holds the record for most superbike race wins with 59 between 1992 and 1999.

MOST POLE POSITIONS

The most pole positions achieved in the World Superbike Championship is the 25 recorded by Troy Corser (Australia) up to March 2001.

MOST RACES WON BY A MANUFACTURER

Ducati (Italy) has won the most World Superbike Championship races, with a total of 161 victories between 1989 to 1999.

SUPERCROSS

MOST SUPERCROSS TITLE WINS

US motorcyclist Jeremy McGrath won the American Motorcycle Association (AMA) 250-cc Supercross Championship title on a record seven occasions between 1993 and 2000.

MOST 250-CC RACES WON IN A CAREER

Jeremy McGrath (USA) had 72 wins in the 250-cc Supercross race class between 1989 and 2001.

MOTOCROSS

WORLD CHAMPIONSHIPS – WINS IN ALL CATEGORIES

Eric Geboers (Belgium) is the only person to have won all three categories of the World Motocross Championships. He won 125-cc in 1982 and 1983, 250-cc in 1987, and 500-cc in 1988 and 1990.

MOST RACES WON IN A CAREER

In a career spanning two decades, Joël Robert (Belgium) won the 250-cc World Motocross Championship title on six occasions – in 1964 and every title between 1968 and 1972.

From April 25 1964 to June 18 1972 Robert won a record 50 Grand Prix races in the 250-cc class.

MOST TITLES WON BY A MANUFACTURER

Italian company Ducati (above) has dominated the World Superbike Championship, taking a record eight titles in all. The manufacturer won every title between 1991 and 1996, and also all those from 1998 to 2000.

YOUNGEST WORLD CHAMPION

Dave Strijbos (Netherlands) is the youngest motocross world champion. He won the 125-cc title when he was 18 years 296 days old on August 31 1986.

MOST TRANS-AMA CHAMPIONSHIP TITLES

The most Trans-AMA Motocross Championship titles won by an individual rider is four by Roger DeCoster (Belgium) between 1974 and 1977, riding a Suzuki.

SIDECAR

MOST EUROPEAN CHAMPIONSHIP TITLES

The most European Sidecar-Cross Championships won by an individual driver is five by Robert Grogg (Switzerland) in 1972, 1974, 1976, 1977, and 1978. Grogg rode a Wasp Norton motorcycle and rode with three different sidecar passengers over the course of his victories.

COUNTRY WITH MOST SIDECAR-CROSS CHAMPIONSHIP TITLES

Drivers and passengers from Switzerland have won more European and World Sidecar-Cross Championships than any other country, claiming a total of 19 titles between 1971 and 2001. The last European victory by a Swiss team was in 1996, when Andreas Führer's Kawasaki, accompanied by Adrian Kaser in the sidecar, took the title.

MOST ROADRACING NATIONAL TITLES

Milcho Mladenov (Bulgaria) is the holder of 16 consecutive Bulgarian national titles in the motorcycle sidecar 500-cc class. His titles came over 18 years between 1981 and 1999. Mladenov has also won the Balkan Championship on three different occasions.

SPEEDWAY

MOST INDIVIDUAL WORLD CHAMPIONSHIP TITLES
The most individual World Speedway Championship wins is six by Ivan Mauger (New Zealand) in 1968, 1969, 1970, 1972, 1977, and 1979.

MOST WORLD CHAMPIONSHIP TITLES
Hans Hollen Nielsen (Denmark) has been the most successful rider in all World Championship competitions with a total of 21 world titles spread over three different disciplines – pairs, team, and individual.

MOST WORLD CHAMPIONSHIP FINALS APPEARANCES
Between 1954 and 1972, New Zealand's Barry Briggs made a record 18 appearances in World Speedway Championship finals.

MOST POINTS BY A TEAM IN WORLD CUP
The most points scored by a team in a Speedway World Cup is 68 by Australia to win the inaugural Ove Fundin trophy in Wroclaw, Poland, held from July 1–7 2001.

MOST WORLD CUP RACE WINS
At the Speedway World Cup in Wroclaw, Poland, in July 2001, Jason Crump (Australia) recorded 10 wins out of 10 races to help his country win the Ove Fundin trophy.

MOST WORLD PAIRS CHAMPIONSHIP TITLES
The World Pairs Championship (instituted unofficially in 1968, officially in 1970 and renamed the World Team Championship in 1994) has been won a record nine times by Denmark – in 1979, every year between 1985 and 1991, and 1995.

MOST WORLD TEAM CUP WINS
The World Team Cup, instituted in 1960, was won a record nine times by England/Great Britain (Great Britain in 1968, 1971, 1972, and 1973; England in 1974, 1975, 1977, 1980, and 1989), and by Denmark in 1978, 1981, 1983 to 1988 and 1991.

TRIAL BIKES

MOST INDOOR AND OUTDOOR WORLD TRIALS CHAMPIONSHIP TITLES
Dougie Lampkin (UK) has won a record 10 Indoor and Outdoor World Trials Championships, claiming both titles every year between 1997 and 2001. Lampkin entered and won his first trials bike competition when he was only nine years old; he was awarded the MBE (Member of the British Empire) in 2002.

MOST WORLD TRIALS CHAMPIONSHIP TITLES
Jordi Tarrés (Spain) has won a world record seven Outdoor World Trials Championship titles in 1987, 1989, 1990, 1991, 1993, 1994, and 1995.

DRAG RACING

FASTEST FUNNY CAR 440-YD STANDING START
Gary Densham (USA) reached a speed of 326.87 mph (526.04 km/h) from a standing start in a Ford Mustang funny car, or dragster, at Pomona, California, USA, in February 2002.

LOWEST FUNNY CAR ELAPSED TIME
The lowest elapsed time to cover 440 yd (402 m) in a drag car is 4.731 sec by John Force (USA), driving a Ford Mustang, at Reading, Pennsylvania, USA, in October 2001. Force is the most successful funny car driver ever, and holds several records including the most NHRA (National Hot Rod Association) Funny Car Championships, the most successive championship wins, and the most career drag car victories. In 1996 Force became the first drag racer to win the national motorsports Driver of the Year award. The NHRA Championships are held as a series of one-on-one elimination races until there are just two drivers left to compete in the final. Up to his hot streak, Force lost nine finals in a row before his first victory, which came in 1987 in Montreal, Canada.

FASTEST SPEED BY PRO-STOCK RACER
For a fuel-driven piston-engined car (Pro-Stock), the highest terminal velocity achieved is 204.35 mph (328.86 km/h) by Mark Osborne (USA) in a Dodge Neon in Reading, Pennsylvania, USA, in October 2001.

LOWEST ELAPSED TIME BY PRO-STOCK RACER
The lowest elapsed time to cover 440 yd (402 m) in a Pro-Stock car is 6.750 sec by Jeg Couglin (USA), driving a Chevrolet Cavalier at Reading, Penn, USA, in October 2001.

FASTEST SPEED BY TOP FUEL RACER
Kenny Bernstein (USA) reached a terminal velocity of 332.18 mph (534.59 km/h) in a Top Fuel drag racer at the end of a 440-yd (402-m) run in October 2001. Bernstein was driving a Hadman dragster powered by a TFX 500 engine.

LOWEST ELAPSED TIME BY TOP FUEL RACER
The lowest elapsed time to cover 440 yd (402 m) in a Top Fuel dragster is 4.477 sec by Kenny Bernstein (USA) in a Hadman dragster with a TTX 500 engine at Chicago, Illinois, USA, in June 2001.

MOST FORMULA 1 INSHORE POWERBOATING WORLD CHAMPIONSHIP TITLES
Guido Cappellini (Italy, above) has won a record six Formula 1 Powerboating World Championship titles from 1993 to 1996 and in 1999 and 2001.

MOST WORLD RALLY CHAMPIONSHIP RACE WINS IN SEASON

France's Didier Auriol (above), a former ambulance driver, won a record six races during the 1992 World Rally Championship season. Auriol won his first World Rally Championship race in the Rally of Corsica in 1988 and claimed his first World Championship title while driving for Toyota in 1994.

RALLYING

LONGEST RALLY

The longest rally is the Singapore Airlines London–Sydney Rally, which originally covered a distance – the route is subject to alteration – of 10,000 miles (16,000 km) between Covent Garden, London, UK, and Sydney Opera House, Sydney, NSW, Australia. It was first held in 1968 and is next due to take place in July 2004. The longest recognized version of the rally is the 1977 race won by Andrew Cowan, Colin Malkin, and Michael Broad (all UK), which covered 19,329 miles (31,107 km) The race is not cheap to enter – it requires a fee of £26,000 ($38,000).

YOUNGEST WORLD RALLY CHAMPION

Britain's Colin McRae was just 27 years 89 days old when he won his first World Championship title in 1995. McRae, who has been awarded an MBE and was born in Scotland, comes from racing stock – his father won the British Rally Championship five times. Following in his father's tire treads, McRae took up rallying in 1986 and entered the World Championship in 1987.

MOST WORLD RALLY CHAMPIONSHIP TITLES BY A MANUFACTURER

Italian car manufacturer Lancia won 11 World Rally Championship titles between 1972 and 1992.

MOST MONTE CARLO RALLY WINS

The most Monte Carlo rally wins is four by: Sandro Munari (Italy) in 1972, 1975, 1976, and 1977 in a Lancia; Walter Röhrl (West Germany) in 1980, 1982, 1983, and 1984, in four different cars; and Finland's Tommi Makinen, who won four races in succession from 1999–2002.

MOST RALLY OF BRITAIN WINS

The RAC Rally of Britain was first held in 1932 and the race has been recognized by the Fédération Internationale de l'Automobile (FIA) since 1957. Hannu Mikkola (Finland) has a record four wins, driving a Ford Escort in 1979 and 1979 and an Audi Quattro in 1981 and 1982.

Mikkola's co-driver in all of his victories, Arne Hertz (Sweden), was also the co-driver when Stig Blomqvist (Sweden) won in 1971.

MOST WORLD RALLY CHAMPIONSHIP RACE WINS

Tommi Mäkinen (Finland, below) won 24 Championship races from 1994–2002. Mäkinen set the record when he won the Monte Carlo Rally in Monaco for a record fourth successive time in 2002. Mäkinen also has a record four successive world titles from 1996–99.

LOWEST WOMEN'S ROUND

Annika Sorenstam (Sweden, below) went around the Moon Valley Country Club in Phoenix, Arizona, USA, in 59 strokes, the lowest 18-hole score by a woman. She was playing in the 2001 Standard Register PING tournament, March 16 2001.

GREATEST MARGIN OF VICTORY IN A MAJOR TOURNAMENT

Tiger Woods (USA) won the US Open in 2000 by a massive 15 shots, the greatest distance a winner of a Major tournament – the Open Championship, US Open, US Masters, and US PGA Championship – has ever finished ahead of the rest of the field. Woods scored 65, 69, 71, and 67 for a 12-under-par total of 272.

MOST OPEN TITLES

Born on the UK-administered Channel Island of Jersey, Harry Vardon won six Open Championships, held in the UK, between 1896 and 1914.

MOST US OPEN TITLES

Willie Anderson (UK), Bobby Jones Jr, Ben Hogan, and Jack Nicklaus (all USA) have each won the US Open four times. Anderson in 1901 and 1903–05; Jones in 1923, 1926, 1929, and 1930; Hogan in 1948, 1950, 1951, and 1953, and Nicklaus in 1962, 1967, 1972, and 1980.

MOST US WOMEN'S OPEN TITLES

Betsy Rawls and Mickey Wright (both USA) both won a record four US Women's Open titles – Rawls's successes came in 1951, 1953, 1957, and 1960, and Wright's were in 1958, 1959, 1961, and 1964.

MOST US AMATEUR TITLES

Bobby Jones Jr (USA) won five US Amateur titles in 1924, 1925, 1927, 1928, and 1930. Jones, who never turned professional, also won the US Open on four occasions, the Open Championship three times, and the British Amateur Championship once before he retired at 28.

MOST BRITISH AMATEUR CHAMPIONSHIP TITLES

John Ball (UK) won eight British Amateur Championship titles, the last at the age of 60, from 1888–1912.

MOST US WOMEN'S AMATEUR TITLES

Glenna Vare (USA) won six US Women's Amateur Championship titles between 1922 and 1935. She remained an amateur until her death.

MOST WORLD CUP TEAM TITLES

The World Cup of Golf, which was instituted as the Canada Cup in 1953, has been won most often by the USA with a record 22 victories between 1955 and 1999.

LOWEST INDIVIDUAL WORLD CUP SCORE

From November 18 to 21 1999 Tiger Woods (USA) completed the four rounds of the World Cup in a record total of 263 strokes at Kuala Lumpur, Malaysia.

MOST WORLD CUP INDIVIDUAL TITLES

The only men to have been on six winning World Cup teams have been Arnold Palmer (USA) in 1960, 1962, 1963, 1964, 1966, and 1967, and Jack Nicklaus (USA) in 1963, 1964, 1966, 1967, 1971, and 1973.

Nicklaus has also taken the individual title a record three times in 1963, 1964, and 1971.

LOWEST WORLD CUP TEAM SCORE

The lowest aggregate score for the World Cup's 144 holes is 536 by the US team of Fred Couples and Davis Love III at Dorado, Puerto Rico, from November 10–13 1994.

HIGHEST US LPGA SEASON'S EARNINGS

Sweden's Annika Sorenstam earned $2,105,868 (£1,477,269) on the US LPGA circuit in 1999, a record for a single season's takings.

HIGHEST US LPGA CAREER EARNINGS

The record career earnings for a woman on the US LPGA Tour is by Annika Sorenstam (Sweden). She had banked a total of $6,957,044 (£4,874,371) up to April 2001.

HIGHEST US PGA CAREER EARNINGS

The career winnings record on the US PGA circuit is held by Tiger Woods (USA). He had earned a total of $23,767,307 (£16,652,285) from August 1996 to April 2001.

OLDEST RYDER CUP PLAYER

The oldest player to compete in the Ryder Cup is Ray Floyd (USA, above), who was 51 years 20 days in 1993. The biennial tournament between the USA and Europe (British Isles or Great Britain prior to 1979) was first held in 1927.

HIGHEST US PGA SEASON'S EARNINGS

The season's record for the US PGA Tour is $9,188,321 (£6,155,504) by Tiger Woods (USA) in 2000.

HIGHEST MEN'S EUROPEAN TOUR SEASON EARNINGS

Lee Westwood (UK) won £1,858,602 ($2,775,822) in European Order of Merit tournaments in 2000.

LONGEST PUTT

Jack Nicklaus (USA), in the 1964 Tournament of Champions, and Nick Price (South Africa), in 1992's US PGA Championship, have both holed 110-ft (33.5-m) putts in professional golf tournaments.

Bob Cook (USA) sank a putt of 140 ft 2.75 in (42.74 m) on the 18th hole at St Andrews, Fife, UK, in the International Fourball Pro-Am Tournament on October 1 1976.

On August 5 2000 Alan Schofield and Robin Kershaw (both UK) both successfully sank a putt measuring 166 ft 8 in (50.79 m) at Fishwick Hall Golf Club, Preston, Lancashire, UK.

MOST RYDER CUP TITLES

The first Ryder Cup match was held in 1927 at the Worcester Country Club, Worcester, Massachusetts, USA. Up to the 1999 event, the USA had won 24 tournaments and Europe seven, with two drawn.

MOST INDIVIDUAL RYDER CUP WINS

Nick Faldo (UK) holds the record for match wins, having won 23 of the 46 Ryder Cup games in which he has played. Faldo also has the overall points record, taking 25 and halving another four. The US record is held by Arnold Palmer (USA), with 22 wins from 32 played. Billy Casper (USA) has the US record points total of 23.5 from 37 matches.

MOST SUCCESSFUL RYDER CUP CAPTAIN

The most successful Ryder Cup captain in the tournament's history is America's Walter Hagen, who skippered four winning US teams in 1927, 1931, 1935, and 1937.

YOUNGEST RYDER CUP PLAYER

Sergio Garcia (Spain) was only 19 years 8 months 15 days old when he played for Europe in 1999.

MOST SOLHEIM CUP TITLES

The Solheim Cup, the women's equivalent of the Ryder Cup, is contested biennially between the 12 top professional players of both Europe and the USA. It was first held in 1990, and the American team has since won on four occasions – 1990, 1994, 1996, and 1998. The European team was successful in 1992 and 2000.

MOST INDIVIDUAL SOLHEIM CUP WINS

The most wins by a player in the history of the Solheim Cup is 13 by Laura Davies (UK) from 23 matches between 1990 and 2000, and also by Dottie Pepper (USA), who played 20 matches over the same period. Both have scored a record 14 points.

MOST CURTIS CUP TITLES

The biennial women's Curtis Cup match between amateur players from the USA against their contemporaries from Great Britain

and Ireland was first held in 1932. The USA has won 22 up to 2000, with Britain and Ireland taking six. Three matches have been tied.

MOST CURTIS CUP INDIVIDUAL WINS

Carole Semple-Thompson (USA) played a record 11 ties and won a record 16 matches from 1974–2000.

Mary McKenna (UK) played her ninth match in 1986, a record for Great Britain and Ireland, and for the first time finished on the winning side.

WOMEN'S LOWEST US LPGA TOURNAMENT SCORE

The lowest four-round total in a US LPGA Championship event is 261. It is shared by Se Ri Pak (South Korea) with scores of 71, 61, 63, and 66 at the Jamie Farr Kroger Classic, Sylvania, Ohio, USA, on July 9–12 1998 and also by Annika Sorenstam (Sweden) with scores of 65, 59, 65, and 68 in the 2001 Standard Register PING tournament at Moon Valley Country Club in Phoenix, Arizona, USA, on March 15–18 2001.

OLDEST COMPETITOR IN A MAJOR EVENT

Ed Alofs (Netherlands) took part in the 1997 Compaq World Putting Championship in Orlando, Florida, USA, at 95 years 289 days old.

MOST NATIONALITIES AT A TOURNAMENT

A record 72 different nations were represented at the 2000 Junior Open Championship at Crail Golf Club, Fife, UK, in July 2000. The event was organized by the Royal and Ancient Golf Club of St. Andrews, Fife, UK.

MOST RYDER CUP MATCHES PLAYED

Nick Faldo (UK, above) played 11 Ryder Cup tournaments between 1977 and 1997. The US record is a shared eight – Billy Casper from 1961 to 1975, Ray Floyd between 1969 and 1993, and Lanny Wadkins from 1977 to 1993.

LOWEST
NINE-HOLE ROUND
Nine holes were completed in 25 strokes (4, 3, 3, 2, 3, 3, 1, 4, 2) by AJ "Bill" Burke in a round of 57 (32 and 25) on the Normandie course at St. Louis, Missouri, USA, on May 20 1970.

The tournament record is 27 strokes and has occurred on eight occasions. The first recorded nine-hole 27 was by Mike Souchak (USA), on the closing nine holes of his opening round in the 1955 Texas Open.

Most recently, Billy Mayfair (USA) scored 27 on the final nine holes of the fourth round of the 2001 Buick Open at Warwick Hills, Grand Blanc, Michigan, USA, on August 12 2001.

FASTEST ROUND
BY AN INDIVIDUAL
The fastest round played by one player, with the ball coming to a rest before each new stroke, is one of 27 min 9 sec by James Carvill (Ireland) at Warrenpoint Golf Course, Co Down, Ireland, on June 18 1987.

FASTEST ROUND
BY A TEAM
On September 9 1996 the Fore Worcester's Children team of golfers completed a round of 18 holes in 9 min 28 sec at the Tatnuck Country Club, Worcester, Massachussets, USA. Collectively, the team went around for an impressive score of 70.

LONGEST CONTROL
OF GOLF BALL
Rick Adams (UK) used a sand wedge to keep a ball aloft for 1 hour 17 min on March 21 2002 in London, UK.

On November 17 2001 in Brisbane, Queensland, Australia, Henry Epstein (Australia) took alternate touches with two sand wedges to keep a golf ball aloft for 33 min 33 sec.

MOST HOLES IN 12 HOURS
Using a cart to get around the course, Brennan Robertson (USA) played 476 holes in 12 hours at Foxfire Golf Club, Sarasota, Florida, USA, on August 19 2000.

MOST HOLES
IN SEVEN DAYS
Colin Young (UK) used a golf cart to get around 1,706 holes in seven days at the Hill Valley Golf Club in Whitchurch, Shropshire, UK, from July 26 to August 2 1999.

MOST HOLES IN A YEAR
The most holes of golf played in one year is 10,550 by Leo Fritz (USA) of Youngstown, Ohio, USA, in 1998.

MOST HOLES PLAYED BY
A FOURSOME IN 24 HOURS
A team of Harold Hagens, Piet van Schaijk, Daniel Kameier, and John Neophytou (all Sweden) achieved

a total score of 5,861 in 24 hours, when they played a record 290 holes as a foursome at the Ronnbacken Golf Club, Skelleftea, Sweden. Each round took an average of 1 hr 24 min.

LONGEST THROW
OF A GOLF BALL
Stefan Uhr (Sweden) threw a golf ball 394 ft 5 in (120.24 m) at Prästholmen, Mora, Sweden, on August 20 1992.

LONGEST SINGLE "HOLE"
COMPLETED IN 12 HOURS
The longest "hole" completed in under 12 hours measured 44 miles (70 km) from South Ice Cave, Lake County, Oregon, USA, to the ninth green of the Meadows Course at Sunriver, Oregon, USA. It was played on September 25 2000 by John Bladholm, Gene Molenkamp, Sean Guard, and Mike O'Connell (all USA) in 1,187 strokes. They lost 147 balls in the process.

MOST GOLFERS ON ONE
COURSE IN 24 HOURS
A record 605 golfers completed a round in one day at the Rhodes Ranch Country Club, Las Vegas, Nevada, USA, on June 21 1998.

NORTHERNMOST COURSE
The island of Uummannaq, located to the west of Greenland at a longitude of 70ºN, is the location of the annual World Ice Golf Championship. The course varies considerably in layout from year to year, in accordance with variations in ice floes and snow distribution. Frostbite is a constant hazard for competitors.

FIRST
TRANS-AMERICAN ROUND
Floyd Satterlee Rood (USA) used the whole of North America as a course when he played a coast-to-coast round from the Pacific to the Atlantic between September 14 1963 and October 3 1964. This 3,397.7-mile (5,468-km) journey took 114,737 strokes and cost Rood 3,511 balls.

GREATEST DISTANCE
TRAVELED BETWEEN TWO
ROUNDS ON SAME DAY
Nobby Orens (USA) played two 18-hole rounds – at Stockley Park, Uxbridge, London, UK, and at Braemar Country Club, Tarzana, California, USA – on July 20 1999. This involved traveling a distance of 5,954 miles (9,582 km).

Orens is an avid golfer – during 1999 he played 134 rounds on 36 courses in 27 cities, five states, six countries, and two continents.

HIGHEST SHOT
Vladímír Mysík (Czech Republic) played a shot from the peak of Gasherbrum I – a height of 26,470 ft (8,068 m) – in the Karakoram Range, Kashmir, on July 9 1997.

HIGHEST EUROPEAN TOUR CAREER EARNINGS
Between 1986 and 2001, Britain's Colin Montgomerie (above) took part in the European Order of Merit, earning a record £8,424,498 ($12,008,908). In his European tour career, Montgomerie had won 25 titles as of April 2002.

HIGHEST WOMEN'S EUROPEAN TOUR SEASON EARNINGS

The record for a season's earnings on the women's European Tour is £204,522 ($330,818) by Laura Davies (UK, above crouching) on the 1999 tour. In 1994 Davies became the first European golfer to be ranked women's world No.1.

LIGHTEST CLUB

The lightest full-size club is the driver JBeam Win.1 manufactured by Japan Golf Equipment Co Ltd of Tokyo, Japan. It weighs just 7.75 oz (220 g) in total. The titanium head weighs 5.64 oz (160 g), the carbon fiber shaft is 1.23 oz (35 g), and the grip is 0.88 oz (25 g). The club is specially embossed with the *Guinness World Records* logo.

LONGEST USABLE CLUB

The longest club that can be used by an individual to hit a golf ball is a driver owned by Brad Denton (USA), which is 11 ft (3.36 m) long. The definition of "usable" is that the club must be able to be used from a regular stance, have a normal-sized head, and be capable of hitting the ball at least 100 yd (91 m).

LARGEST BUNKER

The world's biggest bunker, or sand trap, is Hell's Half Acre on the 585-yd (535-m) seventh hole of the Pine Valley course, Clementon, New Jersey, USA. The course, which covers 623 acres (253 ha), was designed in 1912 by George Crump (USA), and is regarded by most experts as the world's greatest and most challenging golf course.

LONGEST HOLE

The longest hole in the world is the par-seven seventh hole of the Satsuki Golf Club, in Sano, Japan, which measures 964 yd (881 m).

MOST HOLES-IN-ONE BY HUSBAND AND WIFE AT SAME HOLE

Elmer James and his wife Marilyn (both USA) scored consecutive holes-in-one on the 16th at Halifax Plantation Golf Club, Ormond, Florida, USA, on April 19 1998.

MOST BALLS HIT IN ONE HOUR

The most balls driven by a single golfer in a time of one hour, over a distance of 100 yd (91 m) and into a designated target area, is 2,146 by Sean Murphy (Canada) at Swifts Practice Range, Carlisle, Cumbria, UK, on June 30 1995.

MOST PARTICIPANTS IN A LESSON

The most people to take part in a single golf lesson is the 389 pupils who were taught by Scotland-born professional golfer Colin Montgomerie in a lesson that took place at the Army Golf Club in Aldershot, Hampshire, UK, on February 16 1999.

LONGEST CARRY

Karl Woodward (UK) hit a ball a record 408 yd (373 m) at Golf del Sur, Tenerife, Spain, on June 30 1999.

A golf ball has been hit farther than this – Jack Hamm (USA) recorded a drive of 458 yd (418.79 m) at Highlands Ranch, Colorado, USA, on July 20 1993. This shot, though, came at an altitude of more than 3,280 ft (1,000 m), where the thinner atmosphere would have significantly helped the ball carry a greater distance than it would if hit at an altitude closer to sea level.

LARGEST GOLF BALL COLLECTION

Ted Hoz (USA) has collected a total of 70,718 golf balls since 1986. Each bears a different logo covering 7,014 different courses, 51 countries, and 1,689 different tournaments and they are on display at his home in Baton Rouge, Louisiana, USA. If the balls were set side-by-side they would cover a distance of almost 2 miles (3.2 km), and their total weight is estimated at 5.1 tons.

MOST VALUABLE BALL

On July 1 1995 Jaime Ortiz Patiño (Spain) paid $31,855 (£19,995) for a Victorian golf ball that was made of leather and stuffed with feathers.

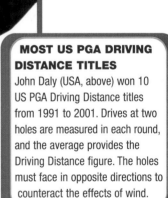

MOST US PGA DRIVING DISTANCE TITLES

John Daly (USA, above) won 10 US PGA Driving Distance titles from 1991 to 2001. Drives at two holes are measured in each round, and the average provides the Driving Distance figure. The holes must face in opposite directions to counteract the effects of wind.

BEST WIMBLEDON WILDCARD PERFORMANCE

Goran Ivanisevic (Croatia, below) was ranked 125th in the world when he was invited by the All England Club to take part in the Wimbledon Championships in 2001. Despite his lowly status, Ivanisevic reached his fourth final, beating Pat Rafter (Australia) 6-3, 3-6, 6-3, 2-6, 9-7 to claim the title.

TENNIS

HIGHEST ATTENDANCE

A record total of 30,472 people were at the Astrodome, Houston, Texas, USA, for the "Battle of the Sexes" exhibition match on September 20 1973 when Billie-Jean King beat Robert Riggs (both USA).

The competitive match record is the 25,578 who saw Australia's Davis Cup Challenge Round contest against USA in Sydney, NSW, Australia, on December 27 1954.

MEN'S GRAND SLAM

The first man to have won all four of the world's major championship singles titles – Wimbledon and the US, Australian and French Opens – was Fred Perry (UK) when he won the French title in 1935.

The first man to hold all four championships simultaneously was Don Budge (USA) in 1936. Having won Wimbledon and the US Open in 1937, he won six successive grand slam tournaments.

The first man to achieve the grand slam twice was Rod Laver (Australia) as an amateur in 1962 and again in 1969 when the titles were open to professionals.

WOMEN'S GRAND SLAM

Four women have achieved the grand slam, and the first three won six successive grand slam tournaments: Maureen Connolly (USA) in 1953; Margaret Court (Australia) in 1970, and Martina Navrátilová (USA) in 1983–84. The fourth was Steffi Graf (Germany) in 1988, when she also won the women's singles Olympic gold medal.

Pam Shriver (USA) and Navrátilová won a record eight successive women's grand slam doubles titles and 109 successive matches in all competitions between April 1983 and July 1985.

MOST GRAND SLAM SINGLES TITLES

The most successful player in terms of grand slam singles titles is Margaret Court (Australia), who won 24 titles

between 1960 and 1973. She won the Australian Open 11 times, five US Open titles, five French Open titles, and three Wimbledon titles.

MOST MEN'S WIMBLEDON SINGLES TITLES

The first Lawn Tennis Championships were held at Wimbledon, London, UK, in 1877. The men's title has been won seven times by Pete Sampras (USA) – every year from 1993 to 1995 and from 1997 to 2000.

MOST MEN'S WIMBLEDON TITLES

The most Wimbledon titles won by a man is 13 by Laurie Doherty (UK). He won five singles titles from 1902 to 1906 and eight men's doubles titles between 1897 and 1906.

MOST WOMEN'S WIMBLEDON TITLES

Billie-Jean King (USA) won 20 titles between 1961 and 1979 – six singles, 10 women's doubles, and four mixed doubles titles.

YOUNGEST MEN'S WIMBLEDON CHAMPION

Boris Becker (West Germany) won the men's singles title in 1985 at the age of 17 years 227 days.

YOUNGEST WOMEN'S WIMBLEDON CHAMPION

Martina Hingis (Switzerland) was 15 years 282 days old when she won the women's doubles in 1996.

LONGEST WIMBLEDON CAREER

Jean Borotra (France) took part in the men's singles competition 35 times between 1922 and 1964. He then went on to compete in the men's veteran doubles and mixed doubles events from 1965 to 1977. Borotra retired when he was 78 after 55 years of competition.

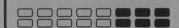

YOUNGEST WOMEN'S WORLD NO.1

Martina Hingis (Switzerland, above) was 16 years 182 days old when she became women's world No.1 on March 31 1997. Hingis had turned professional less than three years before, on October 14 1994.

MOST MEN'S US OPEN SINGLES TITLES

The US Open was first held in 1881 and three players have won seven US Open men's titles to date – Richard Sears (USA), from 1881–87; William Larned (USA), in 1901, 1902, and 1907–11; and Bill Tilden (USA), from 1920–25 and 1929.

MOST WOMEN'S US OPEN SINGLES TITLES

Molla Mallory (Norway) won eight US Open women's singles titles in 1915–18, 1920–22, and 1926. She also won two women's doubles titles and three mixed doubles titles.

YOUNGEST MEN'S US OPEN SINGLES CHAMPION

"Pistol" Pete Sampras was 19 years 28 days old when he won the US Open singles championship on September 9 1990.

YOUNGEST WOMEN'S US OPEN SINGLES CHAMPION

The youngest woman to win the US Open singles title is Tracy Austin (USA), who was 16 years 271 days old on September 9 1979.

OLDEST US OPEN SINGLES CHAMPION

William Larned (USA) was 38 years 242 days old when he won the men's singles title in 1911.

OLDEST US OPEN CHAMPION

Margaret Du Pont (USA) won the mixed doubles title at the age of 42 years 166 days in 1960.

YOUNGEST US OPEN CHAMPION

Vincent Richards (USA) was age 15 years 139 days when he won the US Open men's doubles title in 1918.

MOST MEN'S AUSTRALIAN OPEN SINGLES TITLES

The Australian Open Championships were first held in 1905 in Melbourne, Victoria, Australia. Roy Emerson (Australia) won a record six titles in 1961 and 1963–67. In total, Emerson won 12 grand slam singles titles and 16 grand slam doubles titles.

MOST MEN'S AUSTRALIAN OPEN TITLES

Adrian Quist (Australia) won 13 titles at the Australian Open – the men's singles title three times in 1936, 1940 and 1948, and 10 consecutive doubles titles from 1936 to 1950.

MOST WOMEN'S AUSTRALIAN OPEN TITLES

The most Australian Open tennis titles is 21 by Margaret Court (Australia), who won the women's singles title 11 times (1960–66, 1969–71, and 1973), the women's doubles eight times (1961–63, 1965, 1969–71, and 1973), and the mixed doubles twice (1963 and 1964).

YOUNGEST MEN'S AUSTRALIAN OPEN SINGLES CHAMPION

Rodney Heath (Australia) was just 17 years old when he won the first men's singles title in 1905.

YOUNGEST WOMEN'S AUSTRALIAN OPEN SINGLES CHAMPION

Martina Hingis (Switzerland) won the women's singles title at the age of 16 years 117 days in 1997. Hingis also went on to take the women's titles in the following two years.

MOST WOMEN'S FRENCH OPEN SINGLES TITLES

The most French Open singles tennis titles won by a woman is seven by Chris Evert (USA) in 1974, 1975, 1979, 1980, 1983, 1985, and 1986.

LONGEST TENNIS MATCH

The longest match in a grand slam tournament is one that lasted an exhausting 5 hr 31 min between Alex Corretja (Spain) and Hernán Gumy (Argentina) in the third round of the French Open on May 31 1998. Corretja won 6-1, 5-7, 6-7, 7-5, 9-7.

MOST DAVIS CUP TITLES

The most wins in the Davis Cup, the men's international tennis team championship, is 31 by the United States between the first tournament in 1900 and 1995.

The most individual appearances in winning Davis Cup teams is eight by Roy Emerson (Australia) from 1959 to 1962 and 1964 to 1967.

Bill Tilden (USA) played in a record 28 matches in the final, winning a record 21 – 17 out of 22 singles and four out of six doubles. He was in seven winning sides (1920–26) and then four losing sides (1927–30).

OLDEST DAVIS CUP PLAYER

The oldest player to feature in the Davis Cup is Yaka-Garonfin Koptigan (Togo), at age 59 years and 147 days on May 27 2001 against Mauritius.

YOUNGEST DAVIS CUP PLAYER

Kenny Banzer (Liechtenstein) played for Liechtenstein against Algeria at 14 years 5 days on February 16 2000.

FASTEST WOMEN'S SERVE

The fastest service recorded by a woman in competitive play is one of a scorching 127.4 mph (205 km/h) by Venus Williams (USA, above), during the European Indoor Championships in Zurich, Switzerland, on October 16 1998.

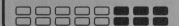

RACKET SPORTS
SPORT

TENNIS

FASTEST MEN'S SERVE
The fastest service by a man (measured with modern equipment) is 149 mph (239.8 km/h) by Greg Rusedski (UK) during the ATP Champions' Cup at Indian Wells, California, USA, on March 14 1998. Rusedski was born in Canada of a British mother and was granted British citizenship in May 1995.

LONGEST RALLY
The longest contrived rally is one that lasted 17,062 strokes between Ray Miller and Rob Peterson (both USA) at Alameda, California, USA. The attempt took 9 hr 6 min and was set during the United States Tennis Association's "Tennis Festival" on July 4 2001.

MOST VALUABLE RACKET
A racket used by the legendary Fred Perry (UK) at Wimbledon was sold at Christie's auction house, London, UK, in June 1997 for a record £23,000 ($37,724). Perry was also world singles table tennis champion in 1929.

MOST BALLS VOLLEYED IN A THREE-HOUR LESSON
The most balls volleyed during a single three-hour lesson is 6,177 by John Forster (USA). He was teaching a group of 456 students at the Cornwall Elementary School, Cornwall, Pennsylvania, USA, on May 14 2001.

MOST CONSECUTIVE SERVES
The most consecutive serves landed successfully without recording a double fault is 8,017 by Rob Peterson (USA) at Port Aransas, Texas, USA, on December 5 1998. Peterson was hitting tennis balls for a grueling 10 hr 7 min during his record-breaking performance.

REAL TENNIS

OLDEST COURT
Real tennis, or court tennis, is the world's oldest racket sport, with a recognizable ancestry that dates back to the 11th century. The most noticeable difference to lawn tennis, which was defined by its own regulations in around 1875, is that the court in real tennis is walled. The oldest active court in the UK is at Falkland Palace in Fife, UK, built by King James V of Scotland in 1539.

MOST MEN'S WORLD CHAMPIONSHIP TITLES
The first recorded real tennis world champion was Clerg (France) in around 1740. Jacques Edmond Barre (France) held the title for a record 33 years from 1829 to 1862. Pierre Etchebaster (France) holds the record for the greatest number of successful defenses of the title, with eight between 1928 and 1952.

MOST WOMEN'S WORLD CHAMPIONSHIP TITLES
The women's World Championship (instituted 1985) has been won five times by Penny Lumley (UK) in 1989, 1991, 1995, 1997, and 1999.

RACQUETBALL

MOST MEN'S WORLD CHAMPIONSHIP TITLES
The Racquetball World Championship was held for the first time in 1981, and the tournament has taken place biennially since 1984. Since its institution, the USA has won nine team titles – 1981, 1984, 1986 (jointly won with Canada), 1988, 1990, 1992, 1994, 1996, and 1998.

MOST WOMEN'S WORLD CHAMPIONSHIP TITLES
The most titles won by an individual is three by Michelle Gould (USA) in 1992, 1994, and 1996.

TABLE TENNIS

LONGEST MATCH
Danny Price and Randy Nunes (both USA) played for 132 hr 31 min at Cherry Hill, New Jersey, USA, on August 20–26 1978.

LONGEST DOUBLES MATCH
The longest doubles marathon is one of 101 hr 1 min 11 sec by brothers Lance, Phil, and Mark Warren, and Bill Weir (all USA) at Sacramento, California, USA, on April 9–13 1979.

MOST OLYMPIC GOLD MEDALS
Deng Yaping (China) has won four Olympic gold medals – the women's singles in 1992 and 1996, and the women's doubles (both with Qiao Hang) in 1992 and 1996.

MOST OLYMPIC MEDALS
As well as Deng Yaping (China), who took four medals – all gold – in the Games of 1992 and 1996, Yoo Nam-kyu (South Korea) has also won four Olympic medals – one gold and three bronze from 1988–96.

MOST MEN'S OLYMPIC GOLD MEDALS
The most men's Olympic titles is two by Liu Guoliang (China) in the singles and doubles competitions in 1996.

LONGEST RALLY
John Duffy and Kevin Schick (New Zealand) achieved a 5 hr 2 min 18.5 sec rally at Whangarei, New Zealand, on November 5 1977.

The longest rally in competition was in a 1936 Swaythling Cup match in Prague, Czechoslovakia (now Czech Republic), between Alex Ehrlich (Poland) and Paneth Farcas (Romania). It lasted 2 hr 12 min.

FASTEST 5,000 COUNTER-HITTING
With a paddle in each hand, S Ramesh Babu (India) completed 5,000 consecutive volleys over the net in 41 min 27 sec at Jawaharal Nehru Stadium, Swargate, India, on April 14 1995.

SQUASH

SHORTEST MATCH
Philip Kenyon (UK) beat Salah Nadi (Egypt) 9-0, 9-0, 9-0 in 6 min 37 sec in the British Open at Lamb's Squash Club, London, UK, on April 9 1992.

YOUNGEST TENNIS MEN'S WORLD NO.1
When Marat Safin (Russia, above) won the President's Cup tournament in Tashkent, Uzbekistan, on September 17 2000 he became the world men's No.1 at the age of just 20 years 234 days.

MOST WORLD OPEN TITLES

Jansher Khan (Pakistan) has won a record eight World Open titles in 1987, 1989, and 1990, and from 1992 to 1996. The Khan family has dominated squash, winning 29 British Opens since 1950 and 14 World Opens since 1975.

MOST CLUB CHAMPIONSHIPS

The most club championships won by an individual at the same club is 19 by Pauline Brown (UK) at the Leamington Spa Lawn Tennis and Squash Club, Leamington Spa, Warwickshire, UK, from 1978–93 and 1995–97. Her 16 consecutive titles is also a record.

FASTEST SQUASH BALL

At Wimbledon Squash and Badminton Club in January 1988, Roy Buckland (UK) hit a ball with an overhead service at a measured speed of 144.6 mph (232.7 km/h) against the front wall. This is equivalent to an initial speed at the racket of a remarkable 150.8 mph (242.6 km/h).

BADMINTON

MOST WOMEN'S TEAM WORLD CHAMPIONSHIP TITLES

The most wins at the women's World Championships for the Uber Cup (instituted in 1956) is eight by China in 1984, 1986, 1988, 1990, 1992, 1998, 2000, and 2002. The only other nations to have won the biennial competition are the USA, Japan, and Indonesia, who have shared the remaining 11 trophies.

LONGEST MATCH

In the men's singles final at the World Championship at Glasgow, Strathclyde, UK, on June 1 1997, Peter Rasmussen (Denmark) beat Sun Jun (China) 16-17, 18-13, 15-10 in a match that lasted 124 minutes.

SHORTEST MATCH

Ra Kyung-min (South Korea) needed just six minutes to beat Julia Mann (UK) 11-2, 11-1 during the 1996 Uber Cup in Hong Kong on May 19 1996, a record for a competitive badminton match.

MOST OLYMPIC MEDALS

Badminton was first contested at the 1992 Olympic Games in Barcelona, Spain, and since its inauguration no individual has won more than one gold medal. The most medals of any color won to date is the three taken by Gil Young Ah (South Korea). She has claimed the full complement – a gold medal in the mixed doubles in 1996, a silver medal in the women's doubles in 1996, and a bronze medal in the women's doubles in 1992.

FASTEST SHUTTLECOCK

On November 5 1996 at Warwickshire Racquets and Health Club, Coventry, Warwicks, UK, Simon Archer (UK, above) smashed a badminton shuttlecock at a world record measured speed of 162 mph (260 km/h).

MOST WORLD CHAMPIONSHIP SINGLES TITLES

Four Chinese players have won two individual world titles – in the men's singles the record goes to Yang Yang, who was successful in 1987 and 1989. Three players have made this achievement in women's singles – Li Lingwei in 1983 and 1989; Han Aiping in 1985 and 1987, and Ye Zhaoying in 1995 and 1997.

MOST WORLD CHAMPIONSHIP TITLES

A record five titles have been won by Park Joo-bong (South Korea) in the men's doubles in 1985 and 1991 and mixed doubles in 1985, 1989, and 1991.

MOST THOMAS CUPS

The most wins at the World Team Championships – or Thomas Cup – is 13 by Indonesia between 1958 and 2002. Hendrawan (below) was a key member of the team of 2002.

MEN'S 4 X 200-M SHORT-COURSE FREESTYLE RELAY
An Australian team made up of William Kirby, Ian Thorpe, Michael Klim, and Grant Hackett (above) completed the men's 4 x 200-m short-course freestyle relay in a record time of 6:56.41 in Perth, WA, Australia on August 7 2001.

GREATEST DISTANCE SWUM
Between June 25 and August 23 2000 Martin Strel (Slovenia) swam the length of the Danube River followed by three other stages to complete a record total distance of 1,866.6 miles (3,004 km).

FARTHEST DISTANCE SWUM IN 24 HOURS IN 25-M POOL
Anders Forvass (Sweden) swam 63.3 miles (101.9 km) in the 25-m Linköping public swimming pool, Sweden, on October 28–29 1989.

MEN'S FARTHEST DISTANCE SWUM IN 24 HOURS IN 50-M POOL
Grant Robinson (Australia) swam a world record distance of 62.82 miles (101.1 km) in a 24-hour period in a 50-m pool at the Mingara Leisure Centre, Tumbi Umbi, NSW, Australia, on June 28–29 1997.

WOMEN'S FARTHEST DISTANCE SWUM IN 24 HOURS IN 50-M POOL
Kelly Driffield (Australia) swam a world record total distance of 59.44 miles (95.657 km) in a period of 24 hours in a 50-m pool at the Mingara Leisure Centre, Tumbi Umbi, NSW, Australia on June 28–29 1997.

FASTEST 50 M SWUM UNDERWATER
Maarten Sterck (Netherlands) swam 164 ft (50 m) underwater in 38.98 sec on March 11 2001 at Valkenswaard, The Netherlands.

HIGHEST SHALLOW DIVE
Danny Higginbottom (USA) dove from 29 ft 1 in (8.86 m) into 12 in (30 cm) of water at the Therme Erding Spa, Munich, Germany, on April 1 2000.

MOST CONTINUOUS ROTATIONS UNDERWATER WITH ONE BREATH
Marta Fernández Pèrez (Spain) completed 28 rotations in one breath in a tank in Madrid, Spain, on October 18 2001.

MOST DIVING WORLD CHAMPIONSHIP TITLES
Greg Louganis (USA) won five world titles – highboard in 1978, and both highboard and springboard in 1982 and 1986 – as well as four Olympic gold medals in 1984 and 1988.

Philip George Boggs (USA) won three gold medals in one event, the springboard, in 1973, 1975, and 1978.

MOST PARTICIPANTS IN ONE-HOUR SWIMATHON
The most people to take part in an hour-long swimathon charity event is 2,533. The event was organized by BT Swimathon 2000 and occurred at more than 500 British pools from 6 to 7 pm on March 18 2000.

MEN'S SHORT-COURSE WORLD RECORDS
Men's 50-m backstroke
23.42
Neil Walker (USA)
Athens, Greece
March 16 2000

Men's 100-m backstroke
50.75
Neil Walker (USA)
Athens, Greece
March 19 2000

Men's 200-m backstroke
1:51.17
Aaron Peirsol (USA)
Moscow, Russia
April 7 2002

Men's 50-m breaststroke
26.20
Oleg Lisogor (Ukraine)
Berlin, Germany
January 26 2002

Men's 100-m breaststroke
57.47
Ed Moses (USA)
Stockholm, Sweden
January 23 2002

Men's 200-m breaststroke
2:03.17
Ed Moses (USA)
Berlin, Germany
January 26 2002

Men's 50-m butterfly
22.74
Geoff Huegill (Australia)
Berlin, Germany
January 26 2002

Men's 100-m butterfly
50.10
Thomas Rupprath (Germany)
Berlin, Germany
January 27 2002

Men's 200-m butterfly
1:51.21
Thomas Rupprath (Germany)
Rostock, Germany
December 1 2001

Men's 50-m freestyle
21.13
Mark Foster (UK)
Paris, France
January 28 2001

Men's 100-m freestyle
46.74
Alexander Popov (Russia)
Gelsenkirchen, Germany
March 19 1994

Men's 200-m freestyle
1:41.10
Ian Thorpe (Australia)
Berlin, Germany
February 6 2000

Men's 400-m freestyle
3:35.01
Grant Hackett (Australia)
Hong Kong
April 2 1999

Men's 800-m freestyle
7:25.28
Grant Hackett (Australia)
Perth, WA, Australia
August 3 2001

Men's 1,500-m freestyle
14:10.10
Grant Hackett (Australia)
Perth, WA, Australia
August 7 2001

Men's 4 x 50-m freestyle relay
1:26.78
USA (Bryan Jones, Matt Ulricksson, Robert Bogart, Leffie Crawford)
Minneapolis, Minnesota, USA
March 23 2000

Men's 4 x 100-m freestyle relay
3:09.57
Sweden (Johan Nystrom, Lars Frolander, Mattias Ohlin, Stefan Nystrand)
Athens, Greece
March 16 2000

Men's 4 x 200-m freestyle relay
6:56.41
Australia (William Kirby, Ian Thorpe, Michael Klim, Grant Hackett)
Perth, WA, Australia
August 7 2001

Men's 100-m medley
52.63
Peter Mankoc (Slovenia)
Antwerp, Belgium
December 15 2001

Men's 200-m medley
1:54.65
Jani Sievinen (Finland)
Kuopio, Finland
April 21 1994
Atilla Czene (Hungary)
Minneapolis, Minnesota, USA,
March 23 2000

Men's 400-m medley
4:04.24
Matthew Dunn (Australia)
Perth, WA, Australia
September 24 1998

Men's 4 x 50-m medley relay
1:35.51 (achieved in same race)
Germany (Thomas Rupprath, Mark Warnecke, Alexander Luderitz, Stephan Kunzelmann)
Sweden (Daniel Carlsson, Patrik Isaksson, Jonas Akesson, Lars Frolander)
Sheffield, S Yorks, England
December 13 1998

Men's 4 x 100-m medley relay
3:29.00
USA (Aaron Peirsol, David Denniston, Peter Marshall, Jason Lezak)
Moscow, Russia
April 7 2002

WOMEN'S SHORT-COURSE WORLD RECORDS

Women's 50-m backstroke
26.83
Hui Li (China)
Shanghai, China
December 2 2001

Women's 100-m backstroke
57.08
Natalie Coughlin (USA)
New York City, USA
November 28 2001

Women's 200-m backstroke
2:03.62
Natalie Coughlin (USA)
New York City, USA
November 27 2001

Women's 50-m breaststroke
29.96
Emma Igelström (Sweden)
Moscow, Russia
April 4 2002

Women's 100-m breaststroke
1:05.38
Emma Igelström (Sweden)
Moscow, Russia
April 6 2002

Women's 200-m breaststroke
2:19.25
Hiu Qi (China)
Paris, France
January 28 2001

Women's 50-m butterfly
25.36
Anna-Karin Kammerling (Sweden)
Stockholm, Sweden
January 25 2001

Women's 100-m butterfly
56.55
Martina Moravcova (Slovakia)
Berlin, Germany
January 26 2002

Women's 200-m butterfly
2:04.16
Susan O'Neill (Australia)
Sydney, Australia
January 18 2000

Women's 50-m freestyle
23.59
Therese Alshammar (Sweden)
Athens, Greece
March 18 2000

Women's 100-m freestyle
52.17
Therese Alshammar (Sweden)
Athens, Greece
March 17 2000

Women's 200-m freestyle
1:54.04
Lindsay Benko (USA)
Moscow, Russia
April 7 2002

Women's 400-m freestyle
4:00.03
Claudia Poll (Costa Rica)
Gothenburg, Sweden,
April 19 1997

Women's 800-m freestyle
8:14.35
Sachiko Yamada (Japan)
Tokyo, Japan
April 2 2002

Women's 4 x 50-m freestyle relay
1:38.21
Sweden (Annika Lofstedt, Therese Alshammar, Johanna Sjöberg, Anna-Karin Kammerling)
Valencia, Spain, December 15 2000

Women's 4 x 100-m freestyle relay
3:34.55
China (Le Jingyi, Na Chao, Shan Ying, Nian Yin)
Gothenburg, Sweden
April 19 1997

Women's 4 x 200-m freestyle relay
7:46.30
China (Xu Yanvei, Zhu Yingven, Tang Jingzhi, Yang Yu)
Moscow, Russia, April 3 2002

Women's 100-m medley
59.30
Jenny Thompson (USA)
Hong Kong
April 2 1999

Women's 200-m medley
2:07.79
Allison Wagner (USA)
Palma de Mallorca, Spain
December 5 1993

Women's 400-m medley
4:27.83
Yana Klochkova (Ukraine)
Paris, France
January 19 2002

Women's 4 x 50-m medley relay
1:48.31
Sweden (Therese Alshammar, Emma Igelström, Anna-Karin Kammerling, Johanna Sjöberg)
Valencia, Spain
December 16 2000

Women's 4 x 100-m medley relay
3:55.78
Sweden (Therese Alshammar, Emma Igelström, Anna-Karin Kammerling, Johanna Sjöberg)
Moscow, Russia
April 5 2002

WOMEN'S 50-M SHORT-COURSE BREASTSTROKE

Emma Igelström (Sweden, left) holds the world record for the fastest women's 50-m short-course breaststroke with a time of 29.96 sec in Moscow, Russia, achieved on April 4 2002. In Moscow two days later (April 6 2002) Igelström also swam a world record time of 1:05.38 in the women's 100-m short-course breaststroke competition.

FASTEST WOMEN'S SINGLE SCULLS – 2,000 M
The women's single sculls record over 2,000 m is 7 min 11.68 sec by Ekaterina Karsten (Belarus, above) at St Catharines, Ontario, Canada, on August 28 1999. Her average speed during the race was 10.36 mph (16.68 km/h).

ROWING

MOST MEN'S OLYMPIC GOLD MEDALS
Steven Redgrave (UK) holds the record for winning the most gold medals in rowing at the Olympic Games, with a total of five. His victories have come in the coxed fours of 1984 and 2000 and the coxless pairs of 1988, 1992, and 1996. For winning five golds in five successive Olympics in such a physically demanding sport, many experts consider Redgrave the greatest Olympian of the modern era.

MOST WOMEN'S OLYMPIC GOLD MEDALS
Canadian pair Kathleen Heddle and Marnie McBean have both won three Olympic gold medals for rowing – in the coxless pairs and the eights in the 1992 Games in Barcelona, Spain, and in the double sculls in 1996 in Atlanta, Georgia, USA.

MOST UNIVERSITY BOAT RACE WINS
The first University Boat Race, which Oxford won, was from Hambledon Lock to Henley Bridge, London, UK, on June 10 1829. Outrigged eights were first used in 1846, and the course now goes along the Thames from Putney to Mortlake, London, UK. In the 148 races to 2002, Cambridge has won 77 times, Oxford 70 times, and there was one dead heat, on March 24 1877.

UNIVERSITY BOAT RACE – MARGINS OF VICTORY
The closest finishes to the boat race were in 1952 and 1980. Oxford won both by a deck – 6 ft (1.8 m).

Apart from when one boat had sunk, the greatest winning margin was by Cambridge with 20 lengths in 1900.

OLDEST UNIVERSITY BOAT RACE PARTICIPANT
The oldest rower is Cambridge's Donald MacDonald, who was 31 years 3 months when he took part in the 1987 race. However, Cambridge cox Andrew Probert was 38 years 3 months in 1992.

YOUNGEST UNIVERSITY BOAT RACE PARTICIPANT
Robert Ross was 18 years 200 days when he rowed for Cambridge in the 1977 University Boat Race.

LONGEST SEA ROWING RACE
The longest rowing race held on the open sea is the biennial Celtic Challenge, which takes participants across the Irish Sea. The course taken by the rowers measures a record 78 nautical miles (144.5 km) from Arklow, Co Wicklow, Ireland, to Aberystwyth, Ceredigion, UK.

FASTEST MEN'S EIGHT – 2,000 M
The record for 2,000 m on non-tidal water is 5:22.80, at an average speed of 13.85 mph (22.30 km/h), by The Netherlands at the World Championships at St Catharines, Ontario, Canada, on August 28 1999.

FASTEST WOMEN'S EIGHT – 2,000 M
The women's record for 2,000 m on non-tidal water is 5:57.02 by Romania at Lucerne, Switzerland, on July 9 1999. Their average speed was 12.53 mph (20.16 km/h).

FASTEST ROWING FROM LONDON TO PARIS
A team of 21 Jersey Rowing Club members rowed from Westminster Bridge, London, UK, to the Eiffel Tower, Paris, France, in a time of 90 hr 33 min 33 sec. The journey took from September 25 to 28 2000 and is the fastest time such a trip has ever been completed.

CANOEING

MOST OLYMPIC GOLD MEDALS
Birgit Fischer (East Germany to 1990, then Germany) won seven Olympic gold medals between 1980 and 2000. She also won three silvers for a record total of 10 medals.

In addition to her seven Olympic titles, Fischer has won 29 world titles for a record total of 36 titles overall.

The men's record is held by Gert Fredriksson (Sweden), who won a record six Olympic gold medals between 1948 and 1960. He also won a silver and a bronze to make a record eight medals in total.

Fredriksson also won seven World Championship titles, giving him a combined total of 13 Olympic and World titles between 1948 and 1960. He shares this record with Rüdiger Helm (East Germany), whose successes came between 1976 and 1983, and Ivan Patzaichin (Romania), who won his titles from 1968 to 1984.

FASTEST UNIVERSITY BOAT RACE
The race record time for the 4 miles 374 yd (6.779 km) University Boat Race on the Thames River, London, UK, is 16 min 19 sec by Cambridge (above) on March 28 1998. Their average speed was 15.49 mph (24.93 km/h).

LARGEST CANOE RAFT

A total of 776 canoes and kayaks were held together to form a giant raft on Hinckley Lake in Hinckley, Ohio, USA, on May 19 2001 at an event organized by Cleveland Metroparks. The rules for this record state that the craft must be held by participants and not tied together.

MOST ESKIMO ROLLS BY HAND

Colin Hill (UK) achieved 1,000 eskimo rolls by hand in a record 31 min 55.62 sec at Consett, Durham, UK, on March 12 1987.

He also managed 100 rolls in 2 min 39.2 sec at Crystal Palace, London, UK, on February 22 1987.

MOST ESKIMO ROLLS BY A MAN

Ray Hudspith (UK) achieved 1,000 eskimo rolls with a paddle in a record 34 min 43 sec at Elswick Pool, Newcastle, Tyne and Wear, UK, on March 20 1987.

Hudspith also completed 100 rolls in a record time of 3 min 7.25 sec at Killingworth Leisure Centre, Tyne and Wear, UK, on March 3 1991.

MOST ESKIMO ROLLS BY A WOMAN

Helen Barnes (UK) completed 100 eskimo rolls in 3 min 42.16 sec on August 2 2000.

FASTEST MEN'S SINGLE SCULLS – 2,000 M

The single sculls world record for completing a distance of 2,000 m on non-tidal water is a time of 6 min 36.38 sec – at an average speed of 11.28 mph (18.16 km/h) – by Robert Wadell (New Zealand, right) at St Catharines, Ontario, Canada, on August 28 1999.

GREATEST DISTANCE IN CANOE IN 24 HOURS

Ian Adamson paddled 203.3 miles (327.1 km) along the Colorado River from Gore Canyon, Kremmling, Colorado, USA, to Potash, near Moab, Utah, USA, on June 7–8 1997.

FASTEST TIME TO COMPLETE 200 M

At the 1998 World Championships at Szeged, Hungary, the Hungarian four-man team claimed the 200-m title in a time of 31.155 sec, which represents an average racing speed of 14.36 mph (23.11 km/h).

FASTEST TIME TO COMPLETE 1,000 M

The 1996 German four-man kayak Olympic champions covered a distance of

1,000 m in 2 min 51.52 sec to win gold on August 3 1996 at Atlanta, Georgia, USA. This is an average speed of 13.04 mph (20.98 km/h).

LONGEST FREE-FALL WATERFALL DESCENT

The longest free-fall descent over a waterfall is 64 ft 8 in (19.7 m) achieved by Shaun Baker (UK) over the Aldeyjarfoss on the Skjalfandafljot, a glacial river in Iceland, on September 25 1996.

LONGEST RACE

The Canadian Government Centennial Voyageur Canoe Pageant and Race from Rocky Mountain House, Alberta, Canada, to the Expo 67 site at Montreal, Quebec, Canada, covered 3,283 miles (5,283 km). Ten canoes represented each of the Canadian provinces and territories. The winner of the race, which took from May 24 to September 4 1967, was the *Radisson*, the canoe from the province of Manitoba.

FASTEST 75-FT VERTICAL DESCENT

The fastest time to descend a vertical height of 75 ft (22.86 m) on a river in a canoe is 19.9 sec by Shaun Baker (UK) in Snowdonia, Gwynedd, UK, on August 26 2000.

PUNTING

LONGEST JOURNEY

The longest known journey that has been completed by punting – pushing a boat using a pole – is a trip of 721 miles (1,160 km) between Oxford, UK, to Leeds, W Yorks, UK, and back to Oxford by John Pearse (UK) – who was accompanied by four crew members – from June 19 to August 10 1965.

YACHTING

MOST PARTICIPANTS IN AN OCEAN RACE
The largest trans-oceanic race was the 1989 Atlantic Rally for Cruisers (ARC), when 204 boats of the 209 starters from 24 nations completed the race from Las Palmas, Canary Islands, Spain, to Barbados, West Indies.

MOST INDIVIDUAL AMERICA'S CUP RACES
Dennis Conner (USA) has raced in six America's Cups as a member of the afterguard, more than anybody else. He made his debut in 1974, was a winning skipper/helmsman in 1980, 1987, and 1989, and a losing skipper in 1983 and 1995.

Charlie Barr (USA) who defended in 1899, 1901, and 1903 and Harold S Vanderbilt (USA) in 1930, 1934, and 1937, each steered the successful winner three times in succession.

NARROWEST AMERICA'S CUP FINISHING MARGIN
The closest finish to an America's Cup race was on October 4 1901, when *Shamrock II* (UK) crossed the finish line 2 seconds ahead of the American boat *Columbia*.

FASTEST SOLO CIRCUMNAVIGATION
Yachtsman Michel Desjoyeaux (France) circumnavigated the globe in 93 days 3 hr 57 min 32 sec during the 2000 Vendée Globe single-handed yacht race in his yacht *PRB*, starting and finishing at Les Sables d'Olonne, France. He covered 24,000 miles (38,600 km) between November 5 2000 and February 10 2001.

MOST YACHTING OLYMPIC GOLD MEDALS
The first sportsman ever to win individual gold medals in four successive Olympic Games was Paul Elvstrøm (Denmark) in the Firefly yachting class in 1948 and the Finn class in 1952, 1956, and 1960. He also won eight other world titles.

GREATEST DISTANCE KITE SURFING
Kite surfing (above) involves using surfboards pulled by kites. On December 21 2001 Neil Hutchinson, Kent Marincovik, and Fabrice Collard (all USA) traveled a record distance of 88 nautical miles (101.3 miles or 163 km) between Key West, Florida, USA, and Varadero, Cuba.

OLDEST ROUND-THE-WORLD RACE
The oldest regular sailing race around the world is the quadrennial Whitbread Round the World Race (instituted in August 1973, now called the Volvo Round the World Race), originally organized by the Royal Naval Sailing Association. It starts in the UK, and the route taken and the number of legs varies from race to race. The distance covered by the 1997–98 race was 31,600 nautical miles (59,239 km) from Southampton, Hants, UK, and back. The winning boat, *EF Language*, was skippered by Paul Cayard (USA), the first American to win the race.

SAILBOARDING

LONGEST SAILBOARD
The longest sailboard measures 165 ft (50.2 m) and was made in Fredrikstad, Norway. It first sailed on June 28 1986.

LONGEST SAILBOARD SNAKE
The world's longest sailboard snake was made up of 70 windsurfers in tandem at the Sailboard Show '89 event at Narrabeen Lakes, Manly, NSW, Australia, on October 21 1989.

MOST AMERICA'S CUP WINS
There have been 30 challenges for the America's Cup since 1851 at Cowes, Isle of Wight, UK, with the USA winning every time except in 1983 (to Australia), in 1995 and in 2000 (both times to New Zealand – shown above).

WINDSURFING AT THE HIGHEST LATITUDE

Gerard-Jan Goekoop (Netherlands) windsurfed alongside the pack-ice of the Arctic Ocean at 80º 40.3' N, 13º 43' E, north of the Spitsbergen archipelago on July 14 1985. Goekoop was ship's doctor on board the *MS Plancius* and went surfing when the boat got stuck in the ice.

MOST WINDSURFING WORLD CHAMPIONSHIPS

World Championships were first held in 1973, and the sport was added to the Olympics in 1984 when the winner was Stephan van den Berg (Netherlands) who also won five world titles between 1979 and 1983.

SURFING

LONGEST RIDE ON A RIVER BORE

The Official British Surfing Association holds the record for the longest ride on a river bore, set on the Severn Bore, UK. The record on a surfboard is 5.7 miles (9.1 km), from Windmill Hill to Maisemore Weir, by David Lawson (UK) on August 29 1996.

LONGEST RIDE ON SEA WAVES

About four to six times each year rideable surfing waves break in Matanchen Bay near San Blas, Nayarit, Mexico, which make rides of around 5,700 ft (1,700 m) possible.

MOST WOMEN'S SURFING WORLD CHAMPIONSHIPS

The women's professional surfing World Championship was instituted in 1979 and has been won on four occasions by three women: Frieda Zamba (USA) from 1984 to 1986 and in 1988; Wendy Botha (Australia, formerly South Africa) in 1987, 1989, 1991, and 1992, and Lisa Andersen (USA) from 1994 to 1997.

WATER-SKIING

LONGEST WATER-SKI JUMP

The official International Water Ski Federation record for the longest ski-jump is 232 ft 7 in (70.9 m). This was achieved by Jimmy Siemers (USA) at the Tri-Lakes Late Bloomer event at Zachary, Louisiana, USA, on October 22 2000.

The same record for the longest water-ski jump achieved by a woman is 180 ft 9 in (55.1 m) by Elena Milakova (Russia) at Lincoln, UK, on July 27 2001.

LONGEST WATER-SKI FLY DISTANCE

The official International Water Ski Federation record for ski-flying is a distance of 298 ft 10 in (91.1 m), by Jaret Llewellyn (Canada) at the Big Air Challenge event at Orlando, Florida, USA, on May 14 2000. Ski-flying is a similar discipline to regular ski-jumping, but participants have a longer rope, travel behind faster boats, and leap off extended ramps to achieve greater distances.

The women's record is 218 ft 6 in (66.6 m), a distance achieved by both Toni Neville and Emma Sheer (both Australia) at the America's Cup event at West Palm Beach, Florida, USA, on September 23 and 24 2000 respectively.

MOST WATER-SKIERS TOWED BEHIND A BOAT

A record 100 water-skiers were towed on double skis over a distance of a nautical mile (1.852 km) by the cruiser *Reef Cat* at Cairns, Queensland, Australia, on October 18 1986. This feat, which was organized by the Cairns and District Powerboating and Ski Club, was then replicated by 100 skiers on single skis.

HIGHEST RIDEABLE SURFING WAVES

Waimea Bay, Hawaii, USA (above), reputedly provides the most consistently high waves, often reaching a rideable limit of 30–35 ft (9–11 m). The highest wave ever ridden was a tsunami of "perhaps 50 feet," which struck on April 3 1868.

MOST MEN'S PRO SURFING WORLD CHAMPIONSHIPS

The World Professional series began in 1975. Since then, the men's title has been won six times by Kelly Slater (USA, right) in 1992 and 1994–1998. Slater began competing at age eight and won his first competition the same year.

HIGHEST POLO SCORE

The highest aggregate number of goals scored in an international match is 30, during Argentina's 21-9 defeat of the USA at Meadowbrook, Long Island, New York, USA, in September 1936.

MOST POLO WORLD CHAMPIONSHIPS

Five Polo World Championships have been contested and three have been won by Argentina, in 1987, 1992, and 1998. The World Championships are held every three years under the auspices of the Federation of International Polo (FIP).

MOST CHUKKAS IN ONE DAY

The most chukkas – a period of continuous play, generally lasting 7½ minutes – played on one ground in a day is 43. This total was achieved by the Pony Club on the No. 3 Ground at Kirtlington Park, Oxon, UK, on July 31 1991.

HIGHEST JUMP

The official Fédération Equestre Internationale (FEI) high-jump record is 8 ft 1.25 in (2.47 m) by *Huaso*, ridden by Capt Alberto Larraguibel Morales (Chile) at Viña del Mar, Santiago, Chile, on February 5 1949.

The indoor high-jump record is 7 ft 10.5 in (2.4 m) by *Optibeurs Leonardo*, ridden by Franke Sloothaak (Germany) at Chaudefontaine, Switzerland, on June 9 1991.

LOWEST OLYMPIC SHOW-JUMPING SCORE

The lowest Olympic show-jumping score obtained by a winner is that of no faults, and the record is shared by Frantisek Ventura (Czechoslovakia, now Czech Republic) on *Eliot* in 1928, Alwin Schockemöhle (West Germany) on *Warwick Rex* in 1976, and Ludger Beerbaum (Germany) on *Classic Touch* in 1992.

MOST SHOW-JUMPING OLYMPIC GOLD MEDALS

The most Olympic show-jumping gold medals won by a rider is five by Hans Günter Winkler (West Germany) – four team medals in 1956, 1960, 1964, and 1972 and the individual Grand Prix in 1956. Winkler also won team silver in 1976 and team bronze in 1968, giving him a record seven medals overall.

MOST INDIVIDUAL DRESSAGE OLYMPIC GOLD MEDALS

Henri St Cyr (Sweden) won a record two individual Olympic gold medals in 1952 and 1956. Nicole Uphoff (Germany) has also won a record two gold medals, with successes in 1988 and 1992.

LARGEST PLAYING FIELD

The largest standard playing field for any ball game is the 12.4 acres (5 ha) for polo (below). This area is accounted for by a maximum length of 300 yd (274 m) and a width, without side boards, of 200 yd (182 m). With boards the width is 160 yd (146 m).

MOST CAREER
WINS BY A JOCKEY
Laffit Pincay Jr (USA, above) has ridden 9,311 winners from May 16 1964 to date. He broke the previous record, by Bill Shoemaker (USA), with a win on October 12 1999, taking his then total to 8,834. Pincay won the Eclipse Award five times, in 1971, 1973–74, 1979, and 1985, the Belmont Stakes three times, and the Kentucky Derby once, in 1984.

MOST TEAM
SHOW-JUMPING
OLYMPIC GOLD MEDALS
The most team wins in the Prix des Nations at the Olympic Games is seven by Germany in 1936, 1956, 1960, 1964, and 1996, and as West Germany in 1972 and 1988.

MOST TEAM DRESSAGE
OLYMPIC GOLD MEDALS
Germany have won a record 10 team gold medals, in 1928, 1936, 1964, 1968, 1976, 1984, 1988, 1992, 1996, and 2000. The country competed as West Germany from 1968 to 1990.

MOST SHOW-JUMPING
WORLD CHAMPIONSHIPS
Two men have won the Show-Jumping World Championships twice: Hans Günter Winkler

(Germany) in 1954 and 1955 and Raimondo d'Inzeo (Italy) in 1956 and 1960.

MOST SHOW-JUMPING
WORLD CUPS
The greatest number of Show-Jumping World Cup wins is three by Hugo Simon (Austria) in 1979, 1996, and 1997, and Rodrigo Pessoa (Brazil) in 1998, 1999, and 2000.

MOST THREE-DAY-EVENT
OLYMPIC GOLD MEDALS
Charles Ferdinand Pahud de Mortanges (Netherlands) won four three-day-event Olympic gold medals (team event in 1924 and 1928, and individual in 1928 and 1932, when he also won a team silver medal).

BEST RACEHORSE
WIN-LOSS RECORD
The best career win-loss record for a racehorse is 100% wins by *Kincsem*, a Hungarian mare foaled in 1874, who was unbeaten in all of her 54 races throughout Europe, including the Goodwood Cup of 1878.

HIGHEST PRICED HORSE
The largest amount of money paid for a yearling is $13.1 million (£9 million) for *Seattle Dancer* on

July 23 1985 at Keeneland, Kentucky, USA, by Robert Sangster and Partners. Part ownership of potential stallions often vastly inflates their value before they go to stud, when in fact the horse would not command that price if it were available on the open market.

FASTEST RACE
The highest speed recorded in a horse race is 43.26 mph (69.62 km/h) over a distance of 0.25 mile (402 m) by *Big Racket* at Mexico City, Mexico, on February 5 1945, and also by *Onion Roll* at Thistledown, Cleveland, Ohio, USA, on September 27 1993.

The record speed over 1.5 miles (2,413 m) is 37.82 mph (60.86 km/h) and was achieved by *Hawkster* at Santa Anita Park, Arcadia, California, USA, on October 14 1989.

OLDEST RACE WINNER
The oldest horses to win on the flat have been the 18-year-olds *Revenge* at Shrewsbury, Shropshire, UK, on September 23 1790, *Marksman* at Ashford, Kent, UK, on September 4 1826 and *Jorrocks* at Bathurst, NSW, Australia, on February 28 1851. At the same age *Wild Aster* won three

hurdle races in six days in March 1919, and *Sonny Somers* won two steeplechases in February 1980.

MOST CAREER WINS
BY A RACEHORSE
Chorisbar (foaled in 1935 in Puerto Rico) won 197 out of 324 races between 1937 and 1947.

MOST CONSECUTIVE
WINS BY A HORSE
The longest winning sequence for a racehorse is 56 races by *Camarero* (foaled 1951 in Puerto Rico) from April 19 1953 to August 17 1955.

MOST RACES WON IN
A YEAR BY A JOCKEY
The most races won in a year by a jockey is 598 from 2,312 rides by Kent Desormeaux (USA) in 1989.

MOST WINNERS IN ONE DAY
Chris Antley (USA) rode nine winners on October 31 1987, consisting of four in the afternoon at Aqueduct, New York, USA, and five in the evening at the Meadowlands, New Jersey, USA.

The most winners ridden on one card is eight by six riders, most recently (and from fewest rides) by Patrick Day (USA) from nine rides at Arlington International, Illinois, USA, on September 13 1989.

The longest winning streak is 12 by Sir Gordon Richards (UK) in 1933 (one race at Nottingham, UK, on October 3, six out of six at Chepstow, Gwent, UK, on October 4, and the first five races next day at Chepstow); and by Pieter Stroebel (Zimbabwe) at Bulawayo, Southern Rhodesia (now Zimbabwe), from June 7 to July 7 1958.

RICHEST DAY'S RACING
The Dubai World Cup meeting on March 23 2002 at Nad Al Sheba, Dubai, UAE (above), had $15.25 million (£10.4 million) in prize money on offer. The seven races included the world's richest race, the Dubai World Cup.

GLIDING

HIGHEST ALTITUDE
The absolute altitude record in a glider is 49,009 ft (14,938 m) by Robert Harris (USA) over California City, USA, on February 17 1986.

For women, the single-seater world record is 41,460 ft (12,637 m) by Sabrina Jackintell (USA) over Black Forest Gliderport, Colorado Springs, USA, on February 14 1979.

GREATEST ALTITUDE GAIN
The greatest height gain in a glider is 42,303 ft (12,894 m) by Paul Bikle (USA) over Lancaster, California, USA, on February 25 1961.

GREATEST DISTANCE
The greatest free distance flown in a glider is 907.7 miles (1,460.8 km) by Hans Werner Grosse (Germany) from Lübeck, Germany, to Biarritz, France, on April 25 1972.

Karla Karel (UK) flew 590.1 miles (949.7 km) in New South Wales, Australia, to achieve the women's record on January 20 1980.

FASTEST GLIDER SPEED
The official FAI world record speed for a glider is 153.96 mph (247.49 km/h) by James and Thomas Payne (both USA) over California City, USA, on March 3 1999.

Pamela Kurstjens-Hawkins (UK) set a women's record of 95.58 mph (153.83 km/h) over Tocumwal, NSW, Australia, on January 3 2000.

MOST WORLD CHAMPIONSHIP TITLES
The most World Individual Gliding Championships won is four, by Ingo Renner (Australia) in 1976 (Standard class), 1983, 1985, and 1987 (Open).

GREATEST PARAGLIDING ALTITUDE GAIN
The paragliding height gain record is 14,849 ft (4,526 m) by Robbie Whittal (UK, above) at Brandvlei, South Africa, on January 6 1993.

The women's record is 14,189 ft (4,325 m) by Kat Thurston (UK) over Kuruman, South Africa, on January 1 1996.

PARAGLIDING

GREATEST DISTANCE
The men's paragliding distance record is 208.16 miles (335 km) by Godfrey Wenness (Australia) from Mt Borah to Ennera Station, Queensland, Australia, on November 16 1998.

GREATEST DISTANCE FLOWN IN A TANDEM PARAGLIDER
Richard Westgate and Jim Coutts (both UK) piloted a tandem paraglider 136.95 miles (220.4 km) from Quixada, Brazil, on November 30 2000.

HANG-GLIDING

MOST WORLD CHAMPIONSHIP TITLES
First held in 1976, the most individual world championships wins is three by Tomas Suchanek (Czech Republic) in 1991, 1993, and 1995.

The women's world championship was first held in 1987, and the most individual wins is two – Judy Leden (UK) in 1987 and 1991, and Kari Castle (USA) in 1996 and 2000.

The World Team Championships have been won most often by Great Britain (1981, 1985, 1989, and 1991).

GREATEST DISTANCE
The Fédération Aéronautique Internationale (FAI) record for the greatest distance covered in a single flight by a hang-glider is 347.78 miles (559.7 km) by Davis Straub (USA) on August 10 2000.

The FAI straight-line distance record by a woman in a hang-glider is 230.44 miles (370.87 km) by Tove Heaney (Australia) from Garnpung Lake, NSW, to Bealiba, Victoria, Australia, on December 2 1998.

PARACHUTING

LARGEST MASS PARACHUTE JUMP
A total of 588 military and civilian parachutists from five nations parachuted from seven aircraft flying at 12,000 ft (3,660 m) over the Santa Cruz Air Base, Rio de Janeiro, Brazil, on April 18 2000.

MOST PARACHUTE JUMPS IN 24 HOURS
Michael Zang (USA) completed 500 parachute jumps in 24 hours at an airfield near Decatur, Texas, USA, from May 18–19 2001. He completed a 2,100-ft (640-m) jump every 2 min 53 sec on average, raising money for the Special Olympics.

FASTEST PARAGLIDING SPEED
Patrick Berod (France) attained 17.56 mph (28.26 km/h) over Albertville, France, on June 27 1995. Fiona Macaskill (UK, above) holds the women's record with 12.34 mph (19.86 km/h) at Plaine Joux, France, on April 21 2000.

GREATEST ALTITUDE GAIN IN A HANG-GLIDER
The greatest height gain in a hang-glider by a male pilot is 14,250 ft (4,343 m) by Larry Tudor (USA), over Owens Valley, California, USA, on August 4 1985.

Judy Leden (UK, right) holds the women's record, with a gain of 13,025 ft (3,970 m) over Kuruman, South Africa, on December 1 1992.

FREE-FALL

LARGEST FREE-FALL FORMATION
The World Team '99 completed a free-fall formation of 282 skydivers on December 16 1999 above Ubon Ratchathani, Thailand, holding a link for 7.11 seconds. The skydivers fell from 23,000 ft (7,010 m).

LARGEST FREE-FALL EVENT
The 10-day World Free-fall Convention 2000, held in Quincy, Illinois, USA, from August 4–13 2000, attracted 5,732 registered skydivers from 55 countries, who between them made in excess of 63,000 jumps. The busiest day was August 11, when 8,104 jumps were made, requiring flight operations on average every 1.08 minutes.

BALLOONING

MOST TO JUMP FROM A BALLOON
Twenty skydivers from the Paraclub Flevo (Netherlands) jumped from a Cameron A-415 PH-AGT balloon over Harfsen, The Netherlands, on April 22 2000. Two skydivers traveled on top of the balloon and jumped from 4,000 ft (1,219 m). Then the balloon climbed to 6,000 ft (1,828 m) and dropped 12 more skydivers. The six remaining left in two groups of three.

AEROBATICS

MOST WORLD CHAMPIONSHIP WINS
Petr Jirmus (Czechoslovakia, now Czech Republic) is the only man to become world aerobatics champion twice, in 1984 and in 1986. The competition, which is known as the Aresti Cup and has been held biennially since 1960, consists of a known and unknown compulsory and a free program.

Svetlana Kapanina (Russia) has won the overall women's competition, first held in 1986, a record three times – in 1996, 1998, and 2001.

LONGEST INVERTED FLIGHT
The longest inverted flight lasted 4 hr 38 min 10 sec, and was performed by Joann Osterud (Canada) flying from Vancouver to Vanderhoof, Canada, on July 24 1991. Osterud also holds the record for most outside loops – with 208 achieved in a Supernova Hyperbipe over North Bend, Oregon, USA, on July 13 1989.

MOST INSIDE LOOPS
On August 9 1986 David Childs (USA) performed 2,368 inside loops in a Bellanca Decathlon over North Pole, Alaska, USA.

MOST INVERTED FLAT SPINS
The most inverted flat spins performed in one attempt is 78 at 15,000 ft (4,500 m) by Wayne Handley (USA) in super-light stunt plane G202, on April 2 1999. After forcing his plane into an inverted flat spin, he attempted several upside-down rotations per thousand feet. At around 2,000 ft (609.6 m) Handley pulled out of this position and resumed flying as normal.

MEN'S 90-M ARCHERY

Oh Kyo-moon (South Korea, below left) scored 332 points out of a possible 360 at Wonju, South Korea, in November 2000. Kyo-moon also set a record of 1,379 out of a possible 1,440 in Wonju, South Korea, in November 2000. He is shown here with Kim Chung-Tae (below center) and Jang Yong-Ho (below right) with the gold medals they received for winning the team archery competition at the Sydney Olympic Games in 2000.

ARCHERY

OLDEST ORGANIZATION

The oldest archery body in the world is the Ancient Society of Kilwinning Archers, Ayrshire, UK. The Society's first recorded Papingo shoot (in which archers aim at a wooden model of a bird positioned on a pole at the top of a tall tower) was in 1483.

MOST POINTS SCORED FROM HORSEBACK

The greatest number of points scored from horseback in 12 hours is 4,238.18 recorded by Kassai Lajos (Hungary) at Kaposmero, Hungary, on June 6 1998.

HIGHEST MEN'S INDOOR 18-M SCORE

Michele Frangilli (Italy) scored 597 points from a possible 600 at the indoor 18-m distance in January 2001 in Nîmes, France.

HIGHEST MEN'S INDOOR 25-M SCORE

Michele Frangilli (Italy) scored 598 points out of a possible 600 at the indoor 25-m distance in November 2001 in Gallarate, Italy.

HIGHEST WOMEN'S INDOOR 18-M SCORE

Lina Herasymenko (Ukraine) scored 591 points from a possible 600 at the indoor 18-m distance in March 1997 in Istanbul, Turkey.

HIGHEST WOMEN'S INDOOR 25-M SCORE

Petra Ericsson (Sweden) scored 592 points out of a possible 600 at the indoor 25-m distance in March 1991 in Oulu, Finland.

HIGHEST SCORE IN 24 HOURS

The highest score in 24 hours over 18 FITA (Fédération Internationale de Tir à l'Arc) rounds is 26,064 by Michael Howson and Stephen Howard (both UK) at Oakbank Sports College, Keighley, W Yorkshire, UK, on November 11–12 2000.

The highest score in 24 hours by two archers is 76,158 in 70 Portsmouth Rounds (60 arrows per round shot at 60-cm FITA targets from 20 yd, or 18.29 m) by Simon Tarplee and David Hathaway (both UK) at Evesham, Worcs, UK, on April 1 1991. During the attempt Tarplee set an individual record of 38,500.

HIGHEST WOMEN'S 50-M SCORE

In November 1996 Kim Moon-sun (South Korea) scored 345 points from a possible 360 at 50 m in a single FITA round in Ch'ungju, South Korea.

HIGHEST WOMEN'S 70-M SCORE

Lee Hee-Jeong (South Korea) scored 348 points from a possible 360 at 70 m in one FITA round in Ch'ungju, South Korea, in October 2001.

POOL

FASTEST TIME TO CLEAR TWO TABLES

Nicolaos Nikolaidis (Canada) cleared two tables in 1 min 33 sec on August 14 2001 at Bar and Billiard Unison in Québec, Canada. He broke the record on his way to potting the most balls in 24 hours – 16,723.

FASTEST CLEARANCE

The record time for potting 15 balls is 26.5 sec by Dave Pearson (UK) at Pepper's Bar And Grill, Windsor, Ontario, Canada, on April 4 1997.

The women's record is 37.07 sec by Susan Thompson (UK) at the Phoenix Pool & Snooker Club, Wallasey, Merseyside, UK, on December 1 1996.

Pearson also holds the record for most tables cleared (15 balls) in 10 minutes, with 10 in Las Vegas, Nevada, USA, on May 25 1998.

HIGHEST SCORE FOR ARCHERY WOMEN'S INDOOR 36 FINAL

The highest score achieved for a 36 Final is 358 (out of 360) by Natalya Valeeva (Italy, above) at Caorle, Italy, in March 2002.

SNOOKER

FASTEST MAXIMUM BREAK

The fastest 147, or maximum break, recorded in a professional snooker tournament came in 5 min 20 sec. It was achieved by Ronnie O'Sullivan (UK) during the World Championship at the Crucible Theatre, Sheffield, S Yorks, UK, on April 21 1997.

O'Sullivan (UK) is also the youngest player to achieve a competitive maximum break of 147 at the age of 15 years 98 days during the English Amateur Championship (Southern Area) at Aldershot, Hants, UK, on March 13 1991.

HIGHEST BREAK

Wally West (UK) recorded a break of 151 in a match at the Hounslow Lucania, London, UK, in October 1976.

The break involved a free ball, creating an "extra" red, with all 15 reds still on the table, thus making a maximum break of 155 possible.

The only "16 red" clearance in a professional tournament was by Steve James (UK), who made 135 against Alex Higgins (UK) on April 14 1990 in the World Professional Championships at Sheffield, S Yorks, UK.

DARTS

MOST BULL'S-EYES IN 10 HOURS

Perry Prine (USA) hit 1,432 bull's-eyes in 10 hours at the Lake Erie Classic Dart Tournament in Mentor, Ohio, USA, on March 27 1998.

WOMEN'S OUTDOORS MARATHON

Anne Herlihy (New Zealand) played darts outside for a record 64 hours at The Bridge Tavern, Waitara, New Zealand, from March 26–28 1999.

HIGHEST WOMEN'S SCORE IN 24 HOURS

The highest score achieved by a team of eight women is 830,737 by a side from The Cornwall Inn, Killurin, Wexford, Ireland, on August 1–2 1997.

FASTEST DARTS "ROUND THE CLOCK"

Dennis Gower (UK) worked his way around a dartboard clockwise, hitting doubles in a time of 9.2 sec at The Millers Arms, Hastings, E Sussex, UK, on October 12 1975.

Jim Pike (UK) achieved a similar feat, with the distinction that he struck the doubles in numerical order, in 14.5 sec at The Craven Club, Newmarket, Suffolk, UK, in March 1944.

FASTEST TIME TO FINISH THREE GAMES OF 301

The shortest time taken to complete three games of 301, finishing on doubles, is 1 min 37 sec by Mervyn King (UK) on August 29 1997. The successful record attempt was recorded on BBC TV's *Record Breakers* and took place at the BBC TV Centre, London, UK.

PÉTANQUE

LONGEST MARATHON

The longest pétanque, or boules, marathon is one of 24 hours recorded by members of the Half Crown Pétanque Club at The Crown Inn, Stockton, Warwickshire, UK, on June 26–27 1999.

MOST WORLD CHAMPIONSHIP TITLES

Two players have won five World Championships as members of a pétanque team. Didier Choupay (France) took a team gold medal in 1985, 1988–89, 1994, and 1998. Philippe Quintais (France) won in 1991, 1993, 1995–96, and 1998.

MOST WORLD CHAMPIONSHIP TEAM TITLES

France has won the Pétanque World Championship team title 18 times, most recently in 2001.

CLAY SHOOTING

FASTEST TIME TO BREAK 500 CLAY TARGETS

Scott Hutchinson (USA) shot and broke 500 clay targets in a record time of 30 min 31 sec at the Silver Harbor Lodge, Lake Placid, Florida, USA, on September 18 1999.

MOST CLAY TARGETS BROKEN IN ONE MINUTE

Esa Kölegård (Sweden) shot and broke a record total of 29 clay targets in one minute at Bräcke, Sweden, on September 26 2001. The event was filmed by *Guinness Rekord TV*, Sweden.

TRAPSHOOTING

MOST CONSECUTIVE TARGETS HIT

The greatest number of trapshooting targets consecutively hit by one person is 675, achieved by Cathy Wehinger (USA) at a shooting range at Ackley, Iowa, USA, in July 1998.

MOST DARTS WORLD CHAMPIONSHIP TITLES

Phil Taylor (UK, above) has won 10 darts world championship titles, more than any other individual. Taylor took the WDO (World Darts Organization) title in 1990 and 1992, and the PDC (Professional Darts Council) title from 1995 to 2002.

MOST REGAINED WORLD HEAVYWEIGHT TITLES

Three boxers have twice regained the heavyweight title: Muhammad Ali (USA), Evander Holyfield (USA), and Lennox Lewis (UK, below). In 1988 Lewis won an Olympic gold for Canada, where he moved at the age of 12, and first took the World Boxing Council (WBC) title in 1993. He regained it in 1997 and 2001.

BOXING

LONGEST REIGNING WORLD HEAVYWEIGHT CHAMPION

Joe Louis (USA) was world champion for 11 years 252 days, from June 22 1937 when he beat Jim Braddock (USA) in Chicago, Illinois, USA, until March 1 1949. Louis made a record 25 successful defenses of his title.

YOUNGEST WORLD HEAVYWEIGHT CHAMPION

Mike Tyson (USA) was a record age of 20 years 144 days when he beat Trevor Berbick (USA) to win the WBC heavyweight title in Las Vegas, Nevada, USA, on November 22 1986. He added the World Boxing Association (WBA) title when he beat James "Bonecrusher" Smith (USA) at 20 years 249 days on March 7 1987. He became undisputed champion on August 2 1987 when he beat Tony Tucker (USA) for the International Boxing Federation (IBF) title.

LIGHTEST WORLD HEAVYWEIGHT CHAMPION

Bob Fitzsimmons (UK) weighed just 165 lb (75 kg) when he won the heavyweight title by defeating James Corbett (USA) in Carson City, Nevada, USA, on March 17 1897.

HEAVIEST WORLD HEAVYWEIGHT CHAMPION

Primo Carnera (Italy), the "Ambling Alp," weighed 260 lb (118 kg) when he won the world heavyweight title from Jack Sharkey (USA) in New York City, USA, on June 29 1933. His peak weight was 269 lb (122 kg), and his reach was a record 85 in (217 cm) from fingertip to fingertip.

LONGEST FIGHTS

Fighting under Queensberry Rules, lightweights Joe Gans (USA) and Oscar Matthew (Denmark) fought for 42 rounds – a record for a title fight – in Goldfield, Nevada, USA, on September 3 1906. In the end, Gans won on a foul.

The longest recorded duration of a fight with gloves was between Andy Bowen (USA) and Jack Burke (USA) in New Orleans, Louisiana, USA, on April 6–7 1893. It lasted 110 rounds, 7 hr 19 min (9:15 pm to 4:34 am) and was declared a no contest (later changed to a draw).

The most rounds ever recorded was 276 in 4 hr 30 min when Jack Jones beat Patsy Tunney (both UK) in Cheshire, UK, in 1825. Before the Queensberry Rules were introduced in 1867, fights were not timed and rounds were limitless – a round would only end when one of the boxers was knocked down.

MOST KNOCKDOWNS IN ONE FIGHT

Vic Toweel (South Africa) knocked down Danny O'Sullivan (UK) 14 times in 10 rounds during their world bantamweight fight in Johannesburg, South Africa, on December 2 1950.

OLDEST WORLD CHAMPION

Archie Moore (USA) was believed to be between the age of 45 and 48 when his world light heavyweight title was removed on February 10 1962 due to his inactivity. Moore, the only boxer to fight both Rocky Marciano and Muhammad Ali (both USA), had first taken the title in 1952.

SHORTEST REIGNING WORLD CHAMPION

Tony Canzoneri (USA) was world light welterweight champion for 33 days from May 21 to June 23 1933 – the shortest time for a boxer to have won and lost a world title in the ring.

YOUNGEST WORLD CHAMPION

US-born Puerto Rican Wilfred Benitez was 17 years 176 days when he won the WBA light welterweight title in San Juan, Puerto Rico, on March 6 1976.

MOST REGAINED WORLD TITLES

US middleweight "Sugar" Ray Robinson (above) beat Carmen Basilio (USA) in the Chicago Stadium, Illinois, USA, on March 25 1958 to regain the title for the fourth time, a record for a boxer at any weight.

MOST WORLD TITLES SIMULTANEOUSLY HELD AT DIFFERENT WEIGHTS

Henry "Homicide Hank" Armstrong (USA) held world titles at a record three different weights at the same time. He was the world champion at featherweight, lightweight, and welterweight between August and December 1938.

It is claimed that Barney Ross (USA) held the world lightweight, junior welterweight, and welterweight titles simultaneously from May 28 to September 17 1934, but there is some dispute as to exactly when he relinquished his lightweight title.

HIGHEST ATTENDANCE AT A BOXING MATCH

The greatest paid attendance at any boxing match is 132,274 to watch four world title fights at the Aztec Stadium, Mexico City, Mexico, on February 20 1993, headed by the successful WBC super-lightweight defense by Julio César Chávez (Mexico) over Greg Haugen (USA).

The non-paying record is 135,132 to see Tony Zale v. Billy Pryor (both USA) at Juneau Park, Milwaukee, Wisconsin, USA, on August 16 1941.

SMALLEST ATTENDANCE AT A WORLD HEAVYWEIGHT TITLE FIGHT

A meagre 2,434 turned up to see Cassius Clay (USA), who had just converted to Islam and become Muhammad Ali, beat Sonny Liston (USA) at Lewiston, Maine, USA, on May 25 1965. A small arena was chosen because Ali had received death threats before the fight.

LONGEST UNBEATEN RUN

As of March 2002 Ricardo López (Mexico) remained unbeaten throughout his professional career, with 50 wins and 1 draw from 51 fights over 17 years.

MOST CONSECUTIVE KNOCKOUTS

The record for consecutive knock-outs is 44 by Lamar Clark (USA) from 1958 to 1960. Clark once knocked out six opponents in one night (five in the first round) at Bingham, Utah, USA, on December 1 1958.

MOST KNOCKOUTS IN A CAREER

Archie Moore (USA) recorded 145 knockouts (129 in professional fights) in his career.

MOST COMPETITIVE FULL CONTACT ROUNDS

The most competitive full contact rounds fought in boxing and other martial arts is 5,962 by Paddy Doyle (UK) from 1993 to February 1999.

JUDO

MOST WORLD CHAMPIONSHIPS

The most successful man in World Championships history is Yasuhiro Yamashita (Japan), who won five world and Olympic titles from 1977–85 – the world over-95 kg title in 1979, 1981, and 1983, the world Open title in 1981, and the Olympic Open category in 1984. By the time he retired he had recorded 203 successive wins and no defeats.

The women's record is held by Ingrid Berghmans (Belgium), who won six world titles between 1980 and 1989.

KARATE

MOST INDIVIDUAL WORLD KATA CHAMPIONSHIPS

Kata is a form of karate that consists of sequences of specific moves. The most individual world titles ever won is four by Yuki Mimura (Japan). She was victorious in 1988, 1990, 1992, and 1996.

The most men's titles is three by Tsuguo Sakumoto (Japan) in 1984, 1986, and 1988 and Michael Milan (France) in 1994, 1996, and 2000.

MOST INDIVIDUAL WORLD KUMITE CHAMPIONSHIPS

Kumite is a freestyle form of karate. The most successful world champion is Guus van Mourik (Netherlands), who won four titles at over-60 kg in 1982, 1984, 1986, and 1988.

The men's record is three by José Manuel Egea (Spain) at Open (Sanbon) in 1988 and under-80 kg in 1990 and 1992, and Wayne Otto (UK) at Open (Sanbon) in 1990 and under-75 kg in 1992 and 1996.

MOST TEAM WORLD KUMITE CHAMPIONSHIPS

Great Britain has won a record six world titles (instituted 1970) at the men's kumite team event – in 1975, 1982, 1984, 1986, 1988, and 1990.

A women's team competition was introduced to the tournament in 1992 and has been won twice by Great Britain in 1992 and 1996.

MOST JUDO TITLES

David Douillet (France, top right) won six world and Olympic titles – three of each – up to 2000.

WEIGHTLIFTING

MOST OLYMPIC GOLD MEDALS
Naim Suleymanoglü (Turkey) won three weightlifting gold medals at the Olympic Games of 1988, 1992, and 1996. Pyrros Dimas (Greece) accomplished the same feat in 1992, 1996, and 2000.

MOST OLYMPIC MEDALS
Norbert Schemansky (USA) has won the greatest number of Olympic weightlifting medals, picking up four between 1948 and 1964.

MOST WOMEN'S WORLD CHAMPIONSHIP TITLES
The most gold medals won at the women's World Championships is 13 by Li Hongyun (China) in the 60/64-kg class from 1992–96.

MOST WOMEN'S POWERLIFTING WORLD CHAMPIONSHIP TITLES
The winner of the most women's world titles is Natalya Rumyantseva (Russia), who won seven at 82.5 kg between 1993 and 1999.

OLDEST WORLD RECORD BREAKER
The oldest weightlifting record holder is Norbert Schemansky (USA), who was 37 years 333 days old when he snatched a record weight of 164.2 kg in the then unlimited heavyweight class at Detroit, Michigan, USA, on April 28 1962.

YOUNGEST WORLD RECORD BREAKER
Naim Suleymanoglü (Turkey) was just 16 years 62 days old when he set the world records for clean and jerk 160 kg and combined total 285 kg at Allentown, New Jersey, USA, on March 26 1983.

SUMO

GREATEST TOURNAMENT DOMINANCE
Yokozuna Mitsugu Akimoto (Japan), whose sumo name was Chiyonofuji, won one of the six annual tournaments – the Kyushu Basho – for eight years in a row, 1981–88. He also holds the record for the most career wins, with 1,045, and Makunouchi (top division) wins, with 807.

MOST CONSECUTIVE TOP DIVISION BOUTS
Jesse Kuhaulua (Hawaii), known as Takamiyama, was the first non-Japanese to win an official top-division tournament in July 1972. In September 1981 he set a record of 1,231 consecutive top-division bouts.

MOST BOUTS WON
Ozeki Tameemon Torokichi (Japan), or Raiden, won 254 bouts and lost only 10 for the highest winning percentage of 96.2 between 1789 and 1810.

MOST CONSECUTIVE WINS
Sadaji Akiyoshi (Japan), alias Futabayama, holds the all-time record for consecutive sumo wins, with 69 victories from 1937–39.

MOST EMPEROR'S CUPS
Yokozuna Koki Naya (Japan), alias Taiho or "Great Bird," won the prestigious Emperor's Cup 32 times until his retirement in 1971.

WRESTLING

MOST INDIVIDUAL DISCIPLINE OLYMPIC MEDALS
The record is four individual discipline medals by Eino Leino (Finland) at freestyle from 1920–32; Imre Polyák (Hungary) at Greco-Roman from 1952–64; and Bruce Baumgartner (USA) at freestyle from 1984–96.

MOST OLYMPIC GOLD MEDALS
The record is three golds by: Carl Westergren (Sweden) in 1920, 1924, and 1932; Ivar Johansson (Sweden) in 1932 (two) and 1936; Aleksandr Vasilyevich Medved (USSR) in 1964, 1968, and 1972, and Aleksandr Karelin (Russia) in 1988, 1992, and 1996.

MOST WORLD CHAMPIONSHIP TITLES
Aleksandr Karelin (Russia) won a record 12 world titles in the Greco-Roman under-130-kg class between 1988 and 1999.

OLDEST WRESTLING COMPETITION
The world's oldest continuously sanctioned sports competition is the Kirkpinar Wrestling Festival (above), which has been held since 1460. The event is currently staged on the Sarayici Peninsula, near Edirne, Turkey.

WOMEN'S 48-KG SNATCH AND 48-KG TOTAL

On June 6 2000 Liu Xiuhua (China, above) broke the existing world record for the 48-kg snatch by lifting 87.5 kg in Montreal, Quebec, Canada. Liu also holds the record for the 48-kg total – she lifted 197.5 kg on September 6 1999, also in an event in Montreal.

Men's 77-kg clean and jerk
210 kg
Oleg Perepetchenov (Russia)
Trencín, Slovakia
April 27 2001

Men's 77-kg snatch
172.5 kg
Plamen Zhelyazkov (Bulgaria)
Doha, Qatar
March 27 2002

Men's 77-kg total
377.5 kg
Plamen Zhelyazkov (Bulgaria)
Doha, Qatar
March 27 2002

Men's 85-kg clean and jerk
218 kg
Zhang Yong (China)
Tel Aviv, Israel
April 25 1998

Men's 85-kg snatch
181 kg
Georgi Asanidze (Georgia)
Sofia, Bulgaria
April 29 2000

Men's 85-kg total
No record yet set.

Men's 94-kg clean and jerk
232.5 kg
Szymon Kolecki (Poland)
Sofia, Bulgaria
April 29 2000

Men's 94-kg snatch
188 kg
Akakios Kakiashvilis (Greece)
Athens, Greece
November 27 1999

Men's 94-kg total
No record yet set.

Men's 105-kg clean and jerk
No record yet set.

Men's 105-kg snatch
198 kg
Vladimir Smorchkov (Russia)
Antalya, Turkey
November 10 2001

Men's 105-kg total
No record yet set.

Men's over-105-kg clean and jerk
No record yet set.

Men's over-105-kg snatch
212.5 kg
Hossein Rezazadeh (Iran)
Sydney, NSW, Australia
September 26 2000

Men's over-105-kg total
472.5 kg
Hossein Rezazadeh (Iran)
Sydney, NSW, Australia
September 26 2000

Women's 48-kg clean and jerk
113.5 kg
Donka Mincheva (Bulgaria)
Athens, Greece
November 21 1999

Women's 48-kg snatch
87.5 kg
Liu Xiuhua (China)
Montreal, Canada
June 6 2000

Women's 48-kg total
197.5 kg
Liu Xiuhua (China)
Montreal, Canada
September 6 1999

Women's 53-kg clean and jerk
125 kg
Yang Xia (China)
Sydney, NSW, Australia
September 18 2000

Women's 53-kg snatch
100 kg
Yang Xia (China)
Sydney, NSW, Australia
September 18 2000

Women's 53-kg total
225 kg
Yang Xia (China)
Sydney, Australia
September 18 2000

Women's 58-kg clean and jerk
131.5 kg
Ri Song Hui (North Korea)
Osaka, Japan
May 3 2000

Women's 58-kg snatch
105 kg
Chen Yanqing (China)
Athens, Greece
November 22 1999

Women's 58-kg total
235 kg
Chen Yanqing (China)
Athens, Greece
November 22 1999

Women's 63-kg clean and jerk
133 kg
Nataliya Skakun (Ukraine)
Thessaloniki, Greece
July 3 2001

Women's 63-kg snatch
112.5 kg
Chen Xiaomin (China)
Sydney, NSW, Australia
September 19 2000

Women's 63-kg total
242.5 kg
Chen Xiaomin (China)
Sydney, NSW, Australia
September 19 2000

Women's 69-kg clean and jerk
143.5 kg
Valentina Popova (Russia)
Brisbane, Queensland, Australia
September 1 2001

Women's 69-kg snatch
115 kg
Valentina Popova (Russia)
Antalya, Turkey
November 8 2001

Women's 69-kg total
257.5 kg
Valentina Popova (Russia)
Antalya, Turkey
November 8 2001

Women's 75-kg clean and jerk
142.5 kg
Sun Tianni (China)
Osaka, Japan
May 6 2000

Women's 75-kg snatch
116 kg
Tang Weifang (China)
Wuhan, China
September 4 1999

Women's 75-kg total
257.5 kg
Sun Tianni (China)
Osaka, Japan
May 6 2000

Women's over-75-kg clean and jerk
165 kg
Ding Meiyuan (China)
Sydney, NSW, Australia
September 22 2000

Women's over-75-kg snatch
135 kg
Ding Meiyuan (China)
Sydney, NSW, Australia
September 22 2000

Women's over-75-kg total
300 kg
Ding Meiyuan (China)
Sydney, NSW, Australia
September 22 2000

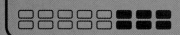
powerboat racing 240
sailing 144–5
bobsleigh
most Championship titles 234
most four-man World Championship
Olympic titles 234
most Olympic gold medals 234
most Olympic medals 234
most two-man titles 234
most women's World Championship
Olympic titles 234
youngest Olympic champion 234
body *see also* births; diseases; human
bodies; medical facts
body cream, largest container 115
body temperature, lowest/highest 54
Boeing 747, greatest distance pulled 34
bombs
earliest use of bouncing 159
heaviest 159
highest death toll 160
largest conventional 160
most accurate 159
nuclear 160–1
Booker Prize wins, most 196
books
best-seller of all time 197
best-selling author 196
best-selling children's book 196
best-selling diary 22
best-selling non-fiction book 196
highest advances 196
highest earnings by author 196
largest book reading attendance 197
largest dictionaries 196
largest library 130
largest library fine 196
largest magazine 196
longest running comic book 197
most Booker Prize wins 196
most overdue 196
most Pulitzer Prize wins 196
most useless inventions 121
most valuable 124
shortest instruction manual 166
smallest 113, 197
youngest author 42
boots, largest 114
bottles
most valuable 124
smallest 112
boules *see* pétanque
bouquets, largest 114
bowls
see also tenpin bowling
bowling ball stacking 44
highest scores 219
longest marathon 219
most titles 219
most World Championships 219
oldest lawn green player 219
box-office gross, highest 182
boxing
heaviest World Heavyweight
champion 264

highest attendance 265
lightest World Heavyweight
champion 264
longest reigning World Heavyweight
champion 264
most consecutive knockouts 265
most knockouts in career 265
most regained World Heavyweight
titles 264
most regained World titles 265
most World titles simultaneously held
265
oldest World champion 264
shortest reigning World champion
264
smallest attendance 265
youngest World champion 264
youngest World Heavyweight
champion 264
brains
earliest cell transplants 55
heaviest 51
largest dinosaur 91
largest tumor 52
lightest 51
bras
largest 114
most expensive 122
breasts
largest natural 50
most enlarged 56
bridesmaid, oldest 43
bridges 132–3
BRIT awards, most 187, 189
Brooks, Garth 186
buildings
fastest run up Empire State Building
40
largest 100, 102–3, 130–1, 134
most expensive 99, 135
offices 99, 128, 129
relocation 132
residential 128, 134–5
sacred 100, 102–3, 128, 130, 131
smallest 102, 112
tallest 128–9
bulldozers, largest 148
buns, most valuable 122
burns, greatest percentage 55

C

cable cars
highest 147
longest 147
caesarean births 54
Cairo, fastest Cape Town to Cairo run 29
Canadian football
longest pass 201
most yards passing in season 201
cancer
largest tumors 52
most survivable 59
cannibalism 106
canoeing

fastest 75-ft vertical descent 255
fastest time 255
greatest distance in 24 hours 255
largest canoe raft 255
largest crews 145
longest free-fall descent 255
most Eskimo rolls 255
most Olympic gold medals 254
Cape Town to Cairo run, fastest 29
capital cities 94
car ferries
fastest 145
largest 144
card games, longest 33
Carey, Maria 186
carnivorous plants 81
carpets, largest 117
carrots, heaviest 114
cars
see also model cars; roads
best-selling 140
drag racing 240
fastest acceleration 140
fastest circumnavigation car 28
fastest reverse driving 40
fastest road race 141
fastest speed 140
Formula 1 236–7
greatest distance driven 140
greatest distance by electric 141
greatest number wrecked 141
highest public highway speed 141
highest traffic density 104
highest ownership rates 104
IndyCar racing 237
land speed records 140
largest engine 141
largest motor shows 141
largest size 140
Le Mans 237
longest power slide 141
longest side-wheel driving 32
longest vehicle 140
lowest emission producing 64
lowest ownership rates 104
most driven on two wheels 35
most expensive 140
most fuel-efficient 140
most powerful 140
most titles by manufacturer 236
most valuable 140
most widespread production 141
NASCAR 237
rallying 241
side-wheel driving 35
smallest 140
stock car racing 237
survived crash 24
cartoons 23, 185
castles, largest inhabited 134
catamarans
fastest 144
fastest Atlantic crossings 145
greatest distance sailed 145
cathedrals 102, 103, 128

cats
earthquake survivor 68
political 96
smallest 112
Cats musical, longest running show 193
causeways, highest 132
caves 77
celebrity hair, largest collection 118
cells 168–9
cemeteries 101
César awards 180
chain-saw juggling 44
chamber pots, largest collection 118
chandelier, largest 114
charities
fundraising concerts 22
largest 20, 21
royal patron 23
sports events 20
charts *see* pop music
chemical weapons, largest stock 160
chimneys, tallest 128
chimpanzees
first to operate computer 85
most numerate 84
most votes for 97
oldest 85
chips, largest bag 116
chocolate
heaviest model 116
longest salami 116
most valuable bar 122
choirs, longest concert 32
chorus line member, oldest 42
Christmas card, most valuable 122
Christmas crackers, largest 115
Christmas trees, largest of lights 114
chromosomes 168–9
churches
see also sacred buildings
smallest 102
tallest spire 128
cigarette consumption 98
cigars, most valuable 124
cinemas
see also films
largest 130
tallest 128
circumnavigation
fastest by car 28
fastest by helicopter 28
fastest microlight 28
fastest yachtswoman 27
first pole-to-pole 28
cities
capital 94
highest cost of living 98
most expensive office space 99
civil rights
see also human-rights organizations
largest gay/lesbian rights march 98
largest racial equality rally 22
civilian aid convoys, largest 153
classical music 190–1
highest note 190

largest choir 191
largest concert attendance 190
largest drum kit 191
largest opera house 190
largest orchestra 190
largest organ 190
largest violin ensemble 190
longest operatic career 190
longest operatic encore 191
longest published hymn 191
lowest note 190
most durable organist 191
most prolific composer 190
most valuable violin 125
oldest opera singer 42
youngest person at No.1 in
 charts 190
youngest violinist 191
clay shooting
 fastest time 263
 most targets broken 263
climate 66–7
 see also weather
Clinton, Bill 96
clones 168, 169
clothing
 see also shoes
 fastest underpants jumper 44
 largest label collection 119
 largest shirts 114
 most surgical gloves inflated 40
 most used fastening 120
 most valuable 122, 123
clouds 67
cocktails
 largest 117
 smallest 112
coconut husker, fastest 40
coffee, highest consumption 98
coins 96, 108–9
collections, largest 118–19, 245
combat sports
 boxing 264–5
 judo 265
 kata karate 265
 sumo 266
 wrestling 266
comets 71, 72
comic strips, most syndicated 197
comics
 longest running comic book 197
 most valuable 124
computer games 176–7
 best-selling driving simulation 176
 best-selling games console 176, 177
 best-selling soccer game 176
 best-selling video games 176
 fastest-selling console 177
 fastest-selling games 177
 greatest market share 177
 most advanced orders for game 176
 most complex games character 177
 most computer sales 177
 most expensive game 176
 most powerful console 176, 177

most successful arcade game 177
most successful games publisher 177
computers
 see also internet
 fastest 166
 first chimpanzee to operate 85
 internet 164, 165
 oldest 164
 programs 166
 screens 166
 shortest manual 166
 viruses 165
Conan the Barbarian, largest memorabilia
 collection 119
CONCACAF (football) Championship 208
condoms, largest collection 118
conjoined twins 100
consultant, youngest 42
container ships, largest 144
continents 76, 94
cook, youngest 42
Copa América 208
cosmetics
 largest body cream container 115
 largest lipstick print collection 118
 most expensive perfume 125
cost of living
 most expensive accommodation 135
 most expensive cities 98
countries 94–5
 boundaries 94
 capital cities 94
 environmental performance 64–5
 governments 96–7
 highest birth/death rate 98
 highest consumption 62, 98
 highest taxes 98
 highest/lowest GNI (GNP) 95
 highest/lowest prison populations 94,
  106
 highest/lowest unemployment 99
 largest 94
 life expectancy 95
 literacy rates 95
 male/female ratios 95
 most/least populous 94, 95
 oldest treaty 96
 oldest/youngest populations 94
courage and endurance 26–7
 deepest seawater scuba diving 27
 fastest seven-summit ascent 27
 fastest solo row across Atlantic 27
 fastest Trans-America walk 26
 first woman to climb Everest 26
 full-body ice endurance 47
 gallantry awards 20
 heroes 20–1
 Le Mans 24-hour endurance race 237
 lifesavers 20–1
 longest distance walked 26
 longest distance walked on stilts 26
 longest scuba dive 26
 most southerly marathon 27
cows, cloned 168
Cox Arquette, Courteney 194

cranes
 largest tower crane 149
 tallest 148
credit cards, most expensive 124
cricket
 fastest double century 215
 highest batting average 214
 highest innings 214
 highest Test scores 214
 largest bat 215
 longest Test match 214
 lowest Test innings 214
 most consecutive test victories 214
 most dismissals 215
 most dismissals by wicketkeeper 214
 most double centuries 215
 most extras conceded 215
 most First-Class centuries 214
 most runs 214, 215
 most Test catches 215
 most Test "ducks" 214
 most wickets 215
 most women's appearances 215
crime
 drug dealing 107
 forgery 108
 kidnap 106
 largest drop 23
 murder 106–7
 speeding 106
 terrorism 21, 24, 25, 106
 theft and robbery 96, 106
criminals
 executions 106, 107
 largest fine 106
 most arrested 106
 prisons 94, 106–7
crocodiles
 largest 87, 90
 most ferocious attack 152
croquet, most hoops scored 218
cross-country, World Championship
 titles 226
crystal bowls, smallest 113
Cup-Winners Cups, most football
 Cups 210
curling
 fastest speed 235
 longest throw 235
 most Olympic gold medals 235
 most World Championships 235
currency 96, 108–9
Curtis Cup, most golf titles 243
cybernetics 166–7
cyberspace, map 164
cycling
 see also bicycles; motorcycles; quad
  bikes; tandems; trikes; unicycles
 fastest completion of three peaks 269
 fastest on snow 269
 fastest team pursuit 269
 fastest Trans-America crossing 269
 fastest unpaced flying start 269
 fastest unpaced standing start 269
 greatest distance cycled 268

longest solo journey 28
most mountain bike cross-country
 World Cup wins 268–9
most mountain bike downhill World
 Cup wins 268
Tour de France 268
cyclones 68

D
dance
 fastest flamenco 192
 fastest tap dancer 193
 largest contra line 192
 largest country dance 192
 largest Irish dance 36
 largest locomotion dance 192
 largest tap dance 192
 longest dance marathon 192
 oldest ballroom dancer 42
 oldest chorus line member 42
darts
 fastest "round the clock" 263
 fastest time 263
 highest women's score 263
 most bull's-eyes 263
 most World Championship titles 263
 women's marathon 263
Davis Cup, youngest tennis player 247
death
 see also battles; man-made
  disasters; mass destruction;
  natural disasters; wars
 funerals and cemeteries 100–1
 highest rate 98
 highest road rate 104
 largest mass suicides 101
 leading cause 58
 most condolences on internet 23
 most executions 107
 murderers 106–7
 terrorist acts 21, 106
deforestation, largest/fastest 64
denim
 most expensive 124
 most valuable 122, 123
deserts 77
diamonds
 most demand 125
 most valuable 124
Diana, Princess of Wales 23, 100, 122
diaries
 best-selling 22
 most valuable 123
dinosaurs 90–1
Dire Straits 187
disasters see man-made...; natural...
disco ball, largest 116
diseases
 biological weapons 160–1
 earliest HIV diagnosis 58
 fastest growing 58
 highest prevalence 58
 largest tumors 52
 leading cause of death 58

most World Championship titles 260
haulage companies, largest fan club 148
hauntings, most systematic study 172
hearts
    survival with exposed 52
    youngest surgery/transplant 54
helicopters
    earliest flight 139
    fastest circumnavigation 28
    fastest speed 138
    first production 120
    largest heliport 105
    largest in production 154
    worst disaster 155
Hepburn, Katharine 180
heroes 20–1
hiccups 52
high jump, dogs 84
hit records *see* pop music
hockey
    see also ice hockey; roller hockey
    fastest international goal 217
    highest score in international 217
    largest attendance 217
    most appearances 217
    most international goals 217
    most Olympics umpired 217
    most World Cup titles 217
Hoffman, Dustin 180
Hollywood 180–1
    largest home 135
home entertainment
    fastest-growing product 166
    largest television audiences 100
    longest video-watching session 32
    smallest televisions 113
homes
    highest residential apartments 134
    largest 134–5
    most expensive 135
    tallest residential building 128
hominids 168, 170
horses
    equestrian sports 258–9
    longest ride in suit of armor 32
horseshoe pitching 270
hostages
    greatest kidnap ransom 106
    longest held 25
    most held 24
hot springs 78
hotels 134–5
house of horrors, longest 179
houses 134–5
hovercraft
    earliest flight 145
    earliest patent 120
    fastest 144
    largest civilian craft 145
    largest naval 157
human bodies 50–9
    see also births; diseases; medical
        facts
    cloned embryos 169
    fewest toes 53

farthest eyeball popper 52
greatest height difference in married
    couple 100
greatest weight changes 50
hairiest family 52
heaviest brain 51
largest bicep 56
largest breasts 50, 56
largest hands 50
largest lip plate 56
lightest brain 51
longest beards 53, 56
longest ear hair 52
longest fingernails 56
longest hair 57
longest lived cell culture 169
longest neck 57
longest nose 50
longest toenails 56
longest tongue 50
most albino siblings 53
most bound feet 57
most detailed dissection 173
most enlarged breasts 56
most fingers and toes 52
most pierced 56
most plastic surgery 57
most rhinestones 56
most tattooed 56
most variable stature 50
oldest ancestors 168, 170
oldest extracted DNA 168
oldest people 50–1
shortest people 51
smallest waist 57
stretchiest skin 52
strongest bite 50
tallest people 50
human-powered vehicles, longest flight
    139
human-rights organizations
    see also civil rights
    largest 98
    oldest 22
hurling
    highest attendance 218
    lowest All-Ireland final score 218
    most All-Ireland Championship titles
        218
    shinty 218
hurricanes 68
Hussein, Saddam 96, 160

I

ICBM *see* Inter Continental Ballistic
    Missiles
ice
    bores 62
    fastest melting glacier 79
    full-body endurance 47
    hail 66, 67, 68, 69
    hotel 134
    largest iceberg 78
    storms 69

ice cream
    largest pyramid 116
    largest sundae 117
ice hockey
    fastest goal 207
    highest percentage wins per
        match 206
    highest score 206
    longest career 207
    most goals 206
    most hat tricks 207
    most matches in career 207
    most men's gold medals 207
    most Olympic gold medals 207
    most penalty minutes 207
    most points in career 206
    most points scored 207
    most shutouts 206
    most Stanley Cups 206
    most wins 206
    most women's team Olympic gold
        medals 206
    most World Championship titles 207
impacts on Earth 76, 77
IndyCar racing
    fastest Indy 500 qualification 237
    most Championship titles 237
    most pole positions 237
    most race wins in career 237
insects 86
    greediest 83
    most expensive 122
    prehistoric 90
instruction manuals, shortest 166
Inter Continental Ballistic Missiles (ICBM),
most destructive nuclear 161
internet 164–5
    most condolences 23
invasion, greatest seaborne 156
inventions 120–1
iron bars, fastest time to bend 39
ironing session, longest 33
islands
    largest man-made 132
    largest uninhabited 94
    most expensive 135
    most remote 77
Isle of Man TT series
    fastest race 238
    most races won in career 238

J

jai-alai ball sport 218
javelin throws 226
jeans
    most expensive 124
    most valuable 123
jellyfish 88, 89
Jenga, fastest tower construction 41
jet aircraft
    see also military aircraft
    most expensive private 138
    most powerful engine 138
    smallest 138

jetstreams 67
jewelry
    see also gems; gold
    largest robbery 106
    most valuable box 124
    most valuable in film 125
jigsaw puzzles, smallest 112
John, Elton 188
judo
    most titles 265
    most World Championships 265
juggling, longest time 33

K

kata karate, most World Championships
265
Kennedy, John F. 23
keyboard playing marathons 32
keyrings, largest collection 118
keys, largest 117
kidnap 106
    see also hostages
kidney stones, most 52
kidney transplants 54
kissing
    longest kiss 32
    most couples kissing 37
kite surfing, greatest distance 256
knives, most penknife blades 120
korfball
    highest team score 216
    largest tournament 216
Kudrow, Lisa 194

L

laboratory experiments 172–3
lacrosse
    highest international scores 217
    highest scores 217
    most women's international
        appearances 217
    most World Championship titles 217
lagoons 79
lakes 78, 79
land boundaries 94
land masses 76
land vehicles, largest 148
land yachting, highest speed 271
landslides 63, 68
languages, most official 94
law and order *see* crime; criminals;
    prisons
Le Mans 24-hour endurance race
    most team wins 237
    most wins 237
length, smallest unit 170
leprosy 58, 59
libraries
    largest fine 196
    largest size 130
    most overdue book 196
lifeboats
    longest journey 28

most medals 21
oldest organization 21
lifeguard, oldest 21
lifesavers 20–1
lifts
longest fall 24
longest fall down shaft 25
longest time trapped 25
light
fastest speed 170
shortest flash 173
slowest 172
light bulbs, largest Christmas tree 114
lighthouse
farthest moved 132
tallest 128
lightning
longest flash 67
most rockets launched 66
most strikes survived 24
worst death toll 68
lights, greatest range 132
Lindbergh, Charles 22
lipstick prints, largest collection 118
literacy rates 95
litter collection, largest 22
lizards 86–7
locks, largest 117
locomotives, fastest steam 147
London Marathon, charity fund-raising 20
lottery wins, largest 99
luge
most Olympic medals 234
most women's World Championship
titles 234
most World Championship and
Olympic titles 234
lyrics, most valuable 122

M

machine guns, highest fire rate 158
Madonna 181, 187
magazines
largest circulation 197
largest size 196
most expensive 124
maggot bathing, longest 32
magnetic field, strongest 173
malaria 58, 59
Mandela, Nelson R. 22
man-made disasters
see also mass destruction; wars
worst air pollution 64
worst helicopter 155
worst landslides 63
worst marine pollution 64
worst nuclear accidents 65
worst submarine 156
worst terrorist act 21, 106
maple syrup bucket, largest 114
maps
cyberspace 164
earliest geological 63
most accurate 3-D map 63

smallest 113
marathons
charity fund-raising 20
fastest athletic 224, 225
fastest stair climb 32
fastest three-legged 35
farthest distance running backward
32
farthest distance walking backward
32
greatest distance dribbling basketball
33
greatest distance sailed in bath tub
33
half 225
highest altitude athletic 224
keyboard playing 32
longest card game 33
longest choir concert 32
longest dance 192
longest DJ 195
longest drumming 34
longest egg-and-spoon distance
run 32
longest handbell ringing session 32
longest ironing session 33
longest kiss 32
longest movie-watching session 32
longest pétanque (boules) 263
longest ride with suit of armor 32
longest tennis ball heading 33
longest time juggling 33
longest time pole-sitting in barrel 33
longest time sitting in shack on
pole 33
longest time spent on bed of nails 33
longest tree sitting 33
longest video-watching session 32
longest wing-walking 33
most southerly 27
oldest finishers 225
marine life 168
maritime boundaries 94
Marley, Bob 186
marriages
see also weddings
greatest height difference 100
longest 100
longest Hollywood 180
most 100, 101
mass destruction
biological weapons 160, 161
earliest use of smallpox 161
first biological attack 161
first use of atomic bomb 160
heaviest nuclear bomb 161
highest death toll 160
highest death toll from chemical
weapons 160
largest conventional bomb 160
largest nuclear explosion crater 160
largest stockpile chemical weapons
160
largest stockpile smallpox
vaccines 161

longest-running environmental
campaign 160
most deadly anthrax epidemic 160
most destructive non-lethal weapon
161
most destructive nuclear ICBM 161
most nuclear weapons detonated at
one time 160
most powerful nerve gas 160
most powerful nuclear explosions 161
nerve gas use 160
smallest nuclear weapon 160
worst submarine accident 161
mass participation 36–7
largest Chinese Whispers game 36
largest clown gathering 36
largest Easter egg hunt 37
largest hug 36
largest human logo 37
largest Irish dance 36
largest mass bungee jump 37
largest cell phone ring 36
largest musical chairs game 36
largest simultaneous jump 36
largest tea party 36
largest Twist 36
largest walk 36
longest distance leap-frogged 37
loudest crowd scream 37
most blowing bubbles 37
most couples kissing 37
most nationalities in sauna 37
most people brushing teeth 36
most people flossing 36
most people skipping simultaneously
36
most people wearing Groucho Marx
glasses 36
matchmaker, most expensive 98
matchstick models, largest instrument
collection 118
mathematics 171
matter
least dense solid 173
most dense 172
medical facts 52–5
see also births; diseases; human
bodies
animal transplants 54, 168
chromosome sequencing 169
earliest transplants 24, 55
greatest percentage burns 55
highest blood sugar level 54
highest body temperature 54
highest g-force survived 24
human clones 169
largest donation to research 21
largest medical charity 21
largest simultaneous blood donation
22
largest tumors 52
leading cause of death 58
life expectancy 95
longest hiccup attack 52
longest lived cell culture 169

longest survival underwater 25
longest survival without food and
water 24
longest survival without pulse 24
longest survived bullet in head 52
longest survived exposed heart 52
longest survived transplants 24, 54
loudest snoring 52
lowest body temperature 54
most artificial joints 54
most blood received 54
most kidney stones 52
most plastic surgeons 95
most plastic surgery 57
most survivable cancer 59
oldest undiscovered twin 52
youngest with bionic arms 55
youngest heart surgery 54
youngest transplant 54
memorabilia
baseball 122
The Beatles 118
Conan the Barbarian 119
film 119, 122
football 123
most valuable 122–3
pop music 118, 122
royal 118
sports 122–3
Star Wars 119
microlight, fastest circumnavigation 28
microorganisms
see also diseases
fastest 171
largest 170
military aircraft
bombers, greatest wingspans 154
fastest bombers 154
fastest combat jets 154
fastest propeller fighter 154
fastest propeller-driven 155
first jet-engined flight 154
greatest wingspan of bombers 154
heaviest bombers 154
largest air force 155
longest range attacks 154
longest runway 155
most complex weapons system 154
most expensive 154
most expensive fighters 154
most flying hours 155
most jets shot down 155
most numerous fighter planes 155
most planes downed 155
most produced tilt rotor aircraft
155
most success against flying bombs
155
most widely deployed 154
smallest spy plane 154
top-scoring female ace 155
top-scoring WWII ace 154, 155
unmanned 154
military buildings, largest fort 134
military forces see armed forces

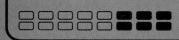
mining
  deepest mine 62
  gold 62, 63
  largest excavation 63
  oldest mine 62
Minogue, Kylie 189
mints (coin)
  largest 108
  smallest 109
missiles *see* Inter Continental Ballistic Missiles
missiles, *see also* mass destruction
mobile cranes, tallest 148
mobile (cell) phones
  country with most 164
  fastest text message 164
  most expensive 124
model aircraft
  fastest radio-controlled 139
  longest duration flight 138
  longest flight by paper plane 139
  radio-controlled, fastest 139
model boats, radio-controlled, farthest distance traveled 144
model cars
  fastest radio-controlled 141
  largest collection 118
  smallest motorized 113
models
  largest collections 118
  smallest 113, 172
monarchs 96–7
money
  banknotes 108–9
  biggest tourist spenders 104
  checks 108
  coins 96, 108–9
  greatest forgery 108
  highest taxes 98
  highest/lowest GNI (GNP) 95
  largest bankruptcy 108
  largest lottery wins 99
  largest single donations 21, 23
  most corporate debt failures 109
  most expensive accommodation 134, 135
  most expensive cities 98, 99
  most expensive objects 122–5
  most per electoral vote 96
  most raised for charity 20, 22
  most stolen 96, 106
  richest monarch 97
  youngest billionaire 42
monkeys
  clones 168
  largest buffet 102
  largest mammal eyes 83
  noisiest land mammal 82
monoliths 76
monoplanes, smallest 138
monorails, longest 146
monster trucks
  largest 149
  longest jumps 149
Monte Carlo, most wins 241

monuments
  largest 131
  tallest 128
Moon, the 73
moons 70
mortars, largest 158
Motocross
  most races 239
  most Trans-AMA titles 239
  World Championships wins 239
  youngest world champion 239
motor boats
  Formula 1 racing 240
  powerboat racing 240
motor sports *see* cars; motor boats; motorcycling and individual sports
motorcycling
  fastest crossing of Americas 29
  fastest production 142
  fastest speed 142
  globe of death, most numbers 142
  highest bunny hop 142
  Isle of Man TT series 238
  longest circuit race 238
  longest hands-free ride 142
  longest trike 142
  longest wheelie 142
  Motocross 239
  oldest motorcyclist 42
  oldest race 238
  sidecar racing 239
  speed records 142
  speedway racing 240
  Supercross 239
  swapping places 142
  three-wheeled, longest 142
  trial bikes 240
  trials, highest wall climb 142
  World Motorcycle Championships 238–9
  World Superbike Championships 239
motorized models, smallest 113
Mount Everest
  fastest ascent 26
  first woman to climb 26
  most conquests 27
mountaineering, seven-summit ascent 27
mountains, highest 76
moustache, longest 56
movie-watching, longest session 32
mud buildings, largest 130
mural, largest 116
murderers 106, 107
muscles, largest bicep 56
museums, largest 130
music *see* classical music; pop music
musical instruments
  largest drum kit 191
  largest guitars 115
  largest organ 190
  matchstick 118
  most valuable violin 125
  oldest 190

N
nail clippers, largest collection 119
nails, longest 56
NASCAR *see* stock car racing
do Nascimento, Edson Arantes (Pelé) 23
national boundaries 94, 95
National Doubles Championship, most rugby fives 270
nations *see* countries
natural disasters 68–9, 79
navy
  earliest stealth ship 157
  fastest destroyer 156
  fastest submarine 156
  fastest warship 156
  greatest ancient battle 156
  greatest battle 156
  greatest invasion 156
  highest death toll 156
  largest 152
  largest aircraft carrier 157
  largest battleship 157
  largest hovercraft 157
  largest surface-effect ship 157
  largest torpedo 156
  largest unmanned submarine 156
  most aircraft 156
  most submarines 156
  most warships 156
neck, longest 57
nerve gas
  most powerful 160
  most recent use 160
nests, largest 83
netball
  highest score 216
  longest match 216
  most World Championship points 216
neutrino observatory, deepest 172
newspapers
  highest circulation 197
  most syndicated comic strips 197
  smallest 113
nightclubs
  largest 130
  smallest 112
Nobel prize winners
  peace 20
  sciences 172, 173
noise, loudest 76
North Pole
  first people to reach 26
  first pole-to-pole circumnavigation 28
  first solo expedition 26
  youngest to visit both Poles 27
noses, longest 50
'NSYNC 189
nuclear explosions
  highest explosion 160
  largest craters 160
  most powerful 161
nuclear reactions, oldest 170
nuclear weapons
  first atomic bomb used 160
  heaviest 161

  highest death toll 160
  most destructive ICBM 161
  most detonated at one time 160
  smallest 160
nude photos, largest 116
numbers, largest prime 171

O
objects
  collections 118–19, 245
  earliest 120–1
  inventions 120–1
  largest 114–17
  most expensive/valuable 122–5
  smallest 112–13
oceans
  deepest 78
  highest temperature 78
  largest 78
  waterspouts 67
  worst tsunamis 68, 78
office buildings, tallest 128
oldest people 25, 42, 50–1
Olsen, Mary-Kate and Ashley 195
Olympics *see* individual sports; Paralympics...
opera singer, oldest 42
Oscar awards 23, 180, 181
oysters, fastest opening 40
ozone layer, largest hole 64

P
paddleboards 34, 270
paintings, largest 117
pantomime horse, fastest 40
parachuting
  escapes 24
  largest mass jump 260
  longest flight 139
  most jumps 260
  oldest person 42
  rescues 20
paragliding
  fastest speed 260
  greatest distance flown 260
  longest journey 138
Paralympic Winter Games
  most biathlon medals 229
  most medal-winning nations 229
  most medals 229
  most Nordic skiing medals 229
  sledge hockey 235
parasites 58, 59
parks *see* theme parks
pasta, longest strand 116
patents
  earliest 120
  largest award 120
pea shooting, most titles 271
peacekeeping
  largest deployment 152
  longest running mission 153
Pelé (Edson Arantes do Nascimento) 23

penknives, most blades 120
penny-farthing bicycles, greatest distance
        covered 143
pens
        earliest 120
        most expensive 124
        most intelligent 167
        most tools 120
        most valuable 124
        most versatile 120
people
        see also human bodies
        largest crowds 98, 102, 103
        life expectancy 94
        male/female ratios 95
        most genetically diverse 168
        most/least populous places 94
        oldest/youngest populations 94
performance 192–3
        Cats musical 193
        fastest flamenco 192
        fastest tap dancer 193
        largest arts festivals 192
        largest chorus line 192
        largest contra line 192
        largest country dance 192
        largest locomotion dance 192
        largest tap dance 192
        largest theater 192
        longest dance marathon 192
        longest running musical 193
        longest running show 192
        longest running West End
                musical 193
        longest Shakespeare play 193
        longest time in bed by couple 193
        most expensive stage production 192
        most one-man show performances
                192
        most stage flights 193
        most Tony Awards 192
        oldest artist 192
        oldest theater 192
perfume, most expensive 125
pétanque (boules) 263
petitions, largest environmental 64
photographs, largest nude 116
pigeon racing
        greatest distance 271
        highest price 271
piggy bank, largest collection 119
pigs
        human transplant material 54, 168
        plant transplants 169
pilgrimages 102, 103
pilot, oldest 43
pingos 77
planets 70, 72
plants 80–1
        gene transplant to animal 169
        largest fruit and vegetables 114
        most chromosomes 168
plate tectonics 76
platinum, largest nugget 62
poisonous, see also venomous

poisonous plants 80
pole-sitting in barrel, longest time 33
police dogs 85
political prisoners 22, 25, 107
politicians 22, 23, 96, 97
pollution 64–5
pool, fastest clearance time 262
pop music
        best-selling albums 186
        best-selling DVD single 187
        biggest record deal 186
        earliest million-selling CD 187
        Elvis Presley 186, 187, 189
        fastest rap artist 41
        fastest video making 41
        largest rap group 187
        longest stay in charts 186
        longest video 188
        memorabilia 118, 122
        most BRIT awards 187
        most concerts 186
        most expensive video 186
        most Grammy awards 186
        most hits by royalty 97
        most No.1 UK Chart singles 187
        most RIAA certificates 187
        most singles 187
        most successful country artist 186
        oldest artist to sell million albums
                186
        oldest records 187
        youngest solo artist 186
pop stars 188–9
        The Beatles 118, 122, 187, 188
        best-selling artists 188
        Britney Spears 188
        Elvis Presley 186, 187, 189
        fastest selling pop album 189
        highest annual earnings 188
        highest earnings 188, 189
        largest attendance at pop concert
                188
        longest music video 188
        most awards won 188, 189
        most BRIT awards 189
        most charts topped 189
        most performers on one single 188
        most pseudonyms used 189
        most successful virtual 188
        most weeks at No.1 189
Post-it notes, most valuable 123
potato peeling, most peeled 34
powerboat racing, Formula 1 240
precious stones, largest 62
prehistoric life 90–1
Premiership (English), most football goals
        211
presidents 96–7
        longest incarcerated 22
        longest serving 97
        youngest 23
Presley, Elvis 186, 187, 189
pretzels, largest 116
prime ministers
        female 22, 97

highest paid 96
        most accessible 97
        youngest 97
Princess Royal 23
Princess of Wales 23, 100, 122
prisons
        highest population 94
        largest jail break 106
        longest incarceration of future
                president 22
        longest survival without food and
                water 24
        lowest population 106
        most escapes 25
propeller-driven aircraft, fastest 155
protein, largest 170
protests
        civil rights 22, 98
        petitions 64
pubs
        see also beer
        most visited 99
        smallest 112
Pulitzer Book Prize, most wins 196
Pulitzer Prize, most wins 196
pumpkins, largest 114
punting, longest journey 255
pyramids, largest 131

Q
quad bikes
        greatest distance jumped 143
        highest speed 143
Queen Elizabeth II 96
Queen Mother 96

R
racial equality, largest rally 22
racing cars see cars; individual sports
racket sports
        badminton 249
        racquetball 248
        real tennis 248
        squash 248
        table tennis 248
        tennis 246–8
racquetball, most World Championship
        titles 248
radar systems, smallest 158
radio
        DJ marathon 195
        earliest broadcast 195
        earliest patent 120
        earliest transmission 121
        largest audiences 23, 194
        largest digital broadcaster 164
        longest running programs 195
        most stations 194
        most successful clockwork 121
        tallest structures 129
radio-controlled model boats, farthest
        distance traveled 144
radio-controlled model cars, fastest 141

rafts, longest survival 24
railways see trains
rain
        see also floods
        most acidic 65
        oldest fossilized raindrops 66
rallying
        longest rally 241
        most Monte Carlo wins 241
        most Rally of Britain wins 241
        most World Championship race
                wins 241
        most World Championship titles 241
        youngest World Champion 241
rangoli pattern, largest 117
ravioli, largest meal 117
reactions, antimatter 171
real tennis
        most World Championship titles 248
        oldest court 248
recording see sound recording;
        video recording; vinyl records
Recording Industry Association of America
        certificates, most 187
recycling, highest rate 64
religion 102–3
        see also bibles; sacred buildings;
sacred objects
        largest radio audience 23
        smallest holy books 113, 197
reptiles 86–7
rescues 20–1
        dogs 84
reservoirs
        largest 132
        worst landslide 63
RIAA (Recording Industry Association of
        America) certificates, most 187
riding
        equestrian sports 258–9
        longest in suit of armor 32
rites of passage 100–1
rivers
        floods 68, 69
        longest 79
        tidal bore 79
RNLI see Royal National Lifeboat
        Institution
road cones, largest collection 119
roads
        densest network 105
        highest traffic 104
        longest 104
        longest road train 148
        tunnels 132
        widest 133
robbery 106
        see also thefts
Roberts, Julia 180, 181
robots 166–7
rocket-powered fire trucks, fastest
        148
rockets
        earliest 158
        first launch 23

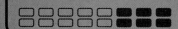
rocks 76
roller coasters 178, 179
roller hockey 216
roller-skating
    fastest 270
    greatest distance on in-line
        skates 29
    most titles 271
roller-skiing relay sport 270
romance
    marriages 100–1, 180
    matchmakers 98
roofs, largest 130
round-the-world walk 26
rowing
    fastest across Atlantic 27
    fastest eight – 2,000 m 254
    most Olympic gold medals
        254
    most University Boat Race
        wins 254
    oldest University Boat Race
        participant 254
    youngest University Boat Race
        participant 254
Royal National Lifeboat Institution
    (RNLI) 21
royalty 96–7
    charity patron 23
    largest memorabilia collection
        118
    most condolences on internet 23
    most hit records 97
    residences 134, 135
Rubik Cube, fastest solver 40
rugby league
    greatest number of World Cup
        wins 212
    highest attendance 212
    highest score 212
    most goals 212
    most hat tricks 212
    most tries 212
    youngest player 212
rugby union
    fastest try 213
    highest attendance 213
    highest score 213
    most international appearances
        213
    most international penalties
        kicked 213
    most international tries 213
    most points 213
    most tries 213
    most World Cup titles 213
running
    see also athletics
    fastest backward 32, 40, 227
    fastest run up Empire State
        Building 40
running backward, farthest
    distance 32
runway, longest military 155
Ryder Cup (golf) 243

S

sacred buildings
    largest 103, 130, 131
    smallest 102
    tallest 128
sacred objects 102, 103
sailboarding
    longest sailboard 256
    longest sailboard snake 256
sailing vessels 144–5
    see also yachting
salmon, fastest filleted 40
sand sculpture, largest 115
sandboarding
    fastest sandboarder 271
    longest backflip 271
sandwich, largest grilled 115
satellites
    highest resolution images 167
    smallest GPS systems 166
sausages, longest 117
schools, largest food drive 23
science 170–3
    see also technology, medical facts
    biological 168–9
    extreme 170–1
    laboratory 172–3
    youngest to publish research 42
scissors, smallest 112
scuba diving
    deepest seawater 27
    longest dive 26
sculptures
    see also statues
    largest 114, 115, 117
    most valuable 124, 125
    smallest 172
sea battles, great 153, 156
search engine, largest 165
September 11th disaster 21, 106
seven-summit ascent, fastest 27
sexual harassment damages 107
shack on pole, longest time sitting 33
Shakespeare, most valuable book 124
sheep 85
    cloned 169
shinty (Scottish "hurling") 218
ships
    see also boats; hovercraft; sub-
marines
    busiest shipping lane 144
    container ships, largest 144
    fastest Atlantic crossing 144
    largest 144, 145, 157
    oldest iron 144
    rescues 20, 21
    sinking largest number of submarines
        156
shirts, largest 114
shoes
    highest heels 114
    largest boot 114
    most energy efficient 120
    most expensive sports 122
    most shined 35

shopping centers, largest 131
shortest people 51
shovel excavators, largest 148
Siamese twins 100
sick-bags, largest collection 119
side-wheel driving, longest 32
sidecar racing
    most European Championship titles
        239
    most roadracing titles 239
    most sidecar-cross titles 239
sieges
    bloodiest 152
    longest 152
signs, largest 130
skating see figure skating; ice hockey;
    roller-skating; speed skating
skeleton
    fastest Cresta Run 234
    most Cresta Run wins 234
    oldest Cresta Run rider 234
skiing
    fastest skier 231
    longest downhill race 231
    longest ski-jumps 231
    most Alpine titles 230
    most biathlon titles 230
    most extensive 229
    most Nordic titles 230
    most Olympic medals 228,
        229
    most people on single pair 35
    most snow-boarding medals
        231
    most "vertical feet" skied 231
    most World Cup wins 230, 231
    most World Freestyle Championships
        titles 231
skittles
    highest alley score 271
    highest tabletop score 271
skydiving, dog 84
skyscrapers 128–9
sled-dog trail, longest 271
sledge hockey
    most Paralympic assists 235
    most Paralympic goals 235
    most Paralympic medals 235
    most Paralympic points 235
smallpox
    earliest use as weapon 161
    largest vaccine stockpile 161
smoking 98
snails 85
snakes 86, 89
snooker
    fastest maximum break 263
    highest break 263
snoring, loudest 52
snowboarding
    most women's biathlon medals
        231
    most World titles 231
snowdrifts, sheep survival 85
snowflakes 66

soccer
    see also football
    best-selling computer games 176
sofa
    fastest 41
    longest 116
solar halos 67
solar roof, largest 65
solar system 70–1
    closest moon 70
    darkest object 71
    densest planet 70
    highest volcanoes 70
    hottest place 70
    largest flood channel 70
    largest solar flare 71
    longest day 70
    smoothest surface 70
Solheim Cup, most golf titles 243
sound recording
    see also vinyl records
    earliest magnetic 121
    oldest recordings 187
    smallest cassette 166
sound systems, most directional 120
South Pole
    first pole-to-pole circumnavigation 28
    youngest to visit both Poles 27
space 70–1
space flight
    earliest manned 27
    first rocket launch 23
    largest audience 22
    oldest astronaut 22
spacecraft 72–3
Spears, Britney 188
special effects 184–5
    earliest black-and-white film
        conversion 185
    largest film stunt budget 184
    largest makeup budget 184
    largest special effects budget 184
    largest stuntman-to-actor ratio in
        film 184
    longest career as cartoon voice 185
    longest feature film 184
    longest makeup job 184
    longest "talkie" cartoon series 185
    most expensive aerial stunt 185
    most expensive cartoon 185
    most expensive explosion sequence
        in movie 184
    most latex feet 185
speed 40–1
    fastest aircraft 138, 154–5
    fastest animals 82, 86
    fastest ball sport 218
    fastest bed pushing 40
    fastest bicycles 143
    fastest boats 144, 145, 156
    fastest cars 140
    fastest catamaran 144
    fastest computers 166
    fastest horse race 259
    fastest men's tennis serve 248

fastest motorcycles 142
fastest possible 170
fastest skier 231
fastest trains 146, 147
speed skating
　fastest men's 500 m 232
　fastest men's 1,000 m 232
　fastest men's 1,500 m 232
　fastest men's 3,000 m 232
　fastest men's 5,000 m 232
　fastest men's short-track 1,000 m
　　233
　fastest men's short-track 1,500 m
　　233
　fastest men's short-track 3,000 m
　　233
　fastest women's 500 m 232
　fastest women's 1,000 m 232
　fastest women's 3,000 m 232
　fastest women's 5,000 m 232
　fastest women's short-track 1,000 m
　　233
　fastest women's short-track 1,500 m
　　233
　fastest women's short-track 3,000 m
　　233
　fastest women's short-track relay
　　233
　most gold medals 232
　most Olympic medals 232
speedway racing
　most points by team 240
　most World Championship
　　appearances 240
　most World Championship titles 240
　most World Cup race wins 240
spice, hottest 81
spirit, most expensive 124
sponges (living) 82, 89
sprites 66
squash
　fastest ball 249
　most Club Championships 249
　most Thomas Cups 249
　most World titles 249
　shortest match 248
stadia, largest 130
stairs, fastest climb 32
Star Wars, largest memorabilia collection
　119
stars 70–1
stations
　highest altitude 146
　largest 146
statues 102, 103
　see also sculptures
　tallest 128
stealth ships
　earliest 157
　largest 157
steam engines
　fastest locomotive 147
　oldest 147
　smallest 113
steamships, oldest iron boat 144

stilts, longest distance walked 26
stinging, see also venomous
stinging plants 80
stock car racing
　highest career earnings 237
　most Championship titles 237
　most race victories 237
storms 66, 67, 68, 69
strength
　fastest barrel roll 38
　fastest time to bend iron
　　bar 39
　fastest tire flipping 38
　fastest world wife-carrying run 38
　greatest weight of bricks lifted 39
　heaviest boat pulled 38
　heaviest bricks on head 39
　heaviest car on head 38
　heaviest deadlift with little
　　finger 38
　heaviest train pulled 38
　heaviest truck pulled 39
　heaviest weight lifted by beard 39
　heaviest weight lifted with
　　teeth 38
　highest beer keg toss 38
　most baseball bats broken 38
　most beer kegs lifted 38
　most bricks lifted 39
　most concrete blocks broken 38
　most weight lifted with ears, nipples,
　　and tongue 38
　sumo 266
　weightlifting 266–7
　wrestling 266
structures
　engineering feats 132–3
　largest 130–1, 132–3
　tallest 128–9
submarines
　accidents 156, 161
　fastest 156
　largest unmanned 156
　Navy with most 156
　rescue 20
　smallest 112
　worst disasters 156, 161
substances
　see also elements
　least dense solid 173
　most dense 172
　smelliest 173
suicides, largest mass 101
sumo
　greatest tournament dominance
　　266
　most wins 266
Sun 71
Superbowl
　most MVP awards 201
　most titles 201
Supercross
　most 250-cc races won 239
　most titles won 239
supernovae 70, 71

surfing
　highest rideable waves 257
　longest rides 257
　most women's World Championships
　　257
survivors
　see also medical facts
　accidents 24–5
　hanging attempts 106
　rescues 20–1
swimming
　dogs 84
　farthest distance swum 252
　fastest 50 m underwater 252
　men's 4 x 200m freestyle relay 252
　men's 50 m backstroke 250
　men's long-course world records 251
　men's short-course world records
　　252
　most Championship medals 250
　most Olympic gold medals 250
　most participants in swimathon 252
　most women's world records 250
　women's 50 m short-course
　　breaststroke 253
　women's 200 m butterfly 250
　women's long-course world records
　　251
　women's short-course world records
　　253
swimming pools, largest 115

T

table football, longest game 34
table tennis
　see also tennis
　fastest 5,000 counter-hitting
　　248
　longest doubles match 248
　longest match 248
　longest rallies 248
　most medals 248
talking
　fastest 41
　fastest backward 41
tallest people 50
tandems, smallest 124
tanks
　earliest 158
　fastest 158
　heaviest 159
　lightest 158
　most heavily armed 159
　most number 153
　most produced 159
tape recording, earliest 121
target sports
　archery 262
　clay shooting 263
　darts 263
　pétanque 263
　pool 262
　snooker 263
　trapshooting 263

team efforts
　fastest 31-legged race 40
　fastest bed push 40
　fastest bed-making 34
　fastest crossing of Florida Straits 34
　fastest three-legged marathon 35
　highest eight-person tightrope
　　pyramid 34
　longest game of table football 34
Technicolor use 183
technology
　biological 168–9
　computers 164, 165, 166
　first rocket launch 23
　games 176–7
　laboratory experiments 172–3
　radio 120, 121, 164
　recording 121, 166
　robots 166–7
　sound systems 120
　telecommunications 164–5, 167
teddy bears
　largest 116
　most valuable 123
　smallest 112
telecommunications
　cell (mobile) phones 124, 164
　largest company 164
　longest telephone cable 165
　telephone calls 164
telescopes 73
television
　see also video
　highest child actor earnings 195
　highest earnings 194
　highest paid actor/actress 194
　largest audiences 100, 194
　largest television phone vote 194
　longest running animated series 194
　longest running drama 194
　longest running pop show 194
　longest running quiz 194
　longest running show 194
　most expensive advertising
　　campaign 194
　smallest sets 113
　tallest transmitting tower 129
temperature
　highest body 54
　highest man-made 172
　lowest body 54
　lowest man-made 172
　lowest possible 171
　ocean 78
　weather 66
temples 102, 103
tennis
　see also table tennis
　best Wimbledon performance
　　246
　fastest men's serve 248
　grand slams 246
　highest attendance 246
　longest rally 248
　longest tennis ball heading 33

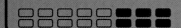
most balls volleyed 248
most consecutive serves 248
most Davis Cup titles 247
most Open singles titles 247
most valuable racket 248
most Wimbledon titles 246
youngest Davis Cup player 247
youngest men's World No. 1 248
youngest Open singles champions 247
youngest Wimbledon champion 246
youngest women's Australian Open Championships 247
youngest women's US Open Tennis Championships 247
youngest women's World No. 1 247
tenpin bowling
see also bowls
most titles 218
most women's titles 218
terrorism
longest held hostage 25
most fire fighters lost 21
most hostages held 24
most people killed 106
text message, fastest 164
thefts 96, 106
see also robbery
theme parks 178–9
country with most roller coasters 178
fastest roller coaster 178
greatest number of roller coasters 179
largest amusement park 179
longest house of horrors 179
oldest carousel 178
oldest roller coaster passengers 178
tallest ferris wheel 179
tallest free-fall drop ride 178
tallest roller coaster 178
tallest speed waters slide 178
thirty one-legged race, fastest 40
three-legged marathon, fastest 35
thunderstorms 66, 67, 68
tidal bores 79
tiddlywinks
fastest potting 271
farthest wink shot 271
most World Championships 271
tie pins, largest collection 118
tightrope pyramid, highest 34
tires, largest 148
toes
fewest 53
longest nails 56
most 52
wrestling 270
tombs, largest 100, 131, 152
tongue, longest 50
Tony Awards, most 192
toothpick sculptures, largest 117
tornados 67, 68
totem poles, tallest 128
tourism 104–5
hotels 134

towers, tallest 128, 129
towns, oldest 94
toys
largest Barbie doll collection 118
largest Star Wars collection 119
largest teddy bear 116
most valuable teddy bear 123
most valuable toy soldier 123
smallest jigsaw 112
smallest teddy bears 112
traffic 104, 105
see also cars
trains
busiest underground railway 146
fastest 146
fastest steam locomotive 147
heaviest 146
highest railway line 146
highest railway station 146
highest speed 146
largest employing railway 98
largest railway system 146
largest station 146
longest 146
longest journey 147
longest monorails 146
longest road train 148
longest straight railroad 147
longest tunnel 146
longest underground platforms 147
narrowest gauge railway 146
oldest 148
oldest trams 146
smallest railway system 146
steepest rail gradient 147
trams, oldest 146
trampoline, most somersaults 34
trams
most extensive system 147
oldest 146
transplants 54, 55
animal 54, 168
earliest heart 24
longest survival artificial heart 24
transport, flight inventions 120
trapshooting, most consecutive targets hit 263
travel 104–5
treaties, oldest 96
tree sitting, longest 33
trees 80
see also forests
largest 80
most remote 80
oldest 80
trial bikes, most World Championship titles 240
trikes 142
trucks
fastest wheelie 148
furthest two-wheel distance 148
heaviest pulled 39
highest monster ramp jump 149
largest dumper trucks 148

largest fork-lift 148
largest front-end loaders 148
largest monster truck 149
longest monster truck jump 149
longest road train 148
most defensive 148
rocket-powered fire trucks 148
truffles, largest 117
tumors, largest 52
tunnels
largest wind 131
longest rail 146
road 132
twins
earliest Siamese 100
oldest undiscovered 52
tallest 50
typewriters, most valuable 197

U
umbrellas, most expensive 123
underground railways
busiest 146
least extensive 146
longest underground platforms 147
most extensive 147
unemployment, highest/lowest 99
unicycles, smallest 113
United Nations 96
universe 70–1
elements 170
forces 170–1
university, largest donation 23
unusual sport
Eton fives 270
heaviest world champion 270
horseshoe pitching 270
land yachting 271
National Doubles Fives Championship 270
paddleboard circumnavigation 270
pea shooting 271
pigeon racing 271
roller-skating 270
roller-skiing 270
sandboarding 271
skittles 271
sled-dog trail 271
tiddlywinks 271
toe wrestling 270
World Elephant Polo 270
useless inventions 121

V
Van de Graff generators, largest 172
vegetables, largest 114
vehicles
see also cars; trucks
largest land vehicles 148
most produced four-wheeled 149
venomous creatures
fish 88

insects 86
jellyfish 89
snakes 86, 89
video games see computer games
video recording
fastest growing product 166
fastest music 41
longest music 188
most expensive music 186
video-watching, longest session 32
vinyl records
largest collection 118
smallest 112
violins
largest ensemble 190
most valuable 125
youngest violinist 191
virtual band, most successful 188
volcanoes 69, 70, 76, 79
volleyball
largest prize money 216
most Championship titles 216
most Olympic titles 216
most women's titles 216
most World Championship titles 216
volunteers, largest ambulance organization 20
vomit, oldest 90

W
waist, smallest 57
walking
fastest Land's End to John O'Groats 227
fastest Trans-America walk 26
farthest round-the-world 26
largest mass walk 36
longest distances 26
most Olympic medals 223
wall climbs, trials motorcycles 142
wallet, most expensive 124
walls, longest 133
wars
see also weapons of war
bloodiest 152
bloodiest battles 153
longest continuous 152
most costly 152
most decorated war hero 20
shortest 152
watches, see also wristwatches
water-skiing
longest fly distance 257
longest jump 257
most skiers towed behind boat 257
oldest barefoot skier 43
water sports 250–7
canoeing 254–5
diving 26, 27
Formula 1 powerboat racing 240
kite surfing 256
punting 255
rowing 254
sailboarding 256

surfing 257
swimming 250–3
water skiing 43, 257
windsurfing 257
yachting 256
waterfalls 78, 79
watering can, largest 116
waterspouts 67
weapons of war
  bouncing bomb 159
  earliest rockets 158
  earliest tank 158
  fastest tank 158
  greatest gun range 158
  heaviest bomb 159
  heaviest tank 159
  highest firing rate machine gun 158
  largest explosion 158
  largest gathering of Ford GPAs 158
  largest gun 158
  largest mortar 158
  largest stockpile chemical weapons
    160
  lightest tank 158
  most accurate anti-aircraft missile
    158
  most accurate bomb 159
  most complex systems 154
  most heavily armed tank 159
  most produced tanks 159
  most widely used firearm 159
  nuclear weapons 160–1
  smallest radar system 158
weather
  best solar halos 67
  disasters 68–9
  driest place 66
  fastest temperature rise 66
  first images of sprites 66
  highest atmospheric phenomena 66
  highest clouds 67
  highest pressure 66
  highest waterspout 67
  hottest place 66
  largest fallen ice 66, 67
  largest hailstones 66, 67
  largest snowflake 66
  least sunshine 66
  lightning 66, 67, 68
  longest fogs 66
  longest rainbow 66
  most powerful climate change 66
  oldest fossilized raindrops 66
  strongest jetstream 67
  warmest year 66
  worst cyclones 68
  worst floods 68, 69
  worst geomagnetic storms 68
  worst hailstorms 66, 68, 69
  worst ice storms 69
  worst thunderstorms 67, 68
  worst tornados 67, 68
weddings
  largest cake 116
  most in city 100

most expensive 101
most simultaneously 101
most valuable piece of cake 100
oldest bride 100
oldest bridesmaid 43
oldest couple 101
weightlifting
  most Olympic gold medals 266
  most Olympic medals 266
  most women's World Championships
    titles 266
  oldest world record breaker 266
  women's/men's snatch 267
  world records 266–7
  youngest world record breaker 266
weird talents 46–7
  arrow shooting 46
  farthest eyeball popping 52
  fastest human crab 46
  full-body ice endurance 47
  hamburger stuffing 47
  most arrows caught 46
  most cigar boxes on chin 46
  most coins regurgitated 46
  most dominoes toppled 46
  most fish caught by hand 47
  most people in car 46
  most rattlesnakes in mouth 46
  most straws in mouth 47
  most swords swallowed 46
  most watches eaten 46
  spinning football on head 47
whales 89
wheelbarrows, fastest race 40
wheelchairs
  greatest distance in 24 hours 26
  longest journey 29
wheelies
  bicycles 143
  motorcycles 142
  trucks 148
whisky, most expensive 124
Williams, Robbie 189
Willis, Bruce 180
Wimbledon see tennis
wind
  see also sailing vessels; yachting
  disasters 68
  strongest jetstream 67
wind farms, largest 65
wind generators, largest 131
wind powered land journey, longest 28
wind tunnels, largest 131
windsurfing
  highest altitude 257
  most World Championships 257
wine
  fastest bottle opener 40
  most expensive glass 125
  most valuable bottle 124
  smallest bottle 112
  smallest glass 113
wing-walking
  marathon 33
  oldest walker 42

Winter Olympics
  see also individual sports;
Paralympic...
  most countries to win Olympic
medals 229
  most gold medals 228
  most Olympic competitors 229
  oldest competitor 228
  Paralympics 229
  youngest competitor 229
winter sports 228–35
  bobsleigh 234
  curling 235
  figure skating 233
  luge 234
  Paralympic Games 229
  skeleton 234
  skiing 229–31
  sledge hockey 235
  snowboarding 231
  speed skating 232–3
women
  deepest free dive 27
  fastest yachtswoman 27
  first to climb Everest 26
  first woman to climb Everest 26
  highest darts score 263
  highest football score 209
  highest golf earnings 245
  highest lacrosse scores 217
  ice hockey 206
  longest beard 53
  longest distance walked 26
  longest football control 211
  lowest golf score 243
  most biathlon medals 231
  most cricket appearances 215
  most cricket dismissals 215
  most lacrosse international
    appearances 217
  most Olympic soccer titles 210
  most Paralympic titles 205
  most surfing World Championships
    257
  most swimming world records 250
  most team Olympic gold medals 206
  most tenpin bowling titles 218
  most volleyball World Championship
    titles 216
  most weightlifting World
    Championships titles 266
  most World Championship luge
    titles 234
  oldest 51
  prime ministers 22, 97
  shortest 51
  tallest 50
  top-scoring female WWII ace 155
  top-scoring WWII ace 155
  wicketkeepers 215
  World Championship bobsleigh
Olympic titles 234
  youngest tennis World No.1 247
Wonder, Stevie 186
wooden buildings, largest 134

world, walking around 26
World Championships
  see also individual sports
  heaviest winner 270
  largest prize money 216
World Cup
  most cycling wins 268–9
  most federations in qualifiers 209
  most football Cups 208
  most freestyle skiing titles 231
  most hockey titles 217
  most rugby league wins 212
  most rugby union titles 213
  most skiing wins 230
  most speedway wins 240
  most Worldloppet titles 230
  oldest player 208
  youngest player 208
  youngest scorer 208
World Elephant Polo 270
World Motorcycle Championships
  most 125-cc titles 238
  most 250-cc titles 238
  most races won in career 238
  most races won in season 238
  most single class wins 239
  most titles 238
  most titles won by manufacturer 239
  oldest world champion 239
  youngest champion 238
World Series
  highest baseball attendance 202
  oldest player 203
World Superbike Championships
  most pole positions 239
  most races won by manufacturer
    239
  most titles 239
World Wide Web 164, 165
wrestling
  most Olympic gold medals 266
  most Olympic medals 266
  most World Championships
    titles 266
  oldest competition 266
wristwatches
  most expensive 124
  smallest GPS 166
  smallest television 113

XYZ

yachting
  fastest Atlantic crossing 144
  fastest circumnavigation 256
  fastest solo circumnavigation 27
  highest speed 256
  longest non-stop race 145
  most America's Cup races 256
  most America's Cup wins 256
  most Olympic gold medals 256
  most participants in ocean
    race 256
  oldest international 145
young and old 42–3

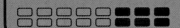
6	AP	28	Nathalie Torline	60	Corbis (2)	99	Jamie Simonds
6	Popperfoto/Reuters	29	Nick Alcock & Hugh Sinclair	62	Dan McKinney	100	Celestis
7	Drew Gardner/Guinness World Records	30	Bayerischer Rundfunk ARD (2)	62	Corbis	100	Corbis
7	Allsport	32	Frank Ryan	63	Corbis	101	Popperfoto/Reuters
8	AP	32	2002 Columbia TriStar	64	Corbis	102	Getty Images/Newsmakers
8	Japan Marine Science & Technology Center	33	Joaquim Cabral	64	Carol Kane	102	AP
8	Allsport	34	The Flying Wallendas	65	Corbis	103	Corbis
8	Rex	34	Ideia Biba	66	Corbis	104	Corbis (2)
8	NASA	35	CP Photo Assignment Services	66	Getty Stone	105	Getty Images/TCL
9	Allsport	36	AP	67	SPL	106	PA
9	Rex (2)	36	Hong Kong College of Cardiology	68	SPL	106	Getty Images/Newsmakers
9	AP	37	Tylo AB	68	Corbis	107	AP
9	Getty Images	38	Drew Gardner/Guinness World Records	69	Corbis	108	Getty Images (2)
10	Matthew Dickens	38	PA	70	NASA	109	Getty Images
10	Tae Oka	39	Pete Fisher	70	ESA	110	Drew Gardner/Guinness World Records (2)
10	Walter Karling	40	Fox Broadcasting	71	NASA	112	Utaho Imaoka
10	Ranjan Saujani	40	Raman Andiappan	72	NASA(2)	112	Jamie Simonds
10	Guy & Liz Shepstone	41	Drew Gardner/Guinness World Records	73	NASA	113	Denso Corporation
10	Robert C Mora/Los Angeles Kings	42	Ken Nolfi/Jimi Miller	74	Bruce Coleman (2)	114	LadyBWear Ltd
12	Ted Stevens	42	Popperfoto/Reuters	76	Corbis (2)	114	Somerfield Stores Ltd
12	Nick Alcock & Hugh Sinclair	43	Corbis	77	Bruce Coleman	115	Holland Sand Sculpture Company
12	Paddy Doyle	44	Mastiff Media/TV3	78	Corbis (2)	116	Baskin-Robbins International
12	Barbara Ackles	44	Nordisk Film & TV/TV4	79	Corbis	116	James A Canfield
13	AP (2)	45	Drew Gardner/Guinness World Records	80	Francois Gohier/Ardea	117	Sheikh Zafar Iqbal
13	Alvin Community College	46	Tom Gregory	80	Wendy Weyforth Schenking	118	Rodolfo Renato Vazquez
13	Ashrita Furman	46	Adi Feichtinger	81	Bruce Coleman	118	Drew Gardner/Guinness World Records
16	Bayerischer Rundfunk/ARD(3)	47	Bayerischer Rundfunk ARD	82	OSF	119	Robert & Patricia Leffler
16	Nordisk Film & TV/TV4	48	Corbis (2)	82	Corbis	120	The Year Knife
17	Bayerischer Rundfunk/ARD(2)	50	Jamie Simonds	83	OSF	120	Corbis
17	Mastiff Media/TV3(2)	50	Nishinihon Newspaper Co.	84	William Munoz	121	Harper Collins
17	Nordisk Film & TV/TV4	51	Popperfoto/Reuters	84	Hulton Archive	122	Popperfoto/Reuters
18	Getty Images (2)	52	Fox Broadcasting	85	Popperfoto/Reuters	122	AP
20	Popperfoto/Reuters	52	BD Tyagi	86	Corbis	123	Mike Schwartz/Irvine World News
20	Getty Images	53	Jamie Simonds	86	SPL	124	AP
21	Getty Images	54	Kristina House	87	OSF	124	Rex
22	Popperfoto/Reuters	54	IRCAD	88	Corbis (2)	125	Getty Images
22	Getty Images/Newsmakers	55	Ross Parry	89	Natural Science Photos	126	Corbis (2)
23	AP	56	Angela Fisher/Robert Estall Photo Agency	90	University of Greenwich	128	Corbis
24	Popperfoto	56	Drew Gardner/Guinness World Records	90	The Field Museum	128	Glasgow Science Centre/Keith Hunter
24	Panos Pictures	57	Corbis	91	Corbis	129	Corbis
25	AP	58	SPL (2)	92	Getty Images (2)	130	Corbis
26	AP	59	Getty Images	94	Corbis (2)	130	Popperfoto/Reuters
26	HMS Endurance			95	Popperfoto/Reuters	131	Corbis
27	Neil M Silverman			96	AP		
28	Popperfoto/Reuters			96	Getty Images		
				97	Getty Images		
				98	Getty Images/Newsmakers		
				98	AP		

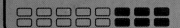

ACKNOWLEDGMENTS

Special thanks go to the following people for their work during the production of this year's edition:

Kat Aalam
Louise Bate
Scott Christie
Ann Collins
Jo Crawford
Neil Hayes
Paul Hearn
Iforce
Joyce Lee
Vicki Miles
Shazia Mirza
Paul Reardon
Amanda Sprague
Caroline Toms
Kate White
Sophie Whiting

The team also wish to thank the following individuals and organisations:

Ernest Adams
Leslie Aiello
American Society of Plastic Surgeons
Amnesty International
Ron Baalke
Healey Baker
Bank of England
Peter Barham
BBC
Guenter Bechly
David Billington, Casella CEL Inc
Biowarfare & Bioterrorism: A Brief History, on www.hospitals-doctors.com
Board of Film Classification
Richard Bourgerie
Bowers and Merena Galleries
James Bradley
Sean Breazeal
Bristol University
British Antarctic Survey
British Geological Survey
British House Rabbit Association
British Telecom
British Tourist Authority
Mike Brown
Lucy Bunker
Caribbean Journal of Science
Clive Carpenter
Mark Carwardine
CERN
Hubert Chanson
Christie's
CIA Factbook
Cinefex
Pamela Clarke, The Royal Archives
Columbia University

Cornell University
Croham Valley Support
Mike Coughlan
Pamela Dalton
Peter D'Amato
Diamond High Council
Martin Dodge
eBay
Economic History Services
Economist Intelligence Unit
Ecoworld
Encyclopaedia Britannica
Louis Epstein
Everestnews.com
FBI
Federation of American Scientists
Forbes
Foreign and Commonwealth Office
Mike Foster, Jane's Defence Weekly
Fremantle media
Geological Society of London
Andy Gillard, Scootering magazine
Simon Gold
Michelle Gonsalves
Google
Stan Greenberg
Richard Gue
Bruce Guettich
Guinness – Die Show Der Rekorde, ARD
Guinness el Show de los Records, Antena 3
Guinness Rekord TV, TV3
Guinness World Records, ITV
Guinness World Record, Nelonen, Channel 4
Guinness World Records, NTV
Guinness World Records: Primetime, Fox Television
David Hancock, Screen Digest
Michael Hanlon
Mary Hanson
Claire Hegarty
Hello! magazine
Carolyn Hewitson
Home and Garden Television website
David Horne
Yvonne Hussey
IMDB
Immigration and Naturalization Service (USA)
Imperial Cancer Research Fund
International Association of Fire Fighters
International Astronomical Union
International Carnivorous Plant Society
International Centre for Prison Studies
International Confederation for Plastic, Reconstructive and Aesthetic Surgery
International Monetary Fund
International Tanker Owners Pollution Federation

International Union for the Conservation of Nature
Kathryn Jenkin
Steve Jones
Ove Karlsson
Nichol Keith
Michael Feldman
Keo Films
Lancaster University
Rolf Landua
Roger Launius
Anthony Liu
Hugh Gene Loebner
Robert Loss
Joe Lynham
Dave McAleer
Jessica Marantz
Giles Marion
Brian Marsden
Koen Martens
Massachusetts Institute of Technology
Peter Matthews
Metro newspaper
Andy Milroy
Eugene Mirman
Edgar Mitchell
Moody's
Rick Moss
Munich Re
NASA
National Bank of Hungary
National Federation of Master Window & General Cleaners
National Geographic
National Museum of Science and Industry
National Science Foundation
Natural History Museum
Nature Magazine and Dr Chris Gunter
NBC
New York City Police Department
Barry Norman, WKVL Amusement Research Library
Numismatic Guarantee Corporation
OANDA
Official Website of the British Monarchy
Organization for Economic Co-operation and Development
Hilary Pearce
People.com
Edwin Perry
David Power-Fardy
PPL Therapeutics
Prison Activist Resource Center
Private Islands online
Rainforest Foundation UK
Rapaport
Simon Rasalingham
Recording Industry Association of America
John Reed, WSSRC

Martin Rees
Rees Entertainment
Dave Roberts
Royal Armouries
Royal Astronomical Society
Royal Horticultural Society
Rutherford Appleton Laboratory
salon.com
Search Engine Watch
Captain Scott Shields and Bear
Bill Slaymaker
Malcolm Smith
Sotheby's
Southampton Oceonography Centre
Standard & Poor's
Jo Steel
Danny Sullivan
Symantec Corporation
TeleGeography
Telescope
Televisual
Texas Department of Criminal Justice
TF1
The Economist
The Met Office
The New York Times
The Nobel Foundation
The Pentagon
The Sun
The World Bank
The World Economic Forum
Ryan Tunstall
Martin Uman
Understanding and Solutions
UN factbook
United Nations
United States Mint
University of Southampton
US Drug Enforcement Agency
US Geological Survey
USA Today
Variety
Anthony Vestal
Ewan Vinnicombe
Joanne Violette
Juhani Virola
Alice Walker
David Wark
Kevin Warwick
Louise Whetter
David Wynn Williams
Martyn Williams
Tom Wood
World Meteorological Organization
World Roads Federation
World Tourism Organization
Yale University
Richard Yarwood
Robert Young
Paul Zajac, Wards Communications